Max Weber
Selections in translation

Max Weber
Selections in translation

Edited by W. G. RUNCIMAN, F.B.A.
Fellow of Trinity College, Cambridge

Translated by E. MATTHEWS
Senior Lecturer in Logic and Metaphysics, University of Aberdeen

 CAMBRIDGE
UNIVERSITY PRESS

PUBLISHED BY THE PRESS SYNDICATE OF THE UNIVERSITY OF CAMBRIDGE
The Pitt Building, Trumpington Street, Cambridge CB2 1RP, United Kingdom

CAMBRIDGE UNIVERSITY PRESS
The Edinburgh Building, Cambridge CB2 2RU, UK   http://www.cup.cam.ac.uk
40 West 20th Street, New York, NY 10011-4211, USA   http://www.cup.org
10 Stamford Road, Oakleigh, Melbourne 3166, Australia

First published 1978
Reprinted 1980, 1982, 1985, 1987, 1988, 1989, 1991, 1992, 1993, 1994, 1995,
1996, 1998

Printed in the United States of America

Typeset in Baskerville

A catalogue record for this book is available from the British Library

Library of Congress Cataloguing-in-Publication Data is available

ISBN 0-521-29268-9 paperback

Contents

Contents

Preface

Max Weber (1864–1920) has come to be widely regarded as the most important European social theorist of the twentieth century. But his writings have only slowly and sporadically become available in English, and have still not been translated in full. This is due in part to the scope and quantity of his work and in part to the interests and purposes of his various editors and translators. But whatever the reasons, there remains a need for a selection which will, so far as is possible within a single volume, give the English-speaking reader an overall picture of Weber's contribution to the remarkably wide range of topics in the social sciences to which he addressed himself over his career. Any selection of this kind will of course be personal and arbitrary. Weber is a difficult author with whom to come to terms. Not only was his major work, *Economy and Society*, incomplete at the time of his death, but much of his earlier writing is unsystematic and on occasion polemical. It has seemed to me better to include a smaller number of longer, continuous extracts than the other way round; and I have been guided in my choice by the wish to cover not only the most significant and influential of Weber's writings but also some of those which have not been translated into English elsewhere. But these aims inevitably conflict, and the result cannot be other than a compromise.

I have also thought it right to keep my own comments to a minimum in order to leave as much as possible of the available space for Weber's own words. Weber is one of those authors who, like Marx, will continue to have as many interpreters as he has readers, and those approaching him for the first time are better advised to make up their minds about him for themselves than to rely on editorial commentary. I have, however, written a brief introduction to each group of selections and appended a summary biography of Weber, together with some suggestions for further reading. These suggestions do not cover more than a fraction of what has by now been written about Weber in English. But they do cover what I think will be found most useful by anyone who wishes to follow up their reading of this volume with more detailed study of one or another aspect of Weber's life and work.

Eric Matthews has sought, in his translation, to keep as close to the original text as is compatible with reasonably idiomatic English. This has

meant some modification in punctuation, sentence structure and the use
of italics. Also, Weber's paragraphs have been broken up wherever they
are much longer than would be found in an English text. Because of
having decided, on principle, against editorial footnotes, we have sometimes had recourse to paraphrase of allusions with which Weber seems
to have assumed that his readers would be familiar. But we have not
otherwise sought to soften the difficulties already present in the original.
The translation was done without reference to other previous translations, where these exist, and I have not attempted any systematic comparison between them. But where I have compared selected passages, I
am bound to say that I have each time found Eric Matthews' translation
not only more readable but also more accurate. Weber is not an easy
author by any standards. But English-speaking readers who complain of
his difficulty can hardly be blamed if his translators have rendered him
more obscure than he already is.

Where semi-technical terms are concerned, we have tried as far as
possible to be consistent in using the same English term throughout.
Thus, for example, we have adopted 'enterprise' for the German *Betrieb*
and retained 'undertaking' for *Unternehmung* even where there is little
or no detectable difference between the two. But where there does arise
a conflict of usage, we have abandoned consistency in favour of whatever
different English term is required, in our view, by the context. Thus, *Stand*
is rendered as 'status group' almost throughout, in contrast with 'class'
(*Klasse*) and the more general 'stratum' (*Schicht*); but where a reference
to 'the Junker Estate' can only be naturally rendered as such, we have
discarded 'status group' without compunction. Similarly, we have rendered *Stadt* as 'city' in most contexts, even where writers in English
on China, or the Roman Empire, or the late Middle Ages in Northern
Italy or Germany might be more likely to use 'town'; but we have not
insisted on retaining it to the point at which the proverbial contrast
between 'town and country' would have to be turned into a quite
unnatural 'city and country'. Where the term in question is in, or
directly derived from, a language other than German, we have adopted
whichever of three alternatives seemed most appropriate for the non-
specialist reader. *Duma*, for example, seems to us a term which can be
left to stand as it is in the context of a discussion of Russia in 1905. But
for *Zyemstvo*, which Weber left as it is, we have thought it better to use
'Council' although making it clear by inserting (*Zyemstvo*) in parentheses
on its first appearance that this is what we have done; and where a
sufficiently precise paraphrase is available, we have adopted the third
alternative of putting it directly into the text even if Weber has not: thus
Decuriones become 'municipal councillors' on the grounds that non-
specialist readers may well never have heard of 'decurions' while

specialists will not (we hope) regard the paraphrase as a distortion. Again, this strategy represents a deliberate compromise, and there are bound to be cases where some readers will feel that the wrong alternative has been chosen. But these examples should at any rate give a fair idea of the principles by which our own decisions have been guided.

Our thanks are due to Dr Jeremy Mynott of the Cambridge University Press, who first engineered our collaboration and saw it through to fruition with patience and understanding; to Dr Peter Garnsey for valuable advice on how best to try to render the selection on the Ancient World; to Dr Anthony Giddens for his comments on the choice of selections and suggestions for further reading; to Dr Paul Gorner for help on many difficult points of German history, language and literature; to Guy Stock, who corrected a particularly glaring error in the draft of one selection; and to Mrs Joan Smith, Logic Department Secretary at the University of Aberdeen, for her invaluable assistance in making the text of the translations presentable.

Trinity College, Cambridge   W.G.R.
February 1977

Publisher's note

In view of the range of literature references in the text, it has not always been feasible to trace which edition Weber was using. In general, titles of English works have been cited in English, but in cases where Weber refers to German editions of works originally published in English his own page references have been retained. German titles have been left in German in the footnotes, but have been translated into English in the text.

Many of the name references in Weber's footnotes are purely bibliographical and it has not therefore seemed useful to index them all. Entries have been selected only when the reference includes some contribution to the discussion in the main text.

Biographical Summary

1864	Born at Erfurt, Thuringia.
1869	Family moves to Berlin.
1882	Student at Heidelberg.
1883	First period of military service at Strasburg.
1884–85	Student at Berlin.
1885–86	Student at Göttingen.
1888	Joins Association for Social Policy.
1889	Doctoral dissertation on medieval trading companies.
1891	Habilitation dissertation on agrarian history of Rome.
1892	Engaged to Marianne Schnitger. Teaches law in Berlin. Publishes major study of labour relations in agriculture in Eastern Germany.
1893	Marriage.
1894	Professor of Political Economy at Freiburg. Publishes first part of article on stock exchange and further article on agricultural labour in Eastern Germany.
1895	Inaugural Lecture. Travels in England and Scotland.
1896	Succeeds Knies as Professor of Economics at Heidelberg. Publishes lecture on decline of Rome and second part of article on stock exchange.
1897	Publishes essay on ancient economic history. Father dies. Nervous breakdown.
1899	Attempts to resume teaching. Further breakdown.
1902	Begins writing on methodology.
1903	Honorary professorship at Heidelberg. Publishes article on Roscher and Knies. Begins work on 'Protestant Ethic'.
1904	Visits the United States. Gives lecture at Congress in St Louis on German rural society. Undertakes jointly with Edgar Jaffé and Werner Sombart editorship of *Archiv für Sozialwissenschaft und Sozialpolitik* and publishes editorial on 'Objectivity'. Also publishes articles on entailment of landed estates and on social structure of ancient Germany.
1905	Publishes two-part article on 'Protestant Ethic'. Disputes with Schmoller over value-judgments in economics at meeting of Association for Social Policy.
1906	Publishes articles on Protestant sects, on the logic of social science and on contemporary political events in Russia.
1907	Publishes methodological critique of Rudolf Stammler. Begins work on empirical study of industrial workers for Association for Social Policy.
1908–9	Publishes articles on methodological problems of industrial worker study.

Biographical Summary

1909   Publishes major, revised essay on ancient economic history.

1910   Attends first conference of German Sociological Society.

1910–14 Works on *Economy and Society*.

1913   Publishes article on 'interpretative' sociology.

1914   Participates in Association for Social Policy's closed debate on value-judgments in social science. Reserve officer in charge of military hospitals

1915   Discharged from hospital administration. Brother Karl killed in action. Works on sociology of religion.

1916   Publishes at length on sociology of religion including 'Confucianism and Taoism' and 'Hinduism and Buddhism'.

1917   Extensive political journalism including article on Russia. Publishes contribution to 1914 debate on values and essay on 'Ancient Judaism'.

1918   Professor of Sociology at Vienna. Lecture to Austrian officers on 'Socialism'. Consultant to drafting commission for Weimar constitution. Refuses nomination for seat in National Assembly. Publishes further long article on political situation in Germany.

1919   Professor of Sociology at Munich. Mother dies. Lectures on 'Politics as a Vocation' and 'Science as a Vocation' to student audiences.

1919–20 Lecture course on general economic history.

1920   Works on sociology of religion. Debates with Oswald Spengler before student audience. Sister Lili commits suicide, leaving children whom Max and Marianne Weber plan to adopt. Dies of influenza in Munich.

I · The Foundations of Social Theory

Introduction

Max Weber has been described as not merely the greatest of sociologists but 'the sociologist'.[1] Yet for most of his career he would not have described himself as a sociologist at all. His own training was in history, economics and law; he was opposed to the creation of professorships of sociology;[2] and in a letter written at the very end of his life he said that his only reason for being a sociologist was to rid the subject of the influence of the collective – or, as it would now be put, 'holistic' – concepts by which it continued to be haunted.[3] It was not until after 1910 that he began to compose the treatise which we now have, still uncompleted, as *Economy and Society*. It is a work of a markedly different kind from his early writings, whether his historical studies of medieval trading companies and Roman agrarian law or his contemporary investigations of the stock exchange and the condition of agricultural labour in the Junker estates to the East of the Elbe. Yet it would be a mistake to read too much discontinuity into the sequence of his writings. His ideas changed over the course of thirty years, as they were bound to do. But his overriding preoccupations did not. The nature of domination in human society, the role of ideas in history, the impact of industrial capitalism first on Europe and then on the world, and the scope and limitations of social science itself – on all these themes Weber's views are, broadly speaking, consistent as well as distinctive. We shall never know what more he might have had to say if he had lived to complete his studies of the social psychology of the great religions, of the sociology of the state and of the methodology of social science. But his work can still be treated as a coherent whole in terms of both method and substance.

Weber's initial unwillingness to see himself as a sociologist sprang partly from his resistance to holistic concepts and his conviction that sociological explanations must relate to the self-conscious actions of individual people, and partly from his distrust of superficial generalisation and his view of typologies as preliminaries to, not substitutes for, the analysis of institutions and events in their own context. But he also recognised that historians can only operate through the use of general concepts and that their explanations must, whether they admit it or not, appeal to some law-like regularities in human conduct. In this qualified sense, therefore, *Economy and Society* can be said to be putting forward a general social theory. Although Weber did not believe in historical laws in the manner of Marxism, he did believe that it is possible to construct trans-cultural and trans-

[1] Raymond Aron, *Main Currents in Sociological Thought*, II (London, 1967), 245.
[2] On the testimony of Karl Jaspers, *Three Essays: Leonardo, Descartes, Max Weber* (New York, 1953), p. 247.
[3] Quoted by Wolfgang J. Mommsen, 'Max Weber's Political Sociology and his Philosophy of World History', *International Social Science Journal*, XVII (1965), 44 n. 2.

temporal concepts in terms of which human history can be categorised and that even if its future course is unpredictable, its course so far can in principle be causally explained.

The relation of Weber's social theory to Marx's is, however, a matter of some dispute. Weber certainly differed from the Marxists on two fundamental and related matters: he did not accept either that ideology is entirely determined by underlying economic causes, or that all conflict in society is class conflict. To Weber, ideas can and sometimes do have an independent and decisive influence on the course of events, and class conflict is only one of the various forms of the unending struggle for domination. He was sceptical of the Marxists' vision of the inevitable triumph of socialism not only because he disbelieved in any kind of theory claiming to prophesy the future but also because he thought that socialism, if it came, would bring about only another form of bureaucratic domination under which the condition of the individual worker would not be significantly changed. But often his attacks are directed more against Marxism than Marx. His own analyses of the nature of class interests, of the transition from slavery to feudalism to capitalism and of the way in which material conditions influence the success or failure of religious and political movements are at many points very close to Marx's own. What is more, his overall view of the modern world as the outcome of an increasingly irresistible process of 'rationalisation' and 'disenchantment' is often reminiscent of what Marx says about 'alienation'.[1] And when one of his colleagues tried to interpret Weber's ideas about the 'Protestant Ethic' as a kind of anti-Marxist idealism, Weber himself protested 'I really must object to this; I am much more materialistic than Delbrück thinks'.[2]

If there is one basic assumption, or set of assumptions, underlying Weber's thought which distinguishes it from that of Marx – or, for that matter, of Comte or Durkheim – it is the assumption deriving from the joint influence of Kant and Nietzsche that reality cannot be objectively grasped by the human mind as a meaningful whole. Any view of the world must, Weber holds, be limited and partial, and such meaning as it has is given to it only in terms of the observer's values. It is not that sociology, economics or history cannot be 'value-free' in the sense that validated statements of cause and effect are true or false irrespective of what may be the moral or political preferences of the sociologist. It is that the sociologist's conceptualisation of the world is, and can only be, formed and directed by what is of historical and cultural significance to him. This therefore makes his task a lonely but at the same time an heroic one. He has to strive for objectivity within his chosen assumptions and values while recognising that these cannot claim any objective validity themselves.

This view of the world and the sociologist's role in it is reflected in both the methodological and substantive parts of *Economy and Society*. The first part of it had, unlike the rest, been revised by Weber before he died and can therefore be taken as a definitive statement of his view of what sociology can and cannot do and how it should set about it. Weber holds that the concepts which sociology

[1] As was first pointed out by Karl Löwith in 'Max Weber und Karl Marx', published in Weber's own journal, *Archiv für Sozialwissenschaft und Sozialpolitik*, in 1932.
[2] Quoted by Paul Honigsheim, *On Max Weber* (East Lansing, Michigan, 1968), p. 45.

employs are directed to the empirical regularities observable in social action, and that it is then for the historian, as opposed to the sociologist, to make use of them in offering a causal explanation of whatever particular events are important to him. These 'ideal type' concepts must, however, even where they refer to collectivities (like 'the state') or epochs (like 'the Renaissance') or forms of society (like 'capitalism'), be reducible to the action or probability of action of individuals; and that action must be understandable both in the sense that it can be seen to relate to some form of rule and in the sense that the meaning of the rule to the agent can be grasped by an external observer. Understanding someone's behaviour is not a substitute for explaining it: on the contrary, it is only a part of the necessary causal account and has itself, like any other hypothesis, to be tested against the evidence. But the need for, and indeed the possibility of, understanding the meaning which behaviour has to the agent performing it is what distinguishes the explanation of behaviour from the explanation of inanimate events (which themselves, of course, may also play a significant causal role in human history).

Much has been written about Weber's use of the term 'ideal type', which he borrowed and adapted from its use in the writings of his contemporary Georg Jellinek, and it is certainly true that his own discussion of it is not so clear as to make further commentary unnecessary. But the main point which he uses it to make is simply that the concepts which the sociologist frames in order to give meaning and coherence to the otherwise chaotic flux of history are logical constructions – constructions, that is, of the sociologist's own adoption or contrivance which furnish a standard in terms of which actual forms of social organisation can be classified and compared. The criticism which this assertion invites is not that it is false – it is, if anything, obvious – but that it leads Weber into an excessive disposition to frame ahistorical typologies which do not, in the event, lead to either the cross-cultural generalisations or the causal explanations which the reader has come to expect. This criticism is, I think, fair. Weber's four-fold typology of social action and his emphasis on 'rationality' as the yardstick against which individual actions and the institutions constituted by them are to be assessed are neither necessary to, nor even very helpful towards, the formulation of his substantive hypotheses about the causes of the decline of the ancient world, the influence of religion on economic activity or the prerequisites for parliamentary democracy. At the same time, however, the need for clear definition and serviceable classification of the types of social relationships with which sociologists, historians, economists and the rest all have to deal is undeniable. Weber's own definitions and classifications may sometimes be both more highly abstract and more strictly individualistic than they either need or should. But then it is up to his critics to improve on them.

This holds particularly for Weber's influential definitions of 'power', 'domination' and 'the state' and his classification of political legitimacy as either 'traditional', 'rational-legal' or 'charismatic'. In accordance with his basic assumption, his definitions reflect his own presuppositions and priorities about the nature of politics. His emphasis on coercion, his insistence that domination is to be defined in terms of obedience to commands on the part of a specified group of people, and his definition of 'the state' in terms of its territorial monopoly of the legitimate use of force irrespective of the purposes to which that monopoly is applied all can be, and have been, challenged by others whose presuppositions differ from his. In particular, his definitions have been argued to make too little allowance for the manipulation as opposed to the coercion by rulers of those over whom they rule and the possibility that domination may be exercised by sustaining a tacit agreement to keep certain kinds of countervailing claims from being articulated at all. But it remains doubtful whether a better alternative set of definitions for the analysis of politics has yet been put forward; and it would be difficult to maintain that Weber's stress on force and nationalism has lost any of its relevance in the decades since he wrote.

Likewise, Weber's analysis of social stratification in terms of a three-fold distinction between the forms of power belonging respectively to classes, status groups and parties has not yet been superseded, despite the controversy which it continues to arouse. It comes, unfortunately, from one of the parts of *Economy and Society* which he left unrevised at his death: even the passage on status groups and classes which is here included as a postscript to the earlier and longer discussion is itself incomplete, as its final sentence makes clear. But his treatment remains the *locus classicus* for all sociologists who see it as necessary to concep-tualise social inequality in a way which does not assume that it can always be reduced without remainder to the relations between classes defined in relation to the forces of production. It is almost certainly a mistake, despite Weber's remark that 'parties are primarily at home in the sphere of power', to understand him as treating class, status (in the sense of social prestige) and power as the three dimensions of stratification, for he sees all competition and conflict between social groups as a struggle for power. But he does not see them as reducible to each other. His view is thus equally far from the 'functionalist' view according to which social stratification reflects the differential value which society as a whole assigns to different occupational roles and from the Marxist view according to which political power derives from ownership of the means of production. The differ-ence between the three is not one which can be settled in the abstract: they can only, as Weber would have agreed, be tested by seeing whether the explanations which they generate stand up more or less well against the evidence which history provides independently of the moral and political preferences of those who subscribe to them. But Weber's view, taken together with his underlying conception of the nature of social action and of the forms which communal action can take, may still turn out in the end to be the most durable of the three.

The four selections which follow, although they are all from *Economy and Society,* are from different parts of it. The first, as Weber's first sub-title indicates, is to be taken as largely methodological. The second comes under his second sub-title 'The Concept of Social Action', and is part of a long sequence of definitional discussions of the forms of social and political relations which leads in turn into a still longer sequence covering economic relations. The third selection comes much later, at the end of a chapter on politics, and the last (which, as I have mentioned, was in fact written earlier) follows a long chapter on the forms of domination. However, they can be read in sequence as complementary to one another even by those unfamiliar with the work as a whole.

1 · *The Nature of Social Action*

'Sociology' is a word which is used in many different senses. In the sense adopted here, it means the science whose object is to interpret the meaning of social action and thereby give a causal explanation of the way in which the action proceeds and the effects which it produces. By 'action' in this definition is meant human behaviour when and to the extent that the agent or agents see it as subjectively *meaningful*: the behaviour may be either internal or external, and may consist in the agent's doing something, omitting to do something, or having something done to him. By 'social' action is meant an action in which the meaning intended by the agent or agents involves a relation to *another* person's behaviour and in which that relation determines the way in which the action proceeds.

I. METHODOLOGICAL FOUNDATIONS

(1) The 'meaning' to which we refer may be either (*a*) the meaning actually intended either by an individual agent on a particular historical occasion or by a number of agents on an approximate average in a given set of cases, or (*b*) the meaning attributed to the agent or agents, as types, in a pure type constructed in the abstract. In neither case is the 'meaning' to be thought of as somehow objectively 'correct' or 'true' by some metaphysical criterion. This is the difference between the empirical sciences of action, such as sociology and history, and any kind of *a priori* discipline, such as jurisprudence, logic, ethics, or aesthetics whose aim *is* to extract from their subject-matter its 'correct' or 'valid' meaning.

(2) No sharp dividing line can be drawn between meaningful action and what we shall call for our present purposes 'purely reactive' behaviour: that is, behaviour with which the agent does not associate any subjectively intended meaning. An extremely important part of all behaviour which is relevant to sociology, especially purely traditional behaviour (see below), straddles this dividing line. In several types of psycho-physical process, action which is meaningful and so understandable is not to be found at all; in others, the meaning can only be discovered by specialists. For instance, mystical experiences which cannot be adequately expressed in words are not fully understandable by those not attuned to them. On the other hand, it is not necessary, in order to

be able to understand an action, that one should be able to perform a similar action oneself: 'It is not necessary to be Caesar in order to understand Caesar.' The ability totally to 're-live' an experience is important if one is to be certain that one has understood it, but is not absolutely necessary in order to interpret its meaning. In any piece of behaviour, those elements which can be understood are often intimately bound up with those elements which can not.

(3) The aim of all interpretation of meanings is, like that of science in general, to achieve certainty. This certainty in our understanding of action may take either a rational form (in which case it may be either logical or mathematical) or the form of empathetically re-living the experience in question (involving the emotions and artistic sensibility). Rational certainty is achieved above all in the case of an action in which the intended complex of meanings can be *intellectually* understood in its entirety and with complete clarity. Empathetic certainty is achieved when an action and the complex of feelings experienced by the agent is completely re-lived in the imagination. Rational intelligibility, which here implies the possibility of achieving an immediate and unambiguous intellectual grasp of meaning, is to be found in its highest degree in those complexes of meaning which are related to each other in the way in which mathematical or logical propositions are. We understand quite unambiguously what is meant when someone asserts the proposition '$2 \times 2 = 4$' or Pythagoras' theorem in thought or argument, or when he completes a logical chain of reasoning in what is – according to our conventions of thought – the 'correct' way. The same is true when someone in his actions derives from 'empirical facts' which we recognise to be the case and from the ends which he has set himself the conclusions which (in our own experience) clearly follow as to the kind of 'means' which he should adopt. Every interpretation of a rationally directed purposive action of this kind attains, in the understanding of the means adopted, the highest possible degree of certainty. We can, however, also achieve a degree of certainty which, although not as high, is quite adequate for the needs of explanation, in our understanding of those 'errors', including the confusion of one problem with another, to which we ourselves are especially liable or whose genesis we are able empathetically to re-live.

On the other hand, there are a number of ultimate 'goals' or 'values' towards which a man's actions may, as a matter of empirical fact, be directed which we very often *cannot* understand with complete certainty, though in some cases we can grasp their meaning at an intellectual level. In such cases, however, the more radically these ultimate values diverge from our own, the more difficult it is for us to understand them by re-living them through an act of empathetic imagination. Indeed, depending on the particular case, we may have to be content either with a merely intellectual understanding or, where even that proves to be unattainable, with a simple acceptance of them as brute facts. In that case, we have to try to make the course of the action motivated by these goals understandable by trying, as far as is possible, to grasp the goals intellectually or to re-live them empathetically in as close an approximation as we can manage. Examples of this kind include attempts by those who are not themselves sympathetic to them to understand many acts of extreme religious devotion or charity. Another example is attempts by those to whom such goals are profoundly abhorrent to understand fanatical supporters of extreme rationalism (such as some campaigners for 'The Rights of Man'). The more we ourselves are susceptible to them, the more certainly we can re-live such emotional states as anxiety, anger, ambition, envy, jealousy, love, enthusiasm, pride, vengefulness, devotion, submissiveness, lust of all kinds, and the reactions which result from them (irrational though they are from the point of view of rationally purposive action). In every case, however, even when such emotions far exceed anything of which we ourselves are capable, we can gain some understanding of their meaning by empathy and we can intellectually allow for their influence on the direction taken by the action and the means used in performing it.

When we adopt the kind of scientific procedure which involves the construction of *types*, we can investigate and make fully comprehensible all those irrational, affectively determined, patterns of meaning which influence action, by representing them as 'deviations' from a pure type of the action as it would be if it proceeded in a rationally purposive way. For example, in explaining a panic on the stock exchange, it is first convenient to decide how the individuals concerned would have acted if they had *not* been influenced by irrational emotional impulses; then these irrational elements can be brought in to the explanation as 'disturbances'. Similarly, when dealing with a political or military enterprise, it is first convenient to decide how the action would have proceeded if all the circumstances and all the intentions of those involved had been known, and if the means adopted had been chosen in a fully rationally purposive way, on the basis of empirical evidence which seems to us valid. Only then does it become possible to give a causal explanation of the deviations from this course in terms of irrational factors. The constructed model of a fully rationally purposive action in such cases can be understood by the sociologist with complete certainty and the total clarity which results from its rationality: as a *type* (an 'ideal type') it thus enables him to understand the real action, influenced as it is by all sorts of irrational facts (emotional impulses, errors), as a 'deviation' from what might be expected if those performing it had behaved in a fully rational way.

9

It is only in these methodological assumptions, and in no other way, that the method of 'interpretative' sociology is 'rationalistic'. It is of course quite wrong to regard this method as expressing any rationalistic prejudices concerning sociology: it is simply a methodological tool and should not therefore be taken as implying any belief that life is in fact dominated by rational considerations. On the question of the extent to which *actual* behaviour is, or is not, governed by rational deliberation about purposes, it has nothing whatsoever to say. That there is always a risk of rationalistic interpretations being proposed in the wrong places is admittedly undeniable. All experience, unfortunately, confirms this.

(4) Events and objects which are in themselves meaningless must be taken into account by all the sciences of action if they are either causes or effects of, or promote or hinder, human action. The term 'meaningless' is not synonymous with 'inanimate' or 'non-human'. Every artefact (e.g. a machine) has a meaning which can be interpreted and understood purely because of its having been produced by human beings and used in human activities (possibly for very different purposes); and unless this meaning is taken into account, the use of the artefact remains totally unintelligible. It is intelligible therefore in virtue of its relationship with human action, either as a means to some end or as an end in itself, which a certain agent or agents had in mind and to which their action was directed. It is only in terms of categories such as these that it is possible to understand such objects. On the other hand, all events or states of affairs, whether animate or inanimate, non-human or human, remain meaningless if no agent has consciously endowed them with meaning and if they do not stand in a 'means–end' relation to any action, but only cause, promote or hinder it. When the River Dollart flooded in the year 1277, this was (perhaps) an event of some 'historical' significance, since it led to movements of population on a scale large enough to be historically important. The way of dealing with death, and the whole cycle of organic life in general, from the helplessness of infancy to that of hoary old age, are naturally of considerable sociological importance because of the various ways in which human action has concerned itself, and continues to concern itself, with these circumstances. Yet another category of cases is constituted by the empirical principles, which have no discernible meaning, governing the course of certain mental and psycho-physiological phenomena, such as fatigue, training, memory, etc., and also such things as states of heightened consciousness induced by some forms of asceticism, or typical variations in reaction in terms of tempo, style, precision and so forth. In the last resort, however, the situation here is the same as in the case of other 'meaningless' facts: both the agent in his actual practice and the sociologist in his attempt at interpretation must simply take them as data with which he has to reckon.

It is possible that future enquiry will bring to light non-meaningful laws underlying meaningful behaviour – however little in this direction has been achieved up to now. For example, differences in biological heredity ('racial' differences and the like) might need to be accepted as sociological data in exactly the same way as physiological facts about variations in nutritional needs or about the effect of ageing on action, if and insofar as reliable statistical evidence were to be produced about their influence on some kind of sociologically relevant behaviour, in particular on the nature of the relationship between a social action and its *meaning*. The recognition of the causal importance of such factors would not in the least, of course, alter the tasks of sociology and of the sciences of action generally. Their task would still be that of interpreting the meanings which men give to their actions and so understanding the actions themselves. It would simply be that at certain points in complexes of motivation which they could interpret and so understand they would interpolate facts which had no intelligible meaning, such as the typical correlations between the frequency with which particular purposive actions occur (or the degree of rationality which actions typically have) and the cranial index or skin-colour or other physiologically inherited qualities of the agents. This already happens at present (see above).

(5) Understanding can be of two kinds. (i) It can consist in *direct* understanding of the intended meaning of an action (including verbal utterances as 'actions'). For instance, we can directly 'understand' the meaning of the proposition '$2 \times 2 = 4$' when we hear or read it: this is a case of direct rational understanding of a thought. Similarly, we can 'understand' an outburst of anger, manifested in a person's facial expression, exclamations, or irrational movements: in this case we have direct non-rational understanding of emotional impulses. Finally, we can 'understand' the behaviour of a woodcutter, or someone's grasping a door-handle in order to shut the door, or someone's aiming a rifle at an animal: this is direct rational understanding of actions. 'Understanding', however, can also mean (ii) *explanatory* understanding. We can 'understand' the meaning of someone's uttering or writing down the proposition '$2 \times 2 = 4$' in the sense of seeing his motive for *acting* in this way at this precise moment and in this context: we may see it as having to do with a commercial calculation, a scientific demonstration, a technical estimate, or some other activity. Because of the connexion between this activity and the meaning of the action, which we can understand, the proposition 'fits in' – that is, it forms part of a complex of meanings which we can make sense of: this constitutes rational understanding of motive. We understand the action of someone cutting wood or aiming a rifle not only directly but also in terms of motive, if we know certain facts about the action: for instance, if we know that someone is cutting wood for a

living or to provide for his own needs or as a form of recreation, these would be examples of rational motivation; on the other hand, if he is simply working off a state of emotional agitation, then this would be an example of irrational motivation. Similarly, if someone fires a rifle because he is ordered to do so in the course of an execution or a battle, this is a rational motive; if he shoots someone for revenge, then this is an affective (and in that sense, therefore, irrational) motive. Finally, we can understand anger in terms of its motives when we know that it springs from jealousy, slighted vanity, or wounded honour, because then we know that it is affectively determined and therefore irrationally motivated. All these are examples of intelligible complexes of meaning: when we have understood them, we consider that we have explained the way in which the action in fact proceeded. To 'explain', therefore, for a science concerned with the meanings of actions, is to grasp the complex of meanings into which a directly intelligible action fits in virtue of its subjectively intended meaning. (For a discussion of the causal significance of this kind of 'explanation' see Section 6.) In all these cases, even in the case of affective processes, we wish to refer to the subjective meaning both of what happens and of the complex of meanings as the 'intended' meaning: in this respect we diverge from ordinary usage, according to which it is customary to speak of 'intending' in this sense only in cases of rationally purposive action.

(6) In all these cases, the term 'understanding' refers to the interpretative grasp of the meaning or pattern of meanings which are either (a) really intended in a particular case (as is normal in historical enquiry) or (b) intended by the average agent to some degree of approximation (as in sociological studies of large groups), or (c) constructed scientifically for the 'pure' or 'ideal' type of a frequently occurring phenomenon (this we can call 'ideal-typical' meaning). Examples of such ideal-typical constructions would be the concepts and 'laws' formulated in pure economic theory. They describe the way a determinate type of human action *would* proceed, *if* the agent were acting in a fully rational way in furtherance of his purposes, undisturbed by errors or emotional impulses and *if*, furthermore, it were quite definitely intended to achieve one and only one goal (an economic one). Actions in the real world proceed in this way only in rare cases (for instance, the stock exchange), and even then they only approximate to the constructed ideal type. (On the purpose of such constructions, see my paper in *Archiv für Sozialwissenschaft*, XIX, pp. 64ff and below, Section 11.)

The aim of every interpretation is indeed certainty (cf. Section 3). But no matter how certain an interpretation may be on the level of meaning, it cannot as such and on that account claim also to be the causally *valid* interpretation. In itself it is rather a causal *hypothesis* which has a particular degree of certainty. For, first, rationalisations of motive and repressions (in other words, failure to avow motives) may often conceal even from the agent himself the real connexions between the things which he does, so that even when he believes himself to be sincerely reporting on his state of mind, his reports may be of only relative value. In a case like this, the task of sociology is to discover these connexions and analyse them in terms of their meanings, *even though* they were not consciously present (or, in most cases, not fully present) as the 'intended' meaning of the action in the particular concrete case. Cases like this are on the borderlines of the interpretation of meaning. Secondly, external processes of action which seem to us to be the 'same' or 'similar' may result from very different complexes of meaning, as seen by the agent or agents; and we can also 'understand' actions which are intended to deal with situations which seem to us to be 'similar', but which differ markedly from each other and may even be totally opposed to each other in meaning. Examples can be found in Simmel's *Problems in the Philosophy of History*. Thirdly, human agents, faced with particular situations, are very often subject to contradictory or mutually conflicting impulses which we can 'understand' collectively. But the relative strength of the various relationships between meanings which may be involved in such 'conflicts of motive' and which are understandable in the same way in relation to each other is something which, judging by all experience, it may be hard in a great many cases to estimate even approximately, and very frequently impossible to be certain about. Only when we see the actual outcome of the conflict of motives do we have the answer.

As with all hypotheses, therefore, it is vital to have some check on our interpretation of meaning by reference to what ensues from the action – to what the outcome actually is. It is only possible to achieve this with relative precision in the regrettably small number of suitable special cases in which it is possible to carry out a psychological experiment. Statistical methods can also give us results, but only to widely varying degrees of approximation, in the equally small number of cases of group phenomena which are measurable and in which numerical relationships can be clearly established. Apart from this, all that it is possible to do is to compare as many events of history or ordinary life as possible, taking events which are similar in all respects except the *one* decisive point, namely the 'motive' or 'cause' which is currently being investigated because of its practical importance. This is an important task for comparative sociology. Often, unfortunately, it has to be accepted that we are left only with that very unreliable instrument, the 'thought-experiment', in which we think away individual elements from the chain of motives and *then* construct the probable course of action, in order to arrive at an attribution of cause.

For example, 'Gresham's Law', as it is called, is a rationally certain interpretation of human actions under given conditions, based on the assumption that the agents are conforming to the ideal type of a purely rational pursuit of their purposes. The extent to which actions *in fact* conform to this type can only be ascertained by producing empirical evidence, which can in principle, and in the last resort, be expressed in some 'statistical' form, about the way in which coinage which is at any given time undervalued in the monetary system in fact tends to disappear from circulation. Such evidence does actually confirm its great accuracy as a generalisation. The way in which this knowledge has actually been acquired has been that first empirical observations were made and then an interpretation was formulated. Without this excellent interpretation our need for a causal explanation would have been plainly unsatisfied. On the other hand, if it had not been shown that the course of behaviour which was constructed – as we assume it was – by pure reasoning also occurs in the real world to some extent, such a 'law', however certain in itself, would remain a worthless construction as far as knowledge of real actions is concerned. In this example, there is absolutely conclusive agreement between adequacy on the level of meaning and empirical validation, and the cases are numerous enough to allow us to see the empirical evidence as sufficiently corroborated. Eduard Meyer has proposed an ingenious hypothesis, deduced on the basis of an interpretation of meanings and supported by the evidence of such symptomatic events as the behaviour of the Greek oracles and of the Persian prophets, about the causal importance of the battles of Marathon, Salamis and Plataea in the development of Greek, and thereby of Western, civilisation. It can only be corroborated, however, by the evidence provided by examples of the way in which the Persians behaved when victorious, as they were in Jerusalem, Egypt and Asia Minor, and the corroboration must remain in many respects necessarily incomplete. In this case, the rational plausibility of the hypothesis in terms of meaning is bound to lend support to it. In a large number of cases of apparently very plausible historical interpretations, however, it is not even possible to apply the kind of test which could be applied in this instance. In these cases, the interpretation must in the end remain at the level of an 'hypothesis'.

(7) A 'motive' is a complex of meanings which seems either to the agent himself or to the observer to provide meaningful grounds for behaving in a certain way. We use the term 'adequate on the level of meaning' to refer to a behaviour pattern to the extent that the relation between the elements of the pattern constitutes a complex of meanings which, in terms of our ordinary conventions of thought and feeling, would be acknowledged as typical (or, as we usually say, 'correct'). We use the term 'causally adequate', on the other hand, to refer to a sequence of events

to the extent that there is a probability, governed by *empirical* laws, of its always in fact following the same course. An example of adequacy on the level of meaning in this sense would be a solution of an arithmetical problem which was *correct* according to our current norms of calculation or reasoning. An example of causal adequacy would be the statistical probability, in accordance with well-confirmed empirical laws, of a solution which was 'correct' or 'false' in terms of those same presently current norms of our society and so of a typical miscalculation or a typical confusion of one problem with another. To give a causal explanation therefore is to establish a generalisation to the effect that a certain observed internal or external event will be followed by (or occur simultaneously with) a certain other event, with a probability which can be estimated in some way or other, and which in the (rare) ideal case can be quantitatively measured.

To give a correct causal interpretation of a particular action is to see the outward course of the action and its motive as appropriate and at the same time as related to each other in a way whose meaning can be understood. To give a correct causal interpretation of a *typical* action (or intelligible type of action) is to show that the occurrence which is said to be typical not only seems to be adequate to some degree or other on the level of meaning but is also to some degree or other causally adequate. Without adequacy on the level of meaning, our generalisations remain mere statements of *statistical* probability, either not intelligible at all or only imperfectly intelligible: this is so no matter how high the probability of outcome (whether in external behaviour or in mental processes) and no matter how precisely calculable in numerical terms it may be. On the other hand, from the point of view of its importance for sociological knowledge, even the most certain adequacy on the level of meaning signifies an acceptable *causal* proposition only to the extent that evidence can be produced that there is a probability (no matter how it may be calculated) that the action in question *really* takes the course held to be meaningfully adequate with a certain calculable frequency or some approximation to it (whether on average or in the 'ideal' case). Only those statistical generalisations which fit in with our interpretation of the intended meaning of a social action are to be taken as intelligible types of action in the sense of that expression used here: in other words, as 'sociological laws'. Only those rationally constructed models of intelligible action which apply, at least to some degree of approximation, to observable situations in the real world constitute a realistic sociological typology. It is far from being the case that the probability of an action's actually following the corresponding course with a certain frequency always increases in proportion to the degree of adequacy on the level of meaning of an interpretation. But only further empirical observation can show in any given case whether this is so. There are statistics of meaningless phenomena (such as death rates, incidence of fatigue, output of machinery, or amount of rainfall) in just the same way as there are of meaningful phenomena. We have *sociological* statistics, however, only when they concern meaningful phenomena (such as crime rates, occupational distributions, tables of prices, or figures for area of land under cultivation). There are, of course, a large number of cases which include *both*, such as harvest statistics.

(8) To say that certain processes and regularities do not count as 'sociological facts' or laws in the sense employed here because they are not meaningful is not, of course, to say that they are for that reason any less *important*. It is not even to say that they have no importance for sociology in the sense used here, according to which it is limited to so-called 'interpretative' sociology – a definition which no one could or should be forced to accept. All that one can say is that they operate (as they inevitably must from the methodological point of view) in an area quite distinct from that of meaningful action – the area of 'conditions', 'stimuli', 'obstacles to' or 'promoters of' action.

(9) In our view, the term 'action', in the sense of behaviour which can be understood in terms of its relation to a meaning, can properly be applied only to the behaviour of one or more *individual* persons.

For the purposes of other disciplines it may be useful or necessary to view a single individual, say, as a community of cells or a system of biochemical reactions, or to think of his 'mental' life as made up of separable elements of some kind or other. There is no doubt that the knowledge acquired in this way, in the form of causal laws, is valuable. But we do not *understand* the behaviour of these elements, as expressed in these laws. This is not even so with mental elements: indeed, the more precisely they are apprehended in terms of natural science, the less intelligible they become. This is certainly *not* the way to obtain an interpretation in terms of intended meaning. For sociology in our sense (and this applies equally to history) it is, however, precisely the complex of *meanings* to which the action belongs which is the object of comprehension. The behaviour of physiological elements such as cells, or of any mental elements, can be observed, at least in principle, and from these observations deductions can be made and rules ('laws') formulated with the help of which individual occurrences can be causally 'explained', that is, subsumed under rules. The sociologist in his interpretation of actions, however, takes no more and no different notice of such facts and laws than of any others (e.g. physical, astronomical, geological, meteorological, geographical, botanical, zoological, physiological, or anatomical facts, meaningless facts of psychopathology or those facts of natural science which provide the foundation for technology).

For the purposes of yet other branches of knowledge (such as jurisprudence), on the other hand, or for practical purposes it may be equally appropriate, and indeed necessary, to treat such social systems as states, associations, limited companies and institutions exactly as if they were individual persons: for example, they may be seen as having rights and duties, as performing *legally* relevant actions, etc. But from the standpoint of the sociological understanding of the meaning of actions such systems are simply outcomes of and relations between specific actions performed by *individual* human beings, who alone, for the sociologist, are the intelligible performers of meaningful actions. Nevertheless, even for its own purposes sociology cannot afford to ignore the collective concepts of other disciplines. This is because the interpretation of action has to refer to these collective concepts in the following three ways:

(*a*) It is often necessary for the sociologist to make use of similar (often even identical) collective concepts in his own work in order, in general, to develop an intelligible terminology. Like everyday language, the language of jurisprudence refers, for instance, to the 'state' in the sense both of the legal concept and of the set of circumstances in terms of social action to which the rules of the law apply. For the sociologist, the set of circumstances which he calls 'the state' does not necessarily consist only or exactly of those elements which are *legally* relevant. And certainly he does not think of there being any collective personality which 'acts' as the state. Rather, when he speaks of a 'state', a 'nation', a 'limited company', a 'family', an 'army corps' or any similar collectivity, he means by such expressions nothing more than a specifically structured outcome of the social actions of individuals, either actually performed or constructed as possible. In short, he imposes a totally different sense on the legal concept, which he makes use of because of its precision and familiarity.

(*b*) In interpreting action, the sociologist must take account of the fundamentally important fact that the collective concepts which we employ in our thinking, whether in legal or other specialist contexts or in everyday life, *represent* something: what they represent is something which in part actually exists and has a normative force in the minds of real men (not only judges and officials, but also the general public) whose actions take account of it. Because of this, they are of great, often absolutely vital, importance in giving a causal explanation of the way in which the actions of real human beings proceed. This is true above all in that they represent in the minds of real human beings something which has (or does not have) binding normative force. (Because of this, a modern 'state' exists to a large extent in the form of a specific complex of collective human action whereby the actions of particular men are governed by their belief that it exists or that it should exist. In other

17

words, their actions result from their acceptance that its regulations have legal validity. There will be further discussion of this later.) If we were concerned only with the particular needs of sociological terminology (cf. (a) above), it would be possible, though extremely pedantic and long-winded, entirely to eliminate such concepts, which are used in ordinary language not only as expressions of legal norms but also as descriptions of what actually happens: we could then substitute completely newly formed words. But at least in this important context it would naturally be out of the question.

(c) The method of 'organic' sociology, as it is called, classically represented by Schäffle's brilliant book *Structure and Life of the Social Organism*, seeks to elucidate collective social action by starting from 'wholes' (e.g. a 'national economy'). The individual and his behaviour are then interpreted within a whole in much the same way that the physiologist interprets the position of a bodily organ in relation to the 'economy' of the organism (in other words, in terms of the contribution which it makes to its 'maintenance'). We might recall the celebrated remark made by a physiologist in one of his lectures: 'Section X. The Spleen. We know nothing of the spleen, gentlemen. So much for the spleen!' Actually, the lecturer in question 'knew' quite a lot about the spleen: where it is situated, what size it is, what shape it is and so on. The only thing he could not tell his students was its 'function', and it is this incapacity to which he referred as 'ignorance'. We cannot here examine the question of the extent to which this kind of *functional* approach, in terms of the relation of the 'parts' to a 'whole', plays a necessarily central role in other disciplines: it is generally accepted that it is in principle inadequate for the purposes of biochemistry and biophysics. In the case of interpretative sociology, such a mode of expression can serve two purposes. First, it can be used for purposes of practical illustration and provisional orientation, and so used can be extremely valuable and necessary (although it must also be said that it can be extremely dangerous if its cognitive value is overestimated and if its concepts are treated in a misleadingly reified way). Secondly, in certain circumstances this approach is the only thing which can enable us to find out which social action it is important to interpret and understand if we are to explain a particular system. But this is the point at which the task of sociology (in the sense defined here) first *begins*. In the case of 'social systems' (as opposed to 'organisms') we are in a position, not only to formulate functional interrelations and regularities (or 'laws'), but also to achieve something which must lie for ever beyond the reach of all forms of 'natural science' (in the sense of the formulation of causal laws governing events and systems and the explanation of individual events in terms of them). What we can do is to 'understand' the behaviour of the individuals involved, whereas we do *not* 'understand' the behaviour of, say, cells. All we can do in the case of cells is to grasp their behaviour in functional terms and then formulate *laws* governing the way it proceeds. A price has to be paid, admittedly, for these advantages which interpretative explanation has over observational: the results obtained by interpretation are necessarily of a more hypothetical and fragmentary character. Nevertheless, this is precisely what is distinctive about the sociological mode of apprehension.

We shall not here consider at all questions about the extent to which animal behaviour has a meaning which we can 'understand' and vice versa: in both cases the term would be highly uncertain in meaning and problematic in scope. Neither, therefore, shall we consider to what extent it would be theoretically possible to have a sociology of the relations between men and animals (as in the cases of domestic and hunting animals). (Many animals 'understand' orders, expressions of anger, affection, aggression and so on, and react to them in many cases in a way which is plainly not simply mechanical or instinctive but is in some degree the expression of a consciously intended meaning and guided by past experience.) The extent to which we can empathetically understand the behaviour of primitive men is essentially no greater. However, it is either impossible for us, or possible only in a very inadequate way, to discover with any certainty an animal's state of mind: as is well known, the problems of animal psychology are as interesting as they are thorny. There are in particular known to be very different kinds of animal community: monogamous and polygamous 'families', herds, packs, even 'states' with a functional division of labour. (The extent to which an animal community is functionally differentiated is not in any way correlated with the extent of differentiation of organs or morphological development in the species in question. This is so with functional differentiation among termites, whose artefacts are, in consequence, much more differentiated than those of ants and bees.) In cases like this, it is obvious that the essential thing, at least for the present, is very often to make a purely functional study, and we must rest content in our researches with a determination of those functions performed by the different types of individuals (kings, queens, workers, soldiers, drones, breeders, substitute-queens, etc.) which are of decisive importance for the preservation (that is, nutrition, defence, reproduction and expansion) of the animal societies in question. Apart from that, there have been for a long time only speculations or else enquiries into the extent to which heredity or environment might be involved in the development of these 'social' tendencies. (For example, the debate between Götte and Weismann, whose 'Omnipotence of Natural Selection' was based on totally non-empirical reasoning.) But serious scientific opinion is, of course, absolutely unanimous on the point that the restriction to functional enquiry is a matter simply of a necessary, and, it is hoped, merely provisional, decision to go no further. (On the state of termite research see e.g. the work by Escherich published in 1909.)

It is obviously desirable to investigate the 'survival value' of the functions of the particular differentiated types (which is relatively easy to understand) and to get some kind of an account of the way in which this differentiation is to be explained, either with or without the assumption of the inheritance of acquired characteristics (and on the various possible interpretations of this assumption). But it would also be useful to know in addition first, what determines the emergence of differentiation from the original still neutral, undifferentiated individuality; and secondly, what makes the differentiated individual behave (on average) in a way which in practice serves the interest in survival of the differentiated group. Wherever there has been some progress in this work, it has come about experimentally, through evidence (or conjectures) about chemical stimuli, or physiological phenomena such as nutrition, parasitic castration, etc., as they affect *particular* individuals. Even specialists themselves could hardly say at the present stage how much hope there is, if any, of obtaining experimental evidence which would make it plausible to suppose that there also exist 'psychological' elements, elements of 'meaning', involved in the direction of behaviour. A testable account of the mental lives of these social animals, based on an 'understanding' of the meaning of their behaviour, seems to be attainable, even as an ideal goal, only within narrow limits. At all events, this is not where we should look for an 'understanding' of human social action: on the contrary, we operate (and have to operate) with human analogies in investigating animal behaviour. Perhaps all that should be hoped for is that these analogies will prove useful in deciding how to evaluate the relationship which must have existed in the early stages of human social differentiation between the kind of differentiated behaviour which was purely mechanical and instinctive and the kind which had an intelligible meaning for the individual concerned and was, moreover, an expression of *conscious* rationality. The sociologist who seeks to 'understand' action must obviously be clear in his own mind that, even in the case of human beings, the former element was overwhelmingly important in the early stages; and he must always remember that it still plays a part even in the later stages of development (indeed, that the part it plays is of decisive importance). All 'traditional' action (see Section 2) and much of that 'charisma' (see *Economy and Society*, Ch. III) which constitutes the germ of psychological 'contagion' and so acts as a stimulus to sociological 'development' are very close to, and indeed merge imperceptibly with, processes of this kind which can only be conceptualised in biological terms, and which cannot (or can only fragmentarily) be said to have a meaning which can be understood and be explained in terms of their motivation. All this, however, does not excuse the interpretative socio-logist, however conscious he may be of the narrow limits within which he is confined, from the task of trying to achieve what only he *can* achieve.

The various writings of Othmar Spann are often rich in good ideas, although it has to be admitted that they also contain occasional misunder-standings and, above all, arguments based on mere value-judgments of a kind which have no place in empirical enquiry. He is, however, undoubtedly right to emphasise (although admittedly no one would seriously dispute it) the importance for all sociology of posing the ques-tion of function as a preliminary (his name for this is the 'universalistic method'). It is certainly necessary to know in the first place what kind of action is functional, from the point of view of 'survival' and also, even more so, of cultural distinctiveness and of continuity of development of a particular type of social action along given lines. Only then can we pose the questions: how does this kind of action come about? what are its underlying motives? It is essential to know what a king, an official, an entrepreneur, a pimp, or a magician does – in other words, what typical 'action' (which alone, after all, marks them out as belonging to a par-ticular category) is important for the purpose of sociological analysis and has to be taken into account – before the analysis itself can begin: this is what Rickert means by 'value-relevance'. But it is only in this analysis that sociology first accomplishes what it *can*, and therefore *should*, achieve by its understanding of the actions of typically differentiated individual human beings (and *only* human beings).

It is a shocking misunderstanding to think that an 'individualistic' methodology implies a certain valuation of 'individualism' (in any pos-sible sense of that word). It is as important to clear up this misunder-standing as to correct the mistaken view that the fact that concept formation takes a more or less rationalistic form implies that rational motives should be held always to predominate or, indeed, any kind of positive valuation of 'rationalism'. Even a socialist economy needs to be understood for the purposes of interpretative sociology in 'individual-istic' terms, that is, in terms of the actions of the individuals and the types of 'functionaries' who are involved in it, in just the same way as in the case of a market economy understood in terms of the theory of marginal utility (or, for that matter, any 'better' method which may be discovered, as long as it is similar in this respect). For the question which must always be asked first before the real empirical work of sociology can begin is: which motives led and continue to lead individual functionaries and members of this 'community' to behave in such a way that it came into being and continues to exist? The formation of functional concepts, in terms of relationship to the 'whole', is simply part of the preliminary work, the usefulness and indispensability of which, if correctly carried out, cannot of course be disputed.

(10) It is usual to refer to various theories of interpretative sociology as 'laws' (for example, 'Gresham's Law'). These 'laws' are observationally verified statements of the probability with which a certain outcome can be *expected* from social action if certain conditions are realised, and they are understandable in terms of the typical motives and typical intended meanings of the agent in question. They are at their most intelligible and unambiguous when the typically observed outcome results from the purely rational pursuit of a goal (or when, on teleological grounds, the typical actions in a methodologically constructed model are attributed to such a motive), and when the means–end relation in the context is clear on empirical grounds (that is, when the means is 'unavoidable'). In this case, it is legitimate to say that if the action *were* performed in a purely rationally purposive way, then it *must* have been performed in that way and no other, since the persons concerned were able, for technical reasons, to use only these and no other means to achieve their clearly defined ends.

It is just this kind of case, moreover, which makes it plain how mistaken it is to think of any kind of 'psychology' as the ultimate 'basis' of interpretative sociology. Everyone nowadays means something different by the term 'psychology'. There are distinct methodological advantages, if certain processes are to be studied by the methods of the natural sciences, in separating the 'physical' from the 'mental': but such a separation, in these terms, is alien to those disciplines which study action. A science of psychology which in practice studies *only* what is classified as 'mental' in terms of the methodology of the natural sciences, uses only the methods of natural science and therefore refrains from the quite different task of interpreting human behaviour in terms of its intended meaning, will yield findings which, whatever form its methodology may take, may of course come to have some importance for sociological enquiry in particular cases just as may those of any other science: indeed they may often be very important. But sociology is not in general related any more closely to such a science than to any other discipline. The mistake lies in a concept of the 'mental' according to which whatever is not 'physical' is 'mental'. But the meaning of an arithmetical problem which confronts someone is certainly not 'mental'. When a man deliberates in a rational way whether certain clearly specified interests would be advanced or not by a particular action, in terms of its likely consequences, and comes to the conclusion which follows from his deliberations, then his action is not made an iota more intelligible by bringing in 'psychological' considerations. But it is on the basis of precisely these kinds of rational presuppositions that sociology (including economics) constructs most of its 'laws'. When the sociologist attempts, on the other hand, to explain the *irrational* elements in action, he can certainly derive valuable assistance from a psychology based on the *understanding* of such elements. But this alters nothing in the fundamental methodological situation.

(11) We have already taken it for granted more than once that the sociologist constructs *type*-concepts and seeks to formulate *general* statements about what happens. This is in contrast with the historian, who aims to provide a causal analysis and an assessment of *individual* culturally significant actions, social systems and persons. The sociologist, in forming his concepts, for the most part (though not by any means exclusively) finds the material which serves him as a paradigm in those same real human actions which are relevant from the point of view of the historian. What is more, he constructs his concepts and formulates his generalisations above all with a view to serving the purposes of the historian in his causal analysis of culturally significant phenomena. As is the case with any generalising science, the very abstract nature of the concepts of sociology means that they must be relatively lacking in content as compared with the concrete realities of history. What sociology can offer in return is greater conceptual clarity. This increase in clarity is achieved by ensuring the greatest possible degree of adequacy on the level of meaning, and it is to this that the sociologist aspires in the formation of his concepts. It can be achieved most completely in the case of *rational* concepts and laws, whether the rationality takes the form of a pursuit of absolute values or of the choice of appropriate means to an end; and it is this which has been our main concern up to now. But the sociologist seeks also to comprehend such irrational phenomena as mysticism, prophecy, inspiration and emotional states by theoretical concepts which are adequate on the level of meaning. In all cases, rational and irrational alike, he abstracts himself from reality and advances our knowledge of it by elucidating the degree of *approximation* to which a particular historical phenomenon can be classified in terms of one or more of these concepts.

For example, the same historical phenomenon can in one respect count as 'feudal', in another as 'patrimonial', in yet another as 'bureaucratic' and in another still as 'charismatic'. In order that these terms should have a *clear* meaning, the sociologist must for his part formulate 'pure' or 'ideal' types of systems of the relevant kind which exhibit the internal coherence and unity which belongs to the most complete possible adequacy on the level of *meaning*. Just because of its internal coherence, however, this ideal *pure* form is perhaps as little likely to be found in the real world as a physical reaction calculated on the assumption of an absolute vacuum. It is only with such *pure* or 'ideal' types that the more subtle sociological distinctions can be drawn. It goes without saying that the sociologist may also, on occasion, make use of *average* types, of the kind found in empirical statistics: such constructions, however, do not require any special methodological clarification. But all talk of 'typical' cases in sociology should, in case of doubt, be taken to concern *ideal* types, which may be either rational or irrational, although they are usually rational and are always so in some cases, such as that of economic theory. In all cases, however, they must be constructed in such a way as to be adequate on the level of *meaning*.

It is important to be clear that in sociology 'averages' and therefore 'average types' can only be formulated with any degree of clarity where it is simply a matter of differences of degree amongst qualitatively similar kinds of meaningful behaviour. Examples of this do occur. In most cases, however, the historically or sociologically relevant action is influenced by a variety of qualitatively different motives which cannot at all be 'averaged' in any legitimate sense. The kind of ideal-typical model of social action which is constructed, for example, for the purposes of economic theory is therefore 'unrealistic' insofar as it normally asks how men *would* act if they were being ideally rational in pursuit of purely economic goals. It does so in order (i) to be able to understand men's real actions, shaped as they are, at least *in part*, by traditional restraints, emotional impulses, errors and the influence of non-economic purposes and considerations, to the extent that they are *also* affected by the rational pursuit of economic goals either in particular cases or on the average; but also (ii) to facilitate knowledge of their *real* motives by making use of this very deviation of the actual course of events from the ideal type. An ideal-typical model of a consistently mystical and other-worldly attitude to life (to politics and economics, for instance) would have to proceed in exactly the same way. The more sharply and clearly constructed the ideal types are – in other words, the more *unrealistic* they are in this sense – the better they perform their function, which is terminological and classificatory as well as heuristic. The historian's task of concrete causal analysis of individual events proceeds in practice in the same way. For instance, when an historian is trying to explain the course of the campaign of 1866, it is absolutely necessary that he should first work out in his own mind how both Moltke and Benedek would have planned the disposition of their forces if they had had full knowledge of their own and the enemy's situation and *if* they had been ideally rational in pursuit of their purposes. His purpose in doing this is then to compare this idealised model with the dispositions which were actually made, and then to give a causal explanation of the observed deviation (whether due to false information, factual error, faulty reasoning, indi-vidual temperament, or considerations which had nothing to do with strategy). In this case, too, even though it may not be obvious, an ideal-typical model constructed on the assumption of a fully rational pursuit of a goal is being employed.

The constructed concepts of sociology, however, are ideal-typical not only in their outward form but also in their internal structure. In the majority of cases in the *real* world, people act in a state of confused half-awareness or total unconsciousness of their 'intended meaning'. The agent has a vague 'feeling' about his meaning rather than knowing it or 'making it clear to himself': in most cases, he acts on impulse or from habit. Only occasionally is the meaning of action, rational or irrational, raised to the level of consciousness: where many people are acting in a similar way, it is often only a few individuals among them of whom this holds. In real life, genuinely effective (in other words, fully conscious and clearly understood) meaningful action is usually only a limiting case. This is a fact which all historical and sociological discussions which aim at an analysis of the real world will always have to take into account. But that should not prevent the sociologist from constructing his concepts on the basis of a classification of possible 'intended meanings': in other words, as if men acted in practice in conscious awareness of the meaning of their actions. The deviation of his models from reality is something which he must always take into account, if he is to give a sufficiently concrete account of the real world: he must always take care to determine the extent and the form of the deviation.

From the methodological point of view, the only choice is often between a terminology which is not clear at all and one which is clear but unrealistic and 'ideal-typical'. In this situation, however, the latter sort of terminology is scientifically preferable. (On this whole question see *Archiv für Sozialwissenschaft*, xix, pp. 64ff and cf. above Section 6.)

II. THE CONCEPT OF SOCIAL ACTION

(1) Social action (which includes failure to act and being acted upon) can be related to the past, present or anticipated future behaviour of other people (for example, revenge for previous attacks, defence against present attacks, or precautionary measures against future attacks). The 'other people' in question may be particular individuals known to the agent, or an indefinitely large group, none of whom is known to the agent: an example of the latter is money, which signifies a medium of exchange which the agent accepts in a transaction because he bases his action on the expectation that a very large number of other people, none of whom is known to him and of whom there may be indefinitely many, will be prepared, for their part, to accept it in exchange in the future.

(2) Not every kind of action, not even every kind of external behaviour,

is 'social' action in our sense. External behaviour is not 'social action' when it results simply from expectations about the behaviour of material objects. Internal behaviour counts as 'social action' only when it has some relation to the behaviour of other people. For example, religious behaviour is not 'social' when it takes the form only of meditation, solitary prayer, etc. The economic behaviour of an individual becomes 'social' only when, and insofar as, he takes account of the behaviour of third parties. We can express this quite generally and in formal terms by saying that it becomes 'social' action when the agent takes into account the willingness of third parties to respect his effective control over economic goods. In more concrete terms it becomes social when, for example, the individual consumer takes into account the future desires of third parties and decides on the form of his own savings in the light of this, or when a producer bases his course of action on the future desires of a third party, etc.

(3) Not every kind of human contact is social in character: it is only social when one person's behaviour is related in its *meaning* to the behaviour of other people. For example, a collision between two cyclists is a mere occurrence, like a natural event. But when they try to give way to each other, or when they engage in insults, fisticuffs, or peaceful discussion after the collision, this does count as 'social action'.

(4) Social action is not to be identified either (*a*) with several people acting in a similar way together, or (*b*) with one person's acting under the influence of the behaviour of others.

(*a*) When a number of people in a street simultaneously put up their umbrellas at the beginning of a shower, their actions are not normally related to each other's; rather, all act in the same way because of a common need for shelter against the rain.

(*b*) It is a familiar fact that an individual who finds himself in the midst of a crowd gathered together in the same place will be strongly influenced in his action by that fact. This phenomenon, which has been the subject of research by 'crowd psychologists' such as Le Bon, is behaviour *conditioned* by membership of a crowd. Moreover, even in scattered groups of people, the behaviour of individual members of the group may be conditioned in this way, in the sense that many other people will be simultaneously or successively acting on them (by means of the press, for example) and they will be aware of this influence. The simple fact that the individual feels himself to be part of a 'crowd' will make some kinds of reaction possible and inhibit others. As a result, a particular event or human action can evoke feelings of the most diverse kinds – euphoria, frenzy, enthusiasm, despair, and passions of all sorts – where these feelings would not have resulted, or would not have been evoked so easily, in a solitary individual. This can be so even though there is not (at least in many cases) any *meaningful* relationship between the behaviour of the individuals and the fact of their being members of a crowd. An action of this kind, whose character is determined or partially determined in a purely reactive way by the mere fact of the existence of a crowd as such, would not be an instance of a 'social action' in the present definition of that concept. In this regard, of course, the distinction is an extremely fluid one. For not only in cases of demagogic leadership, but often also in the crowd behaviour of the general public itself, there can be a greater or lesser, clearer or less clear, relationship between the attribution of meaning and the fact of the existence of a 'crowd'.

Furthermore, the mere 'imitation' of other people's actions (whose significance has rightly been emphasised by G. Tarde) would not count as an instance of specifically 'social action' if it followed the other action in a purely reactive way, and the one person's action was not meaningfully related to that of the other. The dividing line here is so hazy that it often seems scarcely possible to make any distinction. The mere fact of someone's finding a tendency in his own behaviour which seems to him purposeful and which he learned through discovering it in other people's behaviour, is not, however, in our sense a case of social action. The action is not itself related *to* the behaviour of the other person: rather, *through* observing this behaviour the agent has learned to recognise certain objective possibilities, and it is to *these* that his action is related. His action is *caused* by the other person's action, but does not derive its meaning from it. On the other hand, if someone, for example, imitates someone else's behaviour because it is 'the fashion', or because it is traditional or exemplary or the 'smart' thing to do at a particular level in society, then the meaning of his action is related either to the behaviour of the person imitated, or to that of third parties, or both. Between these two extremes there are naturally a number of intermediate cases. Both sorts of cases – the conditioning of behaviour by membership of a crowd and imitative behaviour – constitute ill-defined limiting cases of social action in the form in which they are often encountered, for example in traditional action (see below, §2). The reason for this haziness, in this case as in others, lies in the fact that it is not always possible to determine precisely the relation to another person's behaviour and the meaning attributed by the agent to his own action: moreover, the agent is not always conscious of these things, and even more rarely fully conscious. Mere 'influence', for that reason, cannot always be distinguished with any certainty from meaningful 'relationship'. But conceptually they must be distinguished, although, obviously, purely 'reactive' forms of imitation are at least as sociologically significant as those which represent 'social action' in the strict sense. 'Social action' is by no means the *only* concern of sociology, although it is the central concern of the kind of sociology considered here, the concern which, as it were, defines the kind of science it is. In saying this, however, one implies nothing whatsoever about the *importance* of this fact in relation to other facts.

§2. Social action, like any kind of action, may be (i) *rational* in the sense of employing *appropriate means to a given end* ('*zweckrational*'): that is, the agent may use his expectations of the behaviour of external objects and other human beings as 'conditions' or 'means' to achieve as the outcome his own rationally pursued and calculated purposes, (ii) *rational* in the sense that it is an *attempt to realise some absolute value* ('*wertrational*'): that is, the agent may consciously believe in the unconditional intrinsic value, whether ethical, aesthetic, religious or any other, of a particular sort of behaviour, purely for its own sake and regardless of consequences, (iii) *affectively* (and in particular *emotionally*) determined, that is, the result of current emotional impulses and states of feeling, or (iv) *traditional* behaviour, the expression of a settled custom.

(1) Behaviour which is traditional in a strong sense lies, like purely reactive imitation (see previous section), directly on, and often beyond, the boundary marking out the area of what can in general be called 'meaningful' action. For very often such behaviour is simply a dull reaction to accustomed stimuli along lines laid down by settled habits. Most of our habitual routines of action approximate to this type. In a systematic treatment, this type has to be taken as a limiting case; but also in certain cases it approximates to the type referred to in (ii) above, since, as we shall see later, the agent's conscious awareness of the relation to custom may vary both in degree and meaning.

(2) Behaviour which is strongly affective lies likewise on, and often beyond, the boundary marking out the area of consciously 'meaningful' behaviour: it may simply be a spontaneous response to an unusual stimulus. It is called *sublimation* when the affectively determined action results from the *conscious* discharge of emotion: in most such cases (though not all) it begins to come close to action which is rational either in the sense of realising an absolute value, or in the 'means–end' sense, or both.

(3) The difference between affectively determined action and action which is intended to realise an absolute value is that, in the latter type, the agent consciously decides on the ultimate goal of his action and *in consequence* systematically organises his action to achieve this goal. What, leaving aside this difference, the two kinds of action have in common is that, in both, the meaning of the action does not lie in the consequences which result from it but is inherent in the specific nature of the action itself. An example of affectively determined action is provided by a person who acts in such a way as to achieve immediate satisfaction of a need for

revenge, pleasure, abandonment, blissful contemplation, or the release of emotional impulses, whether directly or in a sublimated fashion.

An example of someone who acts wholly rationally in the sense of attempting to realise an absolute value is a man who, without any concern for foreseeable consequences, acts out of a conviction based on what duty, honour, beauty, religious doctrine, piety or the importance of any kind of 'cause' seem to him to require. In the sense of the term defined here, an action which is 'rational' in this sense is always performed in obedience to 'imperatives' or in fulfilment of 'claims' which the agent believes to be imposed on him. It is only to the extent that human action is directed to meeting such claims that we wish to speak of rationality in the attempt to realise a value; and this normally holds only for a certain proportion of actions which varies in size and is for the most part fairly small. As we shall show later, its significance is sufficiently great to justify setting it apart as a special type; but at present we are in any case not attempting a classification of types of action which would be in any way exhaustive.

(4) A person acts rationally in the 'means–end' sense when his action is guided by considerations of ends, means and secondary consequences; when, in acting, he rationally *assesses* means in relation to ends, ends in relation to secondary consequences, and, finally, the various possible ends in relation to each other. In short, then, his action is *neither* affectively determined (and especially not emotionally determined) *nor* traditional. When, on the other hand, he has to choose between competing and conflicting ends and consequences, his decision may be rational in the sense of being based on his conception of absolute values: in that case, his action is rational in the present sense only in respect of its means. Alternatively, the agent may not take into account absolute values, with their 'imperatives' and 'claims', but treat the competing and conflicting ends simply as subjectively felt needs and order them on a scale of their relative urgency, as consciously *assessed* by himself, so as to act in such a way as will satisfy them as much as possible in this order. (This is the principle of marginal utility.) There can therefore be various kinds of relationship between the two types of rationality to be found in human action, that based on conceptions of absolute value and that based on fitting means to ends. From the standpoint of the 'means–end' kind of rationality, however, the other kind is always *irrational*, and the more so the more it elevates the value by which action is to be guided to the status of an absolute value. It is irrational on the grounds that an agent is bound to reflect less on the consequences of his action the more he considers the intrinsic value which he is attempting to realise as unconditional, as when his action is based on such considerations as purity of intention, beauty, absolute goodness, absolute obedience to duty, etc. *Complete*

rationality in the 'means–end' sense is, however, only to be found in action as an essentially artificial limiting case.

(5) It is very seldom that an action, especially a social action, takes *only* one or other of these several forms. Equally, the list which has been given is of course not intended in *any* way as an exhaustive classification of the different forms which action may take. Rather, the types mentioned are pure abstractions conceived for sociological purposes, to which real action may approximate to a greater or lesser degree or out of which (an even more frequent case) it is compounded. Its usefulness for *our* purposes can only be made clear in what follows.

§3. A 'social relationship' may be said to exist when several people reciprocally adjust their behaviour to each other with respect to the meaning which they give to it, and when this reciprocal adjustment determines the form which it takes. A social relationship therefore is completely and exclusively characterised by the possibilities of a social action's occurring in a manner which is specifiable in terms of its meaning, irrespective of what these possibilities may depend upon.

(1) The criterion for applying this concept, therefore, is that there should be a minimal relationship between each person's action and that of the other. The character of this relationship may be of the most diverse kind: conflict, hostility, sexual attraction, friendship, piety, the market relationship of buyer and seller, 'fulfilment', 'evasion' or 'breach' of an agreement, economic, sexual or other 'rivalry', common membership of a community based on rank, nationality or class (provided that, in this last case, the relationship leads beyond the mere fact of community to 'social action': on this point we shall have more to say later). There is accordingly no implication in the concept either of 'solidarity' between the agents or of the opposite.

(2) In all cases, we are concerned with the meaning which is empirically intended by the parties involved, either in an actual individual case, or on the average in a number of cases, or in a constructed 'pure' type: it is never a matter of a normatively 'correct' or metaphysically 'true' meaning. A social relationship, even when it is a matter of a so-called 'social system' – a 'state', a 'church', a 'guild', or a 'marriage' – consists purely and exclusively in the possibility that someone has acted, is acting or will act in such a way that one agent's meaning varies in relation to another's in a specifiable way. This point must always be insisted on, in order to avoid a 'reified' understanding of this concept. For instance, a 'state' ceases to 'exist' sociologically as soon as there is no longer any *possibility* that certain kinds of meaningful social actions will be performed. This possibility may be either very large or infinitesimally small. The relevant social relationship exists or existed in the sense and

to the degree to which this possibility (approximately) exists or existed. No other *clear* meaning can possibly be given to the assertion that, say, a certain 'state' does or does not any longer 'exist'.

(3) At no point have we said that 'reciprocity' is present in the sense that those who in a particular case relate their actions to each other attach the *same* meaning to their social relationship, or that the meaning which each inwardly attaches to his own action varies in correspondence with that of the other. What is seen as 'friendship', 'love', 'piety', 'fidelity to contract', 'sense of patriotism' by one party to a social relationship may set up totally different attitudes in the other. In a case like this, the parties attach a different meaning to their actions: to that extent, the social relationship is objectively 'unilateral' on both sides. It is, however, mutual insofar as each agent also assumes (perhaps partly or wholly in error) that his partner will see his relationship to him (the agent) in a particular way and bases his own action on these expectations. This can (and usually will) have consequences for the way in which the action is performed and the form which the relationship takes. The relationship is objectively 'bilateral', of course, only to the extent that the meaning of each partner's action 'conforms to' that of the other in accordance with their average expectations. For example, a child's action is related to his father's approximately in the way the father expects it to be (either in a particular case, or in the average case, or in a constructed ideal type). In the real world, a social relationship which is based totally and without remainder on this kind of mutual adjustment of attitudes in relation to their meanings is only a limiting case. In our terminology, however, lack of reciprocity is only said to rule out the existence of a 'social relationship' in those cases where it has the consequence that there is an actual lack of mutual relatedness of reciprocal action. As usual in the real world, intermediate cases of all kinds are the rule here.

(4) A social relationship may be either transient or more enduring. It is more enduring when the relationship is such that a possibility exists of the continual recurrence of behaviour corresponding to its meaning (in other words, giving valid expression to that meaning and being anticipated accordingly). The 'existence' of a social relationship depends on there being such a possibility – in other words, on there being a greater or lesser *probability* that an action corresponding to the meaning will take place; nothing more than this is involved. This point should always be borne in mind if misconceptions are to be avoided. To say that a 'friendship' or a 'state' exists or has existed means therefore purely and simply that *we* (who are concerned with it) judge that a possibility exists or existed that particular men, in the context of a relationship organised in a particular way, will perform certain actions in a way which is specifiable in terms of the meaning which on average they intend; and

it means nothing more than that. (Cf. the end of Section 2.) The decision, unavoidable in jurisprudence, whether a legal proposition with a certain meaning is true (in the law's sense) or not, or whether a *legal* relationship exists or not, has no relevance to sociological research.

(5) The meaning of a social relationship can change: for example, a political relationship can shift from solidarity to a conflict of interests. In that case it becomes only a question of terminological convenience and of the degree of continuity in the transition, whether one should say that a 'new' relationship has come into being or that the old one continues to exist but has acquired a new 'meaning'. The meaning may also be partly permanent and partly changeable.

(6) The meaning constitutive of a permanent social relationship may be formulable in 'maxims'. Then those involved in the relationship will expect from their partner or partners that they should continue to observe such maxims on average and with some approximation to their meaning, and they, for their part, will (on average and approximately) base their actions on these same maxims. The more rational in its general character the action in question is (either in the 'means–end' sense, or in the sense of 'realising absolute values'), the more is this the case. The possibility of a rational formulation of the intended meaning is naturally much smaller in the case of a sexual relationship or an affective relationship in general (a relationship of 'piety', for instance) than in, say, a contractual relationship in commerce.

(7) The meaning of a social relationship may be determined by mutual agreement. This means that the parties make promises about their future behaviour, either in relation to each other or in some other respect. Each party then counts – to the extent that he is thinking rationally – first (with varying certainty) on the other's normally basing his action on the meaning of the agreement as understood by him (the agent). His own actions are rational in two senses: partly in the 'means–end' sense, in that the meaning of his actions is more or less based on 'fidelity' to this expectation; and partly in the sense of trying to realise the absolute value of the 'duty' – to adhere to the agreement which he has entered into in the sense intended by him. This initial discussion will suffice for the moment: for further discussion cf. §9 and §13.

(*Wirtschaft und Gesellschaft*, 4th edn,
Tübingen, 1956, 1, pp. 1–14. First
published in 1922.)

2 · Basic Categories of Social Organisation

§12. The term 'association' should be understood to mean a social relationship whose rules restrict, or exclude, those outside of it and within which there are particular individuals appointed for the specific purpose of securing the maintenance of its regulations. One or more of these individuals will be the '*head*' or '*leader*', and in some cases there will also be an *executive staff* which will normally have delegated powers in appropriate cases. The leadership, or a share in the functions of the executive (what we may call '*governmental powers*'), may either be (*a*) appropriated or (*b*) assigned in accordance with the accepted rules of the association to particular individuals or to persons selected on the basis of particular criteria or in accordance with particular forms. The assignment of powers in this way may be either for a long term or for a period or to deal with specific circumstances. The term 'associational action' will be used to refer (*a*) to actions taken by the executive staff themselves, given legitimacy by their executive or delegated powers and taken in order to preserve the existence of the regulations of the association, or (*b*) to actions taken by members of the association, operating under *instructions* given by the executive. (The latter will be called 'action relative to the association': see Note 3 below.)

(1) It is irrelevant from the point of view of this definition whether the association takes the form of a 'community' or a 'society'. It is enough that there should be some person or persons occupying the position of leadership, whether it be the head of a family, the committee of a club, the managing director of a business, a prince, a president, the head of a church – someone appointed to act in such a way as to maintain the regulations of the association. For this particular sort of action – action whose purpose does not only have a reference to the regulations but also involves their *enforcement* – adds a new sociological characteristic of great practical importance to the situation constituted by a closed 'social relationship'. Not every closed community or society is an 'association': the term cannot, for instance, be applied to sexual relationships or to kinship groups in which there is no head.

(2) The question whether an association can be said to 'exist' depends entirely on the presence of a head and, in the appropriate case, of an executive. That is, to put it more precisely, it depends on whether there

is a possibility that specifiable individuals will act with the intention of maintaining the regulations of the association, which in turn implies that there exist persons who are appointed for the purpose of acting in that sense in particular cases. It is entirely immaterial from the conceptual point of view whether those appointed are motivated by considerations based on tradition, or rationality in the sense of adherence to an absolute value (feudal fealty, professional or official loyalty) or by rationality in pursuit of a purpose (their interest in their salary, etc.). In our terminology, an association does not 'exist' from a sociological point of view except by virtue of the possibility that an action proceeding from such an intention will be performed. If there is no possibility of a specifiable executive body (or a specifiable individual person) acting in such a way, then, in our terminology, this will count only as a 'social relationship', not as an 'association'. But as long as there is such a possibility of action, the association can be said to 'exist' from the sociological point of view, even though the individuals whose actions are guided by reference to its regulations may change. (Indeed, it is part of the purpose of defining the term in this way that it should take into account precisely this fact.)

(3) (a) Apart from actions taken by the executive itself or under its direction there may also typically be cases of action taken by the other members which has a specific reference to the regulations of the association, and whose meaning is to ensure that these regulations are maintained: examples would be the payment of taxes or the performance of civic duties of various kinds by individuals – jury service, military service, etc. (b) It may also be part of the regulations in force that there should be standards laid down in terms of which the members of the association are to regulate their actions in other respects: for instance, in the association we call the 'state', 'civil' law governs the 'private' economic activity of members, in which they act in the furtherance of individual interests rather than in order to enforce the validity of the regulations of the association. Cases of type (a) may be called 'action *relative to* the association', while those of type (b) may be termed 'action *regulated by* the association'. Only action taken by the executive itself, together with all action relative to the association taken under its detailed direction, is to be called 'associational action'. The following are examples of such 'associational action': a war engaged in by a state (this would involve all members); a resolution upon which the committee of a club allows the members to decide; a contract concluded by the head of the association but held to be 'binding' on the members and dependent for its force on them (see § 11); finally, all administration of justice and performance of general administrative functions (see also § 14).

An association may be (a) autonomous or heteronomous; (b) autocephalic or heterocephalic. It is autonomous, as opposed to heteronomous, when its regulations are not imposed from outside the association itself, but laid down by the members of the association in virtue of their membership (other features of the system being irrelevant). It is auto-cephalic when the head and the executive staff of the association are appointed in accordance with the special regulations of the association; it is heterocephalic when they are appointed by outsiders (other features of the method of appointment being irrelevant).

An example of a heterocephalic association is the Canadian provinces, whose governors are appointed by the central government of Canada. A heterocephalic association may be autonomous and an autocephalic association may be heteronomous. An association may also be partly one and partly the other, in both respects. The federated states of the German Empire were autocephalic, but in spite of this they were heteronomous on all matters falling within Imperial jurisdiction, while remaining auto-nomous on matters falling within their own jurisdiction, such as matters of religion and education. During the period when it was a part of Germany, Alsace-Lorraine was autonomous over a limited area, but heterocephalic (the governor being appointed by the Kaiser). All these elements can also be present in part. An association which was both completely heteronomous and heterocephalic (for example, a regiment within an army) would as a rule be considered as a part of a more comprehensive association. Whether this is so, however, depends on the actual degree of independence by which the action is governed in the particular case: from the terminological point of view, the question should be decided purely in terms of convenience.

§ 13. The system of regulations established when forming a society may arise (*a*) from the free acceptance of the members or (*b*) through an imposition to which the members must submit. The executive of an association may claim to have the legitimate power to impose further regulations. By the term 'constitution of an association' we shall under-stand the actual possibility that members will submit to the power of imposition exercised by the existing executive, judged according to degree, kind and preconditions. Depending on the regulations in force, these preconditions may include the requirement that particular groups, or a particular section of the membership of the association, should give their consideration or consent; but a great diversity of other conditions are also, of course, possible.

The regulations of an association may be imposed not only on members but also on certain non-members who satisfy certain stipulated criteria. A particular example of such a criterion is the existence of a territorial relationship: the non-member in question may be present in a region, or have been born in it, or undertake certain activities within it. In such cases we have what I shall call 'territorial validity'. An association whose regulations are enforced on the basis of the principle of territorial validity will be called a 'territorial association', irrespective of the extent to which its regulations also lay claim to no more than territorial validity in their bearing on internal matters affecting members of the association. (This is possible and does indeed occur at least to a limited extent.)

(1) In our terminology a regulation may be said to be 'imposed' in all cases in which it does not arise through the individual free consent of all members. Thus, a 'majority decision' in which the minority acquiesces would also count as 'imposed' in this sense. For this reason, the legitimacy of majority decisions has often not been recognised, or has been regarded as dubious, over long periods (in the Middle Ages, for example, in the case of the Estates, and down to the present day in the case of the Russian peasant commune (*obshchina*)).

(2) As is generally acknowledged, agreements which are 'free' in the formal sense are very often in fact imposed (this is the case in the Russian peasant commune). In such cases, what counts from the socio-logical point of view is what actually happens.

(3) The term 'constitution' is used here in the same sense as that given to it by Lassalle. It is not synonymous with the 'written' constitution, or, in general, with the constitution in the legal sense. The question for the sociologist is simply this: when, for which purposes and within what limits do the members of the association submit to its head? And (in the relevant case) under what particular preconditions – must gods or priests, for example, approve, must electoral bodies consent and so forth? Does the head have control of the executive staff and of the associational action when he issues directives, and especially when he imposes regulations?

(4) The main types of imposed regulation with 'territorial validity' are such things as provisions of criminal law and numerous other sorts of legal injunction, in which the criteria of applicability of the regulation are that the person concerned should be present in, have been born in, should be active in, should have completed some activity in, etc. the territory of the association. This applies particularly to political associations. (Cf. Gierke's and Preuss's concept of the 'territorial corporation'.)

§ 14. The term *administrative system* will be used to refer to a system of regulations governing associational action. The term *regulative system* will be applied to a system of regulations governing other forms of social action which secures for the agents concerned the possibilities opened up by such regulation. When an association involves only systems of the former kind, it will be called an 'administrative association'; when it involves only systems of the latter kind it will be called a 'regulative association'.

(1) Obviously, most associations fall as much into one category as into the other. If there were an association which was purely regulative, it would be a state (which is conceivable in theory) which concerned itself only with the maintenance of law and order, and in which there was otherwise total *laissez-faire*. In such a state, indeed, the implication is that all financial regulation would be left to pure private enterprise.

(2) On the concept of 'associational action' see § 12, Note 3. The term 'administrative system' covers all those rules intended to govern the behaviour both of the executive staff and of the members 'to do with the association', as it is usually expressed. That is, it relates to those goals the achievement of which is supposed to be secured by the regulations of the association through a positively prescribed and systematic allocation of functions to the executive staff and the members. In a totally communist economy, more or less all social action would be of this kind. In a state based on total economic *laissez-faire*, on the other hand, this description would only apply to the functions of judges, police authorities, jurymen and soldiers and to the activities of legislators and electors. In general, though not always in individual cases, the boundary between the administrative and regulative systems coincides with the distinction drawn within a political association between 'public' and 'private' law. (For further details on this point, see the section on the sociology of law (§ 1).)

§ 15. By the term *enterprise*, we shall understand a continuing purposive activity of a particular kind; by *associational enterprise*, an association which has a continuing executive which acts to achieve some end.

The term *voluntary association* will be used to refer to an organised association with an established set of regulations which claim validity only for those who have entered into membership of the association through personal choice.

The term *institution* will be used to refer to an association with an established set of regulations which are imposed with (relative) success within a specifiable sphere of application on all activities satisfying certain definite criteria.

(1) The term 'enterprise' naturally covers also political and religious undertakings, cooperative associations, etc., insofar as they satisfy the criterion of purposive continuity.

(2) The 'voluntary association' and the 'institution' are both associations which have an established set of regulations which are rational in the sense of being systematic. Or it might be more correct to say that, to the extent that an association has a set of rational regulations governing

37

its activity, it is to be called a 'voluntary association' or an 'institution'. The supreme example of an 'institution' is the state, including all its heterocephalic associations; another example is the Church (to the extent that the regulations which govern its activity are rational). The regulations of an 'institution' claim universal validity, in the sense that they apply to all those who satisfy the relevant criteria (place of birth or residence, claims to certain kinds of provision) regardless of whether the person in question has consented (as would be the case in a voluntary association), and certainly without regard to whether he has taken part in drawing up the regulations. Such regulations are, therefore, in a quite definite sense, imposed. The institution is very likely to be a territorial association.

(3) The difference between a voluntary association and an institution is one of degree. The regulations of a voluntary association may touch on the interests of third parties, and in that case the latter may then be forced to recognise the validity of these regulations both by the usurpation and arbitrary action of the voluntary association itself and by the provisions of the law (e.g. company law).

(4) It is hardly necessary to emphasise that the 'voluntary association' and the 'institution' do not completely exhaust between them all the possibilities of types of association. Furthermore, they are only 'polar' opposites (as with the concepts of 'sect' and 'church' in the sociology of religion).

§ 16. The term *power* will be used to refer to every possibility within a social relationship of imposing one's own will, even against opposition, without regard to the basis for this possibility.

The term *domination* refers to the possibility of finding a specified group of people to obey a command of a determinate content; *discipline* means the possibility of finding a specifiable number of people who in virtue of an habitual attitude will obey a command in a prompt, automatic and unthinking manner.

(1) The term 'power' is sociologically diffuse. Any conceivable quality or set of qualities of a person might make it possible for him to enforce his will in a particular situation. The sociological concept of 'domination' must, for this reason, be a more precise one and can only mean the possibility of finding that a command will be obeyed.

(2) The concept of 'discipline' applies, among other things, to uncritical and unresisting obedience by a large group of people to the extent that it is a matter of 'habit'.

Domination exists even where there is only one person successfully giving orders to others: the existence of either an executive staff or an association is not a necessary condition for its exercise. But it is true that in all normal cases, at least, *one* of these conditions is satisfied. To the extent that an association's members, as such and in virtue of its established rules, are subject to relations of domination it will be called an 'authoritarian association'.

(1) The head of a household exercises domination even though he does not have an executive staff. A Bedouin chief who levies tolls on caravans, individual travellers and goods which pass his stronghold exercises domination over all these shifting and indeterminate people who do not form an association with each other. His domination over them lasts from the moment when they get into a particular situation and for as long as they are in that situation, and it rests on his having followers who serve, as the occasion arises, as an executive staff to enforce his will. (But it is also possible, in theory, to imagine an individual's exercising such domination even without any kind of executive staff.)

(2) Associations are always to some extent authoritarian in virtue of having an executive staff. The concept is only a relative one. Normally speaking, any authoritarian association is also, as such, an administrative association. The character of an association depends on how it is administered and by what sort of people, what matters the administration deals with and the area over which its domination is accepted as valid. The first two of these, however, rest in the most fundamental way on the nature of the principles of *legitimacy* on which the domination is based (on this point, see *Economy and Society*, Ch. III).

§17. An authoritarian association will be described as *political* when and insofar as its existence and the validity of its regulations within a specified geographical *area* are continuously secured by the use, or the threat, of physical force by its executive staff. The term 'state' will be used to refer to an institutional enterprise of a political character, when and insofar as its executive staff successfully claims a monopoly of the legitimate use of physical force in order to impose its regulations. Social action, especially associational action, will be described as 'politically related' when and insofar as it aims to influence the leadership of a political association, especially with regard to the appropriation, expropriation, redistribution or allocation of governmental powers.

An authoritarian association will be described as *hierocratic* when and insofar as it employs psychological coercion, involving the granting or withholding of spiritual benefits, as a means of securing that its regulations will continue in force. This may be called 'hierocratic coercion'. The term 'church' will be used to describe an institutional enterprise of a hierocratic character when and insofar as its executive claims a monopoly in the use of legitimate hierocratic coercion.

(1) It goes without saying that force is neither the only nor even the

normal means of administration used by political associations. The heads of such associations have, rather, employed all the methods which are generally feasible in order to achieve their ends. But the threat and, on occasion, the actual use of force is certainly the method which is specific to such associations, and it is always the last resort when all else fails. It is not only political associations who have used, and still use, force as a legitimate method: it has equally been used by tribes, households and other kinds of social unit, and in the Middle Ages it was used by all those entitled to arms in certain circumstances. The political association is distinguished, not only by the fact that it uses force (at least in addition to other methods) in order to secure the continuance of its system of regulations, but also by the characteristic that it lays claim to domination for its executive staff and its regulations over a territory and secures it by force. Whenever associations which use force have this characteristic – whether they are village communes or even individual households or associations of guilds or workers' associations ('soviets') – they must to that extent be described as political associations.

(2) No political association, not even the 'state', can be defined in terms of the goal which it seeks to achieve through its collective action. There has been no purpose, from provision of food supplies to patronage of the arts, which has not been pursued on occasion by some political association; and there has been no purpose, from the guarantee of security of the person to the administration of justice, which *all* political associations have sought to achieve. The 'political' character of an association can therefore be defined *only* in terms of the means which it employs and which is sometimes elevated to the status of an end in itself. This means is not peculiar to the state alone, but it is certainly specific to it and an inescapable part of its essence. I refer to the use of force. This does not conform entirely with ordinary German usage: but ordinary speech cannot be used without being made more precise. We use such expressions as 'the Reichsbank's policy on exchange rates', or the 'financial policy' adopted by those in charge of a club, or the 'educational policy' of a community. What we mean by such expressions is the systematic management and direction of a particular concrete matter of business. We distinguish in terms of essential characteristics between the 'political' aspect or implication of affairs, 'political' officials, 'political' journalism, 'political' revolution, a 'political' club or party, 'political' consequences, and other aspects or characteristics of the persons, things or processes in question (economic, cultural, religious, etc.). What we mean by this is all that has to do with relationships of domination within what we describe in ordinary language as the 'political' association which is the state – all that leads to, hinders or furthers the preservation, alteration or subversion of such relationships, as opposed to persons,

things or processes which are not connected with them. Even in ordinary usage, then, we seek to emphasise the common element in domination as a means, or in other words in the manner in which the powers in the state exercise it, in abstraction from any purpose which this domination may serve. So it is reasonable to claim that the definition here suggested as a basis simply involves making ordinary language more precise, in the sense that it sharply emphasises that feature which is in fact specific, namely the actual or possible use of force. Admittedly, in ordinary language we use the term 'political associations' to refer, not only to those legitimately entitled to use force but also, for instance, to parties or clubs which aim to influence the activities of political associations (in an explicitly *non*-violent way). Our aim here is to distinguish this kind of social activity, which we may call 'politically related', from specifically 'political action' (that is, the *collective* action of political associations themselves in the sense defined in § 12, Note 3).

(3) Since the concept of the 'state', in its fullest development, is an altogether modern one, it is advisable to define it in a way which is consistent with its modern form; but, on the other hand, it is also advisable to leave out of the definition the varying substantive purposes which we find states serving at the present time. In formal terms, the characteristic of the modern state is that it is a system of administration and law which is modifiable by statute and which guides the collective actions of an executive staff: this executive is regulated by statute likewise, and claims authority not only over the members of the association (those who necessarily belong to the association by birth) but within a broader scope over all activity taking place in the territory over which it exercises domination. It is thus an institution with a territorial basis. Furthermore, however, in modern society force may only be 'legitimately' used to the extent that it is permitted or prescribed by the regulations of the state. For instance, the father of a family is allowed to retain a 'right of punishment', a relic of a right which he formerly held as a legitimate personal power extending to the right of life or death over a child or a slave on the part of the head of a household. The monopolistic nature of the state's domination through force is as essential a feature of its present character as its nature as a rational 'institution' and a continuing 'enterprise'.

(4) In the case of the concept of a hierocratic association, we cannot use the nature of the spiritual benefits offered, whether this-worldly or other-worldly, external or internal, as a defining characteristic. What is essential is that the ability to confer such benefits can constitute the basis for spiritual domination over men. On the other hand, it is a characteristic feature of a 'church', according to ordinary usage (which is useful in this context), that it should be a (relatively) rational institution and enterprise,

whose distinctive character is revealed in the form of its regulations and of its executive staff, and that it should claim a monopoly of domination. It is normal for the Church as an institution that its hierocratic domination should extend over a certain territory and that it should have a territorial organisation, in the form of parishes. This means that in different cases different answers may be given to the question by what means this claim to monopoly is sustained. Historically, however, actual territorial monopoly of domination has not been so essential to the Church as to a political association, and it is most certainly not essential today. The character of the Church as an 'institution', especially the fact that one is 'born into' the Church, is what distinguishes it from the 'sect', which is essentially a 'voluntary association' which accepts as members only persons who have the right religious qualifications. (More detailed discussion of this point will be found in the section on the sociology of religion.)

(*Wirtschaft und Gesellschaft*, 4th edn, Tübingen, 1956, 1, pp. 26–30. First published in 1922.)

3 · Classes, Status Groups and Parties

The structure of every legal order (not only the 'state') has a direct influence on the distribution of power, whether economic or of any other kind, within the community concerned. By 'power' we mean very generally the chances which a man or a group of men have to realise their will in a communal activity, even against the opposition of others taking part in it. 'Economically determined' power is not, of course, the same thing as 'power' in general. On the contrary, economic power may result from the possession of power which rests on other foundations. Conversely, men do not only aspire to power for the sake of economic enrichment. Power, even economic power, may be valued for its own sake, and it is very often the case that men seek power in part for the sake of the honorific social 'status' which it brings. Not all power, however, brings status with it. The typical American 'boss', like the typical large-scale financial speculator, consciously renounces such status; and generally speaking it is precisely 'pure' economic power, especially power based on 'naked' cash, which is not accepted in any way as a basis of social 'status'. On the other hand, power is not the only basis of social status. Quite the contrary: social status or prestige can be, and very often has been, the basis of power, even of economic power. The legal system may guarantee both power and status. But, in normal circumstances at least, it is not their primary source; it is merely an extra factor which increases the chances of possessing them but cannot always make it certain. The mode of distribution of social 'status' among typical groups of members of a community will be called the *social order*. Its relation to the 'legal order' is, of course, very similar to that of the economic order. It is not the same as the economic order, by which we mean only the mode of distribution and consumption of economic goods and services. But it is of course very much affected by the economic order and interacts with it.

The distribution of power in a community is reflected in the existence of 'classes', 'status groups' and 'parties'.

Classes are not 'communities' in the sense we have adopted, but merely possible (and frequent) bases of communal action. The term 'class' will be used when (i) a large number of men have in common a specific causal factor influencing their chances in life, insofar as (ii) this factor has to

43

do only with the possession of economic goods and the interests involved in earning a living, and furthermore (iii) in the conditions of the market in commodities or labour. This we shall call 'class situation'. It is an elementary fact of economic life that the manner in which the disposal of property in goods is distributed within a human group whose members encounter one another in the market for purposes of exchange and compete with one another is in itself sufficient to create specific chances in life. In accord ance with the principle of marginal utility, it excludes the propertyless from taking part in the competition for highly valued goods in favour of the propertied and thus in practice gives the latter the exclusive opportunity to acquire such goods. It means that, other things being equal, those who, being already provided with goods, are not dependent on exchange, alone have the exclusive opportunity of profiting from exchange. Thus, in general at least, it increases their power in the price struggle against those who, having no property, have nothing to offer but their labour-power, either in its natural form or in the form of the products of their labour, and so are compelled to sell this labour and its products in order to keep body and soul together. It means that only those who own property have the possibility of shifting what they own from the sphere of benefit as 'wealth' to the sphere of employment as 'capital': hence they alone can become entrepreneurs and have the chance of directly or indirectly participating in capital profit. All this applies in the sphere of pure market conditions. 'Property' and 'propertylessness' are thus the basic categories underlying all class situations, whether in the form of struggles over prices or struggles between commercial competitors.

Within this general framework, however, class situations may be further differentiated in terms of the nature of the property which is a source of income, on the one hand, and in terms of the nature of the services offered on the market, on the other. The class situations of property-owners may be distinguished by the differences in the kind of property which they own: dwelling-houses, workshops, warehouses or shops, agricultural land (this last may be further subdivided in terms of the size of landholdings – a quantitative difference with possible qualitative consequences), mines, livestock, men (slaves), disposal of moveable means of production or industrial tools of all kinds, above all money or objects readily exchangeable for money at any time, products of one's own or other people's labour (this last depends on the stage of development of consumption), or commercially viable monopolies of any kind. Their class situation depends as much on these differences in kinds of property as on the 'meaning' which they can and do give to the use made of their property, especially their property with a money value; such factors determine whether, for instance, they belong to the *rentier* or the entrepreneurial class. There is an equally marked distinction amongst those who have no property but only their labour to offer, depending as much on the nature of the services performed as on whether these services involve them in a continuous or only a casual relationship to the consumer. The element which is always present in all cases where the concept of 'class' is applied, however, is that it is the nature of chances in the market which is the common factor determining the fate of a number of individuals. In this sense, the 'class situation' is ultimately a 'market situation'. It is only a first step towards the formation of genuine 'classes' when in cattle-breeding societies the effect of pure, naked ownership as such is to give over those without property into the power of the cattle-owners as slaves or bondsmen. But it is certainly true that such situations first reveal, in the practice of loaning cattle and the sheer rigour of the law on debt in such communities, the way in which the mere ownership of property as such can determine the fate of an individual: in this there is a sharp contrast with agricultural communities based on labour. The debtor–creditor relationship first formed the basis of 'class situations' in the towns, where a credit market of a rather primitive kind developed, with interest rates which increased in proportion to the degree of distress and with virtual monopolisation of lending by a plutocracy. With this, 'class struggles' began. By contrast, when the fate of a group of men is not determined by their chances of using goods or labour in the market (as in the case of slaves), that group is not in the technical sense a 'class' but a 'status group'.

As we are using the term, then, 'classes' are clearly the product of economic interests, bound up with the existence of the 'market'. Moreover, the concept of 'class interests' becomes ambiguous, indeed ceases to be in any way a clearly empirical concept, as soon as it is taken to mean anything but the actual direction taken by the interests of a specific cross-section of those subject to a class situation, and following from the class situation with a specific probability. In the same class situation, even when other things are equal, the probable direction of the interests of an individual worker will vary greatly according to whether, in terms of native ability, he is highly, averagely or poorly qualified for the occupation in question. It will depend likewise on whether or not there has developed out of the 'class situation' either communal action on the part of a larger or smaller section of those collectively involved in it, or even some form of association, such as a trade union, from which the individual can expect definite results. It is by no means always the case that some form of association or even of communal action emerges from the common class situation. Rather, its effects may be limited to generating an essentially similar reaction: that is, to use the terminology we have adopted, to generating a 'mass action'; and even this may not always result. Often, moreover, such communal action as results is only of an amorphous kind. An example of this is the 'grumbling' by workers which was recognised in ancient Eastern ethical codes – the moral disapproval of their master's behaviour. Presumably this had much the same practical significance as the phenomenon which has once again become increasingly typical within precisely the most recently developed sectors of industry – the 'go-slow', or deliberate restriction of output by tacit agreement among the workers.

The extent to which there emerges from 'mass action' by the members of a class some form of 'communal action', or even possibly of 'association', depends on general cultural conditions, especially of an intellectual kind, and on the extent of the contrasts which have emerged on the basis, above all, of the visibility of the connexions between the causes and the consequences of the 'class situation'. Differences in chances in life, however marked, are certainly not sufficient in themselves, as experience shows, to create 'class action' in the sense of communal action by the members of a class. For that, it must be possible clearly to recognise that they depend on and result from the class situation. Only then can the contrast in chances in life be experienced as something which is not merely given and to be endured, but which results either (i) from the existing distribution of property or (ii) from the structure of the concrete economic order, and only then, therefore, can reactions to it take the form not of sporadic acts of irrational protest but of rational association. 'Class situations' of the first category existed in just such a characteristically blatant and visible form in the ancient world and in the Middle Ages in the towns, especially where great wealth had been accumulated by a virtual monopoly of trade in the local industrial products or food supplies; and they existed also in agricultural societies at various periods when commercial exploitation was on the increase. The most important historical example of the second category is the class situation of the modern 'proletariat'.

Every class may therefore give rise to some form of 'class action', of one of the numerous possible kinds; but it need not do so. In any case, a class itself is not a community, and it is misleading to treat classes as conceptually equivalent to communities. Finally, it is wrong to operate with such concepts as those of 'class' and 'class interest' in the kind of pseudo-scientific way which is all too common today, merely on the strength of the fact that men in the same class situation, faced with situations as emotionally charged as are those of economic life, regularly react by mass action in the direction which best approximates to their average interest – a fact which is as important for the understanding of historical events as it is basically simple. The most classical expression of this pseudo-scientific use of concepts is the contention of a gifted writer that the individual may well mistake his own interests, but the 'class' is 'infallible' about its interests.

If classes are not themselves communities, then, class situations arise only in the context of a community. The collective action which leads to the emergence of a class situation, however, is not in its essence an action undertaken by members of the same class but one involving relations between members of different classes. For example, the forms of communal action which directly determine the class situation of workers and entrepreneurs are the labour market, the commodity market and the capitalist enterprise. The existence of a capitalist enterprise in its turn, however, presupposes the existence of a form of collective action which is ordered in a very special way – one which protects the possession of goods purely as such, and in particular the power of the individual in principle to dispose freely of the means of production: that is, it presupposes the existence of a 'legal order' of a specific kind. Every sort of class situation, since it is primarily based on the power conferred by property as such, is realised in its purest form when all other factors which might determine the significance of the mutual relations between classes are excluded as far as possible, with the result that the use of the power of property on the market holds maximum sway. Amongst the impediments to a consistent realisation of the naked market principle are 'status groups', which for the moment and in the present context are only of interest to us from this point of view. Before dealing briefly with them, we may simply point out that there is not much to be said in a general way about the more specific kinds of opposition between 'classes' (in the sense of that term which we have adopted). The radical change which has taken place between the past and the present may be connected, if a certain imprecision is admissible, with the fact that the struggle by which class situations are brought about has progressively shifted from the area of consumer credit, first to that of competition on the commodity market and then to that of price conflict on the labour market. The 'class struggles' of the ancient world – insofar as they were genuine 'class struggles' rather than conflicts between status groups – were primarily struggles between debtors threatened with debt-slavery (mainly peasants, but also including artisans) and their creditors who lived in the towns. For debt-slavery, both among cattle-breeders and in commercial towns, especially towns engaged in sea-borne trade, is the normal consequence of inequalities of wealth. The debt relationship as such gave rise to class action even as late as the time of Catiline. The next development, which resulted from the increasing tendency for the town's needs to be provided by foreign corn importers, was the struggle over the food supply, in the first instance the provision of bread and its price. This struggle lasted right through antiquity and the whole of the Middle Ages; it grouped together all those without property in opposition to those who had a real or supposed vested interest in a high price for bread, and came more generally to cover all goods essential for the maintenance of life, including those required for artisan production. Conflicts over wages were not an issue in the ancient world or in the Middle Ages; even well into the modern era they existed only in embryonic form and were slow to develop. They took second place in every way not only to slave rebellions but also to struggles in the commodity market.

The objects of protest for those without property in the ancient world and the Middle Ages were such things as monopolies, pre-emptions, cornering of the market, or the holding back of goods from the market in order to raise their price. By contrast, today the central issue is the determination of wage levels. The transitional stage is represented by those struggles over access to the market and the determination of commodity prices which occurred between retailers and artisans working in cottage industry in the earliest days of the modern era. It is a general feature of those class conflicts which result from the market situation, and must therefore be mentioned here because of its generality, that the conflict is usually at its most bitter between those who actually and directly participate as opponents in the price struggle. It is not the *rentier*, the shareholder or the banker who suffers the resentment of the workers, even though it is his coffers which are filled by much more profit (for which he has done much less work) than are those of the manufacturer or the director of the enterprise. Rather it is the latter against whom resentment is directed, as the immediate opponents in the price struggle. This simple fact has often been decisive in determining the role of the class situation in the formation of political parties. It has, for instance, made possible the several varieties of patriarchal socialism and the attempts frequently made, at least in earlier times, to forge an alliance between threatened status strata and the proletariat against the 'bourgeoisie'.

Status groups, in contrast with classes, are normally communities, though often of an amorphous kind. In contrast with the 'class situation', which is determined by purely economic factors, we shall use the term 'status situation' to refer to all those typical components of people's destinies which are determined by a specific social evaluation of 'status', whether positive or negative, when that evaluation is based on some common characteristic shared by many people. This status may also be bound up with a certain class situation: class differences are connected in manifold ways with status differences, and, as remarked earlier, the ownership of property in itself comes to acquire a status value, not in every case, but with remarkable frequency in the long term. In the type of neighbourhood association to be found in subsistence economies in all parts of the world it is very often the case that the richest man as such becomes 'chief', which often means only a certain precedence in status. In modern 'democratic' society in what is called its 'pure' form, that is, in the form in which all explicitly regulated status privileges for individuals are done away with, it is the case, for instance, that only families belonging to broadly similar taxation groups dance with each other: this is reported, for example, of some of the smaller Swiss cities. But 'status' is not necessarily connected with a 'class situation': normally, it stands rather in glaring contradiction to the pretensions of naked property ownership. Furthermore, those who own property and those who do not may belong to the same status group: this frequently happens and its consequences are very noticeable, so precarious may this 'equality' of social assessment become in the long run. The 'equality' of status of the American 'gentleman' finds expression, for instance, in the fact that, outside the context of the 'enterprise', where subordination is determined by purely realistic factors, it would be considered the height of bad taste – wherever the old tradition prevails – for even the richest 'chief' to treat his 'clerk' as in any way at all of unequal rank, even in the evening at the club, over billiards or at the card table. It would be unacceptable to treat him with that kind of condescending affability which marks a difference in position, and which the German chief can never avoid entirely – one of the most important reasons why German club-life has never managed to seem so attractive there as the American club.

In content, social status is normally expressed above all in the imputation of a specifically regulated style of life to everyone who wishes to belong to the circle. This goes together with a restriction of 'social' intercourse – that is, intercourse which does not serve any economic, commercial or other 'practical' purposes – including especially normal intermarriage, to the circle of status equals; this can extend to the point of totally exclusive endogamy. As soon as a communal action of this nature is in question – not a purely individual and socially irrelevant imitation of an alien style of life, but an action based on mutual consent – we say that 'status' development is under way. A typical development of articulated 'status' grouping of this kind on the basis of conventional life-styles is taking place at present in the United States, where it is emerging out of a long-established democracy. One example of this is that only those who reside in a certain street ('The Street') are regarded as belonging to 'society' and as fit for social intercourse, and are accordingly visited and invited. The outstanding example, however, is the strict submission to the fashion prevailing for the moment in 'society', to an extent unknown in Germany, which is taken, even among men, as a sign that the person in question has pretensions to be regarded as a gentleman and so decides at least *prima facie* that he will also be treated as such. This is as important, for instance, for his chances of securing a position in a 'good' company, and above all of mixing socially and intermarrying with 'well-regarded' families, as being qualified to fight a duel is in Germany. For the rest, social 'status' is usurped by certain families who have resided in a certain area for a long time (and who are, naturally, correspondingly well-to-do), such as the 'FFV' or 'first families of Virginia', or the descendants, real or alleged, of the 'Indian princess' Pocahontas or the Pilgrim Fathers, or the Knickerbockers, or the members of some extremely exclusive sect, or all kinds of circles of associates who mark themselves off by some criterion or other. In this case it is a matter of a purely conventional social differentiation based essentially on usurpation (although this is admittedly the normal origin of almost all social 'status'). But it is a short step from this to the legal validation of privilege (and lack of privilege), and this step is usually easy to take as soon as a certain arrangement of the social order has become effectively 'settled' and has acquired stability as a result of the stabilisation of the distribution of economic power. Where the consequences are followed through to the limit, the status group develops into a closed *caste*. That is, distinction of status is guaranteed not only by convention and law, but also by ritual sanction to such an extent that all physical contact with a member of a caste regarded as 'inferior' is held to be ritually polluting for members of the 'superior' caste, a stain which must be religiously expiated. The individual castes, indeed, in part develop quite separate cults and gods.

Status differentiation, to be sure, only as a rule develops into these extreme forms when it is based on differences which are regarded as 'ethnic'. The 'caste' is actually the normal 'societal' form in which ethnic communities which believe in blood-relationship and forbid intermarriage and social intercourse with outsiders live alongside one another. This is true of the 'pariah' peoples which have emerged from time to time in all parts of the world – communities which have acquired specific occupational traditions of an artisan or other kind, which cultivate a belief in their common ethnic origin, and which now live in a 'diaspora', rigorously avoiding all personal intercourse other than what is unavoidable, in a legally precarious situation, but tolerated on the grounds of their economic indispensability and often even privileged, and interspersed among political communities. The Jews are the most striking historical example. A system of 'status' differences which has developed into a 'caste' system differs in structure from a system of purely 'ethnic' differences in that the former creates a vertical social hierarchy out of the horizontal relationships of the latter, in which different groups co-exist side by side in an unsystematic way. To put it more accurately: a more comprehensive consociation unifies the ethnically distinct communities to the point where they can engage in communal action of a specifically political kind. The difference in outcome is that the horizontal relationships of ethnic groups, which lead to mutual repulsion and contempt, permit each ethnic community to consider its own status as the highest, whereas a caste system brings with it a hierarchy of subordination and a recognition of the 'higher status' conferred on the privileged castes and status groups by virtue of the fact that the ethnic distinctions become differences of 'function' within the political sector of the total social system (warriors, priests, craftsmen whose work is of political importance for war, public building and so on). Even the most despised pariah people usually finds some way, moreover, of cultivating the belief in its own specific 'status', which is equally characteristic of both ethnic and status communities. This is true, for instance, of the Jews.

Only amongst underprivileged status groups does the 'sense of worth', the subjective precipitate of social status and of the conventional claims which the privileged status group makes on the life-style of its members, take a specifically deviant turn. Privileged status groups naturally base their sense of their own worth on their 'being', which does not transcend them – their 'beauty and excellence' (καλοκἀγαθία). Their kingdom is 'of this world': they live for the present and on the strength of their glorious past. The underprivileged strata, naturally, can only relate their sense of worth to the future, in this world or the next, but at all events at some point beyond the present: in other words, it must be nourished by a belief in a providential 'mission', in a specific status before God as a 'chosen people', and so by the conviction that there will either be a world beyond in which 'the last shall be first' or there will appear in this world a saviour who will bring out into the light the special status of the pariah people (such as the Jews) or pariah status group, which was hidden from the world which rejected them. It is this simple fact, whose significance is to be discussed in another connexion, and not the '*ressentiment*' which Nietzsche emphasises so strongly in his much-admired account in the *Genealogy of Morals*, which is the source of the type of religion cultivated by pariah status groups – a type of religion which, by the way, as we saw, is found only to a limited extent and, indeed, not at all in the case of one of Nietzsche's chief examples, Buddhism. Moreover, it is by no means normal for status systems to originate from ethnic differences. On the contrary, since it is by no means always the case that subjective feelings of 'ethnic' community are based on objective 'racial differences', it is right that all questions about an ultimately racial foundation for status differentiation should be treated strictly on the merits of the individual case: very often a status group determines by effective exclusion the selection of personal qualities (as when knights select those who are physically and mentally fit for military service) and by so doing creates a pure-bred anthropological type. But selection on the basis of personal qualities is far from being the only, or the predominant, way in which a status group is formed: political membership or class situation is the deciding factor at least as often, and nowadays the latter is by far the most important. After all, the possibility of maintaining the life-style of a status group is usually conditional on economics.

In practice, status differentiation goes together with monopolisation of cultural and material goods and opportunities in the manner we have already acknowledged to be typical. In addition to the specific honorific status, based always on distance and exclusiveness, and its associated privileges, such as the right to certain costumes or kinds of food forbidden by taboo to others, the right to bear arms (so important in its consequences), or the right to engage in certain non-utilitarian or dilettante forms of artistic activity (such as the use of certain musical instruments), there are also material monopolies of various kinds. These are seldom the only motive for the exclusiveness of a status group, but they are almost always to some extent the most effective one. Where intermarriage within a circle of status equals is concerned, the interest of families in monopolising control over their daughters as marriage partners is almost equally matched by their interest in having a monopoly of potential suitors within the circle in order to make provision for these same daughters. As status groups become increasingly exclusive, so the conventional priorities of opportunity for particular appointments develop into a legal monopoly over certain posts for certain groups defined in terms of status. Certain kinds of goods (characteristically, manorial estates), the ownership of bondsmen and serfs, and finally certain sectors of industry come to be the monopoly of particular status groups. This is true both in the positive sense that a particular status group alone has the right to own and exploit them, and in the negative sense that it may not own or exploit them because of the need to maintain its specific life-style. For it is a consequence of the fact that it is life-style which determines social status that status groups are specifically responsible for all 'conventions': all 'stylisation' of ways of life, however expressed, either originates with a status group or is preserved by one.

Despite the enormous differences, there are certain typical features to be seen in the principles on which status conventions are based, especially amongst highly privileged strata. It is very common to find that privileged status groups are disqualified on the grounds of their status from engaging in the usual forms of physical labour: the first signs of this phenomenon can now be seen in America, although it runs counter to the diametrically opposed traditions which have long existed there. It is very often the case that all rational employment of a gainful kind, especially entrepreneurial activity, is regarded as disqualifying a person from high status; furthermore, artistic and literary work, if engaged in in order to earn a living, or if associated with hard physical exertion, is considered to be degrading. For instance, the sculptor, who works in overalls, like a stonemason, is thought to be of lower status than the painter, with his salon-like studio, or than certain kinds of musical performer who have an accepted status.

The extremely frequent disqualification of 'gainful employment' as such is, apart from the particular causes to be discussed later, a direct result of the ordering of society on 'status' principles, in contrast with the regulation of the distribution of power by purely market principles. The market and its economic processes are, as we saw, 'no respecter of persons': it is dominated by 'concrete' interests. It knows nothing of 'status'. The ordering of society in terms of status means precisely the opposite: differentiation in terms of 'social standing' and life-styles peculiar to particular status groups. As such it is fundamentally threatened when purely economic gain and purely economic power, completely naked and clearly displaying the marks of its origin unconnected with status, can confer on everyone who has acquired it the same 'standing' which the interested status groups claim for themselves in virtue of their way of life – or even a consequentially higher standing, given that ownership of property adds an extra element, whether acknowledged or not, to the status of someone who is otherwise of equal standing. The interested parties in every status system therefore react with especial bitterness precisely against the claims of mere economic acquisition as such, and the more they feel threatened, the greater is their bitterness. The respectful way in which peasants are treated in the works of Calderon, in contrast with the open contempt shown by Shakespeare, writing at the same time, for the '*canaille*', is an illustration of these differences in reaction. Calderon was writing within a clearly articulated status system, Shakespeare within one which was economically tottering. Their different reactions are an expression of a universally recurrent situation. Privileged status groups have for that reason never accepted the '*parvenu*' personally, and genuinely without reservations, however completely he has adopted their way of life; it is his descendants who are first accepted, since they have been brought up within the status conventions of their social stratum and have never defiled their standing as members of the status group by their own employment for gain.

In general, then, only one factor, though admittedly a very important one, can be cited as a consequence of status differentiation: the restraint imposed on the free development of the market. This applies, first, to those goods which status groups have directly withdrawn from free trade by either legal or conventional monopolisation: one example is inherited wealth in many Greek cities during the period when considerations of status were dominant and (as the old rule of trusteeship for spendthrifts shows) in the early days of Rome also; other examples are manorial estates, peasant landholdings, church property and above all the goodwill of a craft or trade held by a guild. The market is restricted, and the power of naked property as such, which places its stamp on 'class formation', is held back. The effects of this may be various: they do not necessarily, of course, have any tendency to weaken contrasts in economic situation – often the reverse. At all events, there is no question of genuine free market competition as we nowadays understand it when status differentiation permeates a community as completely as it did in all the political communities of the ancient world and the Middle Ages. But even more far-reaching than this direct exclusion of certain goods from the market is a consequence of the opposition mentioned earlier between the status order and the purely economic order. This is that, in most cases, the concept of honorific 'status' involves a general revulsion from precisely the most characteristic feature of the market, namely bargaining, both between close associates within the status group and occasionally between members of a status group in general. The result is that there are status groups in all societies, and often the most influential of them, which regard all forms of overt participation in trade as totally contaminating.

One might say, therefore (with a certain amount of oversimplification), that 'classes' are formed in accordance with relations of production and the acquisition of wealth, while 'status groups' are formed according to the principles governing their consumption of goods in the context of specific 'life-styles'. An 'occupational status group', furthermore, is still a 'status group': normally, that is, it successfully lays claim to social 'status', by virtue first of all of its specific life-style, which in some cases is determined by the occupation which it pursues. Admittedly, it is often the case that the different types shade into each other, and it is precisely those communities which are most sharply separated in status – the Indian castes – which nowadays display (albeit within very strict and definite limits) a relatively high degree of indifference towards 'trade', which is pursued in the most varied forms, especially by the Brahmins.

In connexion with what has just been said, only one completely general point may be made about the general economic determinants which lead to the prevalence of status differentiation: a degree of relative stability in the bases on which goods are acquired and distributed favours it, whereas all technological and economic convulsions and upheavals pose a threat to it and thrust the 'class situation' into the foreground. Those ages and countries in which the naked class situation is of prevailing importance are generally periods of technological and economic upheaval; while every deceleration of the process of economic change immediately leads to the growth of 'status' structures and restores the significance of 'social standing'.

'Classes' are properly at home in the economic order, 'status groups' in the social order, that is, in the sphere of distribution of status; starting from this point, both reciprocally influence each other and influence the legal order and are in turn influenced by it. *Parties*, on the other hand, are primarily at home in the sphere of power. Their activity is concerned with social power, that is, with exerting influence on communal action, whatever its form: there can in principle be 'parties' in a social 'club' as much as in a 'state'. Communal action by parties, as opposed to classes or status groups, always requires the forming of an association. For it is always directed towards a goal which is pursued in accordance with a plan: the goal may be an 'objective' one, in the sense of the fulfilment of some programme for ideal or material ends, or it may be a 'personal' goal, in the sense of sinecures, power and, as a consequence, status for the leader and members, or, and indeed usually, all these things at once. Such activity is therefore only possible within a community, which, for its part, is in some way or other constituted as an association, that is, which possesses some form of rational organisation and an apparatus of personnel which is ready to bring about the goals in question. For the whole aim of parties is to influence such an apparatus and, wherever possible, to ensure that it is made up of party members. In individual cases, parties may represent interests determined by class situation or status situation and recruit their membership accordingly. But it is not necessary for a party to be purely representative of either a class or a status group: mostly, parties are such only in part, and often not at all. They may be either ephemeral or permanent structures, and their methods of achieving power can be of the most varied kinds: naked force in all its forms, soliciting votes by both crude and subtle means – money, social influence, rhetoric, insinuation, clumsy trickery – or, finally, the use of obstructive tactics, both of the cruder and the more sophisticated kind, within parliamentary bodies. Their sociological structure necessarily differs in its basis, depending on the structure of the communal action which they strive to influence: it depends, indeed, on whether or not the community is, for instance, differentiated by status groups or classes, and above all on the structure of 'domination' within it. For the aim, as far as their leader is concerned, is normally to take control of this structure. Parties, in the sense defined here, did not first emerge from specifically modern forms of domination: we wish to include under the term all ancient and medieval parties, despite the fact that they differ so much in their basic structure from modern examples. At all events, because of this difference in the structure of domination, it is wrong to say anything about the structure of the party, which is always an organisation which

55

strives for domination and so is itself organised, often very rigidly, in terms of domination, without discussing the structural forms of social domination in general. To this central phenomenon of all social life we shall, therefore, now turn.

Before doing so, however, one general point which should be made about classes, status groups and parties is that, in saying that they necessarily presuppose a more comprehensive association, and especially a framework of communal political action within which they function, one is not saying that they themselves are confined within the boundaries of a particular political community. On the contrary, since time immemorial it has always been the case that an association, even an association which aims at the common use of military force, transcends political frontiers. Examples are the solidarity of interests amongst oligarchs and democrats in ancient Greece, or amongst Guelphs and Ghibellines in the Middle Ages, or the Calvinist party in the time of the Wars of Religion, or more recently, the solidarity of landowners in the International Agrarian Congress, or of princes in the Holy Alliance or the Carlsbad Decrees, or of socialist workers or of conservatives (as in the longing of Prussian Conservatives for Russian intervention in 1850). The only reservation is that the goal in such cases is not necessarily to establish a new international political (that is, *territorial*) domination, but usually to influence the existing one.

(*Wirtschaft und Gesellschaft*, 4th edn, Tübingen, 1956, II, pp. 531–40. First published in 1922.)

Postscript: *The Concepts of Status Groups and Classes*

(1) 'Class situation' means the typical chances of material provision, external position and personal destiny in life which depend on the degree and nature of the power, or lack of power, to dispose of goods or qualifications for employment and the ways in which, within a given economic order, such goods or qualifications for employment can be utilised as a source of income or revenue.

'Class' means any group of human beings which shares a similar class situation. A 'property class' is one in which differences in property-ownership primarily determine the class situation. An 'income class' is one in which the chances of utilising goods or services on the market primarily determine the class situation. A 'social class' is the totality of those class situations, between which mobility either within the lifetime of an individual or over successive generations is a readily possible and typically observable occurrence.

Associations based on common class interests (or 'class associations') may arise within any of these three categories of class. But this is not necessarily the case: the terms 'class situation' and 'class' in themselves refer only to situations in which an individual finds himself sharing the same, or similar, typical interests with a number of others. In principle, a particular class situation is always constituted by the power to dispose of consumer goods of any kind, means of production, investments, sources of revenue, or qualifications for employment; and it is only those who have neither property nor skill, and who are dependent on earning what they can by their labour in a situation of uncertain employment, who share a uniform class situation. Ease of movement from one to another is very variable and fluid, and the homogeneity of a 'social' class accordingly varies a great deal.

The main importance of a privileged property class lies (i) in its monopolisation of the purchase of highly priced, or high-cost, consumer goods; (ii) in its monopolistic situation and opportunity to plan mono-polistic policies as a seller; (iii) in its monopolisation of chances to accumulate wealth from unconsumed surpluses; (iv) in its monopolisation of chances for capital accumulation by saving, and hence of possibilities for the investment of wealth in the form of loan-capital and so for control of the leading entrepreneurial positions; (v) in certain privileges of status which depend on education, to the extent that such education costs money.

Privileged property classes consist typically of *rentiers*. Rents may be derived from human beings (as in the case of slave-owners), land, mines, various kinds of installation (as in the case of the owners of plant or machinery), shipping, the giving of credit (in the form of cattle, grain or money), or stocks and shares.

Unprivileged property classes consist typically of slaves or unfree labourers (see under 'status groups'), *déclassés* (or 'proletarians' in the sense meant in the ancient world), debtors, and 'the poor'.

Between these two extremes stand the 'middle'-ranking classes, including all those social strata which draw a livelihood from their property or their educational qualifications. Some of these classes may constitute 'income classes', as do the privileged class of entrepreneurs and the unprivileged class of proletarians. But not all do: for instance, peasants, artisans and officials.

The division of society into classes based purely on property is not 'dynamic': that is, it does not necessarily lead to class struggle and revolution. For instance, the highly privileged property class of slave-owners can co-exist with the much less highly privileged class of peasants (or even *déclassés*), often without any kind of class conflict, and sometimes indeed on a basis of solidarity, for instance against the unfree labourers. The only cases in which a conflict of property classes *may* lead to revolutionary struggle are those in which either landowners are ranged against the *déclassés*, or creditors against debtors (which often means urban patricians against rural peasants or urban artisans). However, such revolutions do not necessarily involve any change in the economic system, but mainly aim at a simple re-allocation or redistribution of property. These might be termed 'property class revolutions'.

A classic instance of lack of class conflict was the relationship of the non-slave-owning whites, or 'poor white trash', to the planters in the southern states of America. Indeed, the poor white trash were much more hostile to the Negroes than the planters, who, because of their situation, were often swayed by patriarchal feelings. It is in the ancient world that we find the main examples, both of conflict between the *déclassés* and those with property, and of struggles between creditors and debtors and between landlords and *déclassés*.

(2) The main importance of a privileged income class lies (i) in its monopolisation of control over the supply of goods in the interests of the income derived by members of the class from this source; (ii) in protecting its chances of income by exercising influence on the economic policy adopted by the political or other associations.

Typical examples of privileged income classes are the various kinds of *entrepreneur* – merchants, ship owners, industrialists, agricultural entre-preneurs, bankers and financiers, some members of the 'liberal pro-fessions' (lawyers, doctors or artists) with specially favoured talents or training, and workers who have a monopoly of certain skills (whether innately or as a result of cultivation or training).

Typical examples of unprivileged income classes are the various qualitatively distinguished kinds of worker – skilled, semi-skilled or unskilled.

Between these extremes, in this case too, stand the 'middle classes' of peasants and artisans. Very often this group also includes officials (public or private), the members of the liberal professions referred to above and the workers with exceptional monopolistic skills (innate, cultivated or trained) also referred to above.

Examples of social classes are: the working class as a whole, as the work process becomes increasingly automated; the petty bourgeoisie; intellectuals without property and trained technical personnel (techni-cians, commercial and other 'employees', and officials, who may be socially very different from each other in such matters as the cost of their training); and the classes of those with property or privileges based on education.

The fragmentary conclusion of Marx's *Capital* was evidently intended to deal with the problem of the unity which is found in the proletariat as a class, in spite of the qualitative distinctions within it. From that point of view, the decisive factor is the increasing importance of workers with only short-term training on the machines themselves, at the expense both of skilled workers and at times also of the unskilled. Nevertheless, skills acquired by this sort of training are also often monopolistic in character (typically, a weaver (*Weber*) sometimes achieves his best performance after five years!). In earlier times, the aspiration of every worker was to become an 'independent' petty bourgeois. But the chance of realising this aim is increasingly small. Over a generation or more it is relatively easiest for members of both the working class and the petty bourgeoisie to 'climb' into the social class of technicians and clerks. Within the class of property-owners and the educationally privileged, money can increas-ingly buy anything, at least over a number of generations. For members of the class of technical personnel there is some possibility of rising to the class of property-owners and the educationally privileged, especially for those employed in banks and joint stock companies and for the higher grades of official.

It is easiest to promote collective action by a whole class (*a*) against those whose interests are directly opposed (for example, workers act against entrepreneurs, not against the shareholders, even though they really draw 'unearned income'; similarly, peasants do not act against landlords); (*b*) only in cases, typically, where the class situation is similar in the mass; (*c*) where it is technically possible to achieve unity of action easily, especially in a community of workers gathered together in a particular locality, such as a factory; (*d*) only where the class is led towards clearly visible goals, which are usually imposed or interpreted by persons who are not members of the class (that is, by intellectuals).

(3) 'Status situation' means a position of positive or negative privilege in social esteem which in the typical case is effectively claimed on the basis of (*a*) style of life, (*b*) formal education, whether based on empirical or rational instruction, together with the corresponding forms of life and (*c*) the prestige of birth or occupation.

In practical terms, status situation is mostly expressed in the form of intermarriage, commensality, in some cases monopolistic appropriation of privileged means of livelihood or repudiation of certain other sources of income and finally in status conventions or 'traditions' of other kinds.

Status situation may depend on class situation, either directly or in a roundabout way. But it is not determined by it alone: possession of money and the position of an entrepreneur are not, in themselves alone, qualifications for status, although they may tend in that direction; conversely, lack of wealth is not in itself a disqualification from status, although it may tend in that direction. On the other hand, status situation, either in combination with other things or by itself, may influence a class situation, without for that reason being identical with it. The class situation of an officer, an official or a student, as determined by his wealth, may be extremely varied without making any difference to his status situation, since the nature of the mode of life formed by education is the same in those respects which are decisive for status.

A 'status group' is a group of human beings who, in the context of some association, effectively claim a special evaluation of their status and possibly also certain special monopolies on the grounds of their status. Status groups may be formed, in the first instance, on the basis of a characteristic mode of life which carries with it a certain status, including especially a particular type of occupation: these may be termed 'life-style' or 'occupational' status groups. Secondly, status groups may be formed on the basis of inherited charisma, that is, on the basis of successful claims to prestige in virtue of a lineage which carries with it a certain status: these may be termed status groups 'by birth'. Finally, status groups may be formed through appropriation on grounds of status of a monopoly of political or hierocratic domination: these may be termed 'political' or 'hierocratic' status groups.

The development of status groups based on birth is normally a form of hereditary appropriation of privileges by an association or by qualified individuals. The firm appropriation of opportunities, especially of opportunities for domination, always tends to result in the formation of status groups. The formation of status groups in turn always tends to result in monopolistic appropriation of powers of domination and sources of income.

Whereas income classes develop in the context of the market economy, status groups mainly emerge and flourish through supplying the requirements of associations, either in the form of the monopolistic performance of public services ('liturgies') or in the manner of feudalism or as a patrimonial obligation of their status. A society may be called a 'status society', when it is structured chiefly in terms of status groups, and a 'class society', when it is structured chiefly in terms of classes. Of the various types of class, the 'social' class is most similar to a 'status group', while the 'income class' is furthest removed. The centre of gravity of a status group is often to be found in a property class.

All status societies are regulated by *convention*, that is, on the basis of rules governing the mode of life. Hence, a status society always creates economically irrational conditions of consumption and so, with its monopolistic appropriations and elimination of the individual's free choice of a means of livelihood, hinders the formation of a free market. More of this elsewhere.

(*Wirtschaft und Gesellschaft*, 4th edn, Tübingen, 1956, I, pp. 177–80. First published in 1922.)

II · The Methodology of the Social Sciences

Introduction

The various papers on methodology which Weber published between 1903 and 1917 have had a strong and continuing influence despite the fact that they were largely directed to the writings of others and their arguments cannot fully be grasped except by readers already familiar with the history of the disputes among German philosophers and social scientists to which they refer. The subjects under dispute, however, have remained of central concern to philosophers and social scientists, and Weber's contribution to them anticipates to a remarkable degree the preoccupations of subsequent writers in Britain and the United States. These preoccupations have centred on the three topics of causality, meaning and values on which those who have asserted that there is a fundamental difference of kind between the natural and the social sciences have rested their arguments. The relation between the three is itself a matter of controversy and those who have made this assertion have done so on a number of different and sometimes incompatible grounds. But they have tended to maintain, first, that human actions cannot be explained in terms of law-like relations of cause and effect; secondly, that to grasp the meaning which human actions have to those performing them requires a different method from any known to, or required by, practitioners of natural science; and thirdly, that the social scientist's moral, political and/or aesthetic values necessarily enter into his conclusions in a way that those of the natural scientist do not. The distinctiveness of Weber's contribution lies chiefly in his reluctance to accept either that there is, after all, no difference between natural and social science or that the difference is such as seriously to undermine the unity of scientific method. This compromise view does not itself escape some serious objections. But it has the overriding merit of taking seriously the most persuasive of the arguments of both sides.

I remarked in the introduction to the previous set of selections that there underlies Weber's thought the assumption that reality cannot be objectively grasped as a meaningful whole, and it is helpful to keep this in mind in tracing his arguments on more specific methodological questions. Thus, although he never questioned the applicability of causal explanations to human affairs, he at the same time rejected any attempt to base the social sciences on a system of laws analogous to those of classical mechanics since such a system could not possibly encompass the historical process which is unendingly generating new cultural forms for which new concepts are required. As he himself put it in 1904, the social sciences (or, as he preferred to call them, the 'cultural' sciences) can only proceed by means of 'a perpetual process of reconstruction of those concepts in terms of which we seek to lay hold of

65

reality.'[1] The concepts in question must in turn be derived from the social scientist's 'cultural value ideas'; and thus, although when they are used *within* an historical explanation the hypotheses framed in terms of them are subject to the standard rules of scientific method, they are still 'value-relevant' in a way that the concepts of classical mechanics are not. What is more, they presuppose a grasp of the 'complexes of subjective meaning' which are taken to be both meaningfully and causally 'adequate' to account for the behaviour described in terms of them,[2] and they must (as we have also seen) be reducible to the action or probability of action of individual persons.

These contrasts on which Weber insists between the social and natural sciences have led some of his interpreters to conclude that he did, in effect, reject the unity of scientific method, whether they then argue (like Nagel)[3] that in doing so he went too far or (like Winch)[4] not far enough. This, I believe, is a mistake. Weber's compromise should be understood more as a recognition of the distinctive features of the 'cultural' sciences within an overall unity of method than as a partial concession to the champions of the unity of science from the side of an anti-Positivist philosophy of action. In particular, any attempt to assimilate Weber's methodology to 'hermeneutics' – that is, to a doctrine substituting understanding for explanation – is misconceived. He himself is quite explicit that when he talks of 're-experiencing' this is not to be taken in the sense used by Wilhelm Dilthey, the leading exponent of 'hermeneutics' as the method for social science, and he quotes several times with approval the saying of his friend and contemporary Georg Simmel that 'one need not be Caesar in order to understand him'.[5] On the contrary, he insists that the understanding which we have of the thoughts and feelings of other people, valuable as it is, can be positively misleading if taken as sufficient by itself for the explanation of their behaviour. He accepts that it is particularly valuable where the social scientist can attribute 'purposive rationality' to those whom he studies and ask himself, therefore, what sequence of reasoning relating to their pursuit of their chosen goals will best account for their choice of means to achieve them. But he has still to test independently the explanation which he offers for its 'causal adequacy'.

The criticisms to which Weber's own arguments have been subject have largely been a function of the standpoint from which they are made. To those of Positivist views, his doctrine of 'ideal types' should simply be assimilated to the role played by limiting cases in the theories of physical science, his talk of 'understanding' should be assimilated to the psychology of hypothesis formation in science generally, and his· notion of 'value-relevance' should be discarded altogether. To anti-Positivists, he is guilty of too readily accepting the Positivists' view of causality, of failing to see that understanding *is* the proper substitute for causal explanation of self-conscious human action and of maintaining that social science can be 'value-free' at all. My own view, for what it is worth, is that the weakest part of his methodology is his concept of 'value-relevance', not because there is not a difference between concept formation in social and natural science,

[1] '"Objectivity" in Social Science and Social Policy', in E. Shils, ed., *The Methodology of the Social Sciences* (Glencoe, Illinois, 1949), p. 105.
[2] Cf. above, pp. 15–16. [3] Ernest Nagel, *The Structure of Science* (London, 1961), Ch. 13.
[4] Peter Winch, *The Idea of a Social Science* (London, 1958), Ch. 4. [5] Cf. above, p. 8.

but because it is misleading to try to link that difference as Weber does to the part played by the social scientist's own 'values'. But the question is too complex to be argued out here.

Of the three selections, the first is taken from a paper published in 1917 which was written, as Weber's own opening footnote states, for a meeting of the Association for Social Policy held in closed session on 5 January 1914. The debate was a heated one, and Weber was on what turned out to be the losing side.[1] But except for those who refuse to accept the logical distinction between fact and value, it is difficult to deny that scientific hypotheses of cause and effect can in principle be disentangled from recommendations about policy, however difficult in practice the disentanglement may, as Weber says, turn out to be; and most social scientists, whether or not they agree in general with what Weber says about values, would, I suspect, agree with him that to the extent that social scientists do mix their advocacy of policy with their purported assertions of fact they ought at least to make it quite clear that they are doing so.

The second selection is taken from the last part of a long and unfavourable review which Weber published in 1907 of the second edition of a book by Rudolf Stammler entitled *Economy and Law according to the Materialist Interpretation of History: a Social-philosophical Investigation*. Weber also singles out Stammler for criticism in the part of *Economy and Society* which deals with the sociology of law. But the exact grounds of Weber's disagreement with Stammler's particular attempt to overturn the historical-materialist view of the relation between economy and law is of less methodological interest than the extended discussion of the concept of 'following a rule' to which it prompted him. The topic has more recently attracted widespread interest among English-speaking philosophers and sociologists, largely as a result of the influence of Wittgenstein's *Philosophical Investigations*. But Weber's treatment, despite his insistence on the role of subjective meaning in human action, is not what would nowadays be called a 'Wittgensteinian' one. For he insists equally on the role of causality in the explanation of action, and it is this which lies behind his argument against Stammler to the effect that the differences between the kinds of 'rule' by which action may be governed do not make any difference to the part they may play in explaining it. The concepts of 'rule', 'regulation', 'rule-governed' and so on cover many different meanings which need to be clearly distinguished: thus, normative principles must be distinguished from empirical generalisations, social rules of behaviour from non-social, and the conscious adherence to a rule accepted as valid (whether normatively or empirically) from imprinted habit or unreflecting imitation. But it does not follow from any of these that social life, because it is rule-governed, is to be explained by a different logic. Here as always, Weber concedes the distinctiveness of human behaviour without at the same time conceding that the unity of scientific method is compromised thereby.

The third selection, like the second, comes from a book review – in this case, a discussion of Eduard Meyer's *On the Theory and Method of History* which had been published in 1902. In it, Weber offers an analysis of causal explanation in history explicitly in terms of what logicians now call the 'counterfactual con-

---

[1] According to the history of the Association published by Franz Boese in 1939, Weber actually walked out of the meeting.

ditional' – that is, the claim that if the antecedent event which is thought to have been contingently sufficient for the occurrence of the subsequent event to be explained had not occurred, then this means that something else would have happened thereafter significantly different from what actually did. He does not on that account modify his view that the social sciences differ from the natural because of the way in which human action can, and natural events cannot, be 'understood' by the observer of them. Nor does he modify his view that the way in which an attempt at historical explanation is framed is a function not of the data themselves but of the theoretical presuppositions (and therefore ultimately, to Weber, the 'cultural value ideas') which the social scientist brings to them. But he continues at the same time to insist that to explain an event is to assign it a cause, and that whatever the role played by 'understanding' in giving the historian access to, or grounds for, the explanation which he offers, that explanation must be tested against the evidence as far as is possible in the same way as in all science.

4 · *Value-judgments in Social Science*[1]

In what follows, except where a different sense is either explicitly mentioned or obvious from the context, the term 'value-judgment' is to be understood as referring to 'practical' evaluations of a phenomenon which is capable of being influenced by our actions as worthy of either condemnation or approval. The problem of the 'freedom' of a particular science from value-judgments of this kind – that is, the acceptability and meaning of this logical principle – is in no way identical with the entirely different question which we shall briefly consider first: the question whether, in the academic context, the teacher's practical value-judgments (whether based on ethical standards, cultural ideals or some other kind of 'world view') ought or ought not to be 'acknowledged'. This question cannot be discussed in scientific terms, since it is itself entirely dependent on practical value-judgments and so irresoluble. Even if we only mention the extremes, two positions have been represented: (*a*) the view that, while it is quite correct to distinguish between, on the one hand, logically demonstrable or empirically observable facts and, on the other, the value-judgments which are derived from practical standards, ethical standards or world views, nevertheless, in spite of (or perhaps even just because of) this, both categories of problem come within the scope of academic teaching; (*b*) the view that, even if this distinction could *not* be carried through with complete logical consistency, nevertheless it is desirable as far as possible to keep all practical value-questions in the background in one's teaching.

View (*b*) seems to me unacceptable. In particular, it seems to me that it is simply impossible to carry through the distinction frequently made in our disciplines between practical value-judgments of a 'party-political' nature and those of any other character, and that the attempt to do so merely serves to disguise the practical implication of the opinion being

---

[1] This is a revised version of a paper presented for internal discussion in the committee of the Association for Social Policy in 1913, and circulated in manuscript form. As far as possible, everything of interest only to this association has been omitted, while the general discussion of methodology has been expanded. Of the other papers presented for discussion in that committee, that by Professor Spranger has been published in *Schmollers Jahrbuch für Gesetzgebung, Verwaltung und Volkswirtschaft.* I confess I find this work, by a philosopher whom I greatly esteem, curiously weak, because insufficiently clear: however, for reasons of space, I shall avoid polemics with him and content myself with presenting my own point of view.

suggested to the audience. Finally, the view that it is an essential feature of the academic approach that it should be 'dispassionate', and that consequently all questions which run the risk of stirring up 'heated' arguments should be excluded, would, once value-judgments in general became a feature of academic teaching, be a merely bureaucratic opinion, which every independent teacher would have to repudiate. Among those scholars who did not believe they ought to renounce the making of practical value-judgments in their empirical discussions, it was precisely the most passionate (such as Treitschke and, in his own way, Mommsen) who were the most tolerable. For precisely because of the force of passion in their words, the hearer was at least put in a position to allow, for his own part, for the way in which the subjectivity of the teacher's value-judgment introduced a possible element of distortion into his statements and so to do for himself what the teacher, because of his emotions, remained incapable of doing. In this way, the influence exercised on the minds of young students would continue to retain the genuine depth of feeling which, I assume, those who support the making of value-judgments in academic teaching would want to ensure, without the audience's being led by misguided teaching into confusing the different domains with each other, as is bound to happen when the statement of empirical facts and the challenge to take up a practical position on the great problems of life are both submerged in the same sea of cool, dispassionate analysis.

View (a) seems to me to be acceptable (even from the point of view of its possible adherents) if and only if the academic teacher imposes on himself the unconditional obligation of rigorously making clear to his audience, and above all to himself, in each individual case (even at the risk of making his lectures boring), which of his statements on that occasion is an assertion of fact, either logically demonstrable or empirically observable, and which a practical value-judgment. To do this certainly seems to me to be a straightforward requirement of intellectual integrity, once the distinction between the two domains is conceded; in this case it is the absolute minimum that is required.

On the other hand, the question whether practical value-judgments are or are not *in general* admissible in academic teaching (even subject to this proviso) is one of practical university policy, which can thus only be settled in the last resort in the light of the individual's views of the functions of the universities, which will be based on *his* value-judgments. Someone who demands of them, and so of himself, in his capacity as a qualified academic teacher, that today they should still fulfil the universal role of forming the minds of men and of propagating political, ethical, aesthetic, cultural or other views, will adopt a different attitude to them from someone who believes that we must accept the fact (with its con-

sequences) that nowadays the really valuable influence of academic teaching consists in the imparting of specialised training by instructors with
specialist qualifications, and hence that the only specific virtue which they
need to inculcate is that of 'intellectual integrity'. The first view can be
derived from as many different fundamental principles as the second.
The latter view in particular (which is the one which I myself accept) may
be derived equally well either from the most extravagant or, on the
contrary, from a very modest estimation of the importance of 'specialist'
training. For instance, one need not hold such a view because one wishes
that all men should inwardly become as pure 'specialists' as possible. It
might rather be for precisely the opposite reason, namely that one does
not wish to see the deepest and most intimately personal decisions in life,
the ones in which a man must rely on his own resources, jumbled up
with specialist training, and that one wishes to see them solved by the
student in the light of his own conscience, not on the basis of any
suggestions from his teachers. One may wish this, however high the value
one may set on the importance of specialised training, not only as a form
of general intellectual discipline, but also, indirectly, as relating to a young
man's self-discipline and moral formation.

Professor von Schmoller is favourably disposed towards the admission
of value-judgments into teaching, and I myself can perfectly well understand this, as an echo of a great age which he and his friends helped
to create. But I think even he cannot have failed to notice that the
situation for the younger generation, simply as a matter of fact, has
changed considerably in one important respect. Forty years ago, the belief
was widespread among scholars in our discipline that, where practical
political value-judgments were concerned, one of the possible positions
must ultimately be the only morally correct one. (Admittedly, Schmoller
himself held this view only with reservations.) This is no longer true; and,
as can easily be shown, it is precisely among those who defend the use
of value-judgments in teaching that the situation has changed. Nowadays,
the legitimacy of such value-judgments is no longer defended in the name
of an ethical imperative demanding, in a (relatively) unpretentious
fashion, that justice be done – a demand which in part really was and
in part seemed to be (relatively) simple and above all (relatively) impersonal because it was unambiguously *supra*-personal, both in the character
of its ultimate foundations and in the consequences to be drawn from
it. Rather, by an inevitable development, it is in the name of a motley
array of 'cultural value-judgments' – which really means subjective demands on culture – or quite openly in the name of the teacher's alleged
'rights as a person'.

It may make some people angry to say this, but, since it too implies
a 'practical value-judgment', it is not really possible to disprove the view

that, of all the varieties of prophecy, *professorial* prophecy, with this tinge of 'the rights of the person', is the only one which is absolutely intolerable. It is certainly a state of affairs without precedent when the state licenses large numbers of prophets, who do not preach on street corners or in churches or some other public place, nor in private, in personally selected conventicles of self-confessed believers, but take it upon themselves to pronounce their authoritative magisterial judgments on the ultimate questions of life 'in the name of science' in the allegedly objective calm of the university lecture hall, where they enjoy the privileges granted by the state and where they are free from any possibility of supervision or discussion and so are carefully protected from all contradiction. It is an old principle, which von Schmoller on one occasion vehemently championed, that what goes on in the lecture hall should be kept separate from public discussion. Although it is possible to take the view that this may occasionally have certain drawbacks even in the domain of empirical science, the general opinion (which I myself share) is that the 'lecture' ought to be something different from a 'public address': that the disinterested rigour, objectivity and reasonableness of discussions among professional colleagues may suffer if the public, for instance in the form of the press, intrude, to the detriment of education. But this privilege of freedom from supervision seems in any case to apply only to the sphere of the teacher's purely specialist qualifications. There is, however, no specialist qualification in personal prophecy, and so it ought not to enjoy that privilege. Above all, however, the teacher ought not to take advantage of the situation in which the student is placed, in which he is compelled, in order to make his way in life, to seek out certain educational establishments, and so their teachers, in order to instil in him not merely what he requires from his education (stimulation and training of his intellectual abilities and powers of reasoning and the acquisition of knowledge) but also, in an atmosphere safe from all contradiction, the teacher's own, occasionally quite interesting but often thoroughly banal, so-called 'world view'.

The university teacher, like anyone else, has at his disposal other opportunities for propagating his practical ideals, and if not he can easily create such opportunities in some suitable form, as experience shows in all cases where it has been honestly attempted. But the teacher should not *as such* lay claim to carrying the baton of the statesman or the cultural reformer in his knapsack, as he does when he exploits the unassailability of his position as an academic in order to express his views on matters of state or of cultural policy. In the press, in congresses and associations, in essays – in short, in any form which is available equally to every other citizen – he may (and ought to) do whatever his god or his demon calls him to do. But what the present-day student should learn from his teachers above all, at least in the lecture hall, is, first, to be able to content himself with the humble fulfilment of a given task; secondly, to first recognise facts – even, and especially, those which he finds personally inconvenient – and then distinguish between stating those facts and taking up an evaluative position towards them; and thirdly, to subordinate his own personality to the matter in hand and so, above all, to suppress the need to display his personal tastes and other feelings where that is not called for. It seems to me that this is much more urgent today than it was forty years ago, when this particular problem did not really exist in this form. It is certainly *not* true that, as some people have maintained, 'personality' is, and ought to be, a 'unity' in the sense that it is bound, so to speak, to wither away if it is not in view on every possible occasion. In all professional work, the task as such has certain claims and must be performed in accordance with its own intrinsic laws. In all professional work, anyone engaged in it must exercise self-restraint and eliminate anything, especially his personal loves and hatreds, which does not strictly form part of the task in hand. It is not true, moreover, that it is a mark of a strong personality to seek out at every opportunity some entirely 'personal note' which is peculiar to it alone. Rather, the hope must be that the generation which is now coming to maturity should once more become accustomed to the idea that 'being a personality' is not an aim which can be intentionally pursued, and that there is only one way in which it can (perhaps!) be achieved – by unreserved devotion to a 'task', whatever shape it and the 'day-to-day demands' which it imposes may take in any particular case. It is bad taste to allow personal concerns to intrude into specialised technical discussions. And the word 'calling' would be stripped of the only part of its meaning which still remains genuinely significant today if there was no exercise of that specific form of self-restraint which it demands. The fashionable cult of personality, whether it flourishes in the palace, the court-room or the university, is nearly always impressive in its outward effects but always equally trivial in its inward influence, and it is always damaging to the matter in hand. I hope, then, that I do not have to make a point of saying that the opponents with whom I am concerned in the present discussion have very little to gain by this kind of cult of personality, for the simple reason that it is 'personal'. In part, they see the function of the university in a different light, in part they have different educational ideals, which I respect but do not share. For the moment, what we must consider is not only what they want but also what effect the views to which they give legitimacy by their authority must necessarily have on a generation which anyway inevitably has a marked pre-disposition to take itself too seriously.

Finally, it scarcely needs to be emphasised that some of those who allegedly oppose the intrusion of (political) value-judgments into academic teaching certainly have very little justification for seeking to discredit discussion of questions of cultural and social policy among the general public *outside* the universities by appealing to the principle of the 'fact-value distinction', which they often grossly misunderstand. Such elements, with their pose of 'value-freedom', their tendentiousness, and their association, in our own subject, with powerful interest groups which stubbornly and methodically pursue the aims of a particular party, do undoubtedly exist, and this makes it perfectly intelligible that a significant number of scholars (precisely among those who are inwardly unattached) continue even now to allow a place to value-judgments in teaching, because they are too proud to join in such mimicry of a purely superficial 'value-freedom'. Personally, I believe that nevertheless what should happen is what (in my view) is correct: that the weight attached to the practical value-judgments of a scholar on the grounds that he confined his advocacy of them to appropriate occasions outside the lecture hall could only increase if it was known that he was austere enough to do within the lecture hall only what 'belonged to his official duties'. However, all these remarks themselves concern issues in which practical value-judgments are involved and which are thus irresoluble.

At all events, it would, in my opinion, be consistent to argue on grounds of principle that teachers have the right to pronounce on questions of value in the course of their teaching only if some guarantee were given at the same time that *all* the different parties should have the opportunity to put their case to the students.[1] In our case, however, emphasis on the rights of teachers in this respect tends, frankly, to be accompanied by a defence of the opposite principle to that of the equal representation of all tendencies (even those thought to be most 'extreme'). For instance, from von Schmoller's personal point of view, it was quite consistent for him to argue that 'Marxists and members of the Manchester School' were disqualified from occupying academic chairs, although he in particular was never guilty of the injustice of discounting the scientific achievements for which these very groups were responsible. But these are just the respects in which I could never follow our revered Master. Obviously, one cannot in the same breath argue for the admissibility of value-judgments in teaching and then, when the logical consequences of this position are pointed out, refer to the fact that the university is a state institution for the training of officials who are 'loyal to

[1] The Dutch approach is far from being adequate for this purpose. In Holland, even the theological faculty is not subject to any confessional requirements, and universities can be freely established as long as financial resources are guaranteed and the regulations governing the necessary qualifications for holding chairs are observed; there is also a private right to found chairs under the personal patronage of the founder. This system merely favours those with money and those authoritarian organisations which are anyway in positions of power: as is well known, only clerical circles have made use of it.

the state' in their thinking. This would make the university not just a 'technical school' (which seems to many lecturers so degrading) but a priests' seminary – except that it could not be given the latter's religious dignity.

Admittedly, attempts have been made to set certain limits on purely 'logical' grounds. One of our leading jurists explained on one occasion, when he was declaring himself against the exclusion of Socialists from university posts, that even he could at least not accept an 'anarchist' as a teacher of law, since an anarchist would deny the validity of law as such; and he clearly thought this argument conclusive. I am of exactly the opposite opinion. An anarchist can certainly be a good legal scholar. And if he is, then it may be precisely that Archimedean point, as it were, outside the conventions and assumptions which seem to us so self-evident, at which his objective convictions (if they are genuine) place him, which equips him to recognise, in the axioms of conventional legal theory, certain fundamental problems which escape the notice of those who take them all too easily for granted. For the most radical doubt is the father of knowledge. It is as little the task of the jurist to 'prove' the value of those cultural goods whose existence is bound up with the existence of 'law', as it is that of the doctor to 'demonstrate' that the prolongation of life is desirable in all circumstances. Neither is even capable of doing so with the means at their disposal. If one wanted to make the university lecture hall into a place where questions of practical value could be discussed, then one would obviously be obliged to allow unrestricted freedom of discussion, from all points of view, of precisely the most fundamental questions of principle. Can this happen? Precisely the most decisive and important questions of practical value in the political sphere are today excluded from academic discussion in German universities by the nature of the political situation. Anyone who considers the interests of the nation to be more important than any of its concrete institutions, without exception, will, for example, consider it to be a question of central importance whether the interpretation of the position of the monarch in Germany which is at present generally accepted is compatible with the world interests of the nation and with the use of the instruments of war and diplomacy to defend these interests. It is not always those who are least patriotic, and certainly not those who are opposed to the monarchy, who are today inclined to answer 'No' to this question and to believe that there can be no lasting success in both those fields as long as there are no fundamental changes in this respect. Everyone knows, however, that these vital national questions cannot be discussed in complete freedom in German universities.[1] In view of the fact

[1] This is not peculiar to Germany. In almost all countries there are limits in practice, whether open or disguised. The only difference is in the kind of value-problems which are ruled out.

that the really decisive issues from the practical political point of view are permanently removed in this way from free academic discussion, however, it seems to me that the only course of action which befits the dignity of a representative of science is to be *silent* even about those value-problems which he is graciously permitted to discuss.

In no case, however, should the question (which is irresoluble, because it is so bound up with value-judgments) whether one may, or must, or ought to defend practical value-judgments in the course of one's teaching, be in any way confused with purely logical analysis of the role played by value-judgments in such empirical disciplines as sociology and economics. Such confusion would necessarily have an adverse effect on the impartiality of the discussion of the properly logical issue, the resolution of which in itself has no bearing on the other question, apart from the purely logical requirement of clarity and sharp separation of the different kinds of problem by the lecturer.

I would rather not discuss any further whether it is 'difficult' to distinguish between statements of empirical fact and practical value-judgments. It is. All of us, the undersigned advocates of this requirement as much as anyone else, are continually offending against it. But at least the adherents of so-called 'ethical' economics could be aware that the moral law too is unrealisable, but that nevertheless it has the status of an 'imperative'. And if we were to examine our consciences we might perhaps find that it is difficult to fulfil the requirements of the postulate mainly because we are reluctant to deny ourselves the chance of entering such an interesting area of value-judgments, especially if we can bring to it that alluring 'personal note'. Every lecturer, of course, observes the way his students' faces light up and assume a more attentive expression when he begins to make a personal 'confession', and also that the attendance figures at his lectures show a marked improvement when such confessions are expected. Everyone knows, furthermore, that, in the competition between the universities for students, a prophet, however minor, who can fill the lecture halls is often given precedence in promotion over others, however considerable their scholarship or substantial their teaching, unless, that is, his prophecy is too far removed from the values which are regarded at the time as politically or conventionally normal. Only the prophet who speaks for material interest groups while posing as value-free has better prospects, because of the influence which these interest groups have on the political powers-that-be. I find all this distasteful, and so I should prefer not to take up the contention that the insistence on a distinction between facts and values is 'petty-minded' and that it would make lectures 'boring'. I offer no opinion on the question whether the chief aim of lectures on a technical, empirical subject must be to be 'interesting', but I am afraid for my own part that at all events the attempt to make lectures attractive by introducing all too interesting personal notes' would in the long run weaken the students' taste for straightforward factual work.

I should like not to discuss the matter further but explicitly to acknowledge that it is possible, precisely when one appears to be eliminating all practical value-judgments, to suggest them very strongly, following the well-known formula, 'Let the facts speak for themselves'. Our parliamentary and electioneering rhetoric of the better sort employs precisely this method, and that is quite legitimate for its purposes. There is no need to waste words in pointing out that, precisely from the point of view of the fact-value distinction, the most contemptible of all abuses would be to follow this practice in university teaching. However, the fact that it is possible to pass off a dishonestly inspired illusion of fulfilling a requirement as if it were the real thing certainly implies no criticism of the requirement itself. But it is relevant to point out at this point that *if* a teacher believes that he ought not to deny himself practical value-judgments, he should make absolutely clear both to his students and to himself that this is what they are.

Finally, the view which must be opposed most decisively of all is the frequently found idea that the way to achieve scientific 'objectivity' is to balance the various value-judgments against each other and thus arrive at a 'statesman-like' compromise between them. Not only is it every bit as impossible to prove the 'middle way' scientifically, by the methods of the empirical disciplines, as it is the most 'extreme' value-judgments, but also, in the domain of value-judgments, it is normatively the least clear. It does not belong in the lecture hall, but in the political programme, the government department and the parliament. The sciences, both normative and empirical, can perform only one invaluable service for the politicians and the opposing parties, and that is to say to them: (i) there are such and such conceivable 'ultimate' positions to be taken on this practical problem; (ii) such and such are the facts which you must take account of in choosing between these positions. At this point, we have arrived at our 'topic'.

Endless misunderstanding and, above all, terminological (and therefore sterile) debate has arisen over the term 'value-judgment', and this has obviously contributed nothing at all towards settling the issue. It is, as was said at the beginning, perfectly clear that the issue in these discussions, as far as our discipline is concerned, is one of the practical evaluation of social facts as practically desirable or undesirable, whether on ethical grounds or on the basis of some attitude to culture or for some other reason. In spite of all that has been said on the matter,[1] such

---

[1] I must here refer to what I have said elsewhere, in my essays on '"Objectivity" in Social Science and Social Policy', 'The Logic of the Cultural Sciences' and 'R. Stammlers'

'objections' have been raised (in all seriousness) as that science seeks to attain 'valuable' results, (i) in the sense of logically and factually correct results and (ii) in the sense of results which are important from the point of view of scientific interest, and that the very selection of material implies a 'value-judgment'. Then again, there is the constantly recurring and almost incredibly wrong-headed misunderstanding of those who think it is being maintained that empirical science cannot treat men's 'subjective' value-judgments as objects (whereas the whole of sociology and, in economics, the whole theory of marginal utility are based on the opposite assumption). What is at issue, however, is exclusively the requirement, utterly trivial in itself, that anyone engaged in research or in presenting its results should keep two things absolutely separate, because they involve different kinds of problem: first, the statement of empirical facts (including facts established by him about the 'evaluative' behaviour of the empirical human beings whom he is studying); and secondly, his own practical value-position, that is, his judgment and, in this sense, 'evaluation' of these facts (including possible 'value-judgments' made by empirical human beings, which have themselves become an object of investigation) as satisfactory or unsatisfactory.

The author of an otherwise valuable paper asserts that a researcher can take even his own value-judgment as 'fact' and proceed to draw the consequences from it. What is meant here is as indisputably correct as the chosen form of expression is misleading. It is of course possible to agree before a discussion that a particular practical measure, such as a plan to meet the costs of an increase in the army out of the pockets of the propertied classes alone, should be 'assumed' in the discussion and that the only topic for discussion should be the means of carrying it out. That is often a perfectly useful thing to do. But a practical purpose which is mutually taken for granted in this way is not called a 'fact', but an 'end fixed *a priori*'. That even this is essentially ambiguous would very soon become apparent in the discussion of the 'means', unless the 'assumed end' held to be outside the scope of the discussion was something as concrete as lighting a cigar now. In that case, admittedly, the means too would only rarely require any discussion. In almost every case of a purpose formulated in more general terms (for example, in the illustration just used), it will be found that in the discussion of the means, not only does it become apparent that the different individuals understand

"Victory" over the Materialist Interpretation of History' [in this volume, see pp. 99–131]. Occasional deficiencies in accuracy in the individual formulations in these papers, which are more than likely, should not affect any essential point. On the 'undecidability' of certain ultimate value-judgments in a particular important problem area, I should like to refer to Gustav Radbruch's *Einführung in die Rechtswissenschaft*, 2nd edn (1913) in particular. I differ from him on a number of points, but they are not important for the problem here being discussed.

something quite different by the supposedly clear end, but in particular it may happen that precisely the same end is desired for very different ultimate reasons and that this has some influence on the discussion of the means. Still, this is by the way. For it has never so far occurred to anyone to dispute that it is possible to start from a certain mutually agreed end and discuss only the means of achieving it and that this *can* result in a discussion which can be settled by purely empirical methods. Rather, the whole discussion turns precisely on the choice of ends (not on that of the 'means' to an already accepted end) – in other words, precisely on the question of the sense in which the individual's fundamental value-judgment can be, not taken as a 'fact', but made the object of a scientific critique. If this is not accepted, then all further discussion is in vain.

The topic for discussion is not really the question of the extent to which practical value-judgments, in particular ethical judgments, may claim for themselves normative status – in other words, whether they are different in character from, for instance, the often cited example of the question whether blondes are preferable to brunettes or any other similarly subjective judgment of taste. These are problems for moral philosophy, not for the methodology of the empirical disciplines. What is important from the methodological point of view is that the validity of a practical imperative as a norm, on the one hand, and the truth claims of a statement of empirical fact, on the other, create problems at totally different levels, and that the specific value of each of them will be diminished if this is not recognised and if the attempt is made to force them into the same category. In my opinion, this is to a large extent what has been done, especially by Professor von Schmoller.[1] It is precisely respect for our Master which makes it impossible to ignore these points at which I believe we should not follow him.

First, I should like to oppose the view that the proponents of 'value-freedom' take the mere fact of the historical and individual variability of the value-positions accepted at particular times to be proof of the necessarily merely 'subjective' character of, for instance, ethics. Statements of empirical fact, too, are often very much disputed, and there may often be considerably greater general agreement about whether someone is to be considered a scoundrel than there is (among the very experts themselves) about the question of the interpretation of a mutilated inscription. Von Schmoller's assumption of an increasing conventional unanimity among all religious denominations and individuals about the most important values is in marked contrast to my impression, which is quite the opposite. However, that seems to me to have no bearing on the

[1] In his article on 'Volkswirtschaftslehre' in *Handwörterbuch der Staatswissenschaften* 3rd edn, VIII, pp. 426–501.

present issue. For it would still be necessary to oppose the view that the fact that certain practical values, however widely held, had come, simply by convention, to be accepted in fact as self-evident could count as an adequate scientific proof. The specific function of science seems to me to be exactly the opposite: for science, what is conventionally 'self-evident' becomes a problem. This is just what von Schmoller and his friends themselves have done in their time. The fact that one investigates the causal influence on economic life of the actual existence of certain ethical or religious convictions, and in certain cases assesses it highly, certainly does not imply that one must therefore share these convictions, which have, perhaps, had a considerable causal influence, or even that one must consider them merely as 'valuable'. Similarly, a high valuation of some ethical or religious phenomenon does not in the least imply a similar positive evaluation of the unexpected consequences which its realisation has had or would have. Such questions cannot be settled by citing facts, and the individual's judgment on them would vary considerably, depending on his own religious and other practical values. All this is completely irrelevant to the question at issue.

On the other hand, I am emphatically opposed to the view that a 'realistic' science of morality, in the sense of a demonstration of the factual influences exercised on the ethical convictions which prevail at any given time in a group of human beings by their other conditions of life and in turn by the ethical convictions on the conditions of life, would produce an 'ethics' which could ever say anything about what *ought* to be the case. Any more than a 'realistic' account of the astronomical ideas of, for instance, the Chinese – one which would show what their practical motives were for studying astronomy and how they went about it, what results they achieved and why – could ever have as its goal to prove the correctness of this Chinese astronomy. Or again, any more than an account of the way in which Roman surveyors or Florentine bankers (the latter even when apportioning quite large inherited fortunes) very often arrived by their methods at results which are incompatible with trigo-nometry or the multiplication table could ever make it a matter for discussion whether the latter were valid. The one and only result which can ever be achieved by empirical psychological and historical investi-gation of a particular value-system, as influenced by individual, social and historical causes, is its *interpretative explanation*. That is no small achievement. Not only is it desirable because of its personal (though not scientific) by-product, of making it easier for the individual to 'do justice to' those who really or apparently think differently. But it is also extremely important from the scientific point of view, in two respects: (i) for the purpose of an empirical causal study of human action, in learning to recognise what are really its ultimate motives; (ii) when one is engaged in discussion with someone who (really or apparently) has a different set of values from oneself, in determining which value-positions are genuinely opposed. For this is the real meaning of any debate about values: to understand what one's opponent (or oneself) really means, in the sense of the value which really, and not just apparently, is important to each of the two parties, and in this way to make it possible to decide one's attitude to this value in general.

Thus, far from its being the case that, from the point of view of the requirement of 'value-freedom' in discussions of empirical matters, debates about value-judgments would be sterile or even meaningless, awareness of the meaning of this requirement is a presupposition of all fruitful discussions of this kind. They presuppose an appreciation, quite simply, of the possibility that ultimate values might diverge, in principle and irreconcilably. For neither is it the case that 'to understand all' means 'to forgive all', nor is there in general any path leading from mere understanding of someone else's point of view to approval of it. Rather, it leads, at least as easily and often with much greater reliability, to an awareness of the impossibility of agreement, and of the reasons why and the respects in which this is so. This very awareness, however, is the recognition of a truth and it is just this recognition which is advanced by 'discussion of values'. What can certainly not be achieved in this way, since it lies in precisely the opposite direction, is any kind of normative ethic or in general any kind of binding 'imperative'. Quite the contrary: everyone knows that the achievement of such a goal is rather made more difficult by the (at least apparently) 'relativising' effect of such discussions. Again, this is naturally not to say that such discussions should be avoided. Quite the opposite. For an 'ethical' conviction which can be undermined by psychological 'understanding' of divergent value-judgments is worth no more than religious opinions which are overthrown, as sometimes happens, by scientific knowledge. Finally, when von Schmoller takes it for granted that the advocates of 'value-freedom' in the empirical disciplines could recognise only 'formal' ethical truths (which obviously means 'formal' in the sense of Kant's *Critique of Practical Reason*), some discussion of his claim is called for, even though the problem is not absolutely relevant to the present issue.

First, the identification which is implicit in von Schmoller's view of ethical imperatives and 'cultural values' must be rejected – even when they are said to be the highest cultural values. For there may be a point of view from which cultural values can be seen as 'given', even insofar as they conflict, inevitably and irreconcilably, with all the requirements of ethics. And contrariwise an ethics which rejects all cultural values is possible without internal contradiction. In any event, the two types of value are not identical. Again, it is a grave (though widespread) misunderstanding to think that 'formal' propositions, like those of Kantian ethics, imply no substantive guidance. The possibility of a normative ethics is by no means called in question merely because there are problems of a practical kind for which normative ethics cannot by itself provide any clear guidance (a very specific example being, in my opinion, certain problems connected with institutions, and so precisely with 'social policy'). Nor is it called in question because ethics is not the only area of values in the world – because, besides ethics, there are other kinds of value, which can in certain cases be realised only by someone who will accept ethical 'responsibility'. A prime example is the area of political action. It would be feeble-minded, in my opinion, to wish to deny the tension with ethics which is inherent precisely in political activity. But it is by no means peculiar to politics, as the usual antithesis of 'private' and 'political' morality would have us believe. Let us go beyond some of the 'limits' of ethics mentioned above.

Among those questions which cannot be clearly resolved by *any* system of ethics are those concerning the consequences of the postulate of 'justice'. For instance, is much owed to the man who achieves much (a view which comes closest to the opinion expressed by von Schmoller in his day)? Or, on the contrary, is much required from the man who can achieve much? Should one then, in the name of justice (for other considerations, such as the necessary 'incentive', would have to be set aside in this case), ensure that those with great talent have the best chances? Or should one rather, like Babeuf, try to compensate for the injustice involved in the unequal distribution of intellectual abilities by making absolutely sure that talent, the very possession of which already confers a beneficial feeling of prestige, cannot also take advantage of its better chances in the world for itself? Such questions would seem to be unanswerable in purely 'ethical' terms. But the ethical aspects of most questions of social policy conform to this type.

Even when purely individual action is concerned, however, there are fundamental problems, of a specifically ethical kind, which cannot be resolved on the basis of purely ethical presuppositions. One example in particular is the fundamental question whether the intrinsic value of a moral action (usually referred to as the 'pure will' or the 'intention') is in itself sufficient to justify the action: this follows the maxim formulated by Christian moralists as, 'The Christian acts rightly and leaves the outcome to God'. Or should some account also be taken of responsibility for the possibly or probably foreseeable *consequences* of the action, once it becomes enmeshed with the ethically irrational world? In the social sphere, all radical revolutionary political tendencies, especially so-called 'syndicalism', base themselves on the former postulate, while all forms of 'political realism' follow the latter. Both appeal to ethical maxims. But these maxims are in permanent conflict with each other, of a kind which simply cannot be resolved by the means of an ethics which relies entirely on its own resources.

Both these ethical maxims are of a severely 'formal' character, and so are similar in that respect to the well-known axioms of the *Critique of Practical Reason*. Because of this formal character, it is widely held that these latter did not in general contain any substantive guidance for the assessment of action. That, as was said above, is by no means true. Suppose we deliberately take an example which is as far removed as possible from anything to do with 'politics': such an example may perhaps clarify the real meaning of the much-discussed 'merely formal' character of Kantian ethics. Suppose a man says of his sexual relationship with a woman, 'At first, our affair was for both of us merely a passion, but now it is a value'. In terms of the cool objectivity of the Kantian ethic, the first half of this sentence would be expressed as 'At first, we were both merely a means for each other', and the whole sentence would thus be claimed as an instance of that well-known principle, which there has been a curious eagerness to represent as a purely historically conditioned expression of 'individualism', whereas in reality it is an extremely original formulation of an enormous number of ethical situations – though one must understand this formulation correctly. In its negative form, and leaving out of account any statement of what is being positively contrasted with treating someone else, in the morally disapproved fashion, 'merely as a means', it evidently contains three elements: (i) the recognition of kinds of values which are independent of ethics; (ii) the demarcation of the ethical domain from these others; and finally (iii) a statement of the fact that, and the sense in which, action in the service of extra-ethical values may nevertheless be connected with differences in ethical worth. In fact, the kinds of values which permit or prescribe the treatment of others 'merely as a means' are quite different in character from ethical values. This matter cannot be pursued any further here, but it is at any rate clear that the 'formal' character of even that, highly abstract, ethical proposition is not indifferent to the content of action.

At this point, however, the problem becomes even more complex. The negative attitude embodied in the words 'merely a passion' may be represented from a certain standpoint as a blasphemy against all that is most authentic and real in life, against the only, or at least the royal, road away from impersonal or *supra*-personal and so life-denying 'value'-mechanisms, from bondage to the lifeless petrification of routine existence and the pretensions of inauthentic values taken as 'given'. At all events, it is possible to conceive of such a view which, although it would certainly disdain to use the word 'value' to describe the kind of totally concrete experience which it has in mind, would yet constitute a domain of values, which, while totally alien and hostile to all conceptions of sanctity or goodness, all forms of ethical or aesthetic legalism, all ideas of the importance of culture or the value of the individual, would yet, and for that very reason, claim its own kind of 'immanent' worth, in the most extreme sense of that word. Whatever our attitude to this claim may be, it is at all events not one which could be either proved or disproved by the methods of any 'science'.

Any empirical consideration of this situation would, as John Stuart Mill remarked, lead to acknowledgement of absolute polytheism as the only metaphysic which would fit the case. A non-empirical approach, concerned more with the interpretation of meanings (in other words, a genuine moral philosophy), would go further than this: it could not fail to recognise that a conceptual scheme of 'values', however well ordered, would fail to do justice to precisely that aspect of the situation which is most decisive. That is to say, it is in the last resort always, and again and again, more than a mere matter of choosing between alternative values: it is rather a matter of an irreconcilable struggle to the death like the conflict between 'God' and the 'Devil'. Between these rivals there can be no question of relativism or compromise – or not, as must be insisted, in the real sense. For, as everyone finds in the course of life, such compromises are made in fact, and so in outward appearance: indeed, they are made at every step. The different domains of value are entwined and entangled in virtually every single important attitude which real men adopt. It is here that we find the levelling effect of 'everyday life' in the truest sense of that word: in the context of everyday routine a man does not become aware (above all, does not even *want* to become aware) of this partly psychological, partly pragmatic confusion of mortally opposed values, and evades the choice between 'God' and the 'Devil' and the decision, which ultimately lies with him, about which of the conflicting values is under the sway of the one and which of the other. The fruit of the Tree of Knowledge, so disturbing to human complacency yet so inescapable, is nothing but this recognition of these oppositions, and of the consequent necessity to accept that every important individual action, indeed life as a whole, if it is not to slip by like a merely natural process but to be lived consciously, is a series of ultimate decisions, by means of which the soul, as in Plato, chooses its own destiny, in the sense of the meaning of what it does and is. The crudest misunderstanding to which the intentions of those who argue for an ultimate conflict of values are occasionally subject is thus that contained in the interpretation of their view as a form of 'relativism', or in other words as a view of life which is based on precisely the opposite conception of the relations between the different value-spheres and is only meaningfully tenable (in any coherent form) on the basis of a metaphysic which is structured in a very special ('organic') fashion.

If we return to our special case, it seems to me to be possible to establish without a shadow of a doubt that, in the area of practical political value-judgments (especially in the fields of economics and social policy), as soon as guidance for a valued course of action is to be sought, all that an empirical discipline with the means at its disposal can show is (i) the unavoidable means; (ii) the unavoidable side-effects; (iii) the resulting conflict of several possible value-judgments with each other in their practical consequences. *Philosophical* disciplines can go further, determining by means of reasoning the 'meaning' of the value-judgments, and so their ultimate structure and consequences from the point of view of meaning: in this way they can assign them their 'place' within the totality of possible 'ultimate' values and mark out their spheres of application from the point of view of meaning. Even such simple questions as: how far should the end justify the necessary means? or again, how far should unintended consequences be taken into account? or finally, how are conflicts between a number of intended or obligatory ends which clash in a particular case to be resolved? – All are entirely matters of choice or of compromise. There is no scientific procedure, either rational or empirical, of any kind which could provide a decision in such cases. Least of all can *our* strictly empirical science presume to spare the individual the necessity of making this choice, and so it should not even give the impression of being able to do so.

One further point which should be explicitly made in conclusion is that the recognition of this state of affairs in relation to our disciplines is completely independent of any attitude one might adopt towards the extremely brief outline of value theory given above. For there is in general no logically tenable point of view from which it could be denied, apart from that of a hierarchy of values clearly prescribed by religious dogmas. I must wait and see whether there are really people who maintain that there is *no* basic distinction in meaning between such questions as: are the facts in a particular case such and such or are they not? why did the particular situation develop as it did, and not in some other way? is a given state of affairs usually succeeded, in accordance with a factual rule, by another state of affairs, and if so with what degree of probability? and such questions as: what should a man do in practice in a particular situation? from which points of view might that situation seem practically desirable or undesirable? are there any general propositions or axioms, of whatever form, to which these points of view are reducible? Again, is there anyone who will maintain that there is the slightest connexion in meaning between the question: in which direction will a particular given factual situation (or more generally, a situation of a particular, sufficiently determinate, type) probably develop, and how great is the probability that it will develop in that direction (or typically tends so to develop)? and the question: should one assist a particular situation to develop in a particular direction (whether that which is inherently probable or the precise opposite or some other)?; or, lastly, between the question: what view will probably (or even certainly) be formed on a problem, of whatever kind, by certain people in particular circumstances, or by an indefinite number of people in similar circumstances? and the question: is this view, which will probably or certainly be formed, *correct*? Can it really be contended that they are, as is said time and time again, 'inseparable from each other'? Or that this latter contention is *not* incompatible with the requirements of scientific thought? Whether someone who admits that the two sorts of question are absolutely heterogeneous in character nevertheless claims the right to express his views on both sorts of problem in one and the same book, on one and the same page, or even in the principal and subordinate clauses of one and the same sentence, is entirely his own affair. What *can* be required of him is simply that he should not unintentionally (or even intentionally, out of a wish to be clever) mislead his readers about the absolute heterogeneity of the problems. Personally I am of the opinion that no means whatsoever is too 'pedantic' to be used in avoiding confusions.

The point of discussions of practical value-judgments (those, that is, of the parties to such discussions) can only be:

(*a*) To work out the ultimate internally 'coherent' value-axioms, from which the opposing opinions are derived. Frequently enough we deceive ourselves, not only about our opponent's fundamental axioms, but also about our own. This procedure essentially begins with the particular value-judgment and its analysis in terms of meaning, and then ascends by stages to more and more fundamental evaluative attitudes. It does not use the methods of any empirical discipline and does not increase our knowledge of facts. It is 'valid' in the same way as logic.

(*b*) To deduce the 'consequences', in terms of evaluative attitudes, which would follow from particular ultimate value-axioms if they and they alone were made the basis of the practical evaluation of factual states of affairs. The argumentation in this case is entirely at the level of meanings, but the procedure depends on empirical enquiry for the most exhaustive possible analysis of those empirical states of affairs which might be generally relevant to a practical evaluation.

(*c*) To ascertain the consequences which would necessarily follow in fact from the practical realisation of a particular practically evaluative attitude to a problem (i) as a result of its being limited to the use of certain unavoidable means, and (ii) as a result of the inevitability of certain, not directly intended, side-effects. This purely empirical enquiry may have the following results, amongst others: (i) that it is absolutely impossible to realise the value-postulate, to however slight a degree of approximation, because no way of realising it can be discovered; (ii) that it becomes more or less improbable that it should be realised, either completely or approximately, either for the same reason or because it is probable that there will be certain unintended consequences of such a kind as directly or indirectly to make its realisation illusory; (iii) that it is necessary to take into account means or indirect side-effects of a kind which the advocate of the practical postulate in question had not considered, so that, even in his own eyes, his evaluative decision between end, means and side-effects becomes a new problem and loses its compelling power over others.

Finally (*d*) new value-axioms, and the postulates derivable from them, may emerge from the discussion, of a kind which the advocate of a practical postulate had not noticed and towards which he had as a result not adopted any attitude, although the realisation of his own postulate conflicts with them either (i) in principle or (ii) because of its practical consequences – in other words, either at the level of meaning or in practice. In case (i) further discussion will concern problems of type (*a*), in case (ii) of type (*c*).

It is thus very far from being the case that discussions of this type about value-judgments are 'pointless'. Rather, it is precisely when their purposes are rightly understood (and in my opinion only then) that they have considerable point.

The utility of a discussion of practical value-judgments, in the right place and in the right sense, is, however, by no means exhausted by the direct 'yield' which it may produce in this way. Rather, when properly conducted, it bears lasting fruit in empirical work, in that it supplies the basic questions for investigation.

The problems posed in the empirical disciplines are, of course, to be answered in a 'value-free' way. They are not 'evaluative problems'. But in the field of our disciplines they are influenced by the relationship of reality 'to' values. For the meaning of the expression 'value-relevance' I must refer to my own earlier discussions and above all the well-known works of Heinrich Rickert. It would be impossible to enter into the discussion again here, so it should simply be recalled that the expression 'value-relevance' refers merely to the philosophical interpretation of that specifically scientific *interest* which governs the selection and formulation of the object of an empirical enquiry.

Within empirical enquiry, this fact, with its purely logical import, does not license any kind of 'practical value-judgments'. But this fact shows, as does all historical experience, that it is cultural (that is, value-) interests which indicate the direction even of empirical scientific work. Clearly, these value-interests may become explicit in the course of discussions about value-judgments. Such discussions may to a large extent remove the need for, or at least facilitate, the scientific researcher's (especially the historian's) task of 'value-interpretation', which is for him such an important preliminary to his genuinely empirical work. Since the distinction, not only between evaluation and value-relevance, but also between evaluation and value-interpretation (in the sense of the development of possible positions at the level of meaning towards a given phenomenon) is often not made with complete clarity, with the result that obscurities arise which have a special bearing on the assessment of the logical character of history, I refer the reader in this regard to the remarks in my paper 'Critical Studies in the Logic of the Cultural Sciences'[1] (without claiming in any way that this is a definitive account).

Instead of entering into yet another discussion of this fundamental methodological problem, I should like to consider in more detail a few specific points of practical importance for our discipline.

There is a recurrent and widespread belief that guidance in practical decisions ought to be, must be, or even may be derived from 'developmental trends'. From such 'trends', however, clear as they may be, clear imperatives for action can be obtained only in regard to the means which will probably be appropriate given a certain end, not in regard to the end itself. The concept of a 'means' which is being used here is, admittedly, as broad as it can conceivably be. For instance, someone whose ultimate end was the power-political interests of the state would, according to the situation, have to regard an absolutist constitution as much as a radical-democratic one as the (relatively) more appropriate means, and it would be ludicrous if a possible change in his assessment of these constitutional contrivances as a means were to be regarded as a change in his 'ultimate' value-position. Obviously, however, as was said earlier, the individual is constantly faced anew with the problem whether to abandon his hopes of realising his practical values in the light of his awareness that there is a clear developmental trend which would either make it possible for him to achieve his end only by using new means which perhaps seem to him morally or otherwise objectionable, or force him to take into account side-effects which he finds abhorrent, or make it so unlikely that he will achieve his end that his work, judged by its chances of success, is bound to seem like fruitless tilting at windmills. But there is nothing very special about the role played by awareness of such more or less easily modifiable developmental 'trends' in all this. Any single new fact may equally mean that a new adjustment has to be made between

---

[1] Original reference: *Archiv für Sozialwissenschaft und Sozialpolitik*, XXII, pp. 168f [in this volume, see pp. 111–131].

end and necessary means, intended end and unavoidable side-effects. But whether this is to happen, and what practical conclusions are to be drawn from it if it does, are questions which not only no empirical science of whatever kind but, as was said earlier, no science at all, however it is constituted, can answer. For instance, one may use the most cogent arguments to show the convinced syndicalist that his action is not only socially 'useless' in that it does not hold out any prospect of success in changing the external class situation of the proletariat, but will undoubtedly make that position worse by creating a 'reactionary' mood: he will still see absolutely no force in such arguments, if he is really committed to his view down to its ultimate consequences. And this would not be because he was mad, but because he may from his own point of view be 'right', as will presently be explained.

On the whole, people have a rather marked tendency to adapt themselves mentally to success, or to what at a particular time holds out the prospect of it, not only, as goes without saying, in regard to the means with which or the extent to which they seek to realise their ultimate ideals at that time, but in their abandonment of these ideals themselves. In Germany, it is thought proper to dignify this attitude with the name of *Realpolitik*. At all events it is incomprehensible why precisely the representatives of an empirical science should feel the need to give this attitude their support, by constituting themselves into a claque of supporters of the current 'developmental trend' and transforming the question of 'adaptation' to the trend from an ultimate problem of values, to be settled only by the individual in the individual case and so a matter for the individual's own conscience, into a principle supposedly guaranteed by the authority of a 'science'.

It is true to say, provided it is rightly understood, that successful politics is always 'the art of the possible'. It is no less true, however, that the possible is very often achieved only by reaching out towards the impossible which lies beyond it. It was not, finally, the only truly consistent ethic of 'adaptation' to the possible (the Confucian bureaucratic morality) which produced the specific qualities of our civilisation, which we probably all (subjectively) value more or less positively, despite all our other differences. I at least should not like to see the nation, as further explained above, systematically deprived of the sense that the value of an action does not only lie in its 'consequences' but also in its 'intentions' – least of all in the name of science. Anyway, failure to appreciate this impedes our understanding of realities. For – to stick to our earlier example of the syndicalist – it is, even from the logical point of view, absurd to 'criticise' a course of action which must, if consistent, take as its guiding thread the value of the agent's intentions by confronting it merely with the value of its consequences. The genuinely consistent syndicalist seeks as much merely to preserve in himself a certain intention which seems to him to be of absolute value, indeed sacred, as he does to arouse, whenever possible, such an intention in someone else. His external actions, in particular those which are doomed from the outset to be totally ineffectual, ultimately have the purpose of assuring him in his own mind that this intention is genuine, that is, has the strength to 'stand the test' in action, and is not an idle boast. That end can (perhaps) only be achieved in the real world by means of such actions. For the rest, his kingdom, if he is consistent, is, like that of any ethics of intention, 'not of this world'. All that can be said from the 'scientific' point of view is that this conception of his own ideals is the only one which is internally coherent and that it cannot be contradicted by external 'facts'.

I should like to think that, in saying this, I have performed a service for supporters and opponents of syndicalism alike, and exactly the service which they rightly require of science. On the other hand, nothing seems to me to be achieved in the sense of any science, however constituted, by 'on the one hand – on the other hand', by seven reasons 'for' and six reasons 'against' a particular phenomenon (such as the General Strike), which are then set against each other in the manner of ancient public administration or modern Chinese memoranda. Once the syndicalist view has been reduced in this way to as rational and internally consistent a form as possible, and once the empirical conditions of its realisation, its chances of success and empirically predictable practical consequences have been stated, the task of value-free science, at any rate in relation to it, is complete. That one should, or should not, be a syndicalist is something that can never be proved in the absence of very definite metaphysical premises, which are not demonstrable, and certainly not by any science of whatever form. Again, for an officer to blow himself and his trench up rather than surrender may in a particular case be absolutely futile in all respects, judged by its consequences. It should not be a matter of indifference, however, whether the intention to act without asking about the usefulness of doing so does or does not exist in general. At any rate, it is no more 'senseless' than that of the consistent syndicalist. If a professor wanted to recommend such Catonism from the comfortable heights of his academic chair, it would not, admittedly, look in particularly good taste. But neither is it necessary for him to extol the opposite attitude and make it into an obligation to adapt one's ideals to the opportunities afforded precisely by current trends and situations.

The expression 'adaptation' has repeatedly been used just now, and in any given case its meaning is sufficiently clear because of the form of expression which has been chosen. But clearly the term is in itself ambiguous: it may refer to the adaptation of the means used in the pursuit of some ultimate end to given situations ('*Realpolitik*' in the narrower sense) or to adaptation, in the choice from among the possible ultimate ends themselves, to the real or apparent momentary chances of one of them at any given time (the form of '*Realpolitik*' which has been so remarkably successful in our policies for the last twenty-seven years). But this is far from exhausting its possible meanings. Hence it would in my opinion be best to avoid employing this much misused concept in any discussions of our problems, whether of questions of 'value' or of questions of any other kind. It is readily liable to misunderstanding as an expression of a scientific argument, as which it is constantly used, both in 'explanation' (for instance, of the empirical emergence of certain ethical views in certain human groups at particular periods) and in 'evaluation' (for example, of the ethical views just referred to as having emerged in practice as objectively 'appropriate' and so objectively 'correct' and valuable). In neither of these respects, however, does it perform any useful function, since it always requires interpretation itself first of all. Its original home is in biology. If it were really understood in the biological sense as referring to the relatively determinable chances, resulting from the environment, which a human group has to preserve its own psycho-physical genetic inheritance through abundant procreation, then, for instance, those social classes which are economically most affluent and regulate their lives in the most rational fashion would be, in terms of the familiar empirical statistics of birth rate, the 'least well adapted'. The few Indians who lived around Salt Lake before the Mormon immigration were as well or as poorly 'adapted' to the conditions of the environment as were the later densely populated Mormon settlements, both in the biological sense and in any other of the numerous possible genuinely empirical senses. Thus we do not increase our empirical understanding in the slightest by using this concept, though it is easy to imagine that we do. And – let it be said at this point – it is only where there are two organisations which are in every other respect absolutely identical that one can say that a concrete difference of detail creates a situation for one of them which is empirically better 'suited' to its continued existence, and is in this sense better 'adapted' to the given conditions. As for evaluation, one person might take the view that the greater numbers of Mormons and the material and other achievements and qualities which they brought to the area and developed there were evidence of their superiority to the Indians; another, who was utterly revolted by the means used by the Mormons and the side-effects of their ethical code, which was at least partly responsible for those achievements, might be just as likely to prefer the plains even if there had been no Indians there, and so to prefer the romantic existence which the Indians led there. No science in the world, however constituted, could claim to be able to convert them. For the issue here is the irresoluble one of balancing ends, means and side-effects against each other.

Only where it is a question of finding the appropriate means to an absolutely unambiguously given end is the problem one which can really be decided empirically. The proposition 'x is the only means to y' is in fact merely the converse of the proposition 'y follows x'. The concept of 'adaptedness', however (and all those linked to it), does not, and this is the main point, give us the slightest information about the ultimate underlying value-judgments, which it rather merely conceals – as does, for instance, the recently fashionable concept of 'human economy', which in my view is fundamentally confused. In the domain of 'culture', either everything is 'adapted' or nothing is, depending on how the concept is used. For no form of civilised life can be without conflict. Its methods, its object, even its basic direction and the people involved in it can be altered, but it cannot be eliminated itself. It may take the form, not of an external struggle between enemies for external things, but of an internal struggle between friends for internal goods, and in the process external compulsion may be replaced by internal control (even in the form of devotion inspired by sexual or charitable feelings). It may, finally, mean an inner struggle of the individual with himself within his own soul. In whatever form, it is always with us. Often, it is all the more fraught with consequence the less it is noticed and the more it appears in the form of apathetic or easy-going tolerance or the illusions of self-deception or takes the form of 'selection'. 'Peace' means nothing more than a shift in the forms of conflict or the parties to conflict or the objects of conflict or, finally, in the chances of selection. Whether and when such shifts stand the test of ethical or other value-judgments is a question about which, obviously, absolutely no generalisation is possible. Only one conclusion undoubtedly follows: without any exception, every ordering of social relationships, whatever its structure, must, if its value is to be assessed, ultimately be judged by the type of human being to which it gives the best chances of becoming dominant in its processes of selection, whether they operate by external criteria or by the internal criterion of motive. For otherwise the empirical enquiry is not exhaustive, nor is there the necessary factual basis for a general evaluation, whether it is consciously subjective or claims objective validity. This fact should be borne in mind at least by those numerous colleagues who think it possible to operate in the determination of social trends with clear concepts of 'progress'. This brings us on to a more detailed examination of this important concept.

The concept of 'progress' can of course be used in a completely value-free way, as when it is identified with the 'progression' of some concrete developmental process considered in isolation. But in most cases the situation is essentially more complicated. We shall now consider some cases drawn from different fields in which the involvement with questions of value is at its most intimate.

In the area of the irrational, emotional or affective aspects of our mental lives, an increase in the number of possible types of behaviour (together with the increase in qualitative variety which is usually associated with it) may be called, in a purely value-free way, progress in mental 'differentiation'. Immediately, however, this becomes associated with the evaluative concept of an increase in the 'range' or 'capacity' of an individual 'mind' or (and here we are already entering the area of ambiguous constructions) of an 'epoch' (as in Simmel's book *Schopenhauer and Nietzsche*).

There is of course no doubt that such 'progress in differentiation' does in fact exist – with the reservation that it does not always really exist in the places where men think it does. The increasing attention paid nowadays to nuances of feeling, resulting both from the increasing rationalisation and intellectualisation of all areas of life and from the increasing subjective importance attributed by the individual to all the expressions of his personal life (often a matter of total indifference in the eyes of others), can easily look like an increase in differentiation. It may even mean or at least advance such differentiation. But appearances are deceptive, and I confess I should be inclined to think that this illusion is in fact fairly widespread. Still, the fact exists. Whether progressive differentiation should be called 'progress' is in itself a question of terminological convenience. Whether it should be assessed as 'progress' in the sense of increasing 'spiritual richness' is anyway not a question which any empirical discipline can decide. For it is not concerned with the question whether the new possibilities of feeling which develop or come to consciousness at a particular time, together with the new 'pressures' and 'problems' which they sometimes bring with them, are to be recognised as 'values'. But anyone who wishes to take up an evaluative attitude towards the fact of differentiation as such (and certainly no empirical discipline can forbid anyone to do so) and seeks a point of view from which to do this, will naturally be forced by several current phenomena to face the question of the price which must be 'paid' for this process, to the extent that it is at the moment anything more than an intellectualist illusion. He will not be able to overlook, for instance, the fact that the pursuit of 'experience', currently so fashionable in Germany, may be to a very large extent a product of a declining ability to cope inwardly with the 'everyday routine', and that the publicity which the individual feels an increasing need to give to his 'experience' could perhaps also be esteemed a loss in the feeling of detachment, and so in feelings of taste and dignity. At all events, where evaluations of subjective

93

experience are concerned, 'progress in differentiation' is identical with an increase in 'value' only in the intellectualistic sense of an enlargement of an increasingly conscious experience or of an increasing ability to express and communicate feelings.

In the field of art, the question of the applicability of the concept of 'progress' (in the evaluative sense) is somewhat more complicated. It is sometimes a matter for passionate controversy, which may be justified or unjustified, depending on the sense intended. No evaluative study of art has been able to make do with the exclusive contrast of 'art' and 'non-art' without also making use of the distinctions between what is attempted and what is actually achieved, between the relative values of different kinds of achievement, or between complete realisation of intentions and a realisation which, though unsuccessful in one or a number of respects (even important ones), was not entirely valueless. These distinctions have indeed been applied not only to particular works of art but also to the art of whole epochs. The concept of 'progress', when applied in such circumstances, has a trivialising effect, because of its use in other cases in relation to purely technical problems. But it is not in itself absurd. Once again, the problem is quite different for the empirical history or sociology of art. For the former there is naturally no 'progress' in art in the sense of the aesthetic evaluation of works of art as achievements at the level of meaning: such evaluation is not possible by the methods of empirical enquiry and so lies entirely outside its scope. On the other hand, empirical art history may employ a concept of 'progress' which is entirely technical and rational and so completely clear. The possibility of using this concept, which we must now discuss in more detail, in empirical art history follows from the fact that it is entirely confined to the determination of the technical means used by a particular kind of artistic impulse to realise a firmly given intention. The significance of such extremely illuminating researches for art history is easily under-estimated or misunderstood, as it is by a certain kind of fashionable, entirely second-rate and inauthentic would-be 'connoisseur', who claims to have 'understood' an artist when he has lifted the curtains of his studio and examined his external methods of representation, his 'manner'. But 'technical' progress, rightly understood, is indeed the province of art history, since such progress and its influence on artistic activity includes those elements in the process of artistic development which can be determined in a purely empirical manner – in other words, without aesthetic evaluation. Let us take a few examples to clarify the real significance for art history of the 'technical' in the true sense of that word.

The emergence of the Gothic style was in the first instance the result of the technically successful solution of what was in itself a pure problem of building technique, that of vaulting over spaces of a certain kind. The problem was to find the technically best way of constructing buttresses to support the thrust of the arch of a cruciform vault, together with certain other details which we shall not go into here. Very concrete problems of construction were solved. The realisation that in this way a particular method of vaulting over non-quadratic spaces had been made possible inspired passionate enthusiasm in those early, and perhaps for ever unknown, architects to whom we are indebted for the development of the new architectural style. Their technical rationalism carried the new principle to its ultimate consequences. Their artistic impulse used it in order to make possible hitherto unsuspected artistic achievements and then dragged sculpture into a new 'feeling for the body', inspired primarily by the new treatment of spaces and surfaces in architecture. The coincidence of this primarily technical revolution with certain developments in human feeling, resulting largely from sociological conditions and the course of religious history, presented the essential elements of that material to the problems on which the artistic creativity of the Gothic period worked. The history and sociology of art have completely fulfilled their purely empirical task when they have made plain these material, technical, social and psychological conditions of the new style. In so doing, however, they do not 'evaluate' the Gothic style in relation to, say, the Romanesque or Renaissance style (itself very closely bound up with the technical problems of the dome and also with the changes, partly resulting from sociological influences, in conceptions of the scope of architecture). Nor does art history, as long as it remains empirical, offer any aesthetic 'evaluation' of the individual work of architecture. Rather, the interest of the works of art and their aesthetically relevant individual peculiarities, and of its object, is something given from outside itself *a priori* by the aesthetic value of the works – something which can certainly not be established by its own methods.

Something similar is true of the history of music. Its central problem, from the point of view of the interests of modern European man ('value-relevance!'), is this: why was harmonic music developed from the almost universal polyphony of folk music only in Europe and only in a particular period, while everywhere else the rationalisation of music took a different path – usually indeed precisely the opposite one, that of the development of intervals by divisions of distance (usually the fourth) rather than by harmonic division (the fifth)? The central problem is thus that of the origins of the third in its harmonic interpretation, as a member of a triad, and furthermore of harmonic chromatics and of modern musical rhythm (strong and weak accents) in place of metronomic timekeeping – a form of rhythm without which modern instrumental music would be unthinkable. Here again it is primarily a matter of a purely technically rational problem of 'progress'. For the ancient chromatic (allegedly even en-

95

harmonic) music for the passionate *dochmiac* verses in the recently discovered fragments of Euripides shows that, for instance, chromatics were known long before harmonic music, as a means of representing 'passion'. Thus it was not in the artistic *urge to* expression, but in the technical *means of* expression, that the difference lay between this ancient music and the chromatics which the great musical experimenters of the Renaissance created in their turbulent rational quest for new discoveries, and therewith for the ability to give musical shape to 'passion'. The technical innovation, however, was that the chromatics took the form of our harmonic intervals and not that of half- and quarter-tone distances, as among the Greeks. And the reason for this development in its turn lay in previous solutions of technically rational problems. This was so particularly in the case of the invention of rational notation, without which no modern composition would be conceivable, and earlier in the development both of certain instruments which provided an impulse towards the harmonic interpretation of musical intervals and, above all, in that of rational polyphonic singing. The major part in these achievements, however, had been played in the early Middle Ages by the monks in the mission fields of north-western Europe, who, without realising the importance which their actions would later have, rationalised the polyphony of folk music for their own ends, instead of following the example of the Byzantine monks who allowed their music to be arranged by a *melopoios* trained in the Greek traditions. Thoroughly concrete characteristics of the external and internal situation of the Christian Church in the West, the result of sociological influences and religious history, allowed a rationalism which was peculiar to Western monasticism to give rise to these musical problems which were essentially 'technical' in character. On the other hand, the invention and rationalisation of rhythmical dancing, the origin of the musical forms which developed into the sonata, resulted from certain modes of social life at the time of the Renaissance. Finally, the development of the piano, one of the most important technical elements in the development of modern music, and its spread among the bourgeoisie, had its roots in the specifically 'indoor' character of North European civilisation. All these represent 'progress' in the technical means of making music, which have had a very marked influence on musical history. The empirical history of music will be able to, indeed must, analyse these factors in historical development without involving itself with the aesthetic evaluation of musical works of art. Technical 'progress' has very often borne extremely meagre fruit in terms of aesthetic value. The direction of interest, or object to be historically explained, is something given from outside music history by its aesthetic significance.

Turning to the development of painting, the refined and diffident way in which the problems are posed in Wölfflin's *Classical Art* is an outstanding example of what can be achieved by empirical work.

The total separation of the domain of values from the empirical sphere is typically revealed in the fact that the use of a particular technique, however 'advanced', implies nothing at all about the aesthetic value of the work of art. Aesthetically, works which employ the most 'primitive' techniques (for instance, paintings produced without any awareness of perspective) may be completely equal in value to the most sophisticated works, created by a rational technique, provided that the artist's intentions have been limited to those forms which are appropriate to such a 'primitive' technique. The invention of new technical means means in the first instance only an increase in differentiation and creates only the possibility of an increase in 'richness' in art, in the sense of heightened value. In practice it has fairly often had the reverse effect, of 'impoverishing' the feeling for form. But from the point of view of an empirical, causal enquiry it is precisely changes in 'technique' (in the highest sense of that word) which constitute the most important generally determinable factor in the development of art.

Not only art historians, but also historians in general, tend to retort that they will neither allow their right of political, cultural, ethical and aesthetic evaluation to be taken away nor are they in a position to be able to do their work without it. Methodology has neither the power nor the intention to dictate to anyone what he should have it in mind to offer in a literary work. It merely claims for its part the right to point out that certain problems are different in nature from each other, that to confuse them with each other results in the parties to a discussion talking at cross purposes, and that a meaningful discussion about the one kind of problem, using the methods either of empirical science or of logic, is possible, but not about the other. Perhaps at this point one further general observation ought to be added, without any proof's being offered for the moment: a careful analysis of historical works shows very easily that the historian's relentless search for empirical causal connexions, right to the end of the causal chain, tends almost always to come to a halt, to the detriment of the scientific results, at the point at which the historian begins to 'evaluate'. He runs the risk at this point of, for example, trying to 'explain' something as the result of a 'fault' or of 'decadence', when it was really perhaps an expression of the agent's ideals, which are simply different from his own: in this way he fails in his essential task of 'understanding'. The misunderstanding can be explained by two causes. First, it is a result of the fact that (to remain in the area of art) the field of art may be approached, not only from the point of view of pure aesthetic evaluation on the one hand and from that of purely empirical causal analysis on the other, but also from a third point of view, that of the interpretation of values: what has been already said in other places on the nature of this third point of view will not be repeated here. Of its inherent value and indispensability for every historian there can be not the slightest doubt. Nor can there be any doubt that the ordinary reader of works of art history expects to be offered this too – indeed this above all. But it is not identical in its logical structure with the empirical approach.

In that case, however, anyone who wants to achieve anything in art history, in however purely empirical a vein, must also have the capacity to 'understand' artistic activity, and this is of course inconceivable if he does not also have the capacity for aesthetic judgment, or in other words the *ability* to evaluate. Parallel things might of course be said of the political or literary historian, or of the historian of religion or philosophy. But obviously this tells us nothing at all about the logical character of historical work.

(*Gesammelte Aufsätze zur Wissenschafts-
lehre*, 2nd edn, Tübingen, 1951, pp.
475–510. First published in 1917.)

5 · The Concept of 'Following a Rule'

The defining characteristic of 'social life', its 'formal' property, according to Stammler, is that it is a '*rule-governed*' communal life, consisting of reciprocal relationships 'governed by external rules'. Let us immediately pause and ask, before following Stammler any further, what might be meant in total by the words 'rule-governed' and 'rule'. 'Rules' might mean first (i) general assertions about causal connexions, or 'laws of nature'. If the term 'laws' is to be reserved, in this context, for general causal propositions of unconditional strictness (in the sense that they admit of no exceptions), then the term 'rule' may be kept only (*a*) for all those empirical propositions which are incapable of this degree of strictness; but no less (*b*) for all those so-called 'empirical laws' to which, on the contrary, no exceptions can be discovered empirically, but for which we lack insight (at any rate of a theoretically adequate kind) into the decisive causal determinants of this lack of exceptions. It is a 'rule' in the sense of an 'empirical law' (sense (*b*)) that men 'must die'; it is a 'rule' in the sense of a general empirical proposition (sense (*a*)) that certain reactions of a specific nature are an 'adequate' response on the part of a student belonging to a fraternity to a slap in the face. The term 'rule' may further mean (ii) a 'norm' against which present, past or future events may be 'measured' in the sense of a value-judgment: that is, the general assertion of a logical, ethical or aesthetic 'ought', as opposed to an empirical 'is', which is all that is referred to by the examples of 'rules' given under (i). The 'validity' of the rule in this second case refers to a general[1] imperative, of which the norm itself provides the content. In the first case, the 'validity' of the rule refers merely to the truth claims of the assertion that the factual regularities corresponding to the rule are either 'given' in empirical reality or may be inferred from what is given by generalisation.

Besides these two basic meanings of the concepts of a 'rule' and 'rule-governedness', which are very simple in sense, there are also others which do not seem without further ado to fit smoothly under one of these two headings. To this group belong, first, what are usually called 'maxims' of action. For instance, Defoe's Robinson Crusoe (whom Stammler occasionally uses in much the same way as the theoretical

---

[1] Let us disregard for the moment the question whether it is *necessarily* 'general'.

economists, as therefore we must likewise) carries on in his isolation an economy which, in terms of the circumstances of his existence, is 'rational': that is, without any doubt whatsoever, he subjects his consumption and production of goods to certain 'rules', indeed to specifically 'economic' rules. From this we see, first, that the assumption that it is conceptually necessary that economic 'rules' can only exist in a context of 'social' life, because they presuppose a large number of subjects who are governed by them and associated through them, is mistaken[1] at any rate in those cases in which it is possible in general to prove something by invoking the example of Crusoe. Admittedly, Robinson Crusoe is a very unreal product of the literary imagination, a purely imaginary being employed in their arguments by 'scholastics': but then Stammler himself is a scholastic and must accept that his readers will treat him as he treats them. Furthermore, once the question becomes one simply of 'conceptual' limits and the concept of a 'rule' is treated as *logically* constitutive of 'social' life, and once 'economic phenomena' are represented as 'conceptually' possible only on the basis of 'social rule-following', as they are by Stammler, then even such a constructed being as Crusoe, which is free of any 'logical' contradiction and (a rather different thing) of any inconsistency with what is generally 'possible' in terms of the rules of experience, ought not to be able to undermine the 'concept'. And it looks extremely bad when Stammler, in his efforts to avoid this conclusion, asserts against it that, precisely from the *causal* point of view, it is possible to construct a Crusoe only as a product of 'social life', from which he has been separated by pure chance. He himself has preached, quite rightly, though with insufficient success precisely in his own case, that the causal antecedents of the 'rule' are entirely irrelevant for its conceptual character. When Stammler goes on to argue that such an individual, conceived of as isolated in this way, is to be explained by the methods of 'natural science', since it is merely 'nature and its technical (N.B.!) mastery' which forms the object to be explained, we should first of all recall the earlier discussion of the variety of meanings of the concepts of 'nature' and 'natural science'. Which of the various meanings is intended here? But then, and above all, we should bear in mind that – if it is simply a question of the concept of a 'rule' – 'technology' is precisely a matter of procedures governed by 'purposefully imposed rules'. The cooperation of the parts of a machine, for instance, takes place in accordance with 'rules imposed by men' in the same 'logical' sense as the cooperation of draught-horses or slaves who

---

[1] As for 'rules' in the sense of moral norms, it is obvious that they are not conceptually limited to 'social beings'. Conceptually speaking, even Crusoe *can* act in a way which is 'contrary to morality' (cf. the moral norm which is made an object of legal protection in paragraph 175 of *RStGB*, second case).

have been forcibly yoked together, or, finally, as that of 'free' human workers in a factory.

It is true that, in the latter case, what keeps the worker in the collective 'machine' is correctly calculated *'psychological* pressure' – exerted by means of 'thoughts' of the closing of the factory gates in the event of any deviation from 'orderly labour', of empty purses, hungry families and so on, but also perhaps by means of all kinds of other ideas, for example of an ethical kind, and finally by means of simple 'habit' – whereas in the case of the material parts of a machine it is their physical and chemical properties. But this does not of course make any difference whatever to the meaning of the concept of a 'rule' in the one case or in the other. The 'worker' has certain ideas in his head: he knows empirically that his food, clothing and heating 'depend' on his uttering certain formulae or giving other tokens of himself in the 'office' (such as are customary for what the 'jurists' call a 'labour-contract') and on his then also becoming a physical part of that mechanism and so performing certain muscular movements; he knows further that, if he does all this, he has the chance of periodically receiving certain metal discs of a specific form or pieces of paper, which, when placed in the hands of other people, bring it about that he can take for himself bread, cabbages, trousers and so on and indeed that the result will be that if anyone thereafter tries to take these objects away from him again, there is a certain probability that men with spiked helmets will appear in response to his cries for help and will assist him to regain possession of them.

This whole sequence of highly complicated trains of thought, which we have here outlined in as crude a fashion as possible, can be counted on to exist in the workers' heads with a certain probability and is taken into account by the factory owners as a causal determinant of the cooperation of human muscle-power in the technical process of production in exactly the same way as the weight, hardness, elasticity and other physical properties of the materials made up by the machines, and the physical properties of those by whom they are set in motion. The one can be considered as causal conditions of a certain 'technical' outcome – for instance, the formation of x tonnes of pig-iron from y tonnes of ore in space z – in exactly the same logical sense as the others. And in the one case 'cooperation according to rules' is a 'precondition' of this technical outcome in exactly the same sense, at any rate *logically* speaking, as in the other: the fact that, in the one case but not in the other, 'conscious processes' are inserted into the causal chain makes not the slightest difference from the 'logical' point of view.

If, therefore, Stammler contrasts 'technical' considerations with 'social-scientific', then at all events the fact that a 'rule of cooperation' exists cannot in itself alone constitute the decisive difference between them. In just the same way as a huntsman takes into account the qualities of his hound, so the factory owner includes in his reckoning the fact that people exist who are hungry and who are prevented by those other people with the spiked helmets from making use of their physical strength simply to take the means of satisfying their hunger wherever they find them, with the result that the trains of thought set out above must arise in their minds. And just as the huntsman counts on his hound's reacting to his whistle in a certain way or performing certain operations after a shot, so the factory owner counts on the fact that posting a sheet of paper printed in a certain way (a 'work-sheet') produces a certain result with more or less certainty. Furthermore, there is a close correspondence between the 'economic' behaviour of Robinson Crusoe with regard to the 'supply of goods' and means of production available on his island and, to take another example, the way in which an individual in present-day society proceeds with the metal discs called 'coins' which he has in his pocket or which he, in his own opinion, whether well- or ill-founded, has the chance of putting into his pocket by certain manipulations (for instance, by scribbling certain marks on a scrap of paper called a 'cheque' or tearing off another scrap of paper called a 'coupon' and presenting it at a certain counter), and which he knows will, when used in a certain way, place at his (actual) disposal certain objects which he observes behind glass windows, refreshment bars and so forth and which he knows, either from personal experience or because someone else has told him, he cannot simply make off with without those people with spiked helmets coming and putting him behind bars.

This modern individual need have as little idea of the precise way in which these metal discs come to have this peculiar capacity as of the way in which his legs enable him to walk; he can content himself with the observation which he has made since childhood that they display the same property in anyone's hands with the same regularity as, at any rate in general, everyone's legs can walk and as a heated oven warms things up and as July is warmer than April. In conformity with this knowledge which he has of the 'nature' of money, he organises his mode of using it, 'regulates' his use of it and 'manages' it. According to Stammler, since it is a question at any given time of explaining the behaviour of the single individual, it must likewise be a problem for treatment by the methods of 'technical' natural science, not those of 'social science', to observe and, as far as the state of the material allows, make sense of the way in which this regulation is in fact undertaken by a concrete individual, or by thousands and millions of his like, in the light of 'experience' (either their own or communicated to them by others) of the 'consequences' of the different possible kinds of 'regulation' and of the different ways in which it is undertaken by each of a number of different distinguishable groups in a given human population in accordance with the distribution of chances of having metal discs of this kind (or scraps of paper of corresponding 'effect') in future in their safe and at their disposal. For the 'rules' by which the individual proceeds are here, exactly as in the case of Robinson Crusoe, 'maxims', whose causal influence on empirical behaviour of the individual is based, in the one case as in the other, on empirical rules, whether acquired by reasoned experience or learned from others, of the type 'If I do x, in accordance with empirical rules, y will result'. It is on the basis of such 'empirical propositions' that the 'rule-governed purposive action' of Robinson Crusoe proceeds, as also does that of the 'possessor of money'.

However enormous the degree of complexity in conditions of life with which the latter has to 'reckon', in comparison with Robinson Crusoe, logically speaking there is no difference. The one, like the other, has to calculate, in the light of experience, the mode of reaction of the 'external world' to certain modes of his own behaviour. It makes not the slightest difference to the 'logical' character of the 'maxims' that in the one case these include human reactions, while in the other they include only reactions by animals, plants and 'inanimate' natural objects. If Crusoe's 'economic' behaviour is, as Stammler maintains, 'merely' technique and hence not an object to which 'social science' can be applied, then this is also true of the behaviour of the individual in relation to a human group of whatever form, to the extent that the enquiry concerns his 'regulation' by 'economic' maxims and their effect. The 'private economy' of the individual is, as we may now express it in ordinary language, governed by 'maxims'. In Stammler's terminology, these maxims would be designated as 'technical' maxims. They 'regulate' the behaviour of the individual empirically with varying constancy, but, judging by what Stammler has said about Robinson Crusoe, they cannot be the 'rules' which he has in mind. Before we attempt a closer examination of what he did have in mind, let us first ask what the relationship is between the concept of the 'maxim', with which we have operated in such detail, and the two 'types' of concept of a 'rule' discussed in the introduction: the 'empirical regularity' on the one hand, and the 'norm' on the other. That requires, once again, a brief general consideration of the way in which the expression 'rule-governed' and related expressions are used with reference to particular forms of behaviour.

When someone says, 'My digestion is governed by rules', he is merely stating in the first instance the simple 'natural fact' that his digestive processes follow a certain temporal sequence. The 'rule' is an abstraction from the course of nature. But he may be reduced to the necessity of 'regulating' his digestion by removing what 'disturbs' it, and if he then utters the same sentence, the outward course of events may be the same as before, but the sense of the concept of a 'rule' has changed. In the first case, the 'rule' was something *observed in* 'nature': in the second, something *pursued for* 'nature'. Observed and pursued 'regularity' may in such a case coincide in fact, and this is then very gratifying for the person concerned, but 'conceptually' they retain distinct senses: one is an empirical fact, the other an ideal which is pursued, a 'norm' against which the facts are 'evaluatively' measured. The 'ideal' rule for its part, however, may play a role in two kinds of enquiry. It may be asked (i) which actual regularity *would* correspond to it, but then also (ii) what degree of actual regularity *is* brought about causally by the attempt to follow the rule. For the fact that, for instance, someone undertakes to 'measure' his behaviour against the hygienic norm just referred to, and 'directs' his behaviour accordingly, is itself one of the causal factors in the empirical regularity to be observed in his bodily condition. This regularity is, in the case which we have supposed, causally influenced by an infinite number of conditions, which also include the medicine which he takes in order to 'realise' the hygienic 'norm'. His empirical 'maxim' is, as can be seen, the representation of the 'norm', which exerts a real causal influence on his action. It is exactly the same in the case of the 'rule-governedness' of men's behaviour in relation to material goods and other men, especially their 'economic' behaviour. The fact that Robinson Crusoe and the possessor of money, of whom we were speaking just now, behave in a certain way in relation to their goods or stocks of money, respectively, to such an extent indeed that this behaviour appears to be 'rule-governed', may lead us to formulate in theoretical terms the 'rule' which we see to 'govern' this behaviour, at least in part: for example, as a 'principle of marginal utility'. This ideal 'rule' would then include a precept on the matter, which would include the 'norm' according to which Crusoe 'would have to' behave, if he wished to adhere strictly to the ideal of 'purposive' action. It may therefore be treated, on the one hand, as an evaluative standard – not, of course, a standard of 'moral' evaluation, but of 'teleological' evaluation, which purposive 'action' presupposes as an 'ideal'. On the other hand, however (and this is more important), it is a heuristic principle, permitting us to discern the actual causal determinants of Crusoe's empirical actions (once we assume *ad hoc* the real existence of such an individual). In this latter case it functions as an 'ideal-typical' construction, and we employ it as an hypothesis, the applicability of which to the 'facts' would have to be 'confirmed' and which would help in determining the actual causes of his actions and the degree of approximation to the 'ideal type'.[1]

---

[1] On the logical sense of the 'ideal type', see my paper on '"Objectivity" in Social Science and Social Policy'.

This 'rule' of purposive action would have a bearing on empirical knowledge of Crusoe's behaviour in two very different senses. First, it might need to be considered as an element in Crusoe's 'maxims', which form the object of the enquiry – that is, as a real determinant of his empirical actions. Secondly, it would be taken into account as an element in the stock of knowledge and concepts with which the investigator comes to his task: his knowledge of the ideally possible 'meaning' of the action makes it possible for him to have empirical knowledge of the action. A sharp logical distinction must be made between the two. In the empirical sphere, the 'norm' is undoubtedly one determinant of the course of events, but from the logical point of view it is *only* one, in just the same way as, in the 'regulation' of one's digestion, the consumption of medicine in accordance with a 'norm' and therefore the 'norm' imposed by the doctor is one, but again *only* one, of the determinants of the actual outcome. And there can be a whole range of degrees of consciousness of the influence exerted on action by these determinants. As the child 'learns' to walk, to keep himself clean, to avoid pleasures which might injure his health, so in general he comes to follow the 'rules' which he sees being followed in the lives of other people, learns to 'express' himself in language and to take part in 'social intercourse'. All this takes place partly (i) without any subjective formulation in thought of the 'rule' in accordance with which he himself in fact acts (with very varying consistency); partly (ii) on the basis of conscious application of 'empirical propositions' of the form 'x is followed by y'; and partly (iii) because the 'rule' is imprinted in his mind by 'upbringing' or simple imitation as a representation of a 'norm' which ought to be observed for its own sake, and is then as a result of his 'experience of life' developed further by his own reflection and becomes one of the determinants of his action. When, in the last two cases (ii and iii), it is said that the rule in question, whether moral, conventional or teleological, is the 'cause' of a certain action, this is of course an extremely imprecise way of putting it: it is not the 'ideal validity' of a norm, but the empirical representation in the mind of an agent that the norm 'ought to be applied' in his behaviour which is the cause. That is as true of 'moral' norms as of rules whose 'validity' is purely a matter of 'convention' or 'worldly wisdom'. For example, it is not of course the conventional rule of greeting personified which raises my hat when I meet an acquaintance, it is my hand. But my hand in turn is caused to do this, either simply by my 'habit' of following such a 'rule' in my actions, or also by my empirical knowledge of the fact that not to do so would be regarded by others as rude and so would cause ill-feeling (that is, by a calculation of 'pain'), or, finally, also by my opinion that it would not be 'fitting' for me to fail to observe a 'conventional rule' which is universally followed and harmless, when there is no compelling reason to do so (in other words, by the 'representation of a norm').[1]

With these last examples we have already arrived at the concept of 'social rule-following', that is, of a rule which is 'valid for' the behaviour of human beings towards each other: in other words, we have arrived at the concept to which Stammler anchors the object 'social life'. We shall not at this point discuss the rights and wrongs of Stammler's definition of this concept, but shall first take our discussion of the concept of a 'rule' a little way further, independently of any reference to Stammler.

Let us begin by taking the elementary example which Stammler, too, occasionally makes use of in order to illustrate the significance of the 'rule' for the concept of 'social life'. Imagine two men who in other respects stand outside any 'social relationship' – say, two savages of different tribes, or a European coming across a savage in darkest Africa. The two men 'exchange' two objects of some kind. What is quite rightly emphasised in such a case is that here we have a pure description of an externally perceptible sequence of events – certain movements of the muscles and, in some cases, when 'speech' is involved, certain sounds, which so to speak constitute the 'physical' nature of the sequence of events, the 'essence' of which would not have been grasped at all. For this 'essence' consists in the 'meaning' which the two men attach to this external behaviour and this 'meaning' attached to their present behaviour in turn represents the 'following of a rule' in their future behaviour. Without this 'meaning', so it is said, an 'exchange' would be neither possible in reality nor conceivable as a concept. Precisely so! The fact that 'external' signs function as 'symbols' is one of the constitutive presuppositions of all 'social' relationships. But the question immediately arises again, is it a presupposition of social relationships *alone*? Obviously not, by any means. When I put a 'bookmark' in a 'book', what is subsequently 'externally' perceptible of the result of that action is obviously merely a 'symbol': the fact that a strip of paper or some other object is inserted between two pages at this point has a 'significance' such that, if I did not know it, the bookmark would have neither use nor meaning for me and the action itself would be 'inexplicable' even in causal terms. And yet no form of 'social' relationship has been entered into here. Or, to return for preference entirely to the domain of Robinson Crusoe, suppose that he has an 'economic' need to manage the forests on his island, and therefore 'marks out' certain trees with his axe which he means to cut down for the coming winter; or suppose that, in the interests of husbanding his supplies of grain, he rations them, stowing

[1] The reader must excuse the almost excessive triviality of this and some subsequent remarks, bearing in mind the necessity of countering at the outset some of Stammler's strongly *ad hominem* arguments.

part of them away as 'seed corn': in all such cases, as in countless others like them, which the reader may make up for himself, the 'externally' perceptible event is, here again, not 'the whole of what is going on'. It is the 'meaning' of this form of action, which certainly includes no element of 'social life', which first impresses upon it its character, which gives it 'significance', in precisely the same way in principle as the 'significance of the sounds' does for the black marks which someone has 'printed' on a bundle of sheets of paper, or as the 'significance of the words' does for the sounds which someone else 'speaks', or finally as the 'meaning' which each of the two men participating in the exchange attaches to his behaviour does for the externally perceptible part of that behaviour.

If we separate in our minds the 'meaning' which we find 'expressed' in an object or event from those elements in the object or event which are left over when we abstract precisely that 'meaning', and if we call an enquiry which considers only these latter elements a 'naturalistic' one, then we get a broader concept of 'nature', which is quite distinct from the previous one. Nature is then what is 'meaningless' – or, more correctly, an event becomes part of 'nature' if we do not ask for its 'meaning'. But plainly in that case the opposite of 'nature', in the sense of the 'meaningless', is not 'social life' but just the 'meaningful' – that is, the 'meaning' which can be attached to, or 'found in', an event or object, from the metaphysical 'meaning' given to the cosmos in a system of religious doctrine down to the 'meaning' which the baying of one of Robinson Crusoe's hounds 'has' when a wolf is approaching.

Having convinced ourselves that the property of being 'meaningful' or of 'signifying' something is certainly not peculiar to 'social' life, let us return to the case of the 'exchange' discussed above. The 'meaning' of the 'external' behaviour of the two parties to the exchange may be considered in two ways which are, logically speaking, very different. First, as an 'idea': we can ask what intellectual consequences can be found in the 'meaning' which 'we' who are considering it attach to a concrete event of this kind, or how this 'meaning' fits into a more comprehensive 'meaningful' system of ideas. From the 'standpoint' thus achieved we can then undertake an 'evaluation' of the empirical course of events. We could ask, for instance, what Robinson Crusoe's 'economic' behaviour would 'have to be' like, if it were pushed to its ultimate logical 'consequences'. That is what the theory of marginal utility does. And we could then 'measure' his empirical behaviour against the standard thus worked out by pure reasoning. And we could likewise ask how the two parties to the 'exchange' would 'have to' go on to behave after the external completion of the transfer of the objects of exchange by both of them, in order that their conduct should conform to the 'idea' of an exchange, that is, in order that we should be able to consider it as conforming to the intellectual consequences of the 'meaning' which we found in their actions. Thus we start from the empirical fact that events of a certain kind have happened, and that these events are in fact associated in conception with a certain 'meaning' which is not clearly thought out in detail but vague and cloudy, but then we abandon the empirical domain and ask how the 'meaning' of the actions of those involved can be constructed intellectually in such a way that an internally coherent pattern of ideas emerges.[1] We then have to do with a 'dogmatics' of 'meaning'.

On the other hand we could ask also whether the 'meaning' which 'we' could attach dogmatically to an event of that kind was at the same time the one which each of the empirical agents involved consciously associated with it, or which alternative meaning each of them associated with their action, or finally whether they consciously associated any 'meaning' at all with their action. We must then first distinguish further between two 'meanings' of the concept 'meaning' itself – this time in the empirical sense which alone concerns us now. In our example, it might mean, first, that the agents consciously wished to adopt a norm which would 'bind' them: in other words, that they were (subjectively) of the opinion that their action as such was of a binding character. In that case, a 'normative maxim' would have been instituted between them.[2] Or, on the other hand, it might mean simply that each of them was pursuing certain 'results' in the exchange, that his action stood, in his 'experience', in the relation of a 'means' towards these, and that the exchange had (subjectively) a conscious 'purpose'. With both kinds of maxims it is, naturally, doubtful in each individual case to what extent they were empirically present: in the case of 'normative maxims' it is in addition doubtful whether they were even empirically present at all. It is open to question (i) to what extent the two parties to the exchange in our

---

[1] All ideas of a 'legal' order should be avoided at this stage, and it goes without saying that several ideal 'meanings' of an act of 'exchange' could if necessary be constructed, many of which would be different from each other.

[2] If the 'meaning' of the act of exchange in this sense (the first of those distinguished here, that of the 'normative maxim') is described as a 'regulation of the relations' of the parties with each other, and their relationship is described as one which is 'rule-governed' in relation to their future behaviour on the basis of the 'norm' which is present in their minds, then it must be stated at the outset that the words 'rule-governed' and 'regulation' here do not necessarily imply any subsumption under a general 'rule', apart from the rule 'that contracts ought to be loyally fulfilled' – which, however, is no more than to say 'that the regulation ought to be treated precisely as a regulation'. The two parties need know nothing of the general 'essence' of the norm of exchange: indeed, we could of course also suppose two individuals to perform an act of which the 'meaning' attached to it by them was absolutely individual and not, as in the case of 'exchange', subsumable under any general type. In other words, the concept of 'being rule-governed' in no way logically presupposes the idea of *general* 'rules' of a definite content. We merely state this fact here: from now on, for simplicity's sake, we shall treat normative regulation entirely as a matter of subsumption under 'general' rules.

example were actually conscious of the 'purposiveness' of their actions, and (ii) to what extent, on the other hand, they had made into their conscious 'maxims' (that is, 'normative maxims') the idea that their relationships '*ought*' now to be 'rule-governed' in such a way that the one object counted as 'equivalent' to the other, that each ought now to 'respect' the other's 'ownership' of the object which he had previously owned, as established by the exchange, and so on. That is, what is questionable is the extent to which the representation of this 'meaning' (i) was causally determinant for the occurrence of the decision to perform this 'act of exchange' itself, and (ii) constituted the motive of their further behaviour *after* the act of exchange. These are obviously questions in which our 'dogmatic' intellectual construction of the 'meaning' of 'exchange' must prove very useful as a 'heuristic principle' for the purpose of framing hypotheses. On the other hand, however, they are of course not at all the sort of questions which would be cleared up by a simple reference to the fact that 'objectively' the 'meaning' of what they have done 'could' once and for all be something specific, to be inferred dogmatically in accordance with definite logical principles.

It would obviously be a pure fiction, matching the hypostatisation of the 'regulative idea' of the 'international treaty', if one simply stipulated that the two men wanted to 'regulate' their reciprocal social relationships in a manner conforming to the ideal 'concept' of 'exchange', because we, the observers, attach this 'meaning' to their conduct from the point of view of a dogmatic classification. One might equally well say, logically speaking, that the dog that barks 'wants' to realise the 'idea' of the protection of property, because of the 'meaning' which this barking may have for his master. The dogmatic 'meaning' of 'exchange' is, as far as empirical enquiry is concerned, an 'ideal type', which we use, partly for 'heuristic' purposes, partly for 'classificatory', because there are large numbers of events in empirical reality which conform to it with a greater or lesser degree of 'purity'. 'Normative' maxims, which treat this 'ideal' meaning of exchange as 'binding', are undoubtedly one of the various possible determinants of the actual behaviour of the parties to an 'exchange', but they are only one. Their empirical presence in a concrete act is an hypothesis, both for the observer and (it should not be forgotten) for each of the two agents in regard to the other. It is very commonly the case, of course, that one or even both of the parties does *not* take as his 'normative maxim' the normative 'meaning' of exchange which, they know, is usually regarded as ideally 'valid', or in other words as obligatory. On the contrary, one, or even both of the parties, commonly speculates on the probability that the other party will do so: in that case, his own maxim is one purely concerned with the 'goal' which he seeks. The assertion that in such a case the event *is* 'rule-governed' in the sense of the ideal norm, and that the agents *have* regulated their relationships in this way is naturally devoid of any empirical meaning. If we nevertheless occasionally express ourselves in this way, this is another example of the same ambiguity of the expression 'following a rule' as we have already seen in the case of the man who artificially 'regulated' his digestion, and as we shall see again in a number of other cases. It is harmless as long as one always keeps before one's mind what is meant by the expression in a particular case. On the other hand, it would be, of course, completely meaningless to wish to call the 'rule' to which the two parties to an exchange ought to have subjected themselves (in accordance with the dogmatic 'meaning' of their behaviour) the 'form' of their 'social relationship', in other words, a 'form' of what did actually happen. For this dogmatically inferred 'rule' itself 'is' in any case a 'norm', which is meant to be ideally 'valid' for the action, but by no means a 'form' of anything empirically 'existent'.

Anyone who wishes to discuss 'social life' as something empirically existent may not, of course, shift his ground into the area of what dogmatically *ought* to be. In the domain of 'fact', the 'rule' in our example exists only in the sense of a causally explicable and causally operative empirical 'maxim' of the two parties to the exchange. In the sense of the concept of 'nature' elaborated in the preceding section, this would be expressed as follows: even the 'meaning' of an external event becomes part of 'nature' in the logical sense when its empirical existence is at issue. For then the question precisely does not concern the 'meaning' which the external event 'has' in some dogmatic sense, but the 'meaning' which the agents either actually associated with it in the particular case or even appeared, by all the perceptible 'criteria', to associate with it. Exactly the same is true, of course, above all in the case of the 'legal rule'.

(*Gesammelte Aufsätze zur Wissenschafts-lehre*, 2nd edn, Tübingen, 1951, pp. 322–37. First published in 1907.)

6 · *The Logic of Historical Explanation*

'The outbreak of the Second Punic War', says Eduard Meyer, 'was the consequence of a deliberate decision by Hannibal; that of the Seven Years War, of a decision by Frederick the Great; and that of the War of 1866, of a decision by Bismarck. All of them might have decided differently, and different personalities would...have decided differently; the consequence would have been that the course of history would have been different.' In footnote 2 he adds, 'This is neither to affirm nor to deny that in such a case the wars in question would never have occurred: that is a completely unanswerable and so an idle question.' Leaving aside the awkward relationship between the second sentence and Meyer's previously discussed account of the relationship between 'freedom' and 'necessity' in history, what is most debatable in this passage is the view that questions to which no answer, or no certain answer, can be given are, for that reason alone, 'idle' questions. Things would be in a bad way even in empirical science if those deep questions to which it gives no answer were never to be raised. To be sure, we are not concerned here with such 'ultimate' problems: rather, it is a case of a question which, on the one hand, has been 'overtaken' by events and, on the other, cannot receive a clear positive answer in the state of our actual and possible knowledge. In addition, looking at the matter from the strict 'determinist' point of view, it is a question concerning the results of something which was 'impossible', given the 'determinants' which were in fact present. And yet, for all that, it is far from being 'idle' to raise the question what might have happened, if, for example, Bismarck had not decided for war. For it is precisely this question which touches on the decisive element in the historical construction of reality: the causal significance which is properly to be attributed to this individual decision within the totality of infinitely numerous 'factors' (all of which must be just as they are and not otherwise) if precisely this consequence is to result, and the appropriate position which the decision is to occupy in the historical account.

If history is to raise itself above the level of a mere chronicle of noteworthy events and personalities, it can only do so by posing just such questions. Indeed, it has proceeded in this way ever since it became a science. What is correct in Meyer's previously quoted view that history considers events from the point of view of 'becoming', so that its object does not fall under the 'necessity' which belongs to 'what has become', is that the historian, in his assessment of the causal significance of a concrete event, proceeds in much the same way as the historical individual himself, with all his attitudes of mind and will, who would not 'act' at all, if his own action seemed to him to be 'necessary' and not merely 'possible'.[1] The difference is simply this: the historical agent, to the extent that he is acting, as we are here assuming, in a strictly 'rational' way, takes into account those 'conditions' of the future course of events which interests him which are 'external' to him and, as far as he knows, given in reality; he then, in his mind, fits into the causal nexus various 'possible' courses of action for himself, together with the consequences to be anticipated from them in combination with those 'external' conditions, in order to decide on one or another of the courses of action appropriate to his 'goal' in accordance with the 'possible' outcomes which he has worked out in his mind. The historian's principal superiority to his hero lies in the fact that he, at any rate, knows empirically whether the agent's assessment of the given, 'externally' existing conditions, in accordance with his knowledge and expectations, in fact corresponded to the real situation at the time: this is shown to him by the actual degree of success of the action.

In this context, where we are simply concerned to elucidate logical questions, we shall, as we are entitled to, take as our theoretical basis an ideally maximum degree of knowledge of such conditions, such as would seldom, if ever, be attainable in real life; equipped with such maximum knowledge, the historian can retrospectively perform in his own mind the same deliberations which his 'hero' performed, or 'might have performed', with more or less clarity, and in this way he can raise the question, with considerably greater chances of success than Bismarck himself, for instance, of the consequences to be 'anticipated' from the making of a different decision. It is clear that such considerations are very far from being merely 'idle'. Meyer himself uses exactly this procedure in dealing with the two shots which, in the 'March days' in Berlin, directly provoked the outbreak of street-fighting. The question of where the shots came from, he argues, is 'historically irrelevant'. But why is it any more irrelevant than discussion of the decisions of Hannibal, Frederick the Great or Bismarck? 'The situation was such that any chance event at all was bound (!) to lead to an outbreak of conflict.' Here we see Meyer himself answering the allegedly 'idle' question, what 'would have' happened *without* those shots, and in this way deciding their

---

[1] This remains correct, in spite of Kistyakovski's criticism (in his essay in Novgorodtsev, ed., *Probleme des Idealismus*, Moscow, 1902, p. 393), which does not at all affect this concept of 'possibility'.

historical 'significance' (in this case, their irrelevance). In the case of the decisions of Hannibal, Frederick and Bismarck, on the other hand, 'the situation' was obviously (at least in Meyer's view) different: in particular, it was not the case that the conflict would have broken out, either in general or in the concrete political conditions of the time which determined its course and outcome, had their decisions been other than they were. For otherwise, these decisions would have been historically as insignificant as the shots were in the other case. The judgment that, if a particular historical fact were thought of as absent from a set of historical conditions, or as present in a modified form, this would have caused historical events to proceed in ways which were different in certain definite, historically important respects, thus seems to be of considerable value in determining the 'historical significance' of that fact (though in practice the historian may not have occasion consciously and expressly to develop that judgment and to support it by argument in any but exceptional cases, particularly those in which there is some dispute about that 'historical significance'). It is clear that this fact would have been bound to call for a consideration of the logical character of judgments which state the consequences which 'would have' resulted if a particular causal factor had been absent from a set of conditions, or present in a modified form, and of their significance for history. We shall attempt to get a little clearer on this question.

The parlous state in which the logic of history[1] still lies is evident, amongst other things, in the fact that the authoritative work on this important question has been undertaken neither by historians nor by methodologists of history, but by specialists in areas far removed from history.

The theory of 'objective possibility', as it is called, to which I am referring here, is based on the work of the distinguished physiologist von Kries,[2] and the current use of this concept is based on works which either acknowledge their relationship to von Kries or are criticised by him. These are works in the first instance by writers on criminal matters, and secondly by legal writers: in particular, Merkel, Rümelin, Liepmann and,

---

[1] The categories discussed in what follows apply, as may be expressly stated, not only in the field of what is customarily called the specialist discipline of 'history', but also in accounting 'historically' for any individual occurrence, even an event in 'inanimate nature'. The category of 'the historical' is here used as a logical concept, not a technical concept belonging to a particular discipline.

[2] *Ueber den Begriff der objektiven Möglichkeit und einige Anwendungen desselben* (Leipzig, 1888). Important foundations for these discussions were first laid by von Kries in his *Prinzipien der Wahrscheinlichkeitsrechnung*. It should be mentioned here at the outset that, because of the nature of the 'object' of history, only the most elementary parts of von Kries' theory are of any importance for the methodology of history. Not only can there be no question, obviously, of any transfer of principles from the 'calculus of probability' strictly so called to the work of causal analysis in history, but great caution is required even in attempting to make an analogous use of its points of view.

most recently, Radbruch.[1] In the methodology of the social sciences, von Kries' line of thought has so far been followed up only in statistics.[2] It is only natural that it was precisely the lawyers, and above all the criminal lawyers, who concerned themselves with this problem, since the question of criminal guilt, to the extent that it includes the problem of the conditions under which it is possible to assert that someone's action was 'responsible' for a certain overt consequence, is a strictly causal question. Indeed, it is obviously of the same logical structure as the question of historical causality. For, as in history, the problems of practical social

[1] The most profoundly radical critique so far of the use of von Kries' theory in relation to legal problems has been made by Radbruch (*Die Lehre von der adäquaten Verursachung*, I, Book 3 (1902) of the *Proceedings* of von Liszt's Seminar – the most important of the other literature is also referred to there). His dissection, on grounds of principle, of the concept of 'adequate causation' can only be examined at a later stage, after the theory has first been expounded in the simplest possible formulation – which means, as will become obvious, only in a provisional and not in a final form.

[2] Among theoreticians of statistics, L. von Bortkiewitsch comes very close to von Kries' statistical theories (*Die erkenntnistheoretischen Grundlagen der Wahrscheinlichkeitsrechnung*, in *Conrads Jahrbücher*, 3rd Series, XVII – cf. also XVIII; and *Die Theorie der Bevölkerungs-und Moralstatistik nach Lexis, ibid.*, XXVII). Another writer who bases himself on von Kries' theory is A. Tschuprow, whose article on moral statistics in the Brockhaus-Ephron *Enzyklopädische Wörterbuch* was unfortunately not available to me. Cf. his article on the tasks of the theory of statistics in *Schmollers Jahrbuch* (1905), pp. 421f. I cannot agree with T. Kistyakovski's criticisms (in the essay cited earlier in *Probleme des Idealismus*, pp. 378ff), which admittedly exist at present only in outline, with provision for more detailed exposition later. He chiefly objects to the theory (p. 379) that it makes use of a false concept of 'cause', based on Mill's *Logic*, and in particular that it employs the category of 'compound' and 'partial' cause, which is in turn based on an anthropomorphic interpretation of causality (in the sense of 'bringing something about'). (The latter point is also made by Radbruch, *Die Lehre von der adäquaten Verursachung*, p. 22.) But the idea of 'bringing something about', or, as it has been expressed in more colourless language which nevertheless is identical in meaning, of 'causal connexion', is inseparable from any view of causality which reflects on individual sequences of qualitative change. The point will be made later that it need not (indeed must not) be burdened with unnecessary and objectionable metaphysical presuppositions. (See, on plurality of causes and elementary causes, Tschuprow's discussion, *Schmollers Jahrbuch*, p. 436.) Here it may simply be noted that 'possibility' is a 'formative' category: that is, it functions in such a way as to determine the selection of the causal links to be admitted into the historical account. The material, on the other hand, once shaped by the historian, contains no element of 'possibility', at least ideally: subjectively, the historical account attains to judgments of necessity only very rarely; but objectively, it is always undoubtedly subject to the presupposition that the 'causes' to which the effect is 'attributed' (in combination, of course, with that infinity of 'conditions' which, as scientifically 'uninteresting', are only summarily indicated in the account) must be regarded as absolutely 'sufficient conditions' of its occurrence. Hence, the use of that category does not in the slightest involve the idea which has long been obsolete in the theory of causality that some terms of real causal relationships have been, so to speak, 'in suspense' up until the time when they entered into the causal chain. Von Kries himself has explained the opposition between his own theory and that of J. S. Mill in a manner which to my mind is absolutely convincing (*Prinzipien der Wahrscheinlichkeitsrechnung*, p. 107). On this point see further below. What is correct is that Mill too discusses the category of objective possibility and has in places formulated also the concept of 'adequate causation' (see his *Works*, German edn by T. Gomperz, III, p. 262).

relationships between human beings, especially those existing in the law, are 'anthropocentric', that is, concerned with the causal significance of human 'actions'. And the historian's problem of causality, like the problem which arises when we are dealing with the question of the causal determination of a particular effect in law, whether an injury to be punished under the criminal law or one to be indemnified under the civil law, is always directed towards the attribution of concrete effects to concrete causes, not to the investigation of abstract 'general laws'. Jurisprudence, especially criminal law, of course diverges from this common path to deal with special problems of its own because of the emergence of the further question whether and when the objective, purely causal, attribution of the effect to the action of an individual also suffices to qualify it as subjectively 'guilty'. For this question is no longer a purely causal problem, to be settled merely by establishing facts which are 'objectively' ascertainable by observation and causal analysis: rather, it is a problem for criminal policy, based on ethical and other values. For it is *a priori* possible, and frequently (indeed, nowadays, normally) the case in fact, that the sense of legal norms, whether explicitly expressed or ascertainable by interpretation, tends to be that the existence of 'guilt', in the sense of the relevant law, should depend in the first instance on certain subjective states of affairs on the part of the agent (intention, subjectively determined 'foresight' and so on), and this can mean a considerable change in the significance of the categorial differences in modes of causal connexion.[1] In the first stages of the discussion, however, this difference in the purpose of the investigation still has no significance. We ask first, in exactly the same way as legal theory, how the attribution of a concrete 'effect' to a particular 'cause' is possible as a matter of general principle, and how it can be achieved in view of the fact that in reality an infinity of causal factors have influenced the occurrence of the particular 'event', and that, for the effect to occur in its concrete form, absolutely all these particular causal factors were necessary.

The possibility of selecting from among the infinity of determinants arises primarily from the nature of our historical interest. When it is said

---

[1] Modern law is directed against the agent, not the act (cf. Radbruch, *Die Lehre von der adäquaten Verursachung*, p. 62), and enquires into subjective 'guilt', whereas history, as long as it wishes to remain an empirical science, enquires into the 'objective' causes of concrete events and the outcome of concrete 'actions', but does not wish to sit in judgment on the 'agent'. Radbruch's criticism of von Kries quite justifiably rests on this fundamental principle of modern (though not of all) law. But this means that he himself admits the validity of von Kries' theory in cases of so-called consequential offences (p. 65), of liability on account of 'abstract possibility of influence' (p. 71), of liability for loss of profits, and of liability of those who are 'not of sound mind': in other words, in all cases where the issue is simply one of 'objective' causality. But this is the very same logical situation in which history finds itself with those cases.

that history has causally to understand the concrete reality of an 'event' in its individuality, that does not of course mean, as we have seen already, that it must 'reproduce' the event, leaving nothing out, in the totality of its individual qualities and causally explain the event in that form: such an undertaking would be not only practically impossible, but absurd in principle. Rather, history has to do exclusively with the causal explanation of those 'elements' and 'aspects' of the event in question which are, from certain points of view, of 'general significance' and on that account of historical interest. In just the same way, the judge in his deliberations concerns himself, not with the total individual course of the events, but with those elements which are essential if the events are to be subsumed under norms. He is not interested in the infinity of 'absolutely' trivial details; nor, leaving that aside, is he interested in everything which might be of interest for other approaches – from the direction of natural science, history or art. He is not interested in whether the fatal thrust caused death with certain 'concomitant' phenomena which might be extremely interesting to the physiologist; nor in whether the attitude of the corpse or the murderer could have been a suitable subject for artistic representation; nor in whether the death helped in the 'promotion' of some 'underling' in the official hierarchy who was not directly involved, and so became causally 'value-laden' from that point of view or occasioned certain measures on the part of the security police, perhaps leading to international conflict and so coming to be of 'historical' significance. For him, all that is relevant is whether the causal chain linking thrust to death was of such a kind, and whether the subjective attitude of the agent and his relationship to his act was such that a particular norm of criminal law became applicable. The historian, on the other hand, in dealing with, for example, the death of Caesar, is interested neither in the criminological nor in the medical problems which the 'case' might have presented; nor in the details of what happened, to the extent that they were of no consequence either in relation to Caesar's 'nature' or to the 'nature' of the party situation in Rome (in which case, they would be of 'heuristic' value), or, finally, in relation to the 'political effect' of his death (in which case, they would be 'real causes'). Rather, he is concerned primarily simply with the circumstance that the death occurred precisely at that time, in a concrete political situation, and he discusses the connected question whether this circumstance has had any definite 'consequences' of any importance for the course of 'world history'.

As in the legal example, so too in that of the problem of attributing historical causes, this makes it possible to eliminate an infinity of constituents of the actual occurrence as 'causally irrelevant'. For, as we saw, an individual circumstance is insignificant, not only when it does not stand in any relation to the event under discussion, so that we can think it away without there being any alteration in the course of events as they actually happened, but even when it does not seem to have played any part in the causation of those elements in the occurrence which were essential in the concrete situation and which were alone of interest.

The real question which we have to ask, however, is this: through what logical operations do we arrive at, and demonstratively support, the insight that such a causal relationship exists between these 'essential' constituents of the effect and certain constituents selected from the infinity of determining factors? Obviously, we cannot do this by simple 'observation' of the occurrence – or not, at any rate, if this means a 'presuppositionless' mental 'photographing' of all physical and psychological occurrences taking place in the region of space and time in question, even if such a thing were possible. Rather, the attribution of causes takes the form of a thought process which encompasses a series of acts of abstraction. The first and most important of these acts involves our thinking of one or several of the actual causal components of the occurrence as altered in a certain direction and asking ourselves whether, if the conditions of the occurrence were to be altered in this way, the same effect (in 'essential' respects) would result, or, if not, which other effect would be 'to be anticipated'. Let us take an example from Eduard Meyer's own practice. No one has expounded as formatively and clearly as he has the significance, in terms of world history, of the Persian Wars for the development of Western civilisation. But how does he do this, from the logical point of view? Essentially, he develops the following argument. There were two 'possibilities': on the one hand, there was the further development of a theocratic religious culture whose origins lay in the mysteries and oracles, under the aegis of the Persian protectorate, which as far as possible always used the national religion, as in the case of the Jews, as an instrument of domination; on the other, there was the victory of the free culture of Greece, with its this-worldly concerns, which has given us those cultural values by which we still live today. Between these two possibilities the 'decision' was made by a skirmish of the miniscule proportions of the so-called 'battle' of Marathon, which in turn was the indispensable 'precondition' of the growth of the Athenian fleet and so of the further course of the struggle for freedom, the preservation of the independence of Greek civilisation, the positive stimulus to the beginnings of specifically Western historiography and the perfection of the drama and of all that unique cultural life which ran its course on this stage of world history, tiny as it was in purely quantitative terms.

Moreover, the fact that that battle 'decided' between those 'possibilities', or had a very important bearing on that decision, is obviously the one and only reason why *our* historical interest (since we are not

Athenians) is in general engaged by it. Without some evaluation of those 'possibilities' and of the irreplaceable cultural values which, to our retrospective gaze, 'hung' on that decision, it would be impossible to determine its 'significance' and to see any reason in fact why we should not equate it with a scuffle between two Kaffir or Indian tribes: in short, why we should not really and thoroughly put into practice the stupid 'fundamental ideas' of Helmolt's *World History*, as has been done in this 'modern' compilation.[1] Thus, the tendency of modern historians to apologise for their use of apparently anti-deterministic categories, as soon as they are obliged by a case to define the 'significance' of a concrete event by means of explicit discussion and exposition of the 'possibilities', has absolutely no logical foundation. For instance, Karl Hampe, in his *Konradin*, gives a very instructive account of the historical 'significance' of the Battle of Tagliacozzo, based on reflection on the various 'possibilities', the 'decision' between which depended on the outcome of the battle – a matter of pure 'chance' in the sense that it resulted from entirely individual tactical incidents. He then suddenly adds in his summary, 'But history does not recognise possibilities'. The answer to this is that when the 'historical process' is thought of as an 'object' governed by deterministic laws, it does not 'recognise' possibilities, because it does not 'recognise' any concepts at all; but 'history', assuming that it aims to be a science, always recognises them. In every line of every historical account, indeed in every selection of archival and documentary material for publication, 'judgments of possibility' are to be found, or, more correctly, must be found, if the publication is to have any value as a contribution to knowledge.

But what, then, does it mean to speak of several 'possibilities' between which these battles are supposed to have 'decided'? First of all, it means at all events the formation of (let us say it calmly) imaginary models by means of the elimination of one or several of the constituents of the 'concrete situation' which were actually present in reality and by means of the construction in thought of an event altered in respect of one or a number of 'conditions'. The very first step towards an historical judgment is thus (and this is the point to be emphasised here) a process of abstraction, which proceeds by means of analysis and isolation in thought of the constituents of what is immediately given, seen as a complex of possible causal relationships, and which should result in a

---

[1] Naturally, this judgment does not apply to the individual essays contained in this work, among which there are some excellent pieces of work, even though they are thoroughly 'outdated' in their 'method'. But the idea of a kind of 'socio-political' justice which would – at long last! – treat the so unfairly neglected Indian and African tribes as being at least as important historically as the Athenians, and which resorts to a geographical organisation of the material in order to make it really clear that justice is being done, is simply childish.

synthesis of the 'real' causal connexions. Already, therefore, this first step transforms the given 'actuality' into an intellectual construct, so as to make it into an historical 'fact': following Goethe, we may say that 'fact' involves 'theory'.

If we now look a little more closely at these 'judgments of possibility' (that is, statements about what 'would' have happened if certain conditions had been eliminated or altered) and ask about them first of all how we can properly arrive at them, then there is no doubt that it is entirely a matter of isolation and generalisation. In other words, we analyse the 'given' into its 'constituents' until it becomes possible to subsume each of these constituents under a 'rule of experience' and so to establish what effect 'would be to be anticipated' from each of them individually in accordance with such an empirical rule, given the presence of the others as 'conditions'. A judgment of 'possibility', in the sense in which the expression is used here, thus always implies some reference to empirical rules. The category of 'possibility' is thus not applied in its negative form, that is, in the sense that it expresses our lack of knowledge, or our lack of complete knowledge, in contrast with assertoric or apodeictic judgments; on the contrary, it implies here reference to a positive knowledge of the 'rules of the historical process', or, as it is usually put, to our 'nomological' knowledge.

When the question whether a particular train has already passed through a station receives the answer, 'Possibly', this statement shows that the person concerned does not subjectively know any fact which would rule out that assumption, but at the same time is not in a position to affirm it as correct: in other words, it means that he does not know. But when, on the other hand, Eduard Meyer judges that a theocratic religious development in Greece at the time of the Battle of Marathon was 'possible' or, given certain eventualities, 'probable', this implies the proposition that certain elements of what was historically given were objectively present (in other words, could be determined by objectively valid methods), and that these were such that, if we think away the Battle of Marathon (and, of course, a considerable number of other constituents of the actual course of events) or think of it as having happened differently, they were, to adapt an expression first used in criminal law, 'capable' of causing such a development in accordance with general empirical rules. The 'knowledge' on which such a judgment relies in order to prove the 'significance' of the Battle of Marathon is, in accordance with all that has been said so far, on the one hand knowledge of certain 'facts' belonging to the 'historical situation', which can be demonstrated from the sources ('ontological' knowledge), and on the other hand, as we have already seen, knowledge of certain familiar empirical rules, especially concerning the way in which men tend to react to given situations ('nomological' knowledge). The way in which these 'empirical rules' are to be 'validated' will be discussed later. At all events, it is established that, to prove his crucial thesis about the 'significance' of the Battle of Marathon, Meyer had, in case of dispute, to analyse that 'situation' into its 'constituents' to such a point that our 'imagination' could apply to this 'ontological' knowledge our empirical 'nomological' knowledge, derived from our own practical experience of life and our knowledge of the behaviour of others. Then we could make a positive judgment to the effect that the joint working of those facts 'could' – in the circumstances thought of as altered in a certain way – have caused the effect claimed to be 'objectively possible'; but that means simply that if we were to 'think' of it as having actually happened, we should recognise the facts so altered in our minds as 'sufficient causes'.

In the interests of avoiding ambiguity, this simple matter has been formulated in a necessarily somewhat laborious way; but this formulation shows not only that the establishment of causal connexions in history involves abstraction in its twin senses of isolation and generalisation, but also that the simplest historical judgment about the historical 'significance' of a 'concrete fact' is far from being a mere matter of registering what is 'given'. Rather, not only does it represent a categorially formed intellectual construct, but also its content can only be validated if we bring to the 'given' reality the whole store of our empirical 'nomological' knowledge.

The historian will object to what has just been said[1] that the actual course of historical work and the actual content of historical accounts are different. He may say that it is the historian's 'hunches' or 'intuition', rather than generalisations and reflection on 'rules', which disclose causal connexions; that the difference from work in natural science is precisely that the historian is concerned to explain events and personalities which can be 'interpreted' and 'understood' by direct analogy with our own mental lives; and that, finally, in the historian's account, it is again a question of the 'hunch', of the suggestive vividness of his narrative which allows the reader to 're-live' the events described, just as the historian himself has experienced and beheld them intuitively, rather than puzzled them out by reasoning. Besides, the argument goes on, a judgment of objective possibility about what 'would have' happened in accordance with general rules of experience, if a particular causal factor were thought of as absent or altered, is very often extremely uncertain and often enough simply cannot be made at all. Thus in practice such a foundation for the attribution of historical causes would always collapse, and so it would be impossible for it to be constitutive of the logical value

[1] For a more detailed account of the points made in the following pages, see my essays on Roscher and Knies.

of historical knowledge. But such arguments confuse a number of different things: in particular, they confuse the psychological process by which scientific knowledge comes into being and the literary form of presentation of knowledge, chosen with a view to 'psychologically' influencing the reader, on the one hand, with the logical structure of the knowledge on the other.

Ranke 'divines' the past, and even an historian of lesser rank is likely to make little progress in knowledge if he does not have this gift of 'intuition' to some degree: he will never be more than a sort of minor clerk in the historical hierarchy. But the situation is absolutely identical in such fields of knowledge as mathematics and the natural sciences, which have made truly major discoveries: they all begin as hypotheses, flashes of imaginative 'intuition', and are then 'verified' against the facts – that is, their 'validity' is tested by means of the empirical knowledge which has already been acquired and they are 'formulated' in a logically correct form. The same is true in history: when it is claimed here that knowledge of what is 'essential' is bound up with the use of the concept of objective possibility, this is not meant to be an answer to the question how an historical hypothesis comes into the mind of the researcher (which, psychologically interesting as it may be, does not concern us here), but to the question of the logical category in which its validity is to be demonstrated in cases of doubt or dispute – for that is what determines its logical 'structure'. And if, in the form of his presentation, the historian communicates to the reader the logical results of his judgments of historical causation without going into details about the logical basis for his conclusions, 'suggesting' the process to him rather than pedantically going through all the reasoning, his account would nonetheless be an historical novel rather than a scientific demonstration if there were not a firm skeleton of causal reasoning behind the external literary form. The dry approach of logic is concerned with this skeleton alone, for historical accounts, too, claim 'validity' as 'truth', and the most important aspect of historical work – the only one we have dealt with so far – namely the causal regress, attains such validity only when in case of dispute it has undergone testing by means of this isolation and generalisation of the individual causal factors, using the category of objective possibility and the synthesis of the different factors to be calculated which is made possible in this way.

It is clear, however, that the causal analysis of personal action logically proceeds in exactly the same way as the causal development of the 'historical significance' of the Battle of Marathon, through isolation, generalisation and the construction of judgments of possibility. Suppose we take a limiting case: the analysis in thought of one's own action. Logically untrained perception is inclined to believe that it certainly does not present any 'logical' problems, since it is given in immediate experience and (on the assumption of mental 'health') can be 'understood' without further ado, and is therefore immediately 'reproducible' in the memory. Very simple considerations show that this is not so, that the 'valid' answer to the question, 'Why did I act in this way?' represents a categorially formed construct, which can only be raised to the level of demonstrable judgment by the use of abstractions – even though in this case the 'demonstration' is conducted before the forum of the 'agent' himself.

Suppose a temperamental young mother, tired of some of her child's rowdiness, boxes his ears soundly, like a good German who does not subscribe to the theory expressed in Busch's fine words, 'A blow touches the surface alone: only the force of the spirit penetrates to the soul beneath'. But suppose further that she is nevertheless so 'sicklied o'er with the pale cast of thought' that she gives a few seconds of further thought, either to the 'educational purpose' of a box on the ears, or to its 'justification' or at least to the considerable 'expenditure of energy' involved in her action. Or, still better, suppose that the child's howls awaken the need in the *paterfamilias* (who, as a German, is convinced of his superior understanding in all things, including the upbringing of children) to rebuke 'her' from a 'teleological' point of view. Then 'she' will, for example, mention the consideration, in excuse for her behaviour, that *if* she had not at that moment been 'irritated' by (say) a quarrel with the cook, she would either not have applied such a disciplinary measure at all or anyway 'not in that form'. He will then be inclined to concede that 'he knows full well that she is not normally like that'. She reproaches him on the grounds of his 'empirical knowledge' of her 'standing motives', which, in the overwhelming majority of all possible circumstances, would have led to a different and less irrational effect. In other words – to anticipate the terminology which will be explained presently – she claims in her own defence that that box on the ears was, for her part, a 'chance' reaction, not an 'adequately caused' one, to the behaviour of her child.

This dialogue between husband and wife has thus already sufficed to make that 'experience' into a categorially formed 'object'; and even if, supposing a logician were to reveal to the young wife that she had performed an 'attribution of causes' like an historian, that she had to this end made 'judgments of objective possibility' and even operated with the category of 'adequate causation', to be discussed in more detail shortly, she would certainly be every bit as astonished as the philistine in Molière who discovered with joyful surprise that he had been speaking prose all his life – even so, this is certainly the case from the logical point of view. Reflective knowledge, even of an experience of one's own, is

The Logic of Historical Explanation

never in any way a genuine 're-living' or a simple 'photographic reproduction' of the experience; the 'experience', once made into an 'object', always acquires perspectives and connexions which were precisely not a 'conscious' part of the experience as it took place. To represent to oneself in reflection a past action of one's own is in this respect no different from representing to oneself a past 'natural event', whether 'experienced' by oneself or reported by someone else. It will not be necessary to illustrate further[1] the universal validity of this proposition

[1] One example, which K. Vossler analyses (in order to illustrate the impossibility of formulating 'laws') (*Die Sprache als Schöpfung und Entwicklung*, Heidelberg, 1905, pp. 101f), may be briefly considered here. He mentions certain peculiarities of language which were developed within his family, 'an island of Italian speech in the sea of German', by the children, and which were then imitated by their elders in speaking with the children, and whose origin goes back to perfectly concrete causes which are still completely clear in his memory. He then asks, 'What is racial psychology (and, we might add, following his line of thought, any science based on 'general laws') meant to explain further in such cases of linguistic development?' The occurrence, considered entirely in itself, is in fact *prima facie* explained in a completely satisfactory manner, though that is not to say that it could not be the object of further treatment and use. The fact that the causal relationship is in this instance definitely ascertainable (in principle, for that is all that is at issue here) could chiefly be used as a heuristic device for investigating whether the same causal relationship can be shown to be probable in other cases of linguistic development: but this, logically speaking, requires the subsumption of the concrete instance under a general rule. Vossler himself has also formulated this rule (p. 102) as follows: 'the more frequently used forms attract the less frequent'. But that is not sufficient. The causal explanation of the present case was satisfactory, we said, '*prima facie*'. But it should not be forgotten that any *individual* causal connexion, even the most apparently 'simple', can be analysed and dissected *ad infinitum*, and that it is only a question of the limits of our causal interests at any given time where we should call a halt. And in the present case nothing has been said to suggest that our causal needs must be satisfied with the account of what 'actually' happened. Precise observation, for instance, might possibly show that the 'attraction' which caused the development in the children's speech, and equally their elders' imitation of their children's linguistic creations, occurred to very different degrees in relation to different word forms, and that might raise the question whether it might not be possible to say something about the reasons why the one or the other occurred more or less frequently or not at all. We should only consider that our causal needs had been satisfied when the conditions governing the occurrence of the different phenomena had been stated in the form of rules and the concrete case had been 'explained' as a particular combination of elements resulting from the joint operation of such rules under concrete 'conditions'. At this point, Vossler would have admitted into his very hearth and home the detested business of chasing after laws, isolation and generalisation. And what is more, it would be his own fault. For his own general dictum that 'Analogy is a question of mental power' forces one necessarily to raise the question whether absolutely nothing can be discovered and stated about the 'mental' conditions of such 'mental power-relationships', and thus, at first sight, it seems in this formulation forcibly to introduce Vossler's very arch-enemy, 'psychology', into the issue. If we content ourselves in the concrete case with a simple description of the concrete event, the reasons for this will be twofold: first, that the 'rules' which might be discovered by further analysis would offer no really new insights for science in the concrete case, and so that the concrete event possesses no very great significance as a 'heuristic device'; and secondly, that the concrete event itself, since it was operative only in a narrow circle, had no universal bearing on linguistic development, and that it remained without significance also as a 'real cause' in history. Thus it is only the limits of our interest, not logical absurdity, which determines that that event in Vossler's family is likely to remain exempt from 'conceptualisation'.

by means of complicated examples or to assert explicitly that our logical procedure is exactly the same in the analysis of a decision by Napoleon or Bismarck as it was in the case of the German mother in our example. The difference that, in her case, the 'inside' of the act to be analysed was given in her own memory, whereas we have to 'interpret' the action of a third person from the 'outside', is, contrary to the preconceptions of the naive, merely a difference in the degree of accessibility and completeness of the 'material'. We are indeed inclined again and again to believe, when we find someone's 'personality' 'complicated' and difficult to interpret, that he himself must at least be in a position, provided only he is willing to be honest, to impart conclusive information about it. That this is not so, and why – why indeed precisely the opposite is often the case – is not a matter we can go into further here.

Let us rather consider in somewhat more detail the category of 'objective possibility', the function of which has so far been characterised only in a very general way, and in particular the question of the mode of 'validation' of the 'judgment of possibility'. Does not the objection suggest itself that to introduce 'possibilities' into 'causal enquiry' implies a renunciation of causal knowledge generally: that, in spite of all that was said above about the 'objective' foundation of the judgment of possibility, in practice, since the determination of the 'possible' course of events must always be left to the 'imagination', to recognise the significance of this category implies precisely the admission that the way is wide open for subjective caprice in the writing of history, and that it, for that very reason, is not a 'science'? It is true that it is often impossible to give a positive answer, with any great degree of probability, on the basis of general empirical rules, to the question what 'would have' happened if a certain factor among the determining conditions were thought of as altered in a certain respect – even when the source material is 'ideally' complete.[1] However, this is not absolutely necessary. The consideration of the causal significance of an historical fact will begin by asking the question whether the exclusion of this fact from the complex of factors considered as co-determinants, or its alteration in a certain sense, could have resulted, in accordance with general empirical rules, in a different turn of events in some way related to those points which are decisive in the light of our interests. For our only concern is with the way in which those 'aspects' of the phenomenon which interest us are affected by the individual co-determining factors. Admittedly, if *no* corresponding 'judgment of objective possibility' is forthcoming in answer to this essentially negative way of framing the question – that is (to say the same thing in different words), if, as far as we can tell, the

---

[1] The attempt positively to reconstruct what 'would have' happened may, when it is made, lead to monstrous results.

course of events in the 'historically important' respects (that is, those which are of interest to us) which was 'to be anticipated' in accordance with general empirical rules would have been precisely the same if that fact had been eliminated or altered as what actually happened – then that fact is in reality without causal significance and has absolutely no place in the chain of events which the causal regress of history is intended to, and ought to, establish.

The two shots on that March night in Berlin belong, according to Meyer, roughly to this category: perhaps not entirely, because even on his interpretation it is at least conceivable that the moment when the fighting broke out was partly determined by them, and if the moment of outbreak had been later this could have meant that events took a different course.

Nevertheless, if our empirical knowledge leads us to assume that a factor has causal relevance in regard to those points which are important for our particular line of enquiry, then the judgment of objective possibility which expresses this relevance admits of a whole scale of degrees of certainty. Meyer's view that Bismarck's 'decision' 'caused' the war of 1866 in a different sense from those two shots involves the contention that, if this decision were eliminated, the other determinants present must allow us to assume a 'high degree' of objective possibility of a development which was different (in the 'essential' respects): for instance, the expiry of the Prussian–Italian Treaty, the peaceful cession of Venetia, coalition between Austria and France or even a shift in the political and military position which would have made Napoleon virtually the 'master of the situation'. Thus, the judgment of objective 'possibility' essentially admits of variation in degree. The logical relationship can be represented in the following way, in terms of the principles used in the logical analysis of the 'calculus of probability': those causal factors to whose 'possible' effects the judgment relates are first thought of as isolated from the totality of all those conditions which can in general be conceived of as working together with them; then the question is asked, how the class of all those conditions, the addition of which makes the factors thus isolated in thought 'apt' to bring about the 'possible' effect, is related to the class of all those the addition of which would 'probably' *not* enable these factors to bring about the effect. Naturally, one cannot by means of this operation obtain a relationship between the two 'possibilities' on which any kind of 'numerical' value at all can be put. Such numerical values can only be obtained in the area of 'absolute randomness' (in the logical sense) – that is, in cases where, as for instance in throwing a die or drawing different coloured balls from an urn which always contains the same mixture of them, certain simple and unambiguous conditions remain absolutely the same over a very large number of cases, while all the others vary in a way which is absolutely unknown to us, and where those 'aspects' of the effect which matter (in throwing a die, the number of spots; in drawing from an urn, the colour of the balls) are determined in their 'possibility' by those constant and unambiguous conditions (nature of the die, distribution of the balls) in such a way that all other conceivable circumstances reveal no other causal relationship to those 'possibilities' of a kind which can be brought under an empirical generalisation. The way in which I take hold of and shake the cup before throwing the die is an absolutely determining factor for the number of spots which I throw in the particular case; but, despite all gambling superstitions, there is no possibility whatever even of thinking of an empirical proposition to the effect that a certain way of doing these two things is 'apt' to favour the throwing of a certain number of spots: thus, the causal relationship in this case is absolutely 'random'. That is, we are entitled to assert that the physical manner of throwing 'in general' does not affect the chances of throwing a certain number of spots: however we throw, the 'chances' of any of the six possible sides of the die falling uppermost are 'equal'. On the other hand, there is an empirical generalisation to the effect that, where the centre of gravity of the die is eccentric, this 'favours' the chances of a certain side of this 'false' die landing uppermost, no matter what other determinants are present in the particular case; and we can even express a numerical value for the degree to which the 'objective possibility' is 'favoured' by means of sufficiently frequent repetition of the throw.

Despite the warnings often, and quite rightly, uttered against transferring the principles of the calculus of probability to other domains, it is clear that this latter case has its analogues in all cases of concrete causality, and thus also in the domain of history. The only difference is that in this case there is absolutely no possibility of numerical determination, which presupposes, first, 'absolute randomness' and, second, certain quantifiable 'aspects' or outcomes as the sole object of interest. But despite this lack, we can not only perfectly well make generally valid assertions to the effect that certain situations 'favour', to a greater or lesser degree, modes of reaction on the part of the human beings confronted with them which are the same in certain respects, but also we are in a position when we formulate such an assertion to point to an enormous number of circumstances which might possibly also be present as *not* being such as to alter that general 'favouring'. And finally, we can estimate the degree to which certain 'conditions' favour a certain outcome. We cannot, to be sure, do so by any means clearly or even in the form of a calculus of probabilities; but we can estimate the relative 'degree' of general favouring by drawing a comparison with the way in which the alteration in thought of other conditions 'would' have 'favoured' it. And if we make this comparison in 'imagination' through sufficiently many conceivable alterations of circumstances, then it is nevertheless conceivable, at least in principle (and this is the only question which concerns us at this stage), that we can achieve a considerable degree of determinateness for a judgment about the 'degree' of objective possibility. Not only in everyday life, but also and precisely in history, we constantly make use of such judgments about the 'degree' of 'favouring': indeed, without them, any distinction between what is causally 'important' and 'unimportant' would simply not be possible, and Meyer too, in the work which has been discussed here, unhesitatingly made use of them. If those two shots which have several times been referred to were causally 'inessential', since 'any chance event at all' (in Meyer's view, which we shall not criticise in substance here) 'was bound to lead to an outbreak of conflict', this means that, in the given historical circumstances, certain 'conditions' could be isolated in thought such that they would have brought about precisely that effect even if there had been an overwhelming preponderance of further conditions which might be conceived of as possibly also being present; while the class of conceivable causal factors such that their presence would make it probable to us that there would be some outcome which was different (in the 'decisive' respects!) seems to us to be relatively very restricted. In view of Meyer's strong emphasis in other places on the irrationality of history, we shall not accept his view that the chances were actually equal to zero, in spite of the expression 'was bound to'.

Such cases in which there is a connexion between certain complexes of 'conditions', unified and considered in isolation by historical reflection, and an 'effect' which has occurred, we shall call, where they conform to the logical type just mentioned, cases of '*adequate*' causation (of those constituents of the effect by those conditions), following the usage which has come to be standard among theorists of legal causality since the work of von Kries. And, just as Meyer does (though he does not formulate this concept clearly), we shall speak of '*chance*' causation in those cases where, in regard to those constituents of the effect which are of historical interest, factors were at work which produced an effect which was *not*, in this sense, 'adequate' to a complex of conditions thus unified in thought.

Thus, to return to the examples used earlier, the 'significance' of the Battle of Marathon as Meyer sees it would be logically determined by saying, not that a Persian victory was bound to have as its consequence a certain totally different course of development for Greek, and so for world, civilisation (such a judgment simply could not be made), but that such a divergent development 'would have' been the 'adequate' consequence of such an event. Likewise, we shall restate Meyer's remarks about the unification of Germany, to which von Below objects, in the correct logical form as follows: that this unification can be made intelligible, on the basis of general empirical rules, as the 'adequate' consequence of certain antecedent events, as can the March revolution in Berlin as the adequate consequence of certain general social and political 'situations'. If, on the other hand, a plausible case were to be made out for saying, for instance, that there was a clearly overwhelming probability, in accordance with general empirical rules, that *without* those two shots in front of Berlin Castle a revolution 'could have' been avoided, because the other 'conditions' taken together, without the intervention of those shots, demonstrably did not 'favour' revolution, in accordance with general empirical rules, or did not 'favour' it to any great extent (in the sense of the word 'favour' elaborated earlier), then we should speak of 'chance' causation: in such a case, which admittedly can be imagined only with difficulty, we should have to 'attribute' the March revolution causally to those two shots. Thus, in this example of the unification of Germany, we should not, as von Below assumes, take the opposite of 'chance' to be 'necessary', but rather 'adequate', in the sense elaborated earlier which follows von Kries' usage.[1] And it must be firmly insisted that when such a contrast is made it is never a matter of differences in the 'objective' causality of the course of historical events and their causal connexions, but always simply of our isolating in the abstract a part of the 'conditions' to be found in the 'material' of events and making them into objects of 'judgments of possibility'; our aim is to gain insight in this way, with the aid of empirical rules, into the causal 'significance' of the individual constituents of the event. In order to gain insight into the real causal connexions, we construct unreal ones.

That it is a matter of abstractions is very often not understood, and that in a very specific form and manner analogous to the theories of certain theorists of legal causality which are based on the views of J. S. Mill – theories which have likewise already been convincingly criticised in the work of von Kries cited earlier.[2] Following Mill, who believed that the mathematical probability quotient referred to the relationship between those causes ('objectively') existing at the given point in time which 'bring about' and those which 'prevent' an effect, Binding assumes that

---

[1] We shall have something to say later on the question whether we have any means, and if so, which, of assessing the 'degree' of adequacy; and also about whether so-called 'analogies' play any role (and if so, what) in this process, especially in the analysis of complex 'combinations of causes' into their 'components' – for which we have absolutely no objectively given 'key' to aid in analysis. The formulation here is necessarily provisional.

[2] I find the extent to which, here as in many previous discussions, I have 'plundered' von Kries' ideas almost embarrassing, especially since the formulation must often fall short in precision of von Kries'. However, for the purposes of this study, both are unavoidable.

between those conditions which 'tend to bring about an effect' and those which 'tend to prevent it' there is an objective relationship which can (in individual cases) be given a numerical value, at least to some degree of approximation, and which in certain circumstances is in a 'state of equilibrium'; and he takes the process of causation to consist in the preponderance of the former.[1] It is quite clear in this instance that the phenomenon of the 'conflict of motives' which occurs as an immediate 'experience' in reflection on human 'actions' has been made into the basis of the theory of causality. Whatever general significance one may ascribe to that phenomenon,[2] it is certain that no rigorous consideration of causality, even in history, can allow such anthropomorphism.[3] Not only is the idea of two 'opposing forces' a physical and spatial image, which can only be applied without self-deception to processes – particularly those of a mechanical and physical kind[4] – in which, of two effects which are 'opposed' in the physical sense, one is caused by one force and the other by the other. But above all it must be insisted once and for all that a concrete effect cannot be regarded as the outcome of a conflict between causes which tend to bring it about and causes which are opposed to it. Rather, the totality of *all* conditions to which the causal regress from an 'effect' leads must 'work together' in exactly the way that they do in order to enable the concrete effect to occur in exactly the way that it does: for any empirical science which operates causally, the occurrence of the effect was certain, not from any particular moment, but 'from all eternity'.

Thus, when there is talk of 'favouring' and 'inhibiting' conditions of a given effect, this cannot mean that certain conditions in the concrete case have sought in vain to hinder the effect which eventually resulted, while others have ultimately achieved it in spite of them. This form of words can always and without exception mean no more than that certain constituents of the actual situation temporally antecedent to the effect, when isolated in thought, generally tend, in accordance with general empirical rules, to 'favour' an effect of the relevant kind. But this means, as we know, that in most cases which we can think of as possible in which

[1] Binding, *Die Normen und ihre Uebertretung*, I, pp. 41f; von Kries, *Prinzipien der Wahrscheinlichkeitsrechnung*, p. 107.

[2] H. Gomperz (*Ueber die Wahrscheinlichkeit der Willensentscheidungen*, Vienna, 1904, reprinted from *Sitzungsberichten der Wiener Akademie, Phil.-hist. Kl.*, vol. 149) has made this the basis of a phenomenological theory of the 'decision'. I could not presume to judge the value of his account of the process. Nevertheless, it seems to me, even leaving this aside, that Windelband's (for his purposes, intentional) identification, in terms of pure conceptual analysis, of the 'stronger' motive with the one in whose favour the decision eventually 'inclines' (*Ueber Willensfreiheit*, pp. 36f) is not the only possible way of approaching the problem.

[3] To this extent, Kistyakovski (*Probleme des Idealismus*) is absolutely right.

[4] See von Kries, *Prinzipien der Wahrscheinlichkeitsrechnung*, p. 108.

they are combined with other conditions, they tend to bring about the effect, while certain others generally tend to bring about, not this effect, but some other. It is a case of an isolating and generalising abstraction, not of the reproduction of a course of events which actually occurred, when we hear Meyer speaking, for instance, of situations in which 'everything pushes towards a certain effect'. When this is restated in its correct logical form, it means simply that we can establish and isolate in thought causal 'factors' to which the anticipated effect must be thought of as standing in the relation of 'adequacy', since we can conceive of relatively few combinations of the factors thus abstracted and isolated with other causal 'factors' from which, in accordance with general empirical rules, we should 'anticipate' a different outcome. We tend, in cases where the situation for our 'apprehension' is of the kind described by Meyer in these words, to speak[1] of a 'developmental tendency' in the direction of the effect in question.

This, like the use of such images as those of the 'driving forces' (or, contrariwise, the 'hindrances') acting on a development such as 'capitalism', or equally the usage whereby a certain 'rule' of causal connexion in a concrete case is neutralised by certain causal chains, or (still more imprecisely) of a 'law' as being 'neutralised' by another 'law' – all such ways of talking are harmless, provided one remains conscious of their conceptual character: that is, provided one bears in mind that they rest[2] on the abstraction of certain constituents of the real causal chain, on the generalisation in thought of the remainder in the form of judgments of objective possibility and on the use of the latter to form the course of events into a causal complex having a certain structure. And it is not enough for us in this case that someone should admit and be aware of the fact that all our 'knowledge' relates to a categorially interpreted reality, and so, for instance, that 'causality' is a category of 'our' thought. For the 'adequacy' of causation is in this respect peculiar.[3] Although it is not our intention here to give an exhaustive analysis of this category, it will be necessary to examine it at least briefly for two reasons: first, to clarify the merely relative nature, determined *ad hoc* by the particular purpose of the enquiry, of the contrast between 'adequate' and 'chance' causation; and secondly, to make intelligible the way in which the often extremely indeterminate

[1] The inelegance of the word does not alter the existence of the logical state of affairs referred to.

[2] Only where this is forgotten – as admittedly is often enough the case – are there any grounds for Kistyakovski's misgivings (*Probleme des Idealismus*) about the 'metaphysical' character of this kind of causal enquiry.

[3] On this point too, the most important points of view have already been either explicitly discussed or referred to in the work cited by von Kries, and, for instance, in Radbruch's work cited above.

content of the assertion contained in a 'judgment of possibility' accords with the claim which it nevertheless makes to 'validity' and with the utility which it nevertheless possesses in the determination of causal connexions in history.

(*Gesammelte Aufsätze zur Wissenschafts-lehre*, 2nd edn, Tübingen, 1951, pp. 266–90. First published in 1906.)

III · Ideology

Introduction

None of Weber's writings has aroused as much controversy both during his lifetime and after it as his two-part article on 'The Protestant Ethic and the "Spirit" of Capitalism', published in 1905, of which the first selection in this section is the concluding part. The extent of the controversy is due partly to the interest of the topic, partly to the complexity of the evidence and partly to the difficulty of specifying precisely the hypothesis which Weber sought to establish. It is clear that he did not claim that Protestantism as such caused the development of industrial capitalism, and that if he had he would have been mistaken. It is also clear that he was right to point out that there is *a* connexion between Protestantism and capitalism which is not merely coincidental. But what sort of connexion is it? Weber does appear to mean more than that the Reformation was one necessary condition of the emergence in Europe but nowhere else of a form of economic and political organisation which came to transform the rest of the world. He argues that there is a particular affinity between certain of the doctrines of Protestantism implying a conception of salvation through the pursuit of a secular calling and the style of life necessary for the successful accumulation of capital through commercial activity. The ideal of 'Christian asceticism' is in his view fundamentally different from that of asceticism as conceived by any of the other great religions, and as a result it alone played a decisive role in the development of a 'rationalised' work ethic without which capitalism would not have developed as it has.

The question whether the influence of Protestantism was decisive in this way is virtually impossible to settle conclusively. The 'Protestant ethic' may well be a plausible example of the way in which, to use a simile of Weber's own, ideas have functioned as 'switchmen' determining 'the tracks along which action has been pushed by the dynamic of interest'.[1] But how are we to estimate the difference which would have been made had the doctrines of Protestantism been other than they were? It seems most implausible to suppose that industrial capitalism would not have emerged at all within a Catholic Europe. Despite his insistence on the importance of material interests, Weber did, in the judgment of the overwhelming majority of later specialists, exaggerate not only the strength of the link between the actual teachings of Calvin and the Puritan Divines and the ethic of economic individualism but also the extent to which a specifically anti-economic ethic is present in the religions of India and China and in Islam. It would perhaps be more plausible to argue that a necessary condition of the emergence of industrial capitalism was an altogether more general ideological

[1] 'The Social Psychology of the World Religions', in H. H. Gerth and C. Wright Mills, eds., *From Max Weber* (New York, 1947), p. 280.

change in the direction of the application of rationality to daily life of which the Calvinist ethic was one notable instance.[1] It may well be that without this the will to exploit the necessary technology and to develop new forms of the division of labour would have been lacking, and that the contribution of Protestantism was more in the indirect promotion of a scientific spirit and (as Weber himself emphasised) the undermining of magic than in the inculcation of an ethic of thrift and hard work.[2]

But whatever the answer may be on the particular question of the 'Protestant ethic', this does not diminish the value of Weber's general analysis of the relation between ideology and social structure. The second selection in this section is taken from the Chapter in *Economy and Society* which deals with the sociology of religion. It is characteristic of Weber in both the density of the argument and the multiplicity of the illustrations adduced in support of it. Weber seeks to maintain on the one hand that religious ideology is never a simple function of social position: not all artisans incline to a rational ethics, not all religions of brotherly love have been influenced by women, and not all urban communities foster congregationalism. On the other hand, he seeks also to show how the spread and influence of religious ideas, although they may owe their origin to a purely spiritual impulse or need, are decisively linked to the social situation of the groups who accept and propagate them. This applies both in the comparisons which he draws between the Judaeo-Christian tradition and the great religions of the East and also in his analysis of the evolution within the Judaeo-Christian tradition of its distinctive modern ethic. The discussion of the Jews as a 'pariah people' particularly brings out the way in which Weber's analysis of religious belief makes selective use of the ideas of Marx and Nietzsche. It is, moreover, an argument which has application not merely in specifically religious contexts but in any context where the situation of an underprivileged stratum generates the need for an ideology which will serve to render that situation more tolerable.

The third selection is the concluding passage of Weber's study of Hinduism and Buddhism published in 1916–17. Here he returns to the question why it was in Europe rather than elsewhere that there emerged the one culture which brought into being what we now think of as 'modern' science and technology and all that goes with it. He summarises the characteristic features of the great Eastern religions which differentiate them from the Judaeo-Christian tradition, and contrasts their ideal of withdrawal from, and rejection of, the world with the 'inner-worldly' asceticism of Protestant Christianity. This contrast still leaves much to be explained. Not merely were the ethics of other religions less anti-capitalist than as Weber presents them, but China, in particular, which by the fourteenth century had 'advanced to the threshold of a systematic experimental investigation of nature and created the world's earliest mechanized

[1] This is the conclusion suggested by David Landes, *Prometheus Unbound* (Cambridge, 1969), pp. 23–4.
[2] It is worth noting that in the paper on 'The Protestant Sects and the Spirit of Capitalism' which he wrote after visiting the United States in 1904, Weber shifted the argument from the level of the influence of religious doctrine on individual motivation to that of the collective interest of the sects in maintaining a distinctive ethic bound up with their social prestige; but even if this is correct, it does not prove that the 'Protestant ethic' itself was necessary for such a process.

industry"[1] cannot possibly be dismissed, as it was by Weber, as lacking 'systematic naturalistic thought' and 'rational technology'. Yet it is hard to deny altogether that there was an ideological element in Hinduism, Confucianism and Islam which in each case, although in very different ways, did inhibit the full development of those two things.

[1] Mark Elvin, *The Pattern of the Chinese Past* (London, 1973), p. 179.

7 · *Protestant Asceticism and the Spirit of Capitalism*

In order to grasp the connexions between the fundamental religious ideas of ascetic Protestantism and its maxims of everyday economic life, it is necessary above all to refer to those theological writings which can be seen to have had their origins in pastoral practice. For, in a time when the next world was everything, when the social position of the Christian depended on his admission to communion, and when the influence exercised by the clergy in the cure of souls, in church discipline and in preaching, was of a kind which (as the merest glance at the collections of '*consilia*', '*casus conscientiae*', etc. will show) we modern men simply cannot any longer begin to imagine, the religious forces at work in pastoral practice are the decisive influences in forming 'national character'.

For the purposes of our discussions in this section, as opposed to later discussions, we may treat ascetic Protestantism as a single undifferentiated whole. But since that kind of English Puritanism which had its roots in Calvinism affords the most consistent attempt to work out the basis of the idea of the 'calling', we may, in accordance with our principle, take one of its representatives as the focus of our discussion. Richard Baxter is distinguished above many other literary representatives of the Puritan ethic by his eminently practical and conciliatory attitude, and also by the universal recognition of his constantly republished and translated works. A Presbyterian and an apologist for the Westminster Synod, he nevertheless gradually, like so many of the best minds of his time, moved away in his doctrinal views from the extreme Calvinist position. He was at heart an opponent of Cromwell's usurpation, as of every revolution, with a distaste for sectarianism, above all for the fanatical zeal of the 'Saints', but a very liberal attitude towards peculiarities of external practice, combined with an objective approach to his opponents. He sought his field of work essentially in the direction of the practical advancement of the moral life of the Church, and in this work he was willing to serve, as one of the most successful pastors known to history,[1] indifferently under the Parliamentary regime, Cromwell or the Restoration. He finally

[1] See the fine character sketch in Dowden's *Puritan and Anglican*. There is a reasonably good guide to Baxter's theology, after he had gradually modified his strict belief in the 'double decree', in the Introduction (by Jenkyn) to the selection of his works printed

retired under the Restoration – before St Bartholomew's day. His 'Christian Directory' is the most comprehensive compendium of Puritan moral theology, relating its theology at every point to his own practical experience as a pastor. For comparison, we have taken Spener's '*Theologische Bedenken*' to represent German Pietism and Barclay's 'Apology' to represent Quakerism, together with other representatives of the ascetic ethic;[1] to save space, these comparisons will be made as far as possible in the footnotes.[2]

To pick up Baxter's 'Saints' Everlasting Rest' or his 'Christian Directory', or some similar works by other writers,[3] is immediately to be struck by the emphasis placed, in the judgments on riches[4] and their acquisition, precisely on the Ebionitic elements in New Testament teaching.[5] Riches

in the *Works of the Puritan Divines*. His attempt to combine 'universal redemption' and 'personal election' satisfied nobody. For us, the crucial point is only that even at that time he remained firm on personal election, or in other words on the ethically decisive feature of the doctrine of predestination. It is important, on the other hand, that he weakened the forensic interpretation of the doctrine of justification, since that represented a move in the direction of the Baptists.

1 Treatises and sermons by Thomas Adams, John Howe, Matthew Henry, J. Janeway, Stuart Charnock, Baxter and Bunyan have been collected in the ten volumes of the *Works of the Puritan Divines* (London, 1845–48), though the selection is often somewhat arbitrary. The work of Bailey referred to is *Praxis Pietatis* (Leipzig, 1724); that of Sedgwick is *Buss- und Gnadenlehre*, in the German translation of 1689; and that of Hoornbeek is *Theologia Practica* (Utrecht, 1663).

2 Voët or other continental representatives of inner-worldly asceticism might equally well have been referred to. Brentano's view that this development was 'merely Anglo-Saxon' is totally mistaken. The choice depends on a wish to give expression, not exclusively but as far as possible, to the ascetic movement of the second half of the seventeenth century, immediately before it turned into utilitarianism. In the framework of this sketch we have unfortunately had to deny ourselves the chance to pursue the fascinating problem of additionally illuminating the style of life of ascetic Protestantism from the biographical literature: the Quaker literature in particular, since it is relatively unknown in Germany, would be worth citing.

3 One might equally well refer to the writings of Gisbert Voët, the proceedings of the Huguenot synods or the Dutch Baptist literature. It is most unfortunate that Sombart and Brentano have singled out precisely those 'Ebionitic' elements in Baxter which I have myself emphasised so strongly, in order to confront me with the undoubted backwardness (from the capitalist point of view) of his teachings. But first of all, one must have a really thorough acquaintance with this literature as a whole in order to make proper use of it; and secondly, it should not be overlooked that I have actually tried to show how, in spite of this 'anti-Mammonistic' teaching, the spirit of this ascetic form of religion, just as in the monastic economies, gave birth to economic rationalism, because it rewarded the ascetically determined rational pursuits which played the decisive role in this process. This alone is the nub of the matter and precisely this is the point of the present argument.

4 It is the same in Calvin, who was certainly no admirer of bourgeois wealth (see the vehement attacks on Venice and Antwerp in *Jes. Opp.*, III 140a, 308a).

5 *Saints' Everlasting Rest*, Chapters X and XII. Compare Bailey, *Praxis Pietatis*, p. 182, or Matthew Henry, 'The Worth of the Soul', *Works of the Puritan Divines*, p. 319: 'Those that are eager in pursuit of worldly wealth despise their soul, not only because the soul is neglected and the body preferred before it, but because it is employed in these pursuits: Psalm 127, 2.' (On the same page, however, can be found the remark to be quoted later about the sinfulness of all forms of wasting time, especially in 'recrea-

as such are a grave danger, their temptations unremitting, the effort[1] to acquire them not only senseless when compared with the surpassing importance of the Kingdom of God, but also morally hazardous. Asceticism seems in these passages to be directed against all striving to acquire temporal goods, to a much greater extent than in Calvin, who found in riches no hindrance to the clergy's activity, but on the contrary a totally desirable means of increasing their authority, and who allowed them to invest their wealth at a profit as long as they avoided scandal. Examples of this kind of condemnation of the pursuit of money and possessions can readily and abundantly be found in Puritan writings, and contrasted with late medieval ethical literature, which was much more free and easy in this respect. Moreover, the intentions behind these reflections were absolutely serious: though it is only on a somewhat closer examination that their decisive ethical meaning and implications become clear. The real object of moral condemnation is, in particular, relaxation in the possession of property[2] and enjoyment of riches, resulting in sloth and the lusts of the flesh, and above all in distraction from the pursuit of a 'holy' life. And it is only because possessions bring with them the risk

tions'.) The same is true of the whole religious literature of English and Dutch Puritanism. See, for example, Hoornbeek's Philippics (*Theologia Practica*, x, Ch. 18, 18) against 'avaritia' (avarice). In the case of the latter writer there are also sentimental influences of a pietistic kind at work: see his praise of a 'tranquillity of spirit' which is pleasing to God, as against the 'cares' of this world. Bailey too (*Praxis Pietatis*, p. 182), alluding to a familiar passage in the Bible, expresses the opinion that 'A rich man is not easily saved'. The Methodist catechisms also warn against 'laying up for oneself treasure on earth'. In Pietism this is absolutely self-evident. And the case is no different with the Quakers. Compare Barclay (*The Apology for the True Christian Divinity*, p. 517), '...and therefore beware of such temptation as to use their callings and engine to be richer'.

[1] Not just riches, but the instinctive pursuit of gain (or what was considered as such) were condemned with equal sharpness. In the Netherlands, the Synod of South Holland in 1574 explained, in answer to an enquiry, that money-lenders, even though their business was carried on legally, should not be admitted to communion; the Provincial Synod of Deventer in 1598 (Article 24) extended this to those employed by money-lenders; the Synod at Gorichem in 1606 laid down harsh and humiliating conditions for the admission of the wives of 'usurers'; and it was still a matter for discussion in 1644 and 1657 whether money-lenders should be admitted to communion. (This is evidence especially against Brentano, who cites his Catholic forebears – although there have been merchants and bankers of foreign birth throughout the European and Asiatic world for millennia.) Finally, Gisbert Voët (*Disp. Theol.*, IV, 1667, *de usuris*, p. 665) could still exclude the 'Trapezites' (that is, the Lombard or Piedmontese money-lenders) from communion. The situation was no different in the Huguenot synods. It was certainly not the capitalist strata of this kind who embodied the frame of mind and the mode of life which are at issue here. What is more, they were nothing new, as compared with the ancient world and the Middle Ages.

[2] A theme which is exhaustively developed in Chapter Ten of the *Saints' Everlasting Rest*. Anyone who would seek lasting rest in possessions, which God gives as merely a 'lodging', is stricken by God even in this life. To rest content on the riches which one has already gained nearly always presages moral failure. Could we have all that we were able to have in this world, would this yet be all that we could hope for? Satisfaction is not to be attained in this world, since God has willed that it should not be.

of this kind of relaxation that they are hazardous. For the 'Saints' everlasting rest' lies in the next world: on earth, however, man too must, if he is to be sure of being in a state of grace, 'work the works of Him that sent him, while it is day'. Not sloth and enjoyment, but only activity, according to the unambiguously revealed will of God, serves to increase His glory.[1]

To waste time is thus the first and, in principle, the worst of all sins. The span of life is infinitely short and precious if one is to 'make sure of' one's election. To lose time through sociability, 'idle talk',[2] extravagance,[3] even through taking more sleep than is necessary for health[4] (six to at most eight hours), is considered worthy of total moral condemnation.[5] Franklin's remark that 'Time is money' is not yet found, but the proposition is true, so to speak, in a spiritual sense: it is infinitely valuable, since every hour lost is taken away from work in the service of God's glory.[6] Hence, passive contemplation is also valueless, indeed

---

[1] *Christian Directory*, I, pp. 375–6, 'It is for action that God maintaineth us and our activities: work is the moral as well as the natural end of power... It is action that God is most served and honoured by... The public welfare or the good of many is to be valued above our own.' Here we see the starting point for the development from the will of God to the purely utilitarian point of view of later liberal theory. On the religious sources of utilitarianism, see further below and above.

[2] Beginning with the Biblical threat of punishment for every idle word, the command to be silent has been, especially since the Cluniac monks, a tried and tested ascetic method for cultivating self-control. Baxter too goes exhaustively into the sinfulness of vain speech. The characterological significance of this has already been assessed by Sanford (*Studies and Reflections of the Great Rebellion*, pp. 90f). The 'melancholy' and 'moroseness' of the Puritans, which made such a deep impression on their contemporaries, were a consequence of the disintegration of the spontaneity of the 'natural state' and the prohibition of thoughtless speech was meant to serve this end.

When Washington Irving (*Bracebridge Hall*, Ch. xxx) seeks the reason which leads to a sense of personal responsibility, partly in the 'calculating spirit' of capitalism and partly in the effects of political freedom, it should be pointed out that the same effect was not produced amongst the Latin nations and that in England the situation was that, first, Puritanism enabled its adherents to create free institutions and so to become a world power, and secondly, that it changed the spirit of 'calculation' (as Sombart calls it), which is indeed constitutive of capitalism, from an economic instrument into the principle of a whole mode of life.

[3] *Op. cit.*, I, p. 111.   [4] *Christian Directory*, I, pp. 383f.

[5] There is a similar point about the preciousness of time in Barclay, *The Apology for the True Christian Divinity*, p. 14.

[6] Baxter, *op. cit.*, p. 79, 'Keep up a high esteem of time and be every day more careful that you lose none of your time, than you are that you lose none of your gold and silver. And if vain recreation, dressings, feastings, idle talk, unprofitable company, or sleep, be any of them temptations to rob you of any of your time, accordingly heighten your watchfulness.' 'Those that are prodigal of their time despise their own souls' is the view of Matthew Henry ('Worth of the Soul', *Works of the Puritan Divines*, p. 315). Here again Protestant asceticism is following well-trodden paths. We usually look on it as specific to modern man in his professional life that he 'has no time', and even, for instance, – as Goethe was already doing in his *Wanderjahren* – measure the extent of capitalist development by the fact that the clocks strike the quarter-hours (as Sombart also says in his *Kapitalismus*). But we should not forget that the first man to take account of

in some cases actually objectionable, at least when indulged in at the expense of work in one's calling.[1] For to God it is less pleasing than the active fulfilment of His will in one's calling.[2] Besides, Sunday exists for that purpose, and it is, according to Baxter, always those who are lazy in their calling who have no time for God even at the hour appointed for that purpose.[3]

Accordingly, Baxter's principal work has as one of its central themes a constantly repeated, at times almost passionate, advocacy of hard, unremitting, physical or intellectual work.[4] Two motifs are combined here.[5]

the divisions of time in his life (in the Middle Ages) was the monk, and that the church bell had first to provide for his need to divide time.

[1] Compare Baxter's discussion of the calling, *op. cit.*, I, pp. 108f, where the following passage is found: 'Question: But may I not cast off the world that I may only think of my salvation? – Answer: You may cast off all such excess of worldly cares or business as unnecessarily hinder you in spiritual things. But you may not cast off all bodily employment and mental labour in which *you may serve the common good*. Everyone as a member of Church or Commonwealth must employ their parts to the utmost for the good of the Church and the Commonwealth. To neglect this and say: I will pray and meditate, is as if your servant should refuse your greatest work and tye himself to some lesser easier part. And *God hath commanded you some way or other to labour for your daily bread and not to live as drones of the sweat of others only.*' God's commandment to Adam, 'In the sweat of thy face shalt thou eat bread', and St Paul's admonition, 'If any would not work, neither should he eat' were cited in this connexion. It has long been known of the Quakers that, even amongst the most wealthy, their sons were put to learn a trade – for ethical, not, as Alberti suggests, for utilitarian reasons.

[2] Here there are some respects in which Pietism, because of its emphasis on feeling, follows a different path. For Spener (see his '*Theologische Bedenken*', III, p. 445), despite his completely Lutheran emphasis on the idea that work in a calling is the service of God, it is settled (and this too is Lutheran) that the agitation of activity in a calling draws one away from God – an extremely characteristic antithesis to Puritanism.

[3] *Op. cit.*, p. 242: 'It's they that are lazy in their callings that can find no time for holy duties'. This is the origin of the view that the towns, the home of the bourgeoisie engaged in rational acquisition, were also pre-eminently the homes of the ascetic virtues. Baxter says of his hand-loom weavers in Kidderminster: 'And their constant converse and traffic with London doth much to promote civility and piety among tradesmen' (in his *Autobiography* – excerpt in the *Works of the Puritan Divines*, p. xxxviii). The idea that the proximity of the capital should have the effect of strengthening virtue would astonish the clergy today, at least in Germany. But there are also similar views to be found in Pietism. Spener, for instance, writes in passing to a young colleague: 'At least it will be seen that, among the great numbers in the towns, though most are utterly wicked, still a few good souls are on the other hand to be found, with whom to achieve something good; but I fear that sometimes in villages there is scarcely anything entirely good to be found in a whole community' ('*Theologische Bedenken*', I, 66, p. 303). The peasant is little fitted for the ascetic rational conduct of life. His ethical glorification is very modern. We will not here go into the significance of these and similar statements for the question of how far asceticism is determined by class.

[4] Consider for example the following passages (*op. cit.*, pp. 336f): 'Be wholly taken up in diligent business of your lawful callings when you are not exercised in the more immediate service of God'. 'Labour hard in your callings'. 'See that you have a calling which will find you employment for all the time which God's immediate service spareth'.

[5] That the specific ethical valuation of work and its 'dignity' was not in origin an idea unique to, or even characteristic of, Christianity has again been strongly emphasised recently by Harnack (*Mitt. des Ev.-Soz. Kongr.*, 14, Folge, 1905, Nos. 3/4, p. 48).

First, work is a well-tried ascetic method, and in the Western Church, in sharp contrast not only with the Eastern, but also with almost all forms of monasticism anywhere in the world,[1] it has been approved as such from earliest times.[2] It is especially the specific prophylactic against all those temptations which Puritanism subsumes under the concept of 'unclean life'; and their role is by no means negligible. Indeed, sexual asceticism differs only in degree, not in underlying principle, from monasticism and precisely because its conception of marriage is more far-reaching. For even in marriage, sexual intercourse is permissible only as the means willed by God to increase His glory, in accordance with the commandment 'Be fruitful and multiply'.[3] The prescription against all

[1] The basis of this important contrast, which has been obvious since the Benedictine rule, can only be clarified by a much more thorough discussion.

[2] So also in Pietism (Spener, '*Theologische Bedenken*', III, pp. 429–30). The characteristic Pietist turn given to the idea is that loyalty to one's calling, which is imposed on us as a punishment because of the Fall, helps to mortify the individual will. Work in a calling, as a form of service expressing love for one's neighbour, is a duty of gratitude for God's grace (a Lutheran conception), and so it is not pleasing to God when it is done unwillingly and with ill humour (III, p. 272). The Christian will therefore 'show himself as diligent in his work as a worldly man' (III, p. 278). That obviously falls short of the Puritan way of thinking.

[3] 'A sober procreation of children' is its purpose according to Baxter. Similarly in Spener, though he makes concessions to the coarse Lutheran view according to which a secondary purpose is to avoid immorality, which cannot be restrained in any other way. Concupiscence, as a feeling which accompanies copulation, is sinful even within marriage and, according to Spener's interpretation, for example, is a consequence of the Fall, which in this way turned a natural and divinely willed process into something unavoidably associated with sinful feelings, and so into something shameful. According to the conception of some pietistic movements, moreover, the highest form of Christian marriage is that in which virginity is preserved, the next highest, that in which sexual relations serve exclusively for procreation, and so on down to those which are entered into for purely sexual motives or simply for the sake of outward appearances and are, ethically regarded, no better than concubinage. Further, among the lower forms of marriage, that which is entered into simply for the sake of outward appearances is preferred to marriage for purely sexual motives, on the grounds that it does still involve rational considerations. The Herrnhut theory and practice need not concern us here. Rationalist philosophy, in the person of Christian Wolff, took over the ascetic theory in the sense that what was ordained as a means to an end (concupiscence and its appeasement) should not be made into an end in itself.

The shift to the purely hygienic concerns of utilitarianism was already complete by the time of Franklin, who adopts the ethical standpoint of the modern doctor, taking 'chastity' to mean the limitation of sexual intercourse to what is desirable on grounds of health, and, as is well known, also expressing views on how that aim should be achieved. This development has begun everywhere as soon as these questions have become a subject for purely rational consideration. The Puritan and the hygienic sexual rationalist follow very different paths, but at this point they 'understand each other'. In a lecture (the theme was brothels and arrangements for regulating them) an enthusiastic advocate of 'hygienic' prostitution supported his claim that 'extra-marital intercourse', because of its hygienic utility, was morally admissible by referring to its poetic glorification in the characters of Faust and Gretchen. Both these notions – that Gretchen should be considered as a prostitute, and that the powerful sway of human passions should be identified with hygienic sex – would be entirely acceptable to Puritan ways of thinking. The same is true, for instance, of the typical specialist's attitude embodied in the view

sexual temptations, as against religious doubt and the torments of excessive self-examination, is (apart from moderation in diet, vegetarianism and cold baths) 'Labour hard in your calling'.[1]

But over and above that, and most important of all, labour is a divinely commanded ultimate end of life as a whole.[2] St Paul's assertion, 'If any would not work, neither should he eat', holds unconditionally and for everyone.[3] Disinclination for work is a symptom of a fall from the state of grace.[4]

The difference from the medieval attitude is clearly to be seen here. Thomas Aquinas had also offered an interpretation of the saying just quoted. But according to him[5] work is necessary only in a naturalistic sense for the preservation of the life of the individual and the community. Where this purpose no longer applies, the commandment is no longer valid. It applies only to the species as a whole, not to every individual

occasionally advocated by very distinguished doctors that a question such as that of the meaning of sexual abstinence, which bears on the subtlest problems of personality and culture, belongs 'exclusively' within the province of the medical man, who is the 'specialist' in this field. For the Puritans, the specialist was the moral theorist, here it is the hygienic expert: but the principle of 'competence' to settle the question, which to us can so easily seem philistine, is the same, though of course it operates in the reverse direction. However, the powerful idealism of the Puritan viewpoint, with all its pruderies, can also point to positive successes, from the point of view of racial conservation and in purely 'hygienic' terms; whereas modern sexual hygiene, because of its inevitable appeal to 'open-mindedness', runs the risk of allowing the very source of its own strength to drain away.

Naturally, it is impossible to discuss here the way in which, in the setting of the rational interpretation of sexual relations to be found in those nations which were influenced by Puritanism, marital relationships ultimately achieved a degree of refinement and permeation by spiritual and ethical ideals, and marital chivalry flourished, in contrast with the patriarchal miasma which still lingers in Germany, often in considerable pockets, through all ranks right up to the intellectual aristocracy. (Baptist influences have also played their part in the emancipation of women; the defence of women's freedom of conscience and the extension to women of the idea of 'the priesthood of all believers' were also among the first breaches in patriarchalism.)

[1] A constantly recurring theme in Baxter. The Scriptural basis is either the passage quoted by Franklin which we already know (Proverbs 22. 29) or the eulogy of work in Proverbs 31. 16. Cf. *Christian Directory*, I, p. 382, p. 377, etc.

[2] Even Zinzendorf says on one occasion: 'One does not work only that one may live, but one lives in order to work, and if one has no more work to do, then one either suffers or dies' (Plitt, I, p. 428).

[3] A Mormon symbol also ends (after quotations) with the words: 'But a lazy or indolent man cannot be a Christian and be saved. He is destined to be struck down and cast from the hive'. However, here it was principally the impressive discipline, following the middle path between monastery and factory, which confronted the individual with the choice between working and perishing and – together, of course, with religious enthusiasm and only made possible by it – produced the astounding economic achievements of that sect.

[4] Hence its symptoms are carefully analysed, Baxter, *Christian Directory*, I, p. 380. 'Sloth' and 'idleness' are such particularly grave sins, just because they have a *dispositional* character. They are regarded by Baxter actually as 'destroyers of grace' (I, pp. 279–80). They are indeed the antitheses of the methodical life.

[5] See Thomas Aquinas, *Quaest. quodlibetal.*, VII, Article 17c.

member. Anyone who can live off his property without work is not included in the commandment, and equally, contemplation, as a spiritual activity in the Kingdom of God, is naturally outside the scope of the commandment in its literal interpretation. For popular theology, finally, the highest form of monastic 'productivity' lay in its contribution to the 'treasury of the Church' through prayer and choral singing. Not only does Baxter, however, naturally not permit such exceptions to the ethical obligation to work: he also preaches with the greatest possible emphasis that even wealth does not excuse anyone from that unconditional commandment.[1] Even the man of property may not eat without working, for, even if he is not compelled to work in order to supply his needs, there is still God's commandment, which he must obey as much as the poor man.[2] For divine providence has prepared for everyone without distinction a particular *calling*, which he must recognise and in which he must work, and this calling is not, as in Lutheranism,[3] a fate to which one must submit and with which one must be content, but a commandment by God to the individual to work to His glory. This apparently slight shade of difference had far-reaching psychological consequences, and went together with the further evolution of that providential interpretation of the economic order which was already current in Scholasticism.

The phenomenon of the division of labour and the distribution of occupations in society had already been interpreted by, amongst others, Thomas Aquinas (to whom we can again most conveniently refer) as flowing directly from the divine plan for the world. But the classification of men within this cosmic order results from natural causes and is, in the Scholastic terminology, 'contingent'. For Luther, as we saw, the classification of men into given estates and occupations resulting from an objective historical order was taken to flow directly from the divine will, and it therefore became for him a religious duty for the individual to persevere in the position and within the limits assigned to him by

---

[1] Baxter, *Christian Directory*, I, pp. 108ff. The following passages are especially striking: 'Question: But will not wealth excuse us? – Answer: It may excuse you from some sordid sort of work, by making you more serviceable to another, but you are no more excused from service of work...than the poorest man', and further, on p. 376: 'Though they [the rich] have no outward want to urge them, they have as great a necessity to obey God...God hath strictly commanded it [work] to all.'

[2] Similarly in Spener ('*Theologische Bedenken*', III, pp. 338, 425), who for this reason is particularly opposed to the tendency to premature retirement, considering it to be morally hazardous; also, in rejecting criticism of the legitimacy of charging interest on the grounds that living on interest leads to idleness, stresses that someone who could live on his interest would still be obliged by God's commandment to work.

[3] Including Pietism. Whenever the question of change of occupation arises, Spener always takes the view that once one has entered upon a certain calling, it is a duty of obedience to God's providence that one should continue in it and reconcile oneself to it.

God.[1] This was all the more true, in that the relationship of Lutheran piety to the 'world' in general was initially, and continued to be, uncertain. It was impossible to extract from Luther's system of ideas, which never entirely shed its Pauline indifference to the world, any ethical principles for the organisation of the world: the world had to be taken as it was, and this alone constituted one's religious duty.

In the Puritan view, on the other hand, there is a different nuance to the providential character of the interplay of private economic interest. True to the Puritan scheme of pragmatic interpretation, the providential purpose of the classification of occupations is to be recognised by their fruits. On these Baxter expresses himself in ways which, at more than one point, are directly reminiscent of Adam Smith's well-known apotheosis of the division of labour.[2] The specialisation of occupations, because it gives scope for the *skill* of the worker, leads to a quantitative and qualitative increase in the performance of work and so serves the common good, or 'common best', which is identified with the good of the greatest possible number. If the motivation is so far purely utilitarian and closely related to a number of views which had already become commonplace in the secular literature of the time,[3] the characteristically

[1] The tremendous emotional power, dominating the whole conduct of life, with which the Indian doctrine of salvation associates occupational traditionalism with the chances of rebirth, has been discussed at length in my essays on 'The Economic Ethics of the World Religions'. This is a particularly good point at which to learn to recognise the difference between merely theoretical ethical concepts and the creation of psychological incentives of a particular kind by religion. The pious Hindu could only secure favourable chances of rebirth by a strictly traditional fulfilment of the obligations of his native caste, and that is the strongest imaginable religious foundation for traditionalism. Indian ethics is in fact in this respect the most consistent antithesis of Puritan ethics, just as in another regard (the traditionalism of its status group structure) it is the most consistent antithesis of Judaism.

[2] Baxter, *Christian Directory*, I, p. 377.

[3] But not for that reason historically derivable from it. A much more important influence in it is the genuinely Calvinist idea that the ordered system of the 'world' serves the glory of God, His Self-glorification. The utilitarian development of this idea, that the economic cosmos ought to serve the purpose of prolonging the life of everyone ('good of the many', 'common good', etc.), resulted from the notion that any other interpretation would lead to a typically aristocratic 'idolatry of the creature', or would serve, not to glorify God, but the purposes of creaturely 'culture'. God's will, however, as expressed in the purposeful ordering of the economic cosmos, may take the form, as far as worldly ends in general come into consideration, only of the well-being of the 'commonwealth', or in other words of an impersonal 'utility'. Utilitarianism is thus, as was said earlier, a consequence of the impersonal construction of the 'love of one's neighbour' and the repudiation of all forms of glorification of the world resulting from the exclusivity of the Puritan conception of '*ad majorem Dei gloriam*'. The degree of intensity to which the whole of ascetic Protestantism was dominated by the idea that all glorification of the creature was detrimental to the glory of God and so utterly objectionable is clearly to be seen in the scruples and mental anguish which it cost even Spener, who certainly could never be suspected of 'democratic' sympathies, to uphold the use of titles as 'indifferent' in the face of numerous enquiries. He reassures himself finally with the reflection that, even in the Bible, the praetor Festus was addressed with the title 'Most Noble' by the Apostle. The political aspect of the matter is not relevant in this connexion.

Puritan overtones become obvious as soon as Baxter begins his discussion with the theme, 'Outside of a well-marked calling the accomplishments of a man are only casual and irregular, and he spends more time in idleness than at work', and when he concludes by saying, 'and he [the worker with a calling] will carry out his work in order while another remains in constant confusion, and his business knows neither time nor place[1]...therefore is a certain calling the best for everyone'. The irregular work in which the ordinary day-labourer is compelled to engage is an often unavoidable, but always regrettable, compromise. The life of those without a calling lacks the systematic and methodical character required, as we saw, by inner-worldly asceticism.

In the Quaker ethic, too, the working life of man is to be a consistent ascetic exercise in virtue, a proof of one's state of grace in the conscientiousness which is apparent in the careful and methodical way in which one follows one's calling.[2] Not work as such, but rational work in a calling, is what God requires. In the Puritan idea of the 'calling' the emphasis is always on this methodical asceticism in the practice of one's calling, not, as in Luther, on contentment with the lot once and for all assigned to one by God.[3] Hence, not only will the question whether anyone can combine several callings be answered with an unconditional 'Yes', provided it is beneficial either for the general good or for one's own[4] and not injurious to anyone else, and provided that it does not lead to unconscientiousness or 'unfaithfulness' in one of the callings so combined. But also it will not be regarded as in any way in itself objectionable to change one's calling, provided it is not done frivolously but in order to take up a calling which will be more pleasing to God,[5] that is, in accordance with the general principle, a more useful one. Above

[1] 'The inconstant man is a stranger in his own house', says also Thomas Adams (*Works of the Puritan Divines*, p. 77).

[2] See especially on this point George Fox's statements in W. and T. Evans, eds., *The Friends' Library* (Philadelphia, 1837), I, p. 130.

[3] It would of course be altogether wrong to look on this turning-point in religious ethics as a mere reflection of the actual economic relationships. The specialisation of occupations had of course gone much further in medieval Italy than in the England of the period under consideration.

[4] For God, as is very often emphasised in the Puritan literature, never commanded man to love his neighbour *more* than himself, but *as* himself. Thus, there is also an obligation to love oneself. For example, if someone knows that he himself uses his possessions more purposefully and so to the greater glory of God than his neighbour could, he is not obliged by his love of his neighbour to give him any of them.

[5] Spener also comes close to this view. But he is still extremely cautious and inclined to be opposed to it even when it is a case of moving from the calling of a merchant, which is morally particularly dangerous, to theology ('*Theologische Bedenken*', III, pp. 435, 443; I, p. 524). The frequent recurrence of answers to precisely this question (about the permissibility of a change of calling) in Spener's naturally well-considered judgment shows, by the way, how distinctly practical in terms of everyday life the various types of interpretation of I Corinthians 7 were.

all, how useful a calling is, and so how pleasing it is to God, depends in the first instance on its moral benefits, secondly on the degree of importance for the community of the goods to be produced in it, and thirdly (and this is naturally the most important from the practical point of view) on its 'profitability' for the individual.[1] For, if the God Whom the Puritan sees at work in all the coincidences of life reveals a chance of profit to one of His own, He has a purpose in so doing. Consequently, the faithful Christian must follow this call, by turning it to good account.[2] 'If God show you a way in which you may lawfully get more than in another way (without wrong to your soul or to any other), if you refuse this, and choose the less gainful way, you cross one of the ends of your calling, and you refuse to be God's steward, and to accept His gifts and use them for Him when He requireth it: you may labour to be rich for God, though not for the flesh and sin'.[3] Riches are only dangerous as a temptation to idle repose and sinful enjoyment of life, and the endeavour to acquire them is only suspect when its purpose is to enable one later to live a life of frivolity and gaiety. When it is engaged in as part of the duties of the calling, however, it is not only morally permissible but positively commanded.[4] The parable of the servant who was rejected

---

[1] Nothing of this kind is to be found in the writings at least of the leading continental Pietists. Spener's attitude to 'profit' vacillates between the Lutheran view, that it has to do with sustenance, and Mercantilist arguments about the utility of commercial prosperity and the like ('*Theologische Bedenken*', III, pp. 330, 332; cf. I, p. 418: the cultivation of tobacco brings money into the country and hence is useful, so not sinful! Cf. also III, pp. 426, 427, 429, 434). He does not fail to point out, however, that, as the example of the Quakers and the Mennonites shows, it is possible to make a profit and remain pious: indeed that specially high profits may – a point we shall return to later – be a direct product of piety and honesty (p. 435).

[2] Such views in Baxter are not a mere reflection of the economic environment in which he lived. On the contrary, his autobiography makes it clear that a decisive element in the success of his home mission was that those tradesmen who lived in Kidderminster were not rich, but only earned enough for 'food and raiment', and that the guild masters had to live no better than their workers, indeed 'from hand to mouth'. 'It is the poor that receive the glad tidings of the Gospel'. Thomas Adams comments on the pursuit of profit, 'He (the knowing man) knows...that money may make a man richer, not better, and thereupon chooseth rather to sleep with a good conscience than a full purse...therefore desires no more wealth than an honest man may bear away' – *but he does want that much* (Thomas Adams, *Works of the Puritan Divines*, LI), and that means that all formally honest means of earning a living are also legitimate.

[3] Thus Baxter, *Christian Directory*, I, Ch. X, Tit. I Dir. 9 (Section 24), p. 378, col. 2. Proverbs 23.4, 'Labour not to be rich' means only 'Riches for our fleshly ends must not ultimately be intended'. Wealth used in the feudal or seigneurial way is what is hateful (cf. the remark in I, p. 380 about 'the debauched part of the gentry'), not wealth as such.

Milton in his first '*Defensio pro populo Anglicano*' puts forward the well-known theory that only the 'middle class' can embody virtue – meaning by 'middle class' the 'bourgeoisie' as opposed to the 'aristocracy', as is shown by the argument that 'luxury' as well as 'distress' may be an obstacle to the exercise of virtue.

[4] This is the decisive point. Once again, the general comment may be made that we are here, of course, concerned, not so much with the intellectual development of theological

because he had not profited from the talent which was entrusted to him seemed to express that idea in explicit terms.[1] To wish to be poor was, as was frequently argued, the same as to wish to be ill:[2] as a form of justification by works, it would be objectionable and detrimental to the glory of God. Finally, begging by anyone fit to work is not only sinful in that it is an instance of sloth, but also, in the Apostle's words, contrary to the love of one's neighbour.[3]

As the teaching of the ascetic significance of a regular calling sheds an ethical aura around the modern specialised expert, so the providential interpretation of the chances of profit does for the business-

ethical theories, as with the morality which had force in the practical life of the believers: in other words, with the practical effect of the religious orientation of the work ethic. Occasionally, at least, it is possible to find discussions in Catholic casuistical literature, especially in Jesuit sources, which for instance on the question of the permissibility of interest, which does not concern us here, have a similar ring to those of many Protestant casuists, which indeed seem to go further than them on the question of what is 'permissible' or 'approvable' (the Puritans have in later times often enough faced the objection that the Jesuit ethics are in principle essentially the same as their own). As the Calvinists often cited Catholic moral theologians – not only Thomas Aquinas, Bernard of Clairvaux, and Bonaventure, but also their own contemporaries – so Catholic casuists frequently took account of heretical ethics (though we shall not go further into this point here). But, quite apart from the decisive fact that the ascetic life was recommended for the laity, the all-important difference even in theory is that these latitudinarian views were in Catholicism the results, not sanctioned by the authority of the Church, of specifically lax ethical theories, repudiated by precisely the most earnest and strictest adherents of the Church, whereas conversely, the Protestant idea of the calling had the effect of leading precisely the most earnest followers of the ascetic life to pursue the life of capitalist acquisition. What in the one case was permissible under certain conditions seemed in the other to be a positive moral good. The fundamental differences between the two ethics, so important in practice, have been finally defined for the modern world, since the time of the Jansenist controversy and the Bull 'Unigenitus'.

[1] 'You may labour in that manner as tendeth most to your success and lawful gain. You are bound to improve all your talents...' Then follows the passage quoted above in the text. A direct parallel is drawn between the pursuit of riches in the Kingdom of God and the pursuit of success in an earthly calling, e.g. in Janeway, 'Heaven upon Earth' (in *Works of the Puritan Divines*, p. 275).

[2] Already in Duke Christoph von Württemberg's Lutheran Confession, which was submitted to the Council of Trent, it was urged against the vow of poverty that, while anyone who is poor in his estate should accept his lot, if he vows to remain so, this is the same as if he vowed to be chronically ill or to have a bad name.

[3] This is to be found in Baxter and e.g. in Duke Christoph's Confession. Cf. further such passages as the following: '...the vagrant rogues whose lives are nothing but an exorbitant course: the main begging...', etc. (Thomas Adams, *Works of the Puritan Divines*, p. 259). Calvin had already strictly prohibited begging and the Dutch synods inveigh against licences and certificates to beg. Whereas the Stuarts, especially Laud's regime under Charles I, had developed the principle of governmental poor relief and provision of work for the unemployed, the Puritan war-cry was 'Giving alms is no charity' (later to be the title of Defoe's well-known work), and towards the end of the seventeenth century there began the system of deterrence, in the form of 'Workhouses' for the unemployed (cf. Leonard, *Early History of English Poor Relief*, Cambridge, 1900, and H. Levy, *Die Grundlagen des ökonomischen Liberalismus in der Geschichte der englischen Volkswirtschaft*, Jena, 1912, pp. 69ff).

man.[1] The aristocratic self-indulgence of the seigneur and the parvenu ostentation of the snob are equally hateful to asceticism. On the other hand, the full radiance of ethical approval falls on the sober bourgeois self-made man:[2] 'God blesseth his trade' is a standard way of referring to those Saints[3] who have successfully followed up the divine dispensation. The whole weight of the Old Testament God, Who rewards His own for their piety precisely in *this* life,[4] was bound to influence in the same direction the Puritan, who, following Baxter's advice, checked his own state of grace by comparing it with the spiritual condition of the Biblical heroes,[5] and in so doing interpreted the statements of the Bible 'as if they were paragraphs in a code of law'.

[1] The president of the Baptist Union of Great Britain and Ireland, G. White, said emphatically in his inaugural address for the assembly in London in 1903 ('Baptist Handbook', 1904, p. 104): 'The best men on the roll of our Puritan churches were men of affairs, who believed that religion should permeate the whole of life.'

[2] This is the characteristic point of contrast with all feudal conceptions. In the feudal view, only the descendants of the political or social parvenu can enjoy the benefits of his success and the line which he founded. (This is characteristically expressed in the Spanish word *hidalgo*, i.e. *hijo d'algo* or *filius de aliquo*, where the *aliquid* (or 'something') is one of the ancestors from whom wealth has been inherited.) However much these differences may be fading today in the rapid transformation and Europeanisation of the American national character, still one occasionally finds there even today the precisely opposite, specifically bourgeois, view which glorifies success in business and acquisition as symptoms of spiritual achievement and which has on the contrary no respect at all for purely inherited wealth. On the other hand, in Europe (as James Bryce has already pointed out in one place) virtually any social position is in effect to be bought for money, provided the man of property has not himself stood behind the counter and carries out the necessary transformation of his property (foundation of trusts, etc.). See the criticism of the honour of lineage, e.g. in Thomas Adams, *Works of the Puritan Divines*, p. 216.

[3] This was so, e.g. already in the case of the founder of the Familist sect, Hendrik Niklaes, who was a merchant. (Barclay, *Inner Life of the Religious Communities of the Commonwealth*, p. 34.)

[4] This is absolutely settled, e.g. for Hoornbeek, since Matthew 5.5 and 1 Timothy 4.8 also made purely earthly promises to the Saints (*Theologia Practica*, 1, p. 193). Everything results from God's providence, but He has a special care for His own: p. 192, '*Super alios autem summa cura et modis singularissimis versatur Dei providentia circa fideles*'. ('Above others, God's providence deals with the faithful with supreme care and in the most singular ways'.) Then follows a discussion about the means of knowing whether a stroke of luck results, not from the '*communis providentia*' (general providence), but from that special provision. Bailey too (*Praxis Pietatis*, p. 191) refers success in one's calling to God's providence. That prosperity is 'often' the reward for godly living is a constantly recurring theme in the writings of the Quakers (see, e.g. a statement of this kind from as late as 1848 in *Selection from the Christian Advices issued by the General Meeting of the Society of Friends in London*, 6th edn, London, 1851, p. 209). We shall return again to the connexion with the Quaker ethic.

[5] As an example of this concern with the patriarchs – which is at the same time characteristic of the Puritan view of life – Thomas Adams' analysis of the quarrel between Jacob and Esau may serve (*Works of the Puritan Divines*, p. 235): 'His (Esau's) folly may be argued from the base estimation of the birthright' (this passage is also important for the development of the idea of the birthright, of which more later), 'that he would so lightly pass from it and on so easy condition as a pottage.' But he was then perfidious in not wanting to recognise the sale as valid on the grounds that he had been cheated. He is

In themselves, indeed, the statements of the Old Testament were not entirely unambiguous. We saw that, linguistically speaking, Luther was the first to use the term 'calling' in the worldly sense in his translation of a passage in Jesus Sirach. The book of Jesus Sirach, however, in spite of the Hellenistic influences at work in it, belongs in its whole atmosphere to the traditionalist sections of the (expanded) Old Testament. It is characteristic that, right up to the present day, this book seems to enjoy a special popularity among the Lutheran peasantry of Germany,[1] just as the fundamentally Lutheran character of the main tendencies in German Pietism used to find expression in the popularity of Jesus Sirach.[2] The Puritans rejected the Apocrypha on the grounds that it was not inspired, in conformity with their strict 'either–or' attitude to the distinction between the divine and the creaturely.[3] This meant that, among the canonical books, the Book of Job had all the greater impact, with its combination of, on the one hand, a sublime glorification of God's absolutely sovereign and totally superhuman majesty – so congenial as it was to Calvinist views – with the sense of certainty which overflows again in the conclusion (as trivial for Calvin as it was important for Puritanism) that God will bless His own also and precisely – and, in the Book of Job, only! – in this life and in material terms.[4] The Oriental quietism which pervades several of the most moving verses of the Psalms and the Book of Proverbs was explained away in the same way as Baxter explained away the traditionalist overtones of the passage in the First Epistle to the Corinthians which was definitive for the concept of the calling. For this reason all the more emphasis was laid on those passages in the Old Testament which extol formal righteousness as the criterion of conduct

indeed a 'cunning hunter, a man of the fields', an irrational barbarian, whereas Jacob 'a plain man, dwelling in tents', represents the 'man of grace'. The feeling of an inner affinity with Judaism, still expressed in Roosevelt's well-known writings, was found by Köhler (*Die Niederl. Ref. Kirche*) to be widespread also among Dutch peasants. On the other hand, however, Puritanism was fully conscious of its opposition to Jewish ethics in its practical dogmatics, as Prynne's pamphlet against the Jews (on the occasion of Cromwell's plan for toleration) clearly shows. See below, Note 4 on p. 152, end.

[1] *Zur bäuerlichen Glaubens- und Sittenlehre.* By a Thuringian parson (2nd edn; Gotha, 1890), p. 16. The peasants here depicted are characteristic products of Lutheran churchmanship. I have again and again written the word 'Lutheran' in the margin, where the esteemed author has imagined he is discussing a general 'peasant' form of religion.

[2] Cf. e.g. the reference in Ritschl, *Pietismus*, II, p. 158. Spener likewise bases his objections to change of occupation and the pursuit of profit in part on remarks of Jesus Sirach, '*Theologische Bedenken*', III, p. 426.

[3] Admittedly, Bailey, for instance, recommends reading them nevertheless, and there are quotations from the Apocrypha to be found here and there, but naturally not often. I do not remember (though this may be just accidental) any such from Jesus Sirach.

[4] Where outward success is the lot of those who are clearly damned, the Calvinist, such as Hoornbeek, consoles himself, in accordance with the 'theory of hardening of the heart', with the certainty that God allows them to prosper in order to harden their hearts and so condemn them to all the more certain perdition.

which is pleasing to God. The theory that the Mosaic Law had only lost its validity under the new covenant to the extent that it contained ceremonial or historically limited prescriptions for the Jewish people, but that otherwise it was an expression of Natural Law and so had always had and still retained its validity,[1] made it possible, on the one hand, to eliminate prescriptions which were simply inappropriate to modern life, while giving free rein to the considerable reinforcement of that spirit of self-righteous and sober legalism so characteristic of the inner-worldly asceticism of this kind of Protestantism, by the many related features of Old Testament morality.[2]

Thus, if several contemporaries, like a number of more recent writers, dubbed the basic ethical temper of English Puritanism in particular 'English Hebraism',[3] this was, rightly understood, a perfectly apt description. It is not, however, the Palestinian Judaism of the time when the Old Testament writings were emerging which should come to mind, but the Judaism which gradually evolved under the influence of many centuries of formalistic education in the Law and the Talmud, and even then one must be extremely cautious about drawing parallels. The temper of ancient Judaism, which was on the whole inclined to the tolerant appreciation of life as such, was very different from the specific character of Puritanism. Equally different – and this should not be overlooked – were the economic ethics of medieval and modern Judaism in those respects which were decisive for the place which both hold in the development of the capitalist ethos. Judaism was on the side of the politically or speculatively orientated 'adventurist capitalism': its ethos was, in a word, that of pariah capitalism. Puritanism, on the other hand, was the vehicle for the ethos of the rational bourgeois enterprise and the rational organisation of labour. It took from the Jewish ethos only what fitted into this framework.

It would be impossible, within the limits of this sketch, to analyse the characterological consequences of this permeation of life by Old Testament standards, though this would be an exciting task, which has not, however, as yet been undertaken even for Judaism itself.[4] Apart

---

[1] We shall not discuss this point in any greater detail in this connexion. The point of interest here is only the formalistic character of 'righteousness'. On the significance of the Old Testament ethic for Natural Law, there is much in Troeltsch's *Soziallehren.*

[2] The ethical standards of the Scriptures are binding, according to Baxter (*Christian Directory*, III, pp. 173f), to the extent that (i) they are merely a 'transcript' of the 'Law of Nature' or (ii) they bear the 'express character of universality and perpetuity'.

[3] For example, Dowden (with reference to Bunyan), *Puritan and Anglican*, p. 39.

[4] There is a more detailed discussion of this in my essays on the 'Economic Ethics of the World Religions'. It is impossible here to analyse the enormous influence exerted on the characterological development of Judaism, on its rationalistic opposition to all cultivation of the senses, by, for instance, the second commandment in particular ('Thou shalt not make unto thee any graven image'). Nevertheless, it is perhaps worth mentioning as

from the connexions already pointed out, one feature of the general mental attitude of the Puritan which above all deserves consideration is that in him there was a spectacular rebirth of the belief that one belonged to God's chosen people.[1] Even the gentle Baxter thanks God for the fact that He has allowed him to be born in England and in the true Church and not anywhere else: and in the same way this gratitude for the

characteristic a remark made to me by one of the leaders of the 'Educational Alliance' in the United States. This is an organisation which with astonishing success and enormous resources attempts the Americanisation of Jewish immigrants, and he told me that the primary aim of the process of assimilation, to achieve which all kinds of artistic and social instruction are used, is 'emancipation from the second commandment'.

In Puritanism there corresponds to the Israelite prohibition of all anthropomorphisation of God the prohibition of all idolatry of the creature, which is somewhat different, but related in its effects. As for Talmudic Judaism, the principal features of Puritan morality are certainly very similar to it. When, for instance, in the Talmud (in Wünsche, *Babyl. Talmud*, II, p. 34) the injunction is found that it is better and more richly rewarded by God when one does something good from a sense of duty than when one does a good deed which one is not obliged to do by the Law – in other words, the loveless fulfilment of duty is ethically higher than emotional philanthropy – the Puritan ethic would accept that in all essentials, just as Kant was later to come close to it, influenced by his Scottish ancestry and his strictly pietistic upbringing. (Several of his formulations are directly derived from the ideas of ascetic Protestantism, though this is a point we cannot discuss here.) Nevertheless, the Talmudic ethic is steeped in Oriental traditionalism: 'Rabbi Tanchum ben Chanilai said, "Let man never alter a custom"' (*Gemara to Mishna*, VII, 1 Fol. 86b, No. 93 in Wünsche: the topic is the diet of day-labourers), and this obligation fails to apply only in relation to strangers.

However, the Puritan conception of 'lawfulness' as a validation, as opposed to the Jewish view of it as the mere fulfilment of commandments, obviously gave a much stronger incentive to positive activity. The idea that success is a sign of God's blessing is of course not unknown in Judaism. But the radically different religious and ethical meaning which it took on in consequence of the double ethical standard, internal and external, in Judaism, ruled out any similarity in outcome precisely in this decisive respect. In relation to 'strangers', actions were permitted which were forbidden in relation to 'brothers'. For this reason alone, it was impossible for success in the area of what was in this way not 'commanded' but only 'permitted' to be a criterion of religious validation and an incentive to a methodical ordering of one's life in the sense it was for the Puritan. On this whole problem, whose treatment by Sombart in his book *Die Juden und das Wirtschaft* is in many ways unsatisfactory, see the essays cited above. Detailed discussion would be out of place here. The Jewish ethic, strange as it may appear at first sight, remained markedly traditionalist. Equally, we cannot here go into the enormous shift in inner attitudes to the world which resulted from the Christian interpretation of the concepts of 'grace' and 'salvation', which always in a unique way concealed within itself the seeds of new possibilities of development. On Old Testament 'legalism', cf. also, e.g. Ritschl, *Rechtfertigung und Versöhnung*, II, p. 265.

To the English Puritans, the Jews of their own time represented the type of capitalism which they themselves found abhorrent – orientated as it was towards war, state contracts, state monopolies, speculative enterprises and princely projects of building and finance. In fact, the contrast can be formulated in general terms, with the always unavoidable reservations, in this way: Jewish capitalism was speculative pariah capitalism; Puritan capitalism was the bourgeois organisation of labour.

[1] The truth of Holy Scripture follows for Baxter ultimately from the 'wonderful difference of the godly and ungodly', the absolute difference between the 'renewed man' and others, and God's obviously special provision for the spiritual welfare of His own (which may, of course, be manifested in the form of 'trials') – *Christian Directory*, I, p. 165, Col. 2, margin.

freedom from sin achieved for the individual by God's grace permeated the attitude to life[1] of the Puritan bourgeoisie and gave rise to that formalistically correct hardness of character typical of the representatives of that heroic epoch of capitalism.

We shall now seek to elucidate the special points at which the Puritan conception of the calling and the requirement of asceticism in one's conduct of life were bound to have a direct influence on the development of the capitalist mode of life. As we saw, asceticism turns with full force against one thing above all – the relaxed enjoyment of life and the pleasures which it has to offer. This feature is well expressed in its most characteristic form in the controversy over the 'Book of Sports',[2] which James I and Charles I sought to enforce by law with the avowed aim of attacking Puritanism, and which Charles I commanded to be read aloud from all pulpits. When the Puritans fought like madmen against the King's decree legally permitting certain traditional popular amusements on Sundays outside the times of church services, it was not only the disturbance of the Sabbath peace which enraged them, but the whole deliberate deviation from the ordered way of life of the Saints. And when the King threatened to impose severe penalties on every attack on the legality of those sports, his purpose was precisely to break that asceticism, which was dangerous to the state because it was anti-authoritarian. The monarchic and feudal society protected those who wanted to amuse themselves against the emergent bourgeois morality and the ascetic conventicle, with its hostile attitude to authority, just as today capitalist society protects those who want to work against the class morality of the workers and the trade union, with its hostile attitude to authority. The Puritans defended against this their most important characteristic, the principle of the ascetic conduct of life. For, apart from this, the antipathy of the Puritans, even of the Quakers, for sport was not a pure matter of principle. They required only that sport should serve a rational

---

[1] To get some sense of this, one has only to read the tortuous attempts made by Bunyan (who after all comes close at times to the mood of Luther's *Freedom of a Christian* – as in 'Of the Law and a Christian', *Works of the Puritan Divines*, p. 254) to come to terms with the parable of the Pharisee and the Publican (see his sermon 'The Pharisee and the Publican', pp. 100f). Why is the Pharisee rejected? He does not truly keep God's commandments: he is obviously a sectarian, concerned only with external trivialities and ceremonies (p. 107); above all, however, he ascribes merit to himself and yet, 'as the Quakers do', thanks God for his virtue, misusing the name of God; he sinfully relies on the merits of his own virtue (p. 126) and in so doing implicitly denies God's election to grace (pp. 139f). His prayer is thus idolatry of the creature and that is what is sinful in it. On the other hand, the Publican, as the sincerity of his confession shows, is inwardly born again, for, as it is expressed, in a characteristic Puritan weakening of the Lutheran idea of conviction of sin, 'to a right and sincere conviction of sin there must be a conviction of the probability of mercy' (p. 209).

[2] Reprinted in Gardiner's *Constitutional Documents*. This struggle against anti-authoritarian asceticism may be compared with Louis XIV's persecution of Port-Royal and the Jansenists.

purpose, the recreation necessary to enable one to be physically capable of work. As a means of pure relaxed enjoyment for unruly instincts, on the other hand, it was suspect to the Puritan; and to the extent that it became a straightforward means of pleasure or aroused competitive jealousy, raw instinct or the irrational desire to gamble, it was obviously utterly objectionable. Instinctive enjoyment of life, which attracts one away from work at one's calling as much as from religious devotion, was equally the enemy of rational asceticism, whether it took the form of 'aristocratic' sport or of the ordinary man's visits to dance halls or taverns.[1]

The attitude to those cultural goods which do not have a directly religious value is correspondingly distrustful, and often hostile. It is not as if a dismal, philistine contempt for culture was any part of the Puritan ideal. Exactly the opposite is true, at least in the case of science – with the exception of the abhorred Scholasticism. The greatest figures of the Puritan movement, moreover, are steeped in the culture of the Renaissance: the sermons of the Presbyterian wing of the movement drip with classicisms,[2] and even those of the Radicals do not disdain that kind of learning in theological polemics, despite the fact that they certainly found it a cause for scandal. Never, perhaps, has any country so abounded in 'graduates' as did New England in the first generation of its existence. The satires of their opponents, such as Butler's 'Hudibras', were directed precisely against the book-learning and sophisticated dialectical skills of the Puritans; and this fits in partly with their religious evaluation of knowledge, which follows from their attitude to the Catholic conception of 'implicit faith'.

Quite a different situation confronts one as soon as one enters the realm of non-scientific literature[3] and even more when one considers the visual

---

[1] Calvin's attitude was in this regard essentially more lenient, at least as far as the more refined aristocratic forms of enjoyment were concerned. The Bible alone determines the limits; anyone who keeps to it and preserves a good conscience is not required anxiously to suspect every impulse in himself to enjoy life. The relevant statements on this point in Chapter x of the *Institution of the Christian Religion* (e.g. *nec fugere ea quoque possumus quae videntur oblectationi magis quam necessitati inservire*) ('and we cannot avoid those things which seem to serve pleasure rather than necessity') could in themselves have opened the door to very lax practices. Along with the increasing anxiety about the certainty of salvation among later generations, another important fact in this respect (which we shall evaluate in another place) is that in the area of the 'church militant' it was the petty bourgeoisie who were responsible for the ethical development of Calvinism.

[2] Thomas Adams (*Works of the Puritan Divines*, p. 3), for example, begins a sermon on 'the three divine sisters' ('But the greatest of these is charity') with the allusion that even Paris gave the apple to Aphrodite!

[3] Novels and the like are 'wastetimes' and should therefore not be read (Baxter, *Christian Directory*, 1, p. 51, Col. 2). The aridity of lyric poetry and folk song, not only of drama, after the Elizabethan period in England is well known. In the visual arts, Puritanism perhaps did not find all that much to suppress. There is, however, a striking decline of musical talent, which seems to have been very good (the part played by England in the

arts. Here, it must be admitted, asceticism lay like a frost on the life of Merry England. And it was not only the secular festivals which were affected by it. The passionate hatred of the Puritan for everything which smelt of 'superstition', for everything reminiscent of magical or ritual means of grace, pursued the Christian festival of Christmas as much as it did the Maypole[1] or the easy-going religious use of art. The fact that there was still room in Holland for the development of a great tradition of often robustly realistic art[2] shows merely how little could be achieved in this direction by the attempt in that country at an authoritarian regulation of morals on its own against the influence of the Court and the Regents (a class of *rentiers*). It also shows, however, the joy in life of the newly rich petty bourgeois, after the brief domination of the Calvinist theocracy had settled down into a more prosaic state church and Calvinism had thus perceptibly lost its power of propaganda in the cause of asceticism.[3]

history of music was not insignificant) until it reached that nadir which we observe among the Anglo-Saxon nations later, and still today, in that regard. Apart from the Negro churches, and except for the professional singers now engaged by the churches as 'attractions' (Trinity Church, Boston, engaged such a singer in 1904 at a fee of $8,000 a year), all that is usually to be heard in America is a kind of caterwauling, unbearable to German ears, which goes by the name of 'community singing'. (To some extent, a similar development has taken place also in Holland.)

[1] It was just the same in Holland, as is clear from the proceedings of the synods. (See the resolution on the Maypole in the Reitsma Collection, VI, 78.139 and *passim*).

[2] It is plausible to suppose that the 'Renaissance of the Old Testament' and the pietistic preoccupation with certain Christian feelings of hostility to beauty, ultimately derived from Deutero-Isaiah and Psalm 22, must have contributed in the arts to the greater possibility of using ugliness as the subject-matter of art, and that the Puritan rejection of all idolatry of the creature must also have played some part in this. But it is still not possible to be certain about all the details. In the Roman Church, quite different, demagogic, motives produced outwardly similar phenomena – but with totally different artistic results. Anyone who stands before Rembrandt's 'Saul and David' in the Maurit-shuis believes himself to be directly experiencing the powerful impact of Puritan feeling. The brilliant analysis of Dutch cultural influences in Carl Neumann's *Rembrandt* probably indicates the extent of what we can know at present about how far positively beneficial artistic effects can be attributed to ascetic Protestantism.

[3] The relatively less extensive penetration of the Calvinist ethic into practical life in Holland, the weakening of the ascetic spirit there, which began as early as the beginning of the seventeenth century (the English Congregationalists who fled to Holland in 1608 found the inadequate observance of the Sabbath in Holland shocking) but was complete by the time of the Stadtholder Friedrich Heinrich, and the smaller power of expansion of Dutch Puritanism generally were caused by a variety of factors which it would be impossible to go into here. They lay in part in the political system, which was a federation of particularistic towns and districts, and in the much less warlike attitude: the War of Independence was fought in the main with the money of Amsterdam and with mercenaries; English preachers used to illustrate the story of the Tower of Babel by referring to the Dutch army. In this way the seriousness of the religious struggle to a large extent affected others, but at the same time their chance of participating in political power was thrown away. By contrast, Cromwell's army, though in part impressed, felt itself to be a citizen army. Admittedly, it was all the more characteristic that it was just this army which included in its programme the abolition of the duty of bearing arms, on the grounds that it was permissible to fight to the greater glory of God in a cause

The theatre was abhorrent to the Puritans,[1] and with the rigorous exclusion of eroticism and nudity from the domain of what was possible, the more radical approach, in literature as in art, could not continue to exist. The concepts of 'idle talk', 'superfluities',[2] 'vain ostentation', all of which referred to forms of behaviour which were irrational and purposeless, and so not ascetic, and serving the glory of man rather than God, were ready to hand to give decisive support to sober purposiveness against every kind of use of artistic motifs. Finally, this applied also to all forms of direct adornment of the person, as, for example, in styles

which could in conscience be known to be right, but not for the whims of princes. The constitution of the English army, which to traditional German ways of thinking is 'immoral', resulted, in its historical origins, from very 'moral' motives and was demanded by soldiers who had never been defeated: only after the Restoration was it used to further the interests of the Crown. The Dutch *schutterijen*, who were the embodiments of Calvinism in the period of the great war, can be seen in Hals' pictures, just half a generation after the Synod of Dordrecht, behaving in a far from 'ascetic' way. The protests from the synods about their manner of life become more and more frequent. The Dutch concept of *Deftigkeit* ('soundness') is a mixture of rational bourgeois 'respectability' and patrician consciousness of status. The gradation of church pews by classes in Dutch churches shows the aristocratic character of this kind of church life even today. The continuation of the town economy retarded industry. It was only through refugees that it received a fresh impetus, and even then it only lasted for a short time in each case. In Holland too, however, the inner-worldly asceticism of Calvinism and Pietism had its effect, and in precisely the same direction as elsewhere. This was true also in the sense of that 'ascetic compulsion to save' which is likewise to be discussed shortly, as Groen van Prinsterer testifies in the passage cited in Note 3 on p. 162 below. The almost complete lack of good literature in Calvinist Holland is naturally no accident. (See on Holland, e.g. Busken-Huët, *Het land van Rembrandt*, which has also been published in German translation by von der Ropp.) The significance of Dutch religion as 'the ascetic compulsion to save' is clearly evident even in the eighteenth century, for example in Albertus Haller's sketches. For the special characteristics of Dutch artistic judgment and its motives compare, for example, Constantine Huyghens' autobiographical sketches (written in 1629–31) in *Oud Holland*, 1891. (Groen van Prinsterer's work already cited, *La Hollande et l'influence de Calvin* (1864) has nothing decisive to say about our problems.) The colony of New Holland in America was socially a half-feudal domination by 'patrons', that is, merchants who advanced capital, and in contrast with New England it was difficult to induce the 'little man' to emigrate there.

[1] It may be recalled that the Puritan town council closed the theatre in Stratford-on-Avon even in Shakespeare's lifetime, indeed while he was spending the last years of his life there. (Shakespeare's hatred and contempt for the Puritans come out at every opportunity.) As late as 1777, the town of Birmingham refused to allow a theatre because it encouraged 'idleness' and so was detrimental to trade. (See Ashley, *Birmingham Industry and Commerce*, 1913, pp. 7–8.)

[2] The decisive point here too is that for the Puritans it was simply a matter of 'either–or' – either the will of God or the vanity of His creatures. For this reason there could be nothing 'indifferent' for them. As already pointed out, Calvin's own attitude was different in this regard: what one eats, what clothes one wears and so forth are matters of indifference, as long as they do not have the consequence of enslaving the soul to the power of desire. Freedom from the 'world' should be expressed, as with the Jesuits, in indifference, that is, in undiscriminating, dispassionate use of those goods which the earth offers (pp. 409ff of the original edition of the *Institution of the Christian Religion*). This is an attitude which obviously comes closer in effect to the Lutheran than the stricter views of his later followers.

of clothing.[1] The powerful tendency towards uniformity in styles of life which is nowadays supported by the capitalist interest in the 'standardisation' of production[2] had its intellectual origin in the rejection of the 'idolatry of the creature'.[3] Certainly, it should not be forgotten in all this that Puritanism contained within itself a world of contradictions, that the instinctive feeling for what is timelessly great in art was certainly stronger among its leaders than in the milieu of the Cavaliers,[4] and that a unique genius like Rembrandt, however far his mode of life may have fallen short of finding complete favour in the eyes of the Puritan God, was certainly greatly influenced in the direction which his creative activity took by his sectarian environment.[5] But that alters nothing in the general picture, to the extent that the powerfully intensified sense of personality, which accompanied and which was, indeed, partly a result of the further development of the Puritan atmosphere, had its most beneficial effects in literature, and even there not until later generations.

[1] Quaker practice in this respect is well known. But already at the beginning of the seventeenth century the exiled congregations in Amsterdam were shaken for a whole decade by the most severe storms over the fashionable hats and dresses of a pastor's wife. (There is an amusing account of this in Dexter's *Congregationalism of the Last Three Hundred Years*.) Sanford (*Studies and Reflections of the Great Rebellion*) has already pointed out that present-day male hair-styles are those of the much-derided 'Roundheads' and that the equally derided style of male clothing of the Puritans is essentially the same, at any rate in underlying principle, as that of the present day.

[2] On this point see again Veblen's book (already cited), *The Theory of Business Enterprise*.

[3] This is an attitude to which we are constantly coming back. It explains statements like the following: 'Every penny, which is paid upon yourselves and children and friends must be done as by God's own appointment and to serve and please Him. Watch narrowly, or else that thievish carnal self will leave God nothing' (Baxter, *op. cit.*, I, p. 108, bottom right). That is the decisive point: anything used for personal purposes is taken away from the service of God's glory.

[4] It is right that we should often be reminded, as we are by Dowden (*Puritan and Anglican*), that, for instance, Cromwell saved Raphael's cartoons and Mantegna's 'Triumph of Caesar' from destruction, while Charles II tried to sell them. As is well known, Restoration society was extremely cool towards English national literature, or even actually rejected it. In courts everywhere the influence of Versailles was indeed all-powerful.

To analyse in detail the influence exercised on the minds of the highest type of Puritans and those who passed through their schools by this turning away from the unreflecting enjoyment of everyday life would be a task impossible to complete, at any rate within the limits of the present essay. Washington Irving (*Bracebridge Hall*) formulates in the customary English terminology the effect which it had: 'It [political freedom, in his opinion: we should rather say, Puritanism] evinces less play of the fancy, but more power of imagination'. It is only necessary to think of the position of the Scots in science, literature, technical invention, even in business life in England, to feel that this comment, though somewhat narrow in its formulation, is on the right lines.

We shall not speak here of its significance for the development of technology and the empirical sciences. The relationship is evident in all aspects of everyday life. For the Quakers, for instance, the following 'recreations' are permissible (according to Barclay): visiting friends, reading works of history, mathematical and physical experiments, gardening, conversation about business matters and other events in the world and so on. The reason is the one explained earlier.

[5] Brilliantly analysed in Carl Neumann's *Rembrandt*, which should in general be read in conjunction with the above remarks.

Without being able to enter into a more detailed discussion here of the influence of Puritanism in all these directions, we should remember only that there was always at least one characteristic limit to the toleration of delight in the kind of cultural goods which are valued only for the sake of aesthetic or sporting pleasure: that was, that they should not cost anything. Man is but the steward of the goods allotted to him by God's grace, and, like the servant in the Bible, he has to give an account of every penny entrusted to him:[1] it is at the very least questionable, therefore, to spend any of his money for a purpose which serves, not God's grace, but his own pleasure.[2] Who is there who keeps his eyes open who has not encountered people who think in this way even in the present day?[3] The thought that man has obligations towards the possessions entrusted to him, to which he subordinates himself either as obedient steward or actually as a 'machine for acquisition', lays its chilly hand on life. The greater the possessions become, the sterner becomes – provided the ascetic attitude to life can stand the test – the sense of responsibility for them, the feeling that one must preserve them undiminished for God's glory and increase them by unceasing labour. The genesis of this way of life, too, like so many elements of the modern capitalist spirit, reaches back in its individual parts to the Middle Ages;[4] but its first coherent ethical foundations are to be found in the ethic of ascetic Protestantism. Its importance for the development of capitalism is clear to see.[5]

[1] Thus Baxter in the passage cited earlier, I, p. 108 bottom.

[2] Compare for example the well-known picture of Colonel Hutchinson in his widow's biography (often quoted, e.g. by Sanford, *Studies and Reflections of the Great Rebellion*, p. 57). After an account of all his chivalrous virtues and his natural tendency towards an unruffled enjoyment of life, it continues: 'He was wonderfully neat, cleanly and genteel in his habit, and had a very good fancy in it; but he left off very early the wearing of anything that was costly...' The ideal Puritan woman depicted in Baxter's funeral oration over Mary Hammer (*Works of the Puritan Divines*, p. 533) is very similar: generous and cultivated, but economical with two things, time and expenditure on 'pomp' and pleasure.

[3] Among many examples, I remember in particular one industrialist, unusually successful in his business life and in his later years very well-to-do, who, when his doctor recommended him to take a few oysters every day for the treatment of a persistent digestive weakness, could only be persuaded to do so with the greatest difficulty. The considerable endowments which he made, during his lifetime, for charitable purposes and his general open-handedness showed, on the other hand, that this was merely a matter of residual 'ascetic' feelings, according to which personal enjoyment of wealth is morally dangerous, and had nothing in common with any form of 'meanness'.

[4] The separation of workplace, office and 'business' in general from private residence, of firm from name and of business capital from private wealth, together with the tendency to make the 'business' into a 'mystical entity' (initially, at least, the corporate wealth), all lay in this direction. On this point, see my *Zur Geschichte der Handelsgesellschaften im Mittelalter*.

[5] In some passages in the first edition of his *Kapitalismus*, Sombart has already rightly alluded to this characteristic phenomenon. However, it should be noted that capital accumulation may stem from two very different psychological sources. One can be found at work far back into the mists of antiquity and is expressed in the form of bequests,

We might summarise what has been said so far by saying that inner-worldly Protestant asceticism used all its power against the relaxed enjoyment of possessions: it set limits to consumption, especially luxury consumption. On the other hand, it had the psychological effect of liberating the acquisition of goods from the restrictions of the tradition-alist ethic: it burst the shackles confining the profit-motive, in that not only did it make it lawful, it even (in the sense described) looked upon it directly as the will of God. The struggle against fleshly lust and the fondness for external goods was, as not only the Puritans but also the great apologist for Quakerism, Barclay, expressly state, not a struggle against rational acquisition, but against the irrational use of possessions. This was, however, above all a matter of the value placed on the luxurious forms of outward display so dear to feudal sensibility, which were to be condemned as 'idolatry of the creature',[1] as opposed to the divinely willed rational and utilitarian use of possessions to serve the ends of life for the individual and the community. It was not mortification of the flesh[2] which Puritanism wished to impose on the rich man, but the use of his possessions for necessary and practically useful purposes. The concept of 'comfort' characteristically encompasses the range of ethically per-missible purposes for which possessions might be used, and it is of course no accident that the development of the style of life associated with that concept is to be observed at its earliest and clearest precisely among the most consistent representatives of this whole view of life, the Quakers. Against the tinsel and show of Cavalier pomp, which, resting as it does on an unsound economic basis, prefers shabby elegance to sober

family estates, trusts and so on as well as, or rather much more purely and clearly than, in the urge to die sometime encumbered with a great weight of material possessions and above all to secure the continued existence of the 'business', albeit by damaging the personal interests of the majority of one's heirs. In these cases, there is not only a wish to prolong one's life (in imagination at least) beyond the grave in one's own creations, but also a desire to uphold the splendour of the family, that is, a form of vanity which, so to speak, applies to the extended personality of the donor: at all events, it is a question of basically egocentric goals. It is quite different in the case of the 'bourgeois' motive with which we have to do here: there, the principle of asceticism, 'Thou shalt deny thyself', is given a positive, capitalist turn, 'Thou shalt acquire', and confronts us, plain and unvarnished in its irrationality, as a kind of categorical imperative. God's glory and the individual's duty, not human vanity, are here, for the Puritans, the only motive; and today, the only motive is duty to one's 'calling'. Anyone who enjoys illustrating ideas by their extreme consequences should remember the theory of certain American millionaires, that the millions one has acquired should not be left to one's children, so that they should not be deprived of the moral benefits of having to work and get rich themselves: today that is admittedly a purely 'theoretical' fancy.

[1] It must be stressed again and again that this is the ultimately decisive religious motive, together with the purely ascetic idea of mortifying the flesh: this is particularly obvious in the case of the Quakers.

[2] Baxter (*Saints' Everlasting Rest*, 12) rejects this, on much the same grounds as were commonly given by the Jesuits: the body should be provided with its needs, or else one will become its slave.

simplicity, they set as their ideal the neat and solid comfort of the bourgeois 'home'.[1]

On the side of the production of private economic wealth, asceticism attacked with equal force both dishonesty and purely impulsive greed: for it was the latter that the Puritans rejected under the name of 'covetousness', 'Mammonism' and so forth – the pursuit of riches for no purpose beyond that of being rich. For possessions were in themselves a source of temptation. In this regard, however, asceticism was a force which 'always wills the good and always creates evil' – by which I mean 'evil' in its own sense, of possessions and the temptations they offer. For not only did it, like the Old Testament and in perfect parallel with its ethical evaluation of 'good works', regard the pursuit of riches as an end in itself as supremely reprehensible, but the achievement of wealth as the fruit of work in a calling as an expression of God's blessing. But also, and still more important, the religious valuation of unceasing, constant, systematic, worldly labour in a calling as simply the highest form of asceticism and at the same time the surest and most visible proof of regeneration and genuineness of faith must certainly have been the most powerful lever imaginable for the expansion of that conception of life which we have here referred to as the 'spirit' of capitalism.[2] And if we

[1] This ideal clearly existed in Quakerism in particular, even in the earliest period of its development, as has been shown in important respects by Weingarten in his '*Englische Revolutionskirchen*'. Barclay's detailed discussions (*The Apology for the True Christian Divinity*, pp. 519ff and 533) also illustrate this very clearly. What is to be avoided is, first, creaturely vanity, and so all forms of ostentation, finery and use of things which have no practical purpose or are valued only for their rarity (that is, out of vanity); secondly, unconscientious use of wealth, as in expenditure on less necessary requirements which is disproportionate in relation to the necessary requirements of life and provision for the future: one might say that the Quaker was thus a walking 'law of marginal utility'. 'Moderate use of the creature' is perfectly legitimate, but, in particular, attention might be paid to the quality and solidity of materials and so forth, insofar as this did not lead to 'vanity'. On all this, cf. *Morgenblatt für gebildete Leser*, 1846, No. 216ff. (For comfort and solidity of materials among the Quakers in particular, cf. Schneckenburger, *Vorlesungen*, pp. 96f.)

[2] It has already been stated above that we shall not consider here the question of the class determinants of religious movements (on this, see my essays on the 'Economic Ethics of the World Religions'). But in order to see that, for instance, Baxter, whom we have used as our principal example, did not see the world through the spectacles of the 'bourgeoisie' of his time, it is sufficient to bear in mind that, even for him, the learned callings were followed in the order of pleasingness to God first by the husbandman, then by mariners, clothiers, booksellers, tailors, etc. in a colourful throng. Moreover, the 'mariners' who are thus characteristically mentioned are perhaps thought of at least as much as fishermen as sailors. In this respect, several of the statements in the Talmud express a different attitude. Cf., e.g. in Wünsche, '*Babyl. Talmud*', II[1], pp. 20, 21, the admittedly not unchallenged statements of Rabbi Eleasar, all to the effect that commerce is better than agriculture. (An intermediate view in II[2], p. 68 on the prudent investment of capital: 1/3 in land, 1/3 in goods, 1/3 as ready money.)

For the sake of those whose conscience cannot be appeased without finding economic ('materialist', as they are unfortunately still called) explanations, it may be remarked here that I consider the influence of economic development on the destiny of systems of

put together the limitation of consumption referred to earlier and this breaking of the shackles on acquisitiveness, then the outward result is obvious: capital accumulation resulting from an ascetic compulsion to save.[1] The restrictions imposed on the consumption of what was acquired were bound to have a beneficial effect on its productive use as investment capital.

The exact extent of this effect naturally cannot be mathematically determined. In New England, the connexion was so palpable that it had already not escaped the notice of such an excellent historian as Doyle.[2] But in Holland, too, which was only really dominated by strict Calvinism for seven years, the greater simplicity of life which prevailed in the religiously more earnest circles led, when combined with enormous wealth, to an immoderate passion for capital accumulation.[3] It is further obvious that the tendency which has always existed, and is still operative amongst us today, to 'ennoble' bourgeois wealth must have been considerably restricted by the antipathy of Puritanism towards feudal forms of life. English mercantilist writers of the seventeenth century attributed

religious ideas to be very important, and that I shall later attempt to examine the way in which, in this case, the processes of mutual adaptation and the general relationships between the two came to be what they were. But the content of those religious ideas can by no means be deduced from the 'economic' influences: they are themselves – let us be quite firm about this – the most powerful formative elements of 'national character', they follow their own laws and have compelling power purely in their own right. And furthermore, the most important differences, those between Lutheranism and Calvinism, are primarily the result of *political* causes, to the extent that any extra-religious factors have any part to play.

[1] This is what Eduard Bernstein is thinking of when he says in his essay in volume I of the *History of Socialism* (p. 681 and p. 625): 'Asceticism is a bourgeois virtue'. His discussion in this work was the first to point out these important connexions in general. The connexion is, however, much more far-reaching than he supposes. For what was central was not the mere accumulation of capital, but the ascetic rationalisation of the whole of working life.

For the American colonies, Doyle has already clearly emphasised the contrast between the Puritan North, where, as a result of the 'ascetic compulsion to save', there was always capital available for investment, and the situation in the South.

[2] Doyle, *The English in America*, II, Ch. I. The existence of iron-working companies (1643), cloth-weaving for the market (1659), and also the flourishing condition of handicrafts in New England in the first generation after the founding of the colony are, from a purely economic point of view, anachronisms. They contrast strikingly, not only with the situation in the South, but also with the non-Calvinist system in Rhode Island, where complete freedom of conscience was enjoyed, and where, despite the excellent harbour, the report of the Governor and Council could still say in 1686, 'The great obstruction concerning trade is the want of merchants and men of considerable Estates amongst us' (Arnold, *History of the State of Rhode Island*, I, p. 490). It can hardly be doubted in fact that some part was played in this by the pressure towards constant re-investment of saved capital exerted by the Puritan limitation of consumption. Some part was also played by church discipline, though we shall not go further into that here.

[3] That these circles in the Netherlands admittedly rapidly declined is shown by Busken-Huët's discussion (*Het land van Rembrandt*, II, Ch. III and IV). For all that, Groen van Prinsterer (*Handb. d. Gesch. v. h. V.*, 3rd edn, Section 303, Note to p. 254) says: '*De Nederlanders verkoopen veel en verbruiken wenig*', even in the period after the Peace of Westphalia.

the greater power of capital in Holland as compared with England to the fact that, in that country, newly acquired wealth did not, as in England, seek ennoblement in the normal course of events through investment in land and (for it was this, and not just the purchase of land in itself, which was at issue) through a change to feudal habits of life, in which it would be withdrawn from capitalist use.[1] Further, the esteem in which the Puritans held agriculture, as a specially important type of industry which was also especially conducive to piety, did not apply (in Baxter for instance) to the big landowner, but to the yeoman and the farmer; and in the eighteenth century, it applied not to the country squire but to the 'rational' farmer.[2] A constant theme in English society ever since the seventeenth century has been the quarrel between the 'squirearchy', who stand for the traditions of 'Merry England', and the Puritan circles, which vary considerably in their social strength.[3] Both traits, that of an uninhibited naive joy in life and that of a severely controlled and reserved self-restraint and subjection to conventional ethical standards, are even today juxtaposed in the portrait of the English 'national character'.[4] An equally persistent theme in the earliest history of North American colonisation is the sharp contrast between the 'adventurers', who ran plantations with the labour of indentured servants and aspired to the life of a seigneur, and the specifically bourgeois attitudes of the Puritans.[5]

[1] For England, it was recommended by, for example, a petition submitted by an aristocratic Royalist after Charles II's entry into London (quoted by Ranke, '*Englische Geschichte*', IV, p. 197) that it should be forbidden by law to acquire landed estates with bourgeois capital, so that such capital would be forced to be applied only to trade.
    The 'Regents' in Holland distinguished themselves as an 'Estate' from the bourgeois patriciate of the towns by buying up the old knightly estates. (See on this point the complaint from the year 1652, cited in Fruin, *Tien jaren uit den tachtigjaren oorlog*, that the Regents were now *rentiers* and no longer merchants.) Admittedly, these circles were never inwardly or seriously Calvinist in their attitudes. And the notorious pursuit of nobility and titles which was widespread among the Dutch bourgeoisie in the second half of the seventeenth century shows in itself that one must be cautious, at least in relation to this period, about accepting that contrast between the English and the Dutch situations. The superior strength of inherited wealth here broke through the ascetic spirit.
[2] The extensive purchase of English landed estates by bourgeois capital was followed by the great age of English agriculture.
[3] Even as late as the present century, Anglican landlords have often refused to accept Nonconformists as tenants. (At present, both church parties are approximately equal in numbers, but in the past the Nonconformists were always the minority.)
[4] H. Levy, in his recent paper in *Archiv für Sozialwissenschaft*, XLVI, pp. 605f, has rightly drawn attention to the fact that the English national character, as it can be inferred from a number of its features, made the English less receptive to an ascetic ethos and bourgeois virtues than other nations; an essential feature of their character was, and still is, a certain robust, if crude, vitality. The power of Puritan asceticism in the period of its dominance can be seen precisely in the astonishing degree to which it was able to moderate this character-trait in its adherents.
[5] A constantly recurring theme also in Doyle's discussion. The decisive influence in determining the Puritans' attitude was always the religious motive (though of course it

IDEOLOGY

Wherever the power of the Puritan conception of life reached, it in all circumstances – and this is, of course, far more important than the mere promotion of capital accumulation – favoured the tendency towards a bourgeois, economically rational, way of life: it gave to that way of life its most essential and, above all, its only consistent support. It stood by the cradle of modern 'economic man'. To be sure, these Puritan ideals gave way under the extreme stresses presented by those 'temptations' of wealth which were so familiar to the Puritans themselves. We usually find the most sincere upholders of the Puritan spirit amongst those strata of petty bourgeois and farmers[1] who are in the early stages of their social ascent, while the '*beati possidentes*', even among the Quakers, are all too often ready to abandon the old ideals.[2] It was, indeed, the same fate to which the predecessor of inner-worldly asceticism, the monastic asceticism of the Middle Ages, succumbed again and again: when the rational conduct of the economy, in a place where life was strictly regulated and consumption restricted, had achieved its full effect, the wealth so acquired either fell directly, as in pre-Reformation times, into the hands of the nobility or else threatened to disrupt monastic discipline and required the institution of one of the numerous 'reformations'. Thus, the whole history of monastic life is in a sense a constantly renewed struggle with the problem of the secularising influence of property.

The same is true, on a larger scale, of Puritan inner-worldly asceticism. The powerful Methodist 'revival' which preceded the full flowering of British industry towards the end of the eighteenth century may be compared in many respects with such a reformation of the monasteries.

was not always the sole determinant). In Massachusetts, the colony, under Winthrop's leadership, tended to permit the immigration of gentlemen, even an upper house with an hereditary nobility, provided the gentlemen joined the church. Settlement was restricted for the sake of church discipline. (The colonisation of New Hampshire and Maine was carried out by great Anglican merchants, who established large cattle plantations. Here there was very much less social cohesion.) There were complaints as early as 1632 about the New Englanders' inordinate desire for profit (see, e.g. Weeden's *Economic and Social History of New England*, I, p. 125).

[1] This has already been emphasised by Petty in his *Political Arithmetick*; all the contemporary sources without exception speak especially about the members of the Puritan sects (Baptists, Quakers, Mennonites) as belonging to a stratum of society which was partly without resources and partly consisted of small capitalists, contrasting them both with the aristocracy of great merchants and with the financial adventurers. It was precisely this stratum of small capitalists, however, not the great financiers, the monopolists, state contractors, state money-lenders, colonial entrepreneurs, promoters and so forth, which was responsible for the characteristic feature of Western capitalism – the bourgeois, private enterprise organisation of industrial labour. (See, e.g. Unwin, *Industrial Organisation in the 16th and 17th Centuries*, London, 1914, pp. 196ff.) This contrast was familiar to contemporaries themselves: cf. Parker's *Discourse concerning Puritans* of 1641, where likewise the contrast with project-makers and courtiers is emphasised.

[2] For the way in which this was expressed in the politics of Pennsylvania in the eighteenth century, especially also in the War of Independence, see Sharpless, *A Quaker Experiment in Government* (Philadelphia, 1902).

A passage from John Wesley himself[1] might well be quoted at this point: it would be a very suitable motto to inscribe over all that has been said so far. For it shows that the leaders of the ascetic movements themselves were clear about the apparently so paradoxical connexions discussed here, and that their understanding of them was throughout along precisely the lines suggested here.[2] Wesley wrote, 'I fear, wherever riches have increased, the essence of religion has decreased in the same proportion. Therefore I do not see how it is possible, in the nature of things, for any revival of true religion to continue long. For religion must necessarily produce both industry and frugality, and these cannot but produce riches. But as riches increase, so will pride, anger and love of the world in all its branches. How then is it possible that Methodism, that is, a religion of the heart, though it flourishes now as a green bay tree, should continue in this state? For the Methodists in every place grow diligent and frugal; consequently they increase in goods. Hence they proportionately increase in pride, in anger, in the desire of the flesh, the desire of the eyes, and the pride of life. So, although the form of religion remains, the spirit is swiftly vanishing away. Is there no way to prevent this – the continual decay of pure religion? We ought not to prevent people from being diligent and frugal; *we must exhort all Christians to gain all they can, and to save all they can; that is, in effect, to grow rich.*' (Then follows the admonition that those who 'gain all they can and save all they can' should also 'give all they can', in order in this way to grow in grace and to lay up treasure in Heaven.) Clearly, the connexions analysed here are present in every detail.[3]

Just as Wesley says here, these powerful religious movements, whose

[1] See Southey's *Life of Wesley*, Ch. 29. The reference, which I did not know, was communicated to me in a letter from Professor Ashley (1913). Ernst Troeltsch, to whom I communicated it for this purpose, has already cited it on occasion.

[2] This passage is recommended reading for all those today who think themselves more informed and cleverer on these matters than the leaders and contemporaries of those movements themselves: as can be seen, they knew very well what they were doing and also what risks they were taking. It really will not do to dispute facts which are absolutely indisputable and have never so far been disputed by anyone, and which I have merely tried to relate a little more closely to their underlying causes, and to dispute them so casually as have, unfortunately, some of my critics. No one in the seventeenth century had any doubts about these connexions (cf. Manley, *Usury of 6% Examined*, 1669, p. 137). Quite apart from the modern writers already cited, poets like Heine and Keats, as well as scholars such as Macaulay, Cunningham, and Rogers or writers like Matthew Arnold have taken them for granted. Among the most recent literature, see Ashley, *Birmingham Industry and Commerce* (1913). Ashley has also subsequently expressed his full agreement with me in correspondence. On the whole problem, see Note 4, p. 194 of H. Levy's article cited above.

[3] Perhaps there could be no clearer proof of the fact that exactly the same connexions were evident already to the Puritans of the classical period than the argument which Bunyan actually puts into the mouth of Mr Money-Love: one may become religious in order to become rich, for instance to increase one's custom. For it does not matter *why* one became religious (p. 114 of Tauchnitz edition).

importance in economic development lay initially in their ascetic educational influence, usually did not achieve their full economic effect until after the peak of purely religious enthusiasm had already passed, when the convulsive quest for the Kingdom of God was beginning gradually to settle down into sober virtue in one's calling and when the religious roots were slowly withering, to give way to a utilitarian concern with this world. This was the time when, as Dowden puts it, the place occupied in the popular imagination by Bunyan's 'Pilgrim', hastening through 'Vanity Fair' in a solitary inward quest of the Kingdom of Heaven, was taken by 'Robinson Crusoe', the isolated economic man who happens also to carry on missionary work.[1] When, as a further step, the principle of 'making the best of both worlds' began to prevail, then, as again Dowden has already put it, a good conscience was liable to become simply one of the means of comfortable bourgeois life, as is neatly expressed too in the German proverb about the 'soft pillow'. The bequest of that religiously lively period of the seventeenth century to its utilitarian heirs, however, was above all an exceedingly good – let us be bold and say, a pharisaically good – conscience about the acquisition of money, as long as it was acquired only by legal means. All relics of the doctrine '*Deo placere vix potest*' had vanished.[2] A specifically bourgeois work ethic had developed. With the consciousness that he stood in God's full grace and was visibly blessed by Him, the bourgeois entrepreneur could and should pursue his acquisitive interests, provided that he kept within the bounds of formal correctness, that his moral conduct was irreproachable and that the use which he made of his riches was not an improper one. The power of religious asceticism, moreover, placed at his disposal workers who were sober, conscientious, extremely industrious and loyal to their job as their divinely appointed purpose in life.[3] It also gave him the soothing

[1] Defoe was a keen Nonconformist.

[2] Spener too ('*Theologische Bedenken*', pp. 426f, 429, 432ff) holds the calling of the merchant to be full of temptations and snares, but he explains in answer to an enquiry, 'It pleases me to see that my dear friend has no scruples as regards trade, but recognises it as a form of life, as it is, in which much that is useful to the human race can be accomplished and so love can be exercised in accordance with God's will'. In various other places there is a more detailed case for this, based on mercantilist arguments. If Spener occasionally, in typically Lutheran fashion, treats the desire to be rich as the principal snare, in accordance with 1 Timothy 6. 8 and 9 and with an appeal to Jesus Sirach (*v. sup.*), and recommends that it should be unconditionally put aside, and if he adopts the view that wealth is only to be pursued as far as is necessary to meet physical needs ('*Theologische Bedenken*', III, p. 435 top), he weakens this position on the other hand by referring to those sectaries who prosper and yet live godly lives (see Note 1 on p. 148 above). Even he does not regard riches as objectionable if they are the result of diligent work in one's calling. Because of the Lutheran elements in his position, it is less consistent than Baxter's.

[3] Baxter (*Christian Directory*, II, p. 16) warns against taking on 'heavy, flegmatic, sluggish, fleshly, slothful persons' as 'servants' and recommends that preference be given to 'godly' servants: not only because 'ungodly' servants would be mere 'eye-servants', but above all because 'a truly godly servant will do all your service in obedience to God, as if *God*

assurance that the unequal distribution of worldly goods was the special work of God's providence, God in these distinctions as in His purely particular grace following His own secret and, to us, unknown ends.[1] Calvin had already uttered the often quoted remark that only when the 'people', in other words, the mass of workers and artisans, was kept poor did it remain obedient to God.[2] The Netherlanders, Pieter de la Court and others, had then 'secularised' this idea, arguing that most men work only when necessity drives them to it, and this formulation of a recurrent theme in capitalist economics then went to swell the flood of theories about the 'productivity' of low wages. In this case too, the utilitarian interpretation was imperceptibly imposed on the idea as its religious roots withered, fully in accordance with the pattern of development which we have observed over and over again. Medieval ethics had not only tolerated begging, but had actually gloried in the mendicant orders. Even non-religious beggars, since they gave the wealthy the opportunity to do good works by giving alms, were sometimes actually singled out and treated as an 'estate'. The Anglican social ethic of the Stuart period was still in essence very close to this attitude. It was left to Puritan asceticism to elaborate the harsh English Poor Laws, which in this respect led to a change in principle. This was possible because begging was in fact unknown among the Protestant sects and the generality of strict Puritan communities in their midst.[3]

Considering matters from the other side, from the workers' point of view, Zinzendorf's variety of Pietism, for instance, glorified the worker who was true to his calling and was not acquisitive as following the model of the Apostles and so as gifted with the charisma of discipleship.[4] Still

Himself had bid him do it'. Others, in contrast, would be inclined 'to make no great matter of conscience of it'. Conversely, among workers it is not the outward confession of religion, but the 'conscience to do their duty' which is the mark of the Saint. As can be seen, the interests of God and the employer here merge suspiciously with each other: Spener too ('*Theologische Bedenken*', III, p. 272), for all his insistent exhortations in other places to set aside time for thinking of God, takes for granted the assumption that workers must be content with the bare minimum of free time (even on Sundays). English writers have rightly called the Protestant immigrants the 'pioneers of skilled labour'. See also the evidence in H. Levy, '*Die Grundlagen des ökonomischen Liberalismus*', p. 53.

[1] The analogy between the predestination of only a few – so 'unjust' by human standards – and the distribution of wealth, equally unjust, but equally the will of God, was brought home continually, e.g. in Hoornbeek, *Theologia Practica*, I, p. 153. Besides, as Baxter says, *op. cit.*, I, p. 380, poverty is very often a symptom of sinful idleness.

[2] In Thomas Adams' opinion, too (*Works of the Puritan Divines*, p. 158), God in particular probably allows so many to remain poor because He knows they are not mature enough to cope with the temptations which riches bring with them. For riches all too often drive religion from men's minds.

[3] See above, Note 3 on p. 149, and the work by H. Levy cited there. Exactly the same point is emphasised by all the accounts (for instance, by Manley for the Huguenots).

[4] Similar phenomena were also found in England. To that category belong, for instance, the kind of Pietism which was associated with Law's *Serious Call* (1728) and which preached poverty, chastity and – initially – separation from the world.

more radical were similar views which spread first among the Baptists. Of course, the whole corpus of ascetic literature of almost all denominations is steeped in the view that faithful work, even at low wages, by those who have otherwise had no chances in life, is something highly pleasing to God. In that respect there is nothing new in Protestant asceticism. But not only did it powerfully add a whole new depth to the view, it also created for that ideal something which was absolutely essential if it was to be effective, namely a psychological stimulus in the form of the conception of such work as a calling, as the most excellent, indeed often in the end the only, means of becoming sure of one's state of grace.[1] And on the other hand, it made it lawful to exploit this specific willingness to work, in that it also interpreted the acquisition of money by the entrepreneur as his 'calling'.[2] It is obvious how greatly the 'productivity' of labour in the capitalist sense must have been advanced by such exclusive pursuit of the Kingdom of God through fulfilment of the duty to work in a calling and the strict asceticism which church discipline naturally imposed precisely on the non-property-owning classes.

The interpretation of work as a 'calling' became as characteristic of the modern worker as the corresponding conception of acquisition became for the entrepreneur. It was in response to this, at that time new, situation that such an acute Anglican observer as Sir William Petty attributed the economic strength of the Dutch in the seventeenth century to the fact that the 'Dissenters' (Calvinists and Baptists) who were specially numerous among them were people who looked on 'Labour and Industry as their duty towards God'. The 'organic' social order in the fiscal-monopolistic form which it took in Anglican thinking under the Stuarts, especially in Laud – that is, the alliance of state and Church with the 'monopolists' on the basis of a Christian social structure – was contrasted

---

[1] Baxter's work in Kidderminster, in a parish which had been going to rack and ruin before his arrival, was not only almost unparalleled in the history of the ministry in its degree of success, but also a typical example of the way in which asceticism prepared the masses for labour (or, in Marxist terms, for 'the production of surplus value'), and so in general first made it possible to use them in conditions of capitalist labour (domestic industry, weaving, etc.). The causal relationship generally takes this form. Seen from Baxter's side, he used this process of fitting his charges into the machinery of capitalism to further his own religious and ethical interests. From the point of view of the development of capitalism, these interests of Baxter's helped to further the development of the capitalist 'spirit'.

[2] One further point: it is open to doubt how much power, as a psychological force, there was in the 'joy' of the medieval craftsman in 'what he had created', of which so much play is made. Nevertheless, there is undoubtedly something in it. At all events, asceticism stripped work of all charms in this world (nowadays capitalism has once and for all destroyed them), and directed it to the other world. Work in a calling as such is the will of God. The impersonality of present-day labour, its joylessness and pointlessness for the individual, is here hallowed by religion. Capitalism in the period of its emergence needed workers who would be available for economic use on grounds of conscience. Today it is in the saddle and can compel their labour without rewards in the next world.

by Puritan thought, whose representatives were all among the passionate opponents of this kind of capitalism based on state privileges, putting out and colonisation, with the individualistic incentives of rational legal acquisition in virtue of one's own ability and initiative. While the monopoly industries of England, with their state privileges, soon vanished again without trace, the Puritans said, rational legal acquisition played a decisive part in the creation of industries which were built up without the support of the governmental authorities, and partly in spite of and contrary to them.[1] The Puritans, such as Prynne and Parker, refused to have anything to do with the 'courtiers and project-makers' of the large-scale capitalist type, whom they looked on as an ethically suspect class; they were proud of their own superior bourgeois business morality, which was the real reason for the persecutions to which they were subjected by those circles. Defoe proposed to win the struggle against Dissent by boycotting bank credit and calling in deposits. The contrast between the two kinds of capitalist activity ran to a large extent in parallel with the contrasts in religion. The opponents of the Nonconformists, even in the eighteenth century, continually scoffed at them as embodiments of the 'spirit of shopkeepers' and persecuted them for undermining traditional English ideals. Here also lay the roots of the contrast between the Puritan and the Jewish economic ethos: contemporaries such as Prynne already knew that it was the former rather than the latter which represented the true bourgeois economic ethic.[2]

One of the constituents of the modern capitalist spirit, and not only of this, but of modern civilisation generally, the rational conduct of life on the basis of the idea of the calling, thus has its origins, as the present discussion should have shown, in the spirit of Christian asceticism. One has only to re-read again now Franklin's treatise cited at the beginning of this essay to see that the essential elements of the frame of mind there referred to as the 'spirit of capitalism' are precisely those to which we have pointed in the foregoing discussion as forming the content of the Puritan asceticism of the calling,[3] only without the religious foundation

---

[1] See, on these conflicts and developments, H. Levy in the book cited earlier. The historical origins of the typically English and very powerful opposition of public opinion to monopolies lay in an association between the political struggle for power against the Crown (the Long Parliament excluded the monopolists from Parliament) and the ethical motives of Puritanism and the economic interests of bourgeois small and middle capitalism against the financial magnates in the seventeenth century. The Declaration of the Army of 2 August 1652 and also the Petition of the Levellers of 28 January 1653 demand, along with the abolition of excises, tolls, and indirect taxes and the introduction of a single tax on estates, above all 'free trade': that is, abolition of all monopolistic limitations on internal and external trade on the grounds that they violate human rights. There had already been something similar in the 'Grand Remonstrance'.

[2] Cf. on this point H. Levy, *Die Grundlagen des ökonomischen Liberalismus*, pp. 51f.

[3] It perhaps would be more appropriate to a somewhat different context to point out that even here those elements which have not yet been traced back to their religious roots,

which had already crumbled even in Franklin's time. The idea that modern work in a calling is ascetic in character is not, indeed, a new one. In his most profound insights, in *Wilhelm Meister's Journeyman Years* and the ending which he gave to his *Faust*, Goethe too[1] sought to teach us that it is in the present-day world a condition of doing anything of value that one should confine oneself to specialised work, with all the renunciation of man's Faustian omnicompetence which that implies; that therefore 'doing' and 'renunciation' are today inextricably linked – which is the ascetic basis of the bourgeois style of life, if indeed it is to be a style of life and not a lack of style. For Goethe, this knowledge meant a renunciatory parting from a time of complete and beautiful humanity, which will no more be repeated in the course of our cultural development than will the period of the flowering of ancient Athens.

The Puritan wanted to be a man with a calling; we are compelled to be. For when asceticism was transferred from the monastic cell to the life of the calling and moral concern with this world began to predominate, this helped to create that powerful modern economic world, bound to the technical and economic conditions of mechanical production, which today shapes the way of life of all who are born into it (not only those who are directly employed in the economy) with overwhelming pressure, and will perhaps continue to do so until the last hundredweight of fossil fuel has been burned to ashes. In Baxter's view, concern for external goods should lie on the shoulders of the Saints only like 'a light cloak, which can be thrown aside at any moment'.[2] But fate has allowed that cloak to become a casing as hard as steel. Because asceticism undertook to rebuild the world and to express itself in the world, the external goods of this world have acquired an increasing and ultimately inescapable power over men, such as they have never had before in history. Today, its spirit (whether finally or not, who knows?) has escaped from

---

especially the dictum that 'honesty is the best policy' (in Franklin's discussion of credit), are of Puritan origin. (See my essay on 'The Protestant Sects and the Spirit of Capitalism'.) Here I shall simply reproduce the following remarks by J. A. Rowntree (*Quakerism Past and Present*, pp. 95–6), to which Eduard Bernstein has drawn my attention: 'Is it merely a coincidence, or is it a consequence, that the lofty profession of spirituality made by the Friends has gone hand in hand with shrewdness and tact in the transaction of mundane affairs? Real piety favours the success of a trader by insuring his integrity, and fostering habits of prudence and forethought: – important items in obtaining that standing and credit in the commercial world, which are requisite for the steady accumulation of wealth'. (See the essay on 'The Protestant Sects'.) 'Honest as a Huguenot' was as proverbial in the seventeenth century as the integrity of the Dutch which Sir William Temple so admired, and as, a century later, was that of the English, compared with the Continentals who had not passed through this ethical school.

[1] Well analysed in Bielschowsky's *Goethe*, II, Ch. 18. For the development of the scientific 'cosmos', cf. the similar view expressed, e.g. by Windelband at the conclusion of his '*Blütezeit der deutschen Philosophie*' (the second volume of his *Geschichte der neueren Philosophie*).

[2] *Saints' Everlasting Rest*, Ch. XII.

these confines. Capitalism in its triumph did not need this support any longer, since it rests on mechanical foundations. Even the rosy disposition of its smiling heir, the Enlightenment, seems finally to be fading, and the idea of 'duty in one's calling' haunts our present life like the ghost of our former religious beliefs. Where 'fulfilment of one's calling' cannot be directly related to the highest spiritual values of culture, or where it is not necessarily felt subjectively as simple economic pressure, the individual today generally ceases to reflect on it. In the United States, where it has been given most freedom, acquisitiveness, stripped of its religious and ethical meaning, tends today to be associated with purely competitive passions, which often give it the character of a sporting contest.[1] No one knows as yet who will live within these confines in future, and whether, at the end of this vast development, totally new prophets will emerge or there will be a powerful revival of old ideas and ideals, or, if neither of these, whether there will be a state of mechanised petrifaction, embellished by a kind of frenzied self-importance. In that case it might indeed become true to say of the 'last men' of this cultural development: 'specialists without soul, hedonists without heart: this cipher flatters itself that it has reached a stage of humanity never before attained'.

At this point, indeed, we enter the domain of value-judgments and confessions of faith, which should not burden such a purely historical discussion as this. The task would rather be to demonstrate the significance of ascetic rationalism, only touched upon in the foregoing sketch, for social and political ethics, and so for the mode of organisation and the functions of social groups from the conventicle to the state. Then there must be an analysis of its relations with humanistic rationalism[2] and its ideals and cultural influences, and further to the development of philosophical and scientific empiricism, to technological development and the spiritual values of our culture. Finally, there should be an historical study of its historical development from its medieval origins through inner-worldly asceticism to the stage where it becomes pure utilitarianism, covering all the different areas in which ascetic forms of

[1] 'Couldn't the old man rest content with his $75,000 a year? No! The front of the store must be widened to 400 feet. Why? That beats everything, he thinks. Evenings, when his wife and daughter read together, he just longs to go to bed; Sundays, he's looking at the clock every five minutes to see when the day will end: what a misguided life!' This was the verdict of the son-in-law (a German immigrant) of the leading dry-goods man of a town in Ohio on his father-in-law – a verdict which no doubt seemed to the 'old man' for his part totally incomprehensible and a symptom of German lack of energy.

[2] This remark (which I have here allowed to stand unaltered) ought to have shown Brentano (*Die Anfänge des modernen Kapitalismus*) in itself that I have never doubted its independent significance. That humanism too was not pure 'rationalism' has recently been strongly emphasised again by Borinski in *Abhandl. der Münchener Ak. der Wiss.* (1919).

religion have played a part. Only in this way could the extent of the cultural significance of ascetic Protestantism in relation to other formative elements of modern culture be established. In the present essay an attempt has been made to refer to their causes the fact and the nature of its influence in one, admittedly important, respect. The way in which the development and the special characteristics of Protestant asceticism have in their turn been influenced by the totality of socio-cultural conditions, especially economic conditions, must then be made clear.[1] For although modern man is on the whole usually incapable, even with the best will in the world, of conceiving the importance which religious ideas and sentiments have had for the conduct of life, for culture and for national character as being as great as it in fact has been, it nevertheless cannot be the intention to substitute for a one-sidedly 'materialist' interpretation of cultural and historical causes an equally one-sidedly 'spiritualist' interpretation. Both are equally possible,[2] but both are of equally little service to the interests of historical truth if they claim to be, not preliminaries to enquiry, but its conclusion.[3]

(*Gesammelte Aufsätze zur Religionssoziologie*, 2nd edn, Tübingen, 1922, I, pp. 163–206. First published in this form in 1920; original publication 1905.)

[1] Not this problem, but that of the Reformation in general, especially Luther, is the concern of von Below's Academic Address, *Die Ursachen der Reformation* (Freiburg, 1916). For the topic treated here, especially the controversies relating to this study, reference may be made to Hermelink's *Reformation und Gegenreformation*, although that is primarily concerned with other problems.

[2] For the foregoing sketch has deliberately concerned itself only with those relationships in which there is no doubt about the influence of religious consciousness on 'material' civilisation. It would have been easy to go on from that to a neat 'construction', in which all that is most 'characteristic' of modern culture would have been logically deduced from Protestant rationalism. But that kind of thing is best left to the type of dilettante who believes in the 'uniformity' of the 'collective psyche' and the possibility of reducing it to a single formula.

It should, however, be remarked that, of course, the period of capitalist development which preceded that considered in our study was everywhere influenced in part by Christianity, which both retarded and advanced it. The nature of these influences belongs in a later chapter. Furthermore, whether any of the wider problems outlined above can be discussed within the framework of the *Archiv für Sozialwissenschaft und Sozialpolitik* is not certain, in view of the type of problems with which the journal deals. But the idea of writing thick tomes which would have to rely as heavily as they would in this case on the works of foreign theologians and historians is not one which fills me with much enthusiasm. (I have allowed these sentences to stand here unaltered.) For the tension between ideals and reality in the 'early capitalist' period before the Reformation see Strieder, *Studien zur Geschichte der kapitalistischen Organisationsformen* (1914), Book II (also against the work by Keller referred to earlier and used by Sombart).

[3] It seems to me that this sentence and the immediately preceding remarks and notes should be more than enough to obviate all misunderstanding of what this study has tried to achieve and I can see no reason to amend it in any way. I have abandoned my original

intention of proceeding directly along the lines of the further programme suggested above, and have now decided, partly for accidental reasons, especially because of the appearance of Troeltsch's *Soziallehren der christlichen Kirchen* (which has settled several of the problems which I should have had to consider in a way which I, as a non-theologian, could not have done), but partly also in order to take these studies out of their isolation and place them in the context of general cultural development, that I shall first set down the results of comparative studies on the connexions between religion and society in world history. These follow here. They are preceded merely by a short essay written for the occasion intended to clarify the concept of a 'sect' used above and also to examine the significance of the Puritan conception of the church for the modern capitalist spirit.

8 · The Soteriology of the Underprivileged

If we turn from the socially or economically privileged strata of society, we find an apparent increase in the variety of religious behaviour. Amongst the petty bourgeoisie, and in particular especially the artisan class, there are to be found the most striking contradictions side by side. It is impossible to conceive of greater contrasts between different styles of religion than those between caste taboo and the magical or mystagogic forms of religion, both sacramental and orgiastic, to be found in India, Chinese animism, Islamic dervish-religion, early Christianity, especially in the Eastern Roman Empire, with its emphasis on congregational enthusiasm and inspiration, primitive superstition coupled with Dionysiac orgiasticism in ancient Greece, Pharisaic legalism in ancient urban Judaism, the essentially idolatrous form of medieval Christianity which existed alongside all kinds of sectarianism and the various forms of Protestantism to be found in the early modern period. Early Christianity was certainly from the beginning a religion specifically for artisans. Its saviour was a small-town artisan, its missionaries itinerant journeymen; indeed, the greatest of them was an itinerant tent-maker, already so completely estranged from the land that in one of his epistles he makes blatantly absurd use of an image taken from the practice of tree-grafting. Finally, the Christian congregations of the ancient world were, as we have already seen, overwhelmingly urban and recruited mainly from the ranks of artisans, both free and unfree. In the Middle Ages, too, the most devout, though not always the most orthodox, stratum of society was the petty bourgeoisie. But even within the Christian tradition a number of different styles of religion drew remarkably strong support from the petty bourgeoisie, apparently on an equal footing with each other: ancient prophetic religion, with its emphasis on divine inspiration and the casting out of demons, medieval institutional religion, with its insistence on absolute orthodoxy, and the mendicant friars, certain forms of medieval sectarian religion, such as, for instance, the order of *Humiliati* (so long suspected of heterodoxy), but equally Baptist sects of all kinds and, on the other hand, the pietism of various Reformed churches, including even the Lutheran. In other words, the picture is extremely variegated, which shows if nothing else that the religion of the artisan class was never the unequivocal result of economic conditions. Nevertheless, it exhibits when compared with the peasantry a clear and marked tendency towards both congregational and salvationist religion, and ultimately towards a rational ethical form of religion. It is important to remember, however, that even this contrast is far from being unequivocally determined: for example, Baptist congregational religion was initially influential to a large extent chiefly in the Low Countries, in Friesia, and it was in the town of Münster that it first took a specifically social-revolutionary form.

The close connexion which usually exists at present in Western societies between congregational religion and the urban middle and lower-middle classes results, of course, primarily from the comparative decline of blood-ties, especially those of kinship, within the Western city. The individual finds a substitute for them both in occupational associations, which in the West, as indeed elsewhere, have cultic significance (though no longer associated with taboo), and in freely created religious communities. This latter connexion is not, however, uniquely determined by the economic character of urban life as such: on the contrary, it is easy to see that very often the reverse is the case. In China, the exclusive significance of the ancestor cult and kinship exogamy keep the individual town-dweller firmly tied for a long time to his kin and his home village. In India, the religious taboos associated with the caste system created difficulties for, or limited the importance of, soteriological congregational religion, in urban communities quite as much as in the countryside. And in both cases, these factors hindered, as we have seen, the development of the town into a 'community' much more than that of the village. Nevertheless, the petty bourgeoisie evidently does have a relatively strong tendency – determined, indeed, by its mode of economic life – towards rational ethical religion, wherever the conditions exist for such a form of religion to emerge. Clearly, the life of the petty bourgeois, especially the urban artisan and small businessman, is much further removed from any kind of connexion with nature than is that of the peasant, so that dependence on the use of magic to influence the irrational forces of nature cannot play the same part in his life as in the peasant's. On the contrary, the economic conditions of his life are essentially more rational: which means, in this context, that they are much more amenable to calculation and to the influence of means rationally chosen to achieve a given end. Furthermore, the character of his economic life suggests, especially to the artisan, but also under certain conditions to the businessman, the thought that to be honest is in his own best interests, that reliable work and fulfilment of obligations are usually 'rewarded', and are indeed 'deserving' of a just reward: in short, it suggests an ethically rational view of the world, in the sense of an ethics based on the idea of recompense, of a kind which is anyway natural to all underprivileged strata of society, as will be shown later. It is, at all events, a good deal more natural to them than it is to the peasants, who only switch to a belief in an 'ethical' recompense when magic has been overthrown by other forces: the artisan, on the other hand, has often played an active part in this very overthrow. Finally, it is a good deal more natural to them than it is to the warrior or the great financial magnates with an economic interest in war and the development of power-politics: such people are the least influenced precisely by the ethically rational aspects of a religion.

It is true that in the early stages of occupational differentiation the artisan is deeply entangled in the limitations of magical ways of thought. For every specialised 'art' which is not a matter of everyday routine and not generally disseminated has the force of a magical charisma, whether specific to the individual or, more often, inherited. The acquisition and preservation of this charisma is guaranteed by magical means; there are taboos, sometimes of a totemic character, which set its possessor apart from the community of ordinary men (the peasants) and often exclude him from ownership of land. Especially in the case of those trades which remain in the hands of peoples who formerly supplied raw materials and first practised their art as 'intruders' or, later, as individual resident aliens, the possession of their skill both condemns them to associate with pariah castes and magically stereotypes the operations involved in the artisan's technique. However, wherever this situation breaks down – which happens most easily in new urban settlements – external conditions bring it about that the artisan must think more rationally about his work, the small businessman more rationally about his business, than any peasant has to do. Furthermore, the artisan in particular has the time and the opportunity, in the course of his work, for reflection – at least in certain trades such as the textile industry which normally, in our climate, are pursued indoors, and as a result are particularly closely associated with sectarian forms of religion. Even in modern machine-loom weaving this is still true to a limited extent in certain circumstances; but it was especially true of the hand-loom weaving of the past. In general, when the bonds of purely magical or purely ritualistic modes of thought are broken by prophets or reformers, artisans and petty bourgeois incline from then on towards some form of ethically and religiously rationalistic attitude of life, admittedly often of a very primitive sort. Moreover, they already, in virtue of their occupational specialisation, follow a uniform 'way of life' of a specific character. The form of their religion is by no means unequivocally determined by these general conditions of their life. Chinese small businessmen, though extremely 'calculating', are not adherents of a rational religion: nor, as far as can be ascertained, are Chinese artisans. They are adherents both of magic and of the Buddhist doctrine of Karma. This lack of an ethically rational form of religion, however, is their chief characteristic in this regard, and seems to have some bearing on the limited degree of rationalism which is to be found in their techniques and which never ceases to be remarkable. The mere existence of a class of artisans and petty bourgeois has never been enough to bring about the growth of an ethical form of religion, of however limited a kind. On the contrary, we have seen how the caste taboo, along with the belief in the transmigration of souls, has influenced and stereotyped the ethical values of Indian artisans. All that can be said is that, where a congregational religion, especially one of an ethically rational character, did develop, it was quite natural that it found it easiest to gain adherents precisely among the urban petty bourgeoisie, and then in turn to influence the way of life of this class in certain circumstances – as has in fact taken place.

Finally, the economically most underprivileged strata of society, the slaves and the free day-labourers, have never in the whole course of history been characterised by a specific form of religion. The slaves in the early Christian congregations were members of the urban petty bourgeoisie. For the Hellenistic slaves, such as those belonging to Narcissus (probably the famous Imperial freedman) mentioned in the Epistle to the Romans, were either (as, probably, in the example just mentioned) relatively well-placed and independent domestic officials and servants belonging to a very rich man; or more often they were independent artisans who paid their master tribute and hoped to earn sufficient money to be able to buy their freedom from their savings, as was normal throughout antiquity and in Russia as late as the nineteenth century; or, finally, they were state slaves, also relatively well-to-do. Mithraism, too, as shown by the evidence of inscriptions, found numerous adherents from among this class. According to a plausible suggestion of Deissmann's, the source of the metaphor which St Paul uses to express the redemption of Christians with the blood of the Saviour from the dominion of the Law and of sin was the function which the Delphic Apollo (and other gods too) frequently performed of being used as a savings bank where slaves could deposit their savings (safely, because of its sacred character) and later withdraw them in order to buy their freedom from their masters. If this suggestion is correct – and it must be remembered that another possible source of the metaphor is the Old Testament phrase *gă'al* or *pădă* – then it shows how much Christian propaganda counted on this unfree petty bourgeoisie, with its industrious, and so economically rational, mode of life. The lowest stratum of slaves, on the other hand, the 'speaking inventory' of the ancient plantations, provided no scope for congregational religion, or indeed for any form of religious propaganda whatever. At all times, it has been the itinerant journeyman, normally only separated from the independent petty bourgeoisie by the waiting period before admission, who has most fully shared the specifically petty bourgeois attitude towards religion. Admittedly, this group has very often shown an even more pronounced tendency towards unofficial sectarian forms of religion, all varieties of which have generally speaking found an extremely fertile field in the industrial underlayers of urban society, struggling with the exigencies of their daily lives, the fluctuations in the price of bread and the chances of earning a living, and forced to rely on 'fraternal assistance'. The numerous secret or half-tolerated communities of 'the poor', with their various forms of religion, sometimes revolutionary, sometimes pacifist and communist, sometimes ethically rationalist and congregational, usually draw their membership precisely from the class of small artisans and artisan journeymen. The main reason for this is the purely technical one that the itinerant artisan journeymen are readily available as missionaries for all forms of popular congregational faith. This process is adequately illustrated by the amazingly rapid expansion of Christianity, which covered the enormous distance from the Middle East to Rome in the course of a few decades.

The modern proletariat, however, to the extent that it has any special position on religious matters, is characterised, like the greater part of the authentic modern bourgeoisie, by indifference to or rejection of religion. The sense of dependence on one's own work is here driven back by or supplemented with the consciousness of depending on purely social arrangements, combinations of economic circumstances and legally guaranteed power relationships. On the other hand, as Sombart has long since recounted with admirable clarity, all thought of dependence on cosmic processes, the weather or other natural phenomena seen as capable of being influenced by magic or providence has vanished. Proletarian rationalism, like its complementary phenomenon, the rationalism of the bourgeoisie of an advanced capitalist system in full possession of economic power, is thus not readily expressible in a religious form: or at any rate, it is hard to see how a religion could develop from it. Rather, religion is normally replaced in such a case by other ideal surrogates. It is true that the lowest, and economically least stable, strata of the proletariat, who find it most difficult to grasp rational processes of thought, and also the 'proletarian-like' strata of the petty bourgeoisie, or those who have suffered impoverishment over a long period and are threatened with sinking to the proletarian level, can succumb particularly easily to religious missionary activity. But the missionary activity is normally of a magical type, or, where genuine magic has been stamped out, it offers a surrogate for the sense of being pardoned for one's sins provided by magical and orgiastic forms of religion: this is found, for instance, in Methodist and similar revivalist orgies, and also in the activities of the Salvation Army. Clearly, it is much easier for the emotional than for the rational elements of a religious ethic to grow in this soil, and at all events an ethical form of religion almost never takes root in or derives its chief nourishment from it. It is only in a limited sense that there is a specific form of religion characteristic of the underprivileged as a 'class'. Insofar as the content of socio-political demands in a religion is based on the will of God, this raises a question to which we shall have to devote some space shortly in our discussion of ethics and of 'natural law'. Insofar as the character of the religion as such is the focus of attention, it can immediately be understood that the need for 'salvation' in the widest sense of that term is by no means exclusively, or even principally, to be found among the underprivileged classes, while within the 'satisfied' or privileged strata of society it is alien at least to warriors, bureaucrats and plutocrats.

A salvation religion may well originate first amongst the socially privileged strata of society. The prophet's charisma is not connected with his social rank: indeed it is quite normal for it to be connected with a certain minimum of intellectual culture. Those prophecies which originate specifically amongst the intellectuals provide sufficient evidence of both. But a prophecy normally changes its character as soon as it spreads to laymen who are not specifically and professionally concerned with intellectualism, and even more when it spreads to those underprivileged strata of society for whom intellectualism is economically and socially unattainable. Indeed, it is possible to characterise in general terms what is normally the salient feature of this change: it is a result of the inevitable adaptation to the needs of the masses that the personal saviour, divine or semi-divine, should come forward as the provider of salvation, and religious relationships with him become a precondition of it. We have already learned to recognise the transformation of cultic religion to pure magic as one kind of adaptation of religion to the needs of the masses. Saviour religion is a second typical form and there is, naturally, a whole range of intermediate stages between it and the transformation to pure magic. The lower one goes down the social ladder, the more radical are the forms usually taken by the need for a saviour, where such a need exists. The Indian Vishnuite sect known as the *Kârtabhajas*, for example, took very seriously the dissolution of the caste taboo (which in theory is a part of many salvation religions) and established at any rate limited commensality among its members, extending to private life as well as cultic contexts, as a consequence of which it has become primarily a sect of poor people. In this sect, the anthropolatrous veneration of the hereditary *guru* is promoted to the fullest extent, even to the point of excluding outsiders from the cult.

Very similar phenomena are to be found in other religions, especially in those recruited from the lowest strata of society or influenced by them.

The result, in almost all cases, of the spread of salvation doctrines to the masses is that a personal saviour arises or comes more strongly to the fore. There are parallels elsewhere, though with variations, for the substitution for the Buddha ideal – the exemplary intellectual release into *Nirvâna* – of the Bodhisattva ideal, the saviour descending to earth and renouncing his own entry into *Nirvâna* in order to save his fellow-men; or again, for the rise in Hindu folk-religion, especially in Vishnuism, of the idea of saving grace mediated by the incarnation of God, and the triumph of this soteriology and its magical sacramental grace, both over the aristocratic atheistic salvation offered by Buddhism and over the old ritualism associated with Vedic culture. In general, the religious needs of the middle and petty bourgeoisie find expression in a more emotional sort of legend, especially in one which promotes inner ardour and devotion, rather than in the form which creates heroic myths. This corresponds to the greater satisfaction and significance found in home and family life by these classes as compared with the upper classes. Examples of this bourgeois domestication of religion can be found in the emergence in all Indian cults, in the creation of the Bodhisattva figure just as much as in the various cults of Krishna, of the 'Bhakti' form of piety, in which the believer is on terms of intimacy with the god; or again in the popularity of the devotional myths about the Dionysus-child, or Osiris, or the Christ-child and their numerous relatives. The rise of the bourgeoisie as a force shaping the forms taken by piety, under the influence of the mendicant friars, is also shown by the substitution for such an excellent example of Imperial art as Nicola Pisano's 'Mother of God' of his son's genre-painting of the Holy Family. Another example is the way in which, in India, the Krishna-child has become the darling of a popular cult. Like magic, the soteriological myth, with its incarnate god or deified saviour, is a specifically popular religious idea and hence one which has arisen spontaneously in the most diverse places. On the other hand, the idea of an impersonal ethical order in the cosmos, transcending any personal deity, and of an exemplary salvation is a purely intellectual conception, suited specifically to the culture of an ethically rational lay élite. The same is true of the concept of an absolutely transcendent deity. With the exception of Judaism and Protestantism, all religions and religious codes of ethics have been forced to revert to the cult of saints, heroes or functional gods in order to accommodate themselves to the needs of the masses. Confucianism allows them to co-exist with itself in the form of the Taoist pantheon; popular forms of Buddhism tolerate the local deities of the Buddhist countries as objects of veneration subordinate to the Buddha; Islam and Catholicism have had to accept local gods, functional gods and occupational gods in the guise of saints, who are the true objects of everyday devotion amongst the masses.

The Soteriology of the Underprivileged

A further characteristic of the religion of the underprivileged, in contrast with the aristocratic cults of the warrior nobility, is the admission of *women* on an equal footing. The wide variation in the extent to which women are admitted to religious cults and participate in them, whether more or less actively or passively, or are excluded from them is in general a function of the degree of relative peacefulness or military activity (either past or present). The existence of priestesses, the veneration of prophetesses or sorceresses – in short, the most extreme devotion paid to individual women to whom supernatural powers and charismata are attributed – does not, of course, furnish the slightest evidence of the equal status of women as such within the cult. Conversely, the acceptance of the principle of equality in relations with God in Christianity and Judaism (and less consistently in Islam and official Buddhism) can co-exist with complete monopolisation of the priestly function and the right to active participation in making decisions about the affairs of the congregation by the men, who (as is in fact the case in these religions) are alone admitted to the special vocational training or accepted as qualified. The special susceptibility of women to all prophecy which is not exclusively military or political in emphasis is clearly evident in the free relationships, quite devoid of prejudice, which almost all prophets have had with women: this is as true of the Buddha as it is of Christ or even of Pythagoras. This situation seldom persists, however, beyond the early period of the congregation's existence, in which esteem is accorded to the charismata of inspiration as the marks of special religious elevation. Then, when the relationships within the congregation become routine and regularised, there is always a reaction against the phenomena of female inspiration, which are now felt to be disruptive and morbid. This view can already be found in St Paul. Finally, all prophecy of a political and military character, like that of Islam, is addressed to men alone. Often, moreover, the cult of some warlike spirit, such as the Duk-Duk cult in the Indian archipelago and other similar periodical epiphanies of a hero-spirit in other parts of the world, is used in order to domesticate and regularise the pillage of the women's houses by the inhabitants of the warrior houses, which are organised along the lines of a club. In general, wherever warriors are or have been subjected to an ascetic course of training, in which the hero is 'reborn', women are treated as lacking in the higher, heroic qualities of soul and so relegated to a lower religious status. This is so in most aristocratic or specifically military cult-communities. Women are totally excluded from the official Chinese cult, as from the Roman and the Brahmin. Buddhist intellectual religion is not feminist. Even as late as the Merovingian period, Christian synods could doubt whether the female soul was of equal value. On the other hand, the admission of and granting of equal status to women has given much of their propagandist impetus to the special cults of Hinduism, to some of the Chinese Buddhist–Taoist sects, and, in the West, above all, to early Christianity and the later inspirational and pacifist sects of Eastern and Western Europe alike. Even in Greece, the Dionysus cult, when it first emerged, offered to the women who participated in its orgies a degree of emancipation from all forms of social convention which was otherwise quite unheard of in that society. Admittedly, as time went on, this freedom became more and more artificial and ceremonially stylised and regulated: as a result it became limited to processions and similar isolated festivals in the different cults, and so in the end ceased altogether to be of any practical significance. The greatest advantage of Christian propaganda amongst the petty bourgeoisie, in its struggle with its most important rival, Mithraism, was that the Mithraist cult, being exaggeratedly masculine, excluded women. During a period of universal peace, this forced its adherents to find a substitute cult for their womenfolk in other mysteries, such as those of Cybele: thus, in stark contrast with Christianity, the uniformity and universality of religious community even within individual families was undermined from the outset. The situation in all genuinely intellectual cults, of a Gnostic, Manichaean or similar kind, though rather different in theory, was in many ways the same in practice. By no means all religions which teach the love of one's brother and of one's enemies have become important through female influence or are of a feminist character: for instance, the Indian Ahimsâ religion is not at all of this kind. Female influence usually adds intensity only to the emotional or hysterical aspects of a religion. This is so in India. But it is certainly no accident that salvation religions tend to glorify the unwarlike or anti-warlike virtues in a way which must come naturally to the underprivileged and to women.

The special significance of salvation religion for the politically and economically underprivileged, as opposed to the privileged, may now be considered in more general terms. A point to be elaborated further in our discussion of 'status' and 'class' is that the most highly privileged strata (other than the priesthood), and especially the nobility, base their sense of their own worth or dignity on their awareness of the 'perfection' of their mode of life as an expression of their qualitative 'being' – a 'being' which depends on them alone and does not point beyond them – as, in the nature of things, it is perfectly possible for them to do. In the case of the underprivileged, however, every feeling they have of their own worth is bound up with some 'promise' which has been made to them, and this promise is in turn bound up with a 'function', 'mission' or 'calling' which has been allotted to them. They make up for their lack of any claim to 'be' anything *either* by insisting on the worth of what they will one day be, of what they are 'called' to be, in future life either in this world or the next, *or* (and usually at the same time) by insisting on their 'significance' and their 'achievements' in the eyes of Providence. Their hunger for a dignity that has not come to them, they and the world being what they are, leads them to form this conception, from which arises the rationalistic idea of a 'Providence' and the importance which they have before a divine court with quite different standards of human worth.

This internal situation gives rise, in their relations with other strata, to a number of further characteristic contrasts in the functions which different strata of society expect religion to perform for them. The need for salvation is always an expression of some 'distress', and so social or economic oppression is naturally a very important source of it, though not by any means the only one. The socially and economically privileged strata of society scarcely feel any need for salvation under similar conditions. Rather, they assign to religion in the first instance the role of giving 'legitimacy' to their own way of life and social position. This virtually universal phenomenon springs from some quite general psychological tendencies. All our everyday experience of human beings teaches us to recognise that a fortunate man, confronted with those who are less fortunate, is not satisfied with the fact of his good fortune, but wants something more, namely the 'right' to it, the consciousness of having 'deserved' it, in contrast with the less fortunate who must in some way have 'deserved' their misfortune; and this need for the spiritual comfort of feeling that one's success is justified is felt equally in political good fortune, in differences in economic position, in physical health, in success in sexual rivalry, or what you will. It is this feeling of 'legitimation' that the privileged inwardly want from religion, insofar as they want anything at all. Not every privileged stratum experiences this need to the same extent. To warrior heroes, the gods are beings who are not strangers to envy. Solon and the ancient Jewish sages are at one on the danger of high position. The hero maintains his position above the common herd in spite of the gods, not with their help – indeed often against their opposition. There is a characteristic contrast between the Homeric epic and some of the Indian epics, on the one hand, and the bureaucratic Chinese and priestly Jewish chroniclers on the other. In the latter, the 'legitimation' of good fortune as a reward for those virtues which please God is expressed with considerably greater force than in the former. On the other hand, the idea of a connexion between misfortune and the anger and envy of demons or gods is extremely widespread. Almost every folk religion, the ancient Jewish as much as the modern Chinese (the latter, indeed, with special emphasis), treats bodily defects as a sign of some transgression, magical or moral, according to circumstances, either on the part of the individual himself or, in Judaism, of his ancestors; anyone burdened with such a defect or otherwise suffering the blows of fate is considered to be the victim of the wrath of the god, and so may not participate in the common sacrifices of the political associations, where he would have to appear in the sight of the god along with those who are fortunate and therefore pleasing to the god. In just the same way, in virtually all ethical religions practised by the privileged and the priests who serve them, the privileged or underprivileged social situation of an individual is regarded as somehow or other religiously deserved: only the form of legitimation of the situation of the fortunate changes.

As one would expect, the situation of the underprivileged is quite the reverse of this. Their specific need is for salvation from suffering. This need for salvation is not always felt in a religious form: compare the modern proletariat, for instance. And their need for *religious* salvation, where it does exist, may take various forms. In particular, it can be combined in markedly different ways with the need for a just 'recompense', both for one's own good works and for the injustice of others. Next to magic, therefore, and associated with it, the most widespread form of popular faith in the world is the expectation of recompense, usually of a fairly 'calculating' kind, and the hope of reward. Furthermore, prophecies which reject at any rate the more mechanical forms of this belief come increasingly to be reinterpreted in accordance with it as they become popularised and routine. The kind and degree of hope for recompense and salvation, however, vary quite considerably, according to the kinds of expectation aroused by the promises of the religion. This is particularly so when these promises are projected beyond the earthly life of the individual into a future quite outside his present existence. An exceptionally important example of the interpretation of the content of religious promises is provided by the exilic and post-exilic religious experience of the Jews.

Since the exile in practice, and from a formal point of view since the destruction of the Temple, the Jews have been a '*pariah people*'. The sense of this term as used here has as little in common with the special position of the 'Pariah castes' in India as does, for example, the concept of 'Kadi-justice' with the actual principles of administration of justice followed by the *Kadi*. In the present context, it means a group which lacks an autonomous political association and which is confined to an hereditary separate community by limitations (originally of a magical, taboo and ritual kind) on commensality and intermarriage with outsiders, on the one hand, and by political and social underprivilege, associated with a radical separation in economic activity, on the other. The underprivileged and occupationally specialised Indian castes, with their exclusiveness towards outsiders, guaranteed by taboo, and the hereditary religious obligations which they have to perform as part of their way of life, are relatively closest to the Jews: in their case, too, their hopes of salvation are bound up with their pariah status as such. Both the Indian castes and the Jews reveal the same consequence of a pariah religion: that it binds its adherents all the more closely to each other and to their pariah status, the more oppressive is the position in which the pariah people finds itself and the more powerful in consequence are its hopes of salvation to be achieved by the fulfilment of its religious obligations, as commanded by its god. As has already been remarked, it was precisely the lowest castes who clung most tenaciously to their caste obligations, as the condition of their rebirth in a higher position. The bond between Yahweh and his people became all the more indissoluble, the more vicious was the contempt and persecution which oppressed the Jews. In marked contrast with the Oriental Christians, for instance, who under the Umayyads were converted in droves to the privileged religion of Islam – in such numbers, indeed, that the political authorities made conversion more difficult in the economic interests of the privileged classes – all the frequent attempts at forcible conversion of the Jews, which would have gained for them the privileges of the ruling class, were in vain. The only means of salvation, for the Indian castes as for the Jews, was the fulfilment of the religious commandments specially enjoined on the pariah people, which no one could avoid without having to fear bad magic for himself and endangering his own or his descendants' chances for the future. The differentiating feature of the Jewish religion, however, as opposed to the Hindu caste religion, lay in the nature of the salvation hoped for. The Hindu expects that if he fulfils his religious obligations he will improve his personal chances of rebirth, and therefore of his soul's ascent or reincarnation into a higher caste. The Jew, by contrast, hopes that his descendants will have a share in a Messianic kingdom, which will release his entire pariah community from its inferior position and make them instead lords of the world. For by the promise that all the peoples of the world will borrow from the Jew, while he will borrow from no one, Yahweh did not mean that he would make the Jews into small-time pawnbrokers and money-lenders in the ghetto: the meaning of the promise was that they would become like a typical powerful ancient city-state, whose debtors and debt-slaves were the inhabitants of the villages and small towns which it had subjugated. The Hindu acts with a view to a future human life, in the form of the future incarnation of his own soul, which concerns him only if one presupposes the animist doctrine of the transmigration of souls, just as the Jew acts on behalf of his biological descendants, in whose relationship to him, understood in animistic terms, his 'earthly immortality' consists. But there is a contrast between the ideas of the Hindu and the Jew. According to the Hindu's conception, the social caste hierarchy and the position of his own caste within it continue to exist, absolutely unquestioned, for ever, and he wishes to better the future destiny of his individual soul precisely within this same hierarchy. The Jew, by contrast, expects his own personal salvation in precisely the reverse way, in the form of an overthrow of the existing social hierarchy in favour of his pariah people. For his people is the one called and chosen by God for the position of highest prestige, not for that of pariahs.

Hence, out of the Jewish ethical salvation religion there has developed a new element of great importance, which was totally absent from all forms of magical and animistic caste religion. This element was first remarked on by Nietzsche, and called by him *ressentiment*. In the sense which Nietzsche gave this term, it refers to a concomitant of the religious ethics of the underprivileged, who, in direct contradiction to the earlier belief, trusted that the unequal distribution of chances in life results from the sin and unrighteousness of the privileged and therefore must sooner or later provoke God's vengeance. Moralism, in this kind of theodicy of the underprivileged, then serves as a means of justifying their conscious or unconscious thirst for revenge. This is primarily connected with 'religions of recompense'. Once there exists in a religion the idea of recompense, suffering itself, since it carries with it powerful hopes of recompense, can begin to be seen as something which is of religious value purely in itself. Particular teachings about ascetic practices, on the one hand, and specific neurotic predispositions, on the other, can play into the hands of this idea. However, the specific character of *ressentiment* enters into religions of suffering only on certain, very distinctive presuppositions: it is not, for instance, found in either Hinduism or Buddhism. For in these religions, a man's suffering is individually merited. In Judaism the situation is quite different. The religion of the Psalms is full of the need for revenge, and the same theme recurs in the priestly revisions of the old Israelite traditions. Most Psalms express in the most blatant form the moralistic satisfaction and self-justification of a pariah people's need for vengeance, whether overt or rigidly suppressed; and from this point of view it is irrelevant whether these elements are perhaps later additions to an older version which was free of them. Either God is reproached with the misfortunes which they suffer despite their observance of His commandments and the good fortune enjoyed, despite their godless deeds, by the arrogant heathen, who consequently scoff at His promises and power. Or, alternatively, their own sins are humbly acknowledged and God is besought finally to desist from His wrath and to bestow His grace once more on that people which is, after all, in the end alone His. In both cases, there is also the hope that God, now finally propitiated, will in His vengeance on some future day make their godless enemies doubly into a footstool for Israel, in the same way as the Canaanite enemies of Israel are treated in the priestly interpretation of history, as long as this does not arouse God's wrath through disobedience and so lead to their humiliation at the hands of the heathen. It may be, as modern commentators think, that some of these Psalms perhaps express the individual anger of pious Pharisees at the persecutions under Alexandros Iannaios. In that case, it is their selection and preservation which is their characteristic feature; and certainly others are quite obviously reactions to the pariah situation of the Jews as such.

In all the religions of the world, there is no universal God who has Yahweh's unparalleled thirst for vengeance, and the historical value of the factual assertions in the priestly revision of history can be sufficiently judged by the fact that the event in question (such as the Battle of Megiddo) is out of place in a theodicy of compensation and vengeance. The Jewish religion has thus become the religion of recompense *par excellence.* The virtues commanded by God are practised for the sake of the hope of recompense. And the recompense in question is in the first instance collective: the people as a whole is to be uplifted, and only thereby can the individual also regain his own dignity. At the same time there is of course bound up with this also an individual theodicy of personal fate, such as has obviously existed from time immemorial. The problems which arise in this context are reflected above all in the book of Job, whose author came from a different stratum of society than the common people. In that work, the renunciation of all attempts to solve the problem and the submission to the absolute sovereignty of God over His creatures prefigure the Puritan idea of predestination, which necessarily developed as soon as the pathos of eternal divine punishment in Hell was added. But this idea had not yet arisen at that time, and the conclusions which the author intended to be drawn from the book of Job, as is well known, met with almost total incomprehension, so rock-hard was the collective belief in recompense within the religion of Judaism. The hope of vengeance which, for pious Jews, was inextricably bound up with the moralism of the Law, since it pervades almost all exilic and post-exilic religious writings, must have been nourished, consciously or unconsciously, for two and a half millennia in almost every divine service of this people with their fixed commitment to the two principles of their religiously hallowed separation from the rest of the world and the this-worldly promises of their God. This hope naturally diminished, in the religious consciousness of intellectuals, as the period of waiting for the Messiah grew longer, and was increasingly replaced by the value of an inward awareness of God as such, or by a bland, emotionally appealing confidence in God's goodness as such, combined with a readiness to be at peace with all the world. This happened especially during periods when the social situation of the communities, condemned as they were to total political impotence, was fairly tolerable. During periods like those of the persecutions at the time of the Crusades, however, there were fresh outbursts of passionate feeling, either in the form of cries to God for vengeance, as vehement as they were fruitless, or in the form of a prayer that the worshipper's own soul might 'become as dust' before the enemies who were cursing the Jews, but that he might restrain himself in the face of evil words and deeds and be satisfied simply with wordless fulfilment of God's commandments and keeping his heart open to God.

Though it would be a grotesque distortion to seek for the true sources of Jewish religious thought, variable as it has been over the course of history, in the feeling of *ressentiment*, yet nevertheless its influence on the fundamental characteristics of Jewish religion should not be underestimated. For, in contrast with those elements which are common to Judaism and other salvation religions, *ressentiment* reveals one of the specific traits of Judaism, and in no other religion of the underprivileged does it play such a conspicuous role. Nevertheless, the theodicy of the underprivileged, in some form or other, is an element in all salvation religions, and such religions find most of their adherents amongst the underprivileged strata of society. The priestly ethic, moreover, in the course of its development, has adapted to such a theodicy wherever it has become an element in a community religion mainly practised by the underprivileged. Its almost total absence, and equally the lack of any religious ethics of social revolution in the religions of the pious Hindu and of Asiatic Buddhism, is explained by the nature of the theodicy of rebirth: the hierarchy of castes as such remains eternal and is absolutely justified. For the virtues or sins of a previous life determine one's birth into a particular caste, while behaviour in the present life determines one's chances of betterment. Above all, therefore, there is no trace of any obvious conflict between the social claims created by the promises of God and the contemptible situation in which one actually finds oneself. In the case of the Jew, living as he did in such a state of permanent tension with his situation in the social hierarchy and in permanent expectation and fruitless hope, this conflict denied him any chance of being at ease in the world and enabled religious criticism of the godless heathen, to which merciless scorn used to be his answer, to turn into a concern with his own virtue according to the Law which was always sustained and often embittered by the constant threat of secret self-criticism. Added to this were casuistical ruminations, the product of life-long training, concerning the religious duties of one's fellow country-men, on whose correct behaviour Yahweh's ultimate mercy depended, and the characteristic mixture, so noticeable in numerous works of the post-exilic period, of despair in every sense over the vanity of the world, submission to the chastisement of God, sorrow at the offence caused to Him by pride, and an anxiety-ridden concern with ritual and moral propriety which compelled the Jews to struggle desperately not, as before, to gain the respect of others, but to achieve a sense of self-respect and of their own dignity. This sense of one's own dignity was always liable to be precarious, once given that the ultimate standard of one's value in the eyes of God at any one time must be the fulfilment of Yahweh's promises, so that one was again exposed to the risk that all sense of meaning in one's own conduct of life might be shattered.

For the Jews of the ghetto, in the event, one tangible evidence of God's personal grace continued to an increasing extent to be success in business. However, the idea of 'confirmation' in a 'calling' willed by God is not appropriate to the Jewish situation in the sense recognised by inner-worldly asceticism. For the benediction of God in Jewish thought was much less rooted than in Puritanism in a systematic, ascetic, rational mode of life as the *only* possible source of the feeling of certainty of salvation. Not only did Jewish sexual ethics, for instance, remain completely anti-ascetic and naturalistic, while the ancient Jewish economic ethic remained strongly traditionalist in the relationships which it laid down and full of an unabashed admiration for wealth which was totally foreign to all forms of asceticism, but also all the outward piety of the Jews was underpinned by ritual and frequently combined with the specific emotional content of their religious creed. As with all ancient systems of ethics, of course, the traditionalistic rules of the economic ethic which applied within the Jewish community were held to be valid to their full extent only in relationships with one's fellow believers, not with outsiders. All in all, however, Yahweh's promises have in fact produced in Judaism a strong infusion of moralising in the spirit of *ressentiment*.

It would be quite false to depict the need for salvation, theodicy, or community religion in general as emerging only from among the underprivileged or only out of *ressentiment*, as if they were merely the product of a 'slave revolt in morality'. That picture does not at all fit the case of early Christianity, even though its promises are directed with greatest force precisely to the spiritually and materially 'poor'. In the opposition to the prophecy of Jesus and its immediate consequences can be recognised much more readily the results which were bound to ensue from the devaluation and undermining of a ritual legalism which deliberately aimed at the exclusion of outsiders, and consequently the *loosening* of the bonds between religion and the position of believers considered as excluded pariah people belonging to a lower caste. It is true that early Christian prophecy does contain definite traces of the idea of 'recompense', in the sense of a future readjustment of destinies (most clearly in the story of Lazarus) and of vengeance, which belongs to God. Further, the Kingdom of God was also thought of at this time as an earthly kingdom, at first, seemingly, a kingdom specially or in the first instance reserved for the Jews who have believed from of old in the true God. But the characteristically vehement *ressentiment* of a pariah people is precisely what is ruled out by the consequences of the new religious promises. Moreover, the motive for pointing out the danger of wealth for one's chances of salvation, at least in the elements in the tradition which are represented as Jesus' own preaching, is not by any means an ascetic one, still less one of *ressentiment*, as is shown by the evidence in the tradition of his association, not only with publicans (usually in Palestine small-time usurers), but also with other rich nobles. Jesus' indifference to the world, springing from his preoccupation with eschatological expectations, was much too great for that. Admittedly, if he wishes to become 'perfect', that is, a disciple, the rich young man must unconditionally separate himself from the 'world'. But it is expressly said that with God all things, however difficult, are nevertheless possible, even the admission to heaven of a rich man who cannot bring himself to part with his wealth.

Jesus was a prophet of other-worldly love, who brought to the spiritually and materially poor the good tidings of the imminent approach of the Kingdom of God and liberation from the power of demons: 'proletarian instincts' were as foreign to him as they were to Buddha, for whom total separation from the world was the absolute precondition of salvation. The limitations of talk of '*ressentiment*' and the seriousness of applying too generally the concept of 'repression' are nowhere so clearly seen, however, as in Nietzsche's mistaken attempt to apply his concept to the completely inappropriate case of Buddhism. Buddhism is, on the contrary, the diametrical opposite of all forms of moralising in a spirit of *ressentiment*: it is much more the salvation doctrine of an intellectual class which proudly and nobly despises the illusions of this world and the next alike, and was initially almost entirely recruited from the privileged castes, especially the warrior caste, so that it can be compared, at least in respect of its social provenance, with the Hellenistic doctrines of salvation, above all Neoplatonism, or even Manichaeism or Gnosticism, however different these may be from it in their fundamental principles. To him who has no wish to be released into Nirvâna, the Buddhist *bhikshu* does not begrudge the whole world, including rebirth in Paradise. It is precisely examples like this which show that the need for salvation and ethical forms of religion have another source than the social situation of the underprivileged and the rationalism of the bourgeoisie as shaped by the practical conditions of the lives they lead. This source is pure intellectualism, just by itself, above all the metaphysical needs of the spirit, which is forced to meditate on ethical and religious questions not through material necessity, but through the personal inner need to grasp the world as a *meaningful* cosmos and to be able to take up a stance towards it.

(*Wirtschaft und Gesellschaft*, 4th edn,
Tübingen, 1956, 1, pp. 293–304.
First published in 1922.)

9 · *The Religions of Asia*

We may summarise what has been said in this survey of Asian civilisation (extremely superficial as it has been in view of the richness of the structures considered) in the following way:

For Asia as a whole, China has played much the same role as France has done in the modern Western world. From China has stemmed all gentlemanly 'polish', from Tibet to Japan and Indo-China. India, on the other hand, has come to have something of the significance that ancient Greece has had in the West. There is little thought about anything beyond purely practical concerns in Asia whose sources are not ultimately to be sought in India. Above all, the Indian salvation religions, both orthodox and heterodox, have had some claim to be considered as playing roughly the role, for the whole of Asia, that Christianity has played in the West. With one big difference: apart from local, and usually short-lived, exceptions, none of them has been elevated for any length of time to the position of the single dominant 'church' in the sense in which this was the case in the West in the Middle Ages and indeed right up to the Peace of Westphalia. Asia was, and remained, in principle the land of free competition between religions, of 'tolerance' in the sense of late Classical antiquity – subject, that is, to due reservations for the limits imposed by reasons of state, which, it should not be forgotten, continue even in the modern world to set bounds to all forms of religious toleration, albeit taking effect in a different direction. Where these political interests were in any way involved, there was no lack, even in Asia, of religious persecution in the grand manner. This was most markedly true in China, but it was also found in Japan and parts of India. As in Athens at the time of Socrates, so in Asia too, superstition could claim its victims at any time. And finally, in Asia too, right up into the nineteenth century, religious wars between the sects and the militarised monastic orders played their part. On the whole, however, we observe otherwise the same kind of co-existence between cults, schools, sects and orders of all kinds which was characteristic of ancient civilisation in the West.

Admittedly, this did not mean that all the competing tendencies were in any way equivalent in the eyes of most members of the ruling strata at any given time, or often in the eyes of the political authorities. There were orthodox and heterodox, and among the orthodox more or less classical, schools, orders and sects. Above all – and this is especially important for us – there were also social distinctions between them. On the one hand (and to a lesser extent), they were distinguished by the social strata to which they were indigenous. On the other hand (and principally), they were distinguished by the nature of the salvation which they bestowed on the different strata of their adherents. The first phenomenon was found in different forms. Sometimes, a socially superior class which sharply rejected all forms of salvation religion would be faced with popular soteriologies among the masses: a typical example of this was China. Sometimes it was rather that different social strata tended towards different forms of soteriology. Then in most cases – that is, in all those in which it did not lead to socially stratified sects – this phenomenon is identical with the second: the same religion bestows different kinds of supernatural benefits, and accordingly the demand for them in the various social strata varies in strength. With very few exceptions, the Asian soteriologies recognised certain promises which were accessible only to those who lived an exemplary (usually, a monastic) life, and others which were valid for the laity. Almost without exception, all soteriologies of Indian origin were of the latter type. The causes of both phenomena were the same; and two of them above all were closely connected. First, there was the chasm separating the 'educated' classes, with their literary culture, from the illiterate mass of philistines. Secondly, and connected with this, there was the common assumption of all Asian philosophies and soteriologies that knowledge (be it literary knowledge or mystical gnosis) is ultimately the one absolute route to the highest salvation in this world and the next. This is not, be it noted, knowledge of the things of this world, of the ordinary course of nature and social life and the laws governing both. Rather, it is philosophical knowledge of the 'meaning' of the world and of life. Such knowledge obviously cannot be replaced by any gained by the methods of Western empirical science, and it is no part of the proper purposes of Western science to pursue it. It lies beyond science. Asia, and that again means India, is typically the land of intellectual struggle directed simply and solely to the attainment of a 'world view' in this true sense – that is, of a 'meaning' for life in the world.

It can be asserted here (and in view of the incompleteness of our discussion, we shall have to be content with this incompletely supported assertion) that in the realm of reflection on the 'meaning' of life and the world there is absolutely nothing which has not already been thought in Asia, in some form or other. This knowledge – which inevitably takes a gnostic form, both because of its own intrinsic meaning and also in most cases as a matter of fact – is the goal of Asian thought, considered in all genuinely Asian (that is, Indian) soteriology as the only path to the highest salvation and at the same time as the only path to correct action. As a result, nowhere has it seemed so self-evidently true that, as is obvious to all forms of intellectualism, virtue can be taught and that correct apprehension produces correct action as its inevitable consequence. Even in the folk legends of Mahayana Buddhism, for instance, which played somewhat the same role in the visual arts as Bible stories did in the West, this is always the absolutely self-evident underlying assumption.[1] Only knowledge gives, according to circumstances, ethical or magical power over oneself or over others. It would be totally wrong to think that that 'teaching' and this 'apprehension' of what has to be known are a rational offer and acquisition of empirical scientific knowledge, which makes possible the rational domination of nature and other men, as in the West. Rather, it is the means of mystical and magical domination over oneself and the world, that is, gnosis. It is to be achieved by means of the most intensive training of body and spirit: either by means of asceticism or, more usually, by exacting, methodically regulated, meditation.

Two important consequences followed from the fact that the knowledge remained of an essentially mystical character. First, there developed a spiritual aristocracy of the soteriology. For the capacity for mystical gnosis is a charisma, and is far from being available to everyone. But secondly, and connected with this, it took on an asocial and apolitical character. Mystical knowledge is not communicable, at least not adequately and rationally. Asian soteriology leads the seeker after the highest salvation always to a realm beyond this world, a realm of rationally unformed (and for that very reason divine) contemplation, of having, possessing and being possessed by a bliss which is not of this world and yet can and should be attained in this life by means of the gnosis. It is experienced in all the highest forms of Asian mystical contemplation as a 'void' – that is, as a realm which has been emptied of the world and of what agitates it. This corresponds entirely to the normal interpretation of mysticism, but only in Asia has it been carried to its ultimate consequences. The devaluation of the world and its strivings is, even from the purely psychological point of view, the inevitable result of this intrinsic meaning of the state of mystical blessedness, which cannot be further interpreted in rational terms. Rationally interpreted, this mystically experienced state of salvation can be seen as the opposition between rest and restlessness. The former is divine, the latter specifically creaturely, and so ultimately either actually illusory or else soteriologically valueless, because bound up with space and time and transitory.

This inner attitude to the world, with its origns in immediate experi-

---

[1] See the *Mahasutasomajataka* (cited earlier) in Grünwendel's translation, *Buddhistische Studien*, V.d. Kgl. M. f. Völkerk., Berlin, v, pp. 37f.

ence, found in the Indian doctrine of *Samsara* and *Karma* its most rational interpretation, and so the one which prevailed almost universally in Asia. Through this doctrine, the soteriologically devalued world of real life acquired a relatively rational meaning. In it (in its most rationally developed version) the law of determinism holds. In external nature, according to the Mahayana doctrine which was developed especially in Japan, there reigns strict causality in our sense. In the destinies of the soul, there reigns *Karma*, which is a determinism of ethical recompense. From it there is no escape save by flight, by means of the gnosis, to the realm beyond the world: the fate of the soul is either conceived of simply as 'dissolution', or as a state of eternal individual repose, akin to dreamless sleep, or as a condition of eternal calm blessedness of feeling in contemplation of the divine, or as absorption into the divine unity. At all events, the idea that the transitory deeds of a transitory being on this earth might result in 'eternal' punishment or reward in the 'next world', and that this should be in virtue of the decree of a God who is at once all-powerful and good, has always appeared, and will always appear, absurd and spiritually second-rate to all genuinely Asian thinking. But that means that there has been none of the heavy emphasis placed on the brief span of earthly life, which there has been, as already remarked, in Western soteriological doctrines about life after death. Indifference to the world was the accepted attitude, whether it took the form of overt escape from the world or that of action which remained within the world but was still indifferent to it – a proving of oneself *against* the world and one's own activity, not in and through them. Whether the supreme divinity was conceived of as personal or, as was naturally more usual, as impersonal, made (and this is not without importance from our point of view) a difference of degree, not of principle, and even the idea of a transcendent personal God, which was rare, but was occasionally found, did not have a profound impact. The decisive factor was the nature of the salvation to be sought. But this was ultimately determined by the fact that the soteriology was the work of a class of *literati* who engaged, simply for its own sake, in reflection on the meaning of the world.

It was this soteriology of the intellectuals which confronted those strata of Asian society who were engaged in the practical business of life. No internal connexion could be made between activity in the world and a totally unworldly soteriology. The only form which was internally completely consistent was the caste soteriology of Vedantic Brahmanism in India. The political, social and economic effects of its conception of the calling were necessarily extremely traditionalist. But it is the only form of 'organic' doctrine of salvation and society to have emerged which was logically completely consistent.

The aristocratic strata of the laity adopted an attitude towards the soteriology which corresponded to their inner disposition. Insofar as they were themselves an aristocratic status group, there were several possibilities. They might be a worldly class of knights, with a literary education, confronting an independent priesthood, also with a literary training, like the ancient *Kshatriya* in India and the court knights in Japan. In that case, they might either participate in the creation of priest-free soteriologies (as happened especially in India), or adopt a sceptical attitude to anything religious, as happened with a section of the ancient Indian aristocratic laity and considerable sections of the Japanese aristocratic intelligentsia. In the latter case, insofar as they had occasion, despite their scepticism, to come to terms with religious practices, they normally treated them in a purely ritualistic and formalistic way. This happened with sections of the ancient Japanese and ancient Indian cultivated aristocracies. Or they were officials and officers, as in India, in which case they simply adopted the last-named attitude. Their own conduct was, in all the cases mentioned so far, ritually regulated in a manner appropriate to their special rules by the priesthood, whenever the priests had the power to do so, as was the case in India. In Japan, after the priesthood had been deposed by the Shoguns, the priests were no longer powerful enough to regulate the conduct of the knights in any but a purely external way. Or the case might be quite the opposite of the one discussed so far: the aristocratic laity were not only worldly officials, incumbents of or candidates for office in a patrimonial bureaucracy, but also officials of the state cult in the absence of competition from a powerful priesthood. In that case, they developed their own mode of life, rigidly ceremonial and directed towards purely inner-worldly concerns, and they also treated the ritual as part of the ceremonial of their status group: Confucianism played this role in China for the (relatively) democratically recruited class of *literati*. In Japan, the cultivated worldly aristocracy, relatively free as it was from the power of the priesthood, did not have, despite the ritual obligations which were also incumbent there on the political rulers as such, the same character as the Chinese: they were not patrimonial officials and candidates for office, but knightly nobles and courtiers. Consequently, they did not have the pedantic and scholarly elements of Confucianism. They were a 'cultivated' class which was especially strongly disposed towards the reception and syncretism of all kinds of cultural elements from all quarters, but which was essentially firmly rooted in feudal conceptions of honour.

The situation of the non-literary 'middle class' in Asia – the merchants and those artisans who belonged to the middle classes – diverged in a peculiar way from the Western situation because of the special character of Asian soteriology. The upper strata of this class partly had a share in the rational development of the intellectual soteriologies, especially to the extent that these soteriologies preached – negatively – the rejection of ritualism and book-learning and – positively – the exclusive importance of the personal pursuit of salvation. But the character of these soteriologies, which was still ultimately gnostic and mystical, offered no basis for the development of a methodically rational, inner-worldly mode of life which would be adequate to them. As a result, to the extent that their religion was sublimated under the influence of the salvation doctrines, they became adherents of the various forms of saviour religion. Here too, however, the decisive influence was the all-pervasive gnostic and mystical character of all Asian intellectual soteriology and the inner relationship of intimacy with God, possession of God and possession by God, of mystics and magicians. In all parts of Asia, except where, as in China and Japan, it was forcibly suppressed, saviour religion took the form of the cult of saints, indeed the cult of *living* saviours, of the *gurus* and their like, whether they were more mystagogic or more magical dispensers of grace. It was this which gave the religion of the non-literary middle class its definitive stamp. The often limitless power of these usually hereditary bearers of charisma was broken to any extent at all only in China and Japan, for political reasons and by the use of force: in China this was done for the sake of obedience to the political class of *literati*, in Japan in order to weaken the prestige of all clerical and magical forces in general. Otherwise in Asia generally it was that charismatic stratum which determined the practical mode of life of the masses and dispensed magical salvation to them: devotion to a 'living saviour' was the characteristic form of Asian piety.

Along with the persistence of magic generally and the power of the kinship group, the persistence of charisma in its oldest interpretation, as a purely magical power, was the typical feature of the Asian social order. The aristocratic *literati*, whether political or hierocratic, generally succeeded in sublimating or denaturing the orgiastic religion of the masses into love for a saviour, private prayer, or the formalised ritual of the cult of a saint – incidentally, with varying degrees of success, being most successful in China, Japan, Tibet and the Buddhist parts of Indo-China, and least successful in India. But it was only occasionally, and generally only with short-lived success, that they aimed or attempted to break the domination of magic. It was not the 'miracle', but the magic 'spell', therefore, which remained at the heart of mass religion, especially the religion of the peasants and manual workers, but also that of the middle class. Both terms, miracle and spell, have an ambiguous meaning. It is easy enough to satisfy oneself on this point by comparing Western and Asian legends. The two may appear very similar to each other; ancient Buddhist legends and revised Chinese legends especially come close at times even in their inner content to those of the West. But if one takes the average on both sides the contrast becomes obvious. The 'miracle', by its very meaning, is always regarded as an act of some sort of being which rationally controls the world, of a divine dispenser of grace; hence it is usually more internally motivated than the 'spell' which, by its very meaning, comes into being because the whole world is full of magical powers working in an irrational fashion, which can be accumulated through ascetic or contemplative practices in beings, whether human or superhuman, who are charismatically qualified and yet act of their own free will. The miracle of the rose of St Elisabeth seems to us significant. On the other hand, if magic is universal, then any kind of connexion of meaning between events is severed. Precisely in the typical average Asian legends, such as those of Mahayana Buddhism, it is possible to see how this inner-worldly *deus ex machina* is combined, seemingly in the most unintelligible way, with the diametrically opposed need, which is equally inartistic, because it is rationalistic, to provide some kind of historical explanation, as sober as possible, for some entirely indifferent details of the legendary event. In this way, the ancient treasury of Indian fairy tales, fables and legends, which was the historical source for the fables of the whole world, was later transformed by this religion of magical saviours into a form of artistic literature of an absolutely inartistic character, whose significance for its readers was similar to the emotions aroused by the popular romances of chivalry against which Cervantes took up arms.

Everyday economic life, too, formed part of this extremely anti-rational world of universal magic, so that no route could be traced from it to a rational mode of conduct in the world. Magic was used, not only as a form of therapy, but as a method for procuring birth, especially the birth of male children, for ensuring a pass in examinations or the achievement of any conceivable earthly goods; against enemies, sexual or economic rivals; to help the orator to win his case; to enable creditors to distrain against their debtors with the aid of spirits; or to influence the god of riches to secure the success of an enterprise. By such means, either in the crude form of coercive magic or in the more refined form of winning the favour of a functional god or demon by means of gifts, the broad masses of Asians, both illiterate and even literate, controlled their everyday lives. There was no rational, practical ethic, no methodical approach to life to lead the way out of this enchanted garden of all life in the 'world'. To be sure, there was that opposition between the divine and the 'world' which in the West was historically responsible for the introduction of that unified systematisation of the conduct of life which is normally called 'ethical personality'. But nowhere[1] in Asia was this an

---

[1] Only in this sense should one understand Percival Lowell's ingeniously elaborated thesis (*The Soul of the Far East*, Boston and New York, 1888) about 'impersonality' as the

opposition between the ethical God and a power of 'sin', of radical evil, which had to be overcome by means of energetic activity in life. Rather, it might be an opposition between ecstatic possession by the god, to be achieved by orgiastic means, and everyday life, in which the divine was not experienced as a living force. This meant an increase in the forces of irrationality, which actually hindered the rationalisation of the conduct of life within the world. Or else it might be an opposition between an emotionless state of ecstatic possession of the god by means of gnosis and the everyday world, seen as the locus of transitory and meaningless activity. This meant a state of neutrality, divorced from all everyday concerns, indeed passive, and, because of its mystical nature, irrational when seen from the standpoint of an inner-worldly ethics, leading away from rational activity in the world.

Where inner-worldly ethics was systematised in a 'specialist' way, as happened with great consistency and with sufficiently effective practical soteriological rewards for the corresponding behaviour in Hindu inner-worldly caste-ethics, it was absolutely stereotyped both traditionalistically and ritualistically. Where this was not the case, hints of an 'organic theory of society' did emerge, but without psychologically effective rewards for the corresponding practical activity; and there was no consistent or psychologically effective systematisation. The laity, to whom the gnosis and so the highest form of salvation is denied, or which itself rejects such gnosis, guides its life by ritual and tradition and in this way looks after its everyday interests. The boundless avarice of the Asian, in small matters as in great, is notorious for being without parallel in the whole world, and this notoriety is generally quite justified. But 'avarice' is what it is, pursued with all the means of cunning and with the assistance of the universal means, magic. What is lacking is precisely the decisive element in Western economic life, the modification of this instinctive avarice, its transformation into a rational pursuit of gain and its integration into a system of rational, inner-worldly ethics of action – that transformation which was achieved in the West by the 'inner-worldly asceticism' of Protestantism, following on the work of a few predecessors to whom it had inner affinities. The preconditions for such a transformation were not present in Asian religious development. How could they emerge against the background of a religion which recommended as religiously meritorious, even to the laity, the life of a *Bhagat*, a holy ascetic; and which recommended this, not merely as a goal for old age, but even, in the form of the life of a wandering

essential feature of the Oriental. As for his dogma about the 'monotony' of Asian life, this must surely, especially when expressed by an American, provoke the well-founded astonishment of all Orientals. A citizen of the United States must surely allow James Bryce to be cited as the classical witness on the question of the true heartland of 'monotony'.

mendicant, during the workless periods of life generally (and not without success[1])?

In the West, the emergence of the rational, inner-worldly ethic is bound up with the appearance of thinkers and prophets who, as we shall see, grew up against the background of political problems of a social structure which was alien to Asian culture – namely the political bourgeoisie of the city, without which neither Judaism nor Christianity nor the development of Greek thought could be conceived. The emergence of the 'city' in this sense in Asia was, however, hindered in part by the persisting power of kinship groups and partly by the division into castes.

The interests of Asian intellectuals, to the extent that they went beyond practical questions of everyday life, usually lay in a direction other than politics. Even the political intellectuals, the Confucians, were aesthetically cultivated *literati* and polished salon conversationalists rather than politicians. Politics and administration were merely their means of earning a livelihood, which they anyway in practice left to their subordinate assistants. The educated Hindu or Buddhist, whether orthodox or heterodox, on the other hand, found his true sphere of interest quite outside the things of this world, in the quest for the mystical, timeless salvation of the soul and escape from the meaningless mechanism of the 'wheel' of existence. Both the Hindu and the Confucian gentleman avoided too close a contact with the Western barbarian – the Hindu in order not to be disturbed in his quest, the Confucian in order not to allow any coarsening of the elegance of his aesthetic gestures. What distinguishes him from the Western barbarian is the latter's lack of restraint in his passions, which seems to him exuberant, but undisciplined and unsublimated, and the lack of decorum which permits him to reveal his inner self in his conduct, gestures and expressions: in other words, it is the lack in this sense of any control over himself.

The specifically Asian form of 'self-control' in its turn, however, has certain peculiar features which must on the whole be evaluated as purely 'negative' by the Westerner. For what was the ultimate goal of that eternally wakeful self-control prescribed by all Asian rules for the conduct of life without exception to the intellectual, the educated man, the seeker after salvation? What was the ultimate content of that intense and concentrated 'meditation' or that lifelong literary study which they insisted on preserving as the highest good against those disturbances from outside, at least where they took on the character of a striving for perfection? The Taoist *Wu wei*, the Hindu conception of an 'emptying' of worldly relationships and concerns, and the Confucian 'detachment' from preoccupation and concern with fruitless problems all lay in the

---

[1] In India, it was especially in April that the members of the lower castes had to perform their periodic ritual duty of living as a wandering mendicant.

same direction. The Western ideal of the busily active 'personality', relating his activity to a centre, be it other-worldly and religious or be it this-worldly, would to all highly developed Asian intellectual soteriologies be either something to be set aside as in itself ultimately self-contradictory or vulgarly specialist or something to be rejected as a mere expression of barbarian vitality. Where it is not the beauty of the traditional gestures, sublimated by the refinement of the salons, purely as such (as in Confucianism), it is the realm beyond this world of release from transitory things, to which all the highest interests point and from which the 'personality' derives its value. In the highest conceptions, not only those of orthodox Buddhism, this is called '*Nirvâna*'. It would be quite unobjectionable, not just from the linguistic point of view, but even in terms of substantive content, to translate this term, as was often popularly done, by the word 'nothing'. For under the aspect of the 'world' and seen from that point of view, it meant in fact just that. Admittedly, from the point of view of the doctrine of salvation, the condition of salvation is usually to be described differently, in terms of more positive predicates. But in the last analysis it should not be forgotten that the goal of the striving of the typical Asian holy man was 'emptying', and that the positive state of unutterable blessedness in this world for those who had escaped death was in the first instance only something expected as a positive concomitant of success, not as something always achieved. On the contrary: really to be able to enjoy such a state, to possess the divine, was the high charisma of those favoured with special grace. But what of the great multitude who did not achieve it? Well, for them it was true in a peculiar sense that 'the goal is nothing, the journey everything', and the journey was in the direction of this 'emptying'.

The Asian, and especially the intellectual or half-intellectual Asian, easily gives the Westerner the impression of being 'enigmatic' and 'mysterious'. Sometimes the attempt is made to get at the supposed 'mystery' by means of 'psychology'. Without of course denying in any way that there exist physical and psychological differences of disposition[1] (there are, by the way, certainly no greater differences than those between Hindus and Mongols, who have nevertheless both been susceptible to the same soteriology), it must nevertheless be emphasised that this is not the primary route to understanding. Those directions of interest which are imprinted by upbringing and imposed by the objective situation, not any 'temperaments', are the first things to be grasped. What the Westerner

[1] For our present purposes, we should especially need a discussion from the point of view of racial neurology of the Indians' presumably extreme liability to hysteria and self-hypnosis. The question would still remain how far any difference in disposition can be ascertained from such neuropathological ecstasies. They are to be found in embryonic form amongst almost all 'primitive peoples'; the difference is that in India the technique has been developed into an art.

finds most irrational in the Asian's behaviour was and is conditioned by ceremonial and ritual practices whose 'meaning' he does not understand; after all, among us as well as in Asia, the original meaning of such customs tends often to be no longer clear even to those who have grown up in them. Furthermore, the reserved, dignified countenance and the seemingly extremely significant silence of the Asian intellectual tends to torment the curiosity of the Westerner. In this regard, however, it would perhaps often be as well to dismiss certain preconceived ideas which may suggest themselves about the inner content which lies behind this silence. We stand before the natural order and think that it must have some 'last word' to say about its 'meaning', either to the analytic thinker or to the contemplative who gazes upon the whole and is stirred by its beauty. The tragedy is, as Dilthey has sometimes remarked, that 'Nature' either has no such 'last word' to divulge or does not see itself as in a position to do so. Very often, something similar is true of the belief that someone who remains silent out of good taste must have much to conceal. But that is not the case – no more with Asians than elsewhere; it is undoubtedly true that the soteriological products of Asian literature have worked on most of the problems which arise in this special area with much greater thoroughness than the West.

The failure of economic rationalism and a rational approach to life in general to emerge in Asia is, to the extent that factors other than those of cultural tradition have been at work, primarily the result of the continental character of the social structure, as determined by geography. The centres of Western civilisation have always developed in places involved in external or passing trade: Babylon, the Nile Delta, the ancient Greek city-state and even the Israelite confederacy on the caravan routes of Syria. It has been otherwise in Asia.

The nations of Asia have predominantly insisted on either forbidding or setting extreme limits to foreign trade. This was true, until they were forcibly opened up, of China, Japan and Korea and is still the case now in Tibet; it has been true to a significantly lesser, but still considerable, extent of most parts of India. The limitation of foreign trade in China and Korea was the result of the process of granting prebends, which automatically led to traditionalist stability in the economy. Any disruption might endanger the interests of a Mandarin in his revenues. In Japan the interests of feudalism had a similar stabilising influence on the economy. Further influence in this direction (and this is also true for Tibet) came from ritual factors: foreigners entering the holy places disturbed the spirits and might result in magical evil; travellers' accounts make it plain (especially for Korea) how the local population tended to be seized with frantic anxiety about the consequences when Europeans appeared in the holy places. In India, the area of least seclusion, the increasingly influential ritual distrust of travel, especially in ritually impure barbarian regions, worked against the export trade, while political hesitations led to the strictest possible limitations being set on the admission of foreigners. Political hesitation was also in all other regions, especially in East Asia, the final reason which decided the political authorities to give free rein to the ritual fear of foreigners.

Did this rigid seclusion permit the indigenous culture to develop into a 'feeling of nationality'? The answer to that question must be 'No'. The peculiar character of the Asian intellectual strata essentially prevented the emergence of 'national' political formations, even of the kind which have developed in the West from the later Middle Ages onward – although even in our case, the full conception of the idea of the nation was first elaborated by the modern Western intellectual strata. The Asian cultural regions lacked – and fundamentally so – any community of language. The language of culture was a religious language or the language of *literati*: Sanskrit amongst aristocratic Indians, the Mandarin dialect of Chinese in China, Korea and Japan. In part, the position of these languages corresponds to that of Latin in the Middle Ages, in part to that of Greek in the ancient Near East or Arabic in the Islamic world, in part to that of Church Slavonic or Hebrew in their respective cultural regions. In the cultural region of Mahayana Buddhism this has continued to be so. In the region of Hinayana Buddhism (Burma, Ceylon and Siam), which recognised the vernacular as a missionary language, the theocracy of the *gurus* was so absolute that there was no possibility of any kind of worldly, political social structures emerging from the intellectual stratum, which was in these areas composed of monks. Only in Japan did the development of feudalism bring with it some hints of a genuinely 'national' consciousness, though this was mainly on the basis of the knightly class's sense of status. In China, however, the gulf which separated the aesthetic Confucian literary culture from all contact with popular traditions was so enormous that there was only a sense of common status, based on education, among the *literati*, and any consciousness of common identity apart from that extended only as far as its immediate influence (which was admittedly not small). The Empire was, as we saw, basically a federation of provinces, fused into some kind of unity only by the periodic governmental exchange of high Mandarins, who were everywhere in their official precincts alienated from the land. For all that, there did exist in China, as in Japan, a stratum devoted to purely political interests and at the same time with a literary education. This was precisely what was lacking, however, in all those parts of Asia where the specifically Indian soteriology set foot – except where, as in Tibet, it imposed itself in the form of a monastic landlord class on the masses, and for that very reason had 'national' relationships with them.

IDEOLOGY

The educated strata of Asia remained, with their own special interests, entirely 'amongst themselves'.

Wherever an intellectual stratum seeks by sheer thought to fathom the 'meaning' of the world and of its own life and – after the failure of this directly rationalistic endeavour – seeks to grasp this meaning in experience and then to raise this experience to consciousness in an indirectly rationalistic way, their path will lead them somehow or other into the quiet pastures of the world beyond of formless Indian mysticism. And where, on the other hand, a status group of intellectuals renounces such concern to escape from the world and instead consciously and deliberately finds in the grace and dignity of beautiful gestures the highest possible goal of inner-worldly perfection, then it belongs in some way to the Confucian ideal of excellence. Of these two elements, however, intersecting and interpenetrating each other, an important part of all Asian intellectual culture is made up. The idea that, by straightforward activity adapted to the 'demands of the day' one can gain that relationship to the real world which is at the basis of all specifically Western conceptions of 'personality', remains as far from it as the purely objective rationalism of the West, which seeks to master the world in a practical way by the discovery of its own impersonal laws.[1] The rigid ceremonial and hieratic stylisation of its mode of life has preserved it from all attempts, in the modern Western fashion, to pursue what is peculiar precisely and only to this individual, in opposition to all others, and so to drag oneself by the forelock from the morass and make oneself into a 'personality' – a concern which is as fruitless as the attempt deliberately to invent one's own artistic form, or 'style'. But the goals of its self-discipline, partly purely mystical, partly purely worldly and aesthetic as they were, could not be pursued in any other way than by emptying them of all the real forces of life, and were far removed from the interests of the 'masses' engaged in practical activity whom they thus left to the unbroken bondage of magic. The social world split asunder into the stratum of the knowledgeable and educated, on the one hand, and that of the uneducated plebeian masses, on the other. The objective inner organisation of the real world, of nature as of art, of ethics as of economics, remained a closed book to the aristocracy, since it seemed to them devoid of any interest. Their mode of life, in its pursuit of goals which lay beyond the everyday,

---

[1] What is characteristic is not, as again Percival Lowell suggests, that certain (though not all) Chinese inventions were used in the service of art rather than economics. In the West, too, experiment was born from art and the majority of inventions originally served the purposes of art, apart from the military and medical purposes which were also important in Asia. The decisive development in the West was that art became 'rationalised' and that then experimentation made the transition from its original sphere to that of science. It was not 'impersonality' but rationally evaluated 'impartiality' which prevented what we call 'progress' to rational specialisation from being made in the East.

revolved around the model of their essentially exemplary prophets and sages. But for the plebeians there appeared no prophets with an ethical mission which might have imposed a rational form on their everyday lives. The appearance of such prophets in the West, on the other hand, above all in the Near East, with all the far-reaching consequences which followed from it, was the result of a very special conjunction of historical circumstances, without which, despite all the differences in natural conditions, development in the West might easily have followed similar paths to those which were followed in Asia, and especially in India.

(*Gesammelte Aufsätze zur Religionssoziologie*, 2nd edn, Tübingen, 1923, II, pp. 363–78. First published in 1917.)

IV · Politics

Introduction

Weber wrote extensively about politics not only from an academic standpoint but also as a committed participant in the controversies of his own country and period. This is, at first sight, out of keeping with his strictures against those 'favourably disposed towards the admission of value-judgments into teaching'.[1] But in his own terms, his commitment to nationalist values and his advocacy of the policies which he believed would best serve the interests of Germany as a major power are perfectly consistent with his rigorous separation of academic from political values. He did not claim scientific objectivity for his personal values, and he acknowledged the entitlement of others to support different values provided only that they were consistently held. It is true to say that his insistence on the duty of the scholar to accept the findings of science whether they accord with his preferences or not has an obvious connexion with his insistence on 'realism' and 'facing facts' in the views which he puts forward about practical politics. His open contempt for those who cherish illusions about peace and progress and his determination to expose hypocrisy and rhetoric among the advocates of Conservatism and Social Democracy alike are both expressions of an underlying commitment to what one of his commentators has called 'the familiar bourgeois values writ large'.[2] It is also true that his academic writings as well as his journalism were visibly influenced by his reactions to contemporary political events: in particular, his view of 'charisma', which he at first regarded as an archaic and irrational form of political legitimacy, changed during the First World War into a view of it as not merely compatible with, but even necessary for, successful leadership of Germany.[3] But this does not constitute a violation of his methodological principles, for it still leaves the validity (or otherwise) of his analysis to be assessed independently of the passions or prejudices which may have inspired it. Nor, it should be added, was his nationalism, extreme as it may have been, of a kind which can plausibly be equated with the 'National Socialism' of the Nazis which he did not live to see. For all his belief in *Realpolitik* and German *Kultur*, Weber was explicitly not a Social Darwinist;[4] he was opposed to a policy of territorial expansionism by Germany during the War;[5] and he was not only not anti-semitic himself but an outspoken opponent of anti-semitism in

[1] Above, p. 71.
[2] David Beetham, *Max Weber and the Theory of Modern Politics* (London, 1974), p. 58.
[3] See Arthur Mitzman, *The Iron Cage: an Historical Interpretation of Max Weber* (New York, 1970), Ch. 8.
[4] This is made clear both in *Economy and Society* and in his Inaugural Lecture of 1895.
[5] See the discussion of Weber's wartime attitudes in D. Beetham, *Max Weber and the Theory of Modern Politics*, pp. 138–44, and Wolfgang J. Mommsen, *The Age of Bureaucracy: Perspectives on the Political Sociology of Max Weber* (Oxford, 1974), Ch. 2.

others.[1] Many of his readers are likely to find his values uncongenial (as I myself do). But that is not a reason to exaggerate those aspects of them which, seen with hindsight, are the least attractive or fashionable.

Weber's attitude to politics is most explicitly and memorably expounded in the lecture on 'Politics as a Vocation' which he delivered to a student audience in Munich in the year before his death. It was extensively revised by him for publication, and it can be read at the same time as a discussion of the changing role of the professional politician in modern society and a personal political testament. Composed at a time when Germany had been defeated in war and was in the throes of attempted revolution and counter-revolution, it could hardly be other than sombre in tone and pessimistic in outlook. But it is consistent with the view of politics which Weber took throughout his life, and it is hard to suppose that that view would have been altered by the events of the subsequent half-century. The passage which I have taken from it is roughly the last third of the lecture.

The following selection on charismatic domination comes from *Economy and Society*. Weber's concept of 'charisma' – which, like 'ideal type', he borrowed but did not invent – as a distinctive type of domination is perhaps his most influential legacy to political science. 'Charismatic' differs both from 'traditional' domination, where obedience is customary, and 'rational-legal' domination, where obedience is secured through acknowledgment of explicitly formulated constitutional rules, in that obedience rests on acceptance of the legitimacy of the person as such to whom it is paid. It is thus inherently unstable. But at the same time, precisely because the circumstances in which it occurs involve a break with routine, it carries the possibility of a revolutionary transformation of social structures and ideologies. It raises a number of difficulties which Weber leaves unresolved, in particular those which stand in the way of clearly diagnosing the residue of charisma which persists, in his view, within political structures after the re-establishment of routine. But two criticisms sometimes made of it can be repudiated without qualification. First, 'charisma' is not to be equated with force of personality: charismatic domination is a product of social circumstances as well as of individual psychology. Secondly, charismatic domination is not a stage in an evolution from primitive, 'traditional' to modern, 'rational-legal' domination: all three types can be found in varying combinations in all historical periods, and it is perfectly possible that the trend towards 'rationalisation', powerful though it may be, may be reversed by a leader who, for better or worse, embodies legitimacy in his own person.

The selection on 'Socialism' is taken from a lecture which Weber gave to an audience of army officers in Vienna in July 1918. In it, he was concerned at the same time to expound to a non-academic audience the content of socialism as conceived by Marx and Engels and also to state his own views on the likelihood of capitalism being succeeded by socialism, and the consequences which might be expected to follow if it were. By this time, the Russian Revolution of October 1917 had of course happened, and Weber refers to it later on in the lecture. But it does not lead him to qualify either of his two main conclusions: first, that the

[1] Eduard Baumgarten, *Max Weber: Werk und Person* (Tübingen, 1964), pp. 610–12.

predictions of the *Communist Manifesto*, work of genius though it is, have not been borne out by subsequent history; secondly, that if the entrepreneurs of bourgeois capitalist society *are* dispossessed, they will merely be replaced by a state bureaucracy which will, if anything, exert a tighter control over the industrial worker.

The selection on 'Economic Policy and the National Interest in Imperial Germany' is taken from the inaugural lecture which he delivered at Freiburg in 1895 under the title 'The Nation State and German Economic Policy'. It was an outspoken statement of the need for economic policy to be guided by the political interests of Germany as a major power, and it was regarded even at the time as an aggressive and controversial statement of liberal-imperialism. Much of it is taken up with two related questions by which Weber was preoccupied during this period: the role of the Junkers as a politically dominant class, and the likely consequences of their importation of migrant workers from Eastern Europe to work their estates. But he goes on from this to enlarge, in a deliberately rhetorical and slightly archaic style, on the general theme of the need for political leadership in Germany and the importance of subordinating short-term, sectional economic interests to long-term, power-political aims. The irony of the contrast between his hopes in 1895 that the Germans of his generation might become 'the forerunners of a greater period' and his vision in 1919 of 'a Polar night of icy darkness'[1] would not be lost on Weber himself.

The final selection on politics is taken from the first of two articles which Weber wrote about the abortive Russian revolution of 1905–6, in which he discussed the proposals for reform which the Constitutional Democrats had put forward. He did not claim for these articles that they were other than more or less instant political journalism. But they show a remarkable knowledge of the situation for a non-specialist – it is characteristic of Weber that he set himself to learn Russian for the purpose – and this extract retains a continuing interest both as a diagnosis of the limitations of democratic liberalism in the Russian context and as an illustration of how Weber's view of the nature of politics coloured his interpretation of the particular events which he was concerned to analyse. His tone is sceptical to the point of cynicism, and he is at different points equally contemptuous of the failings of the reactionaries, the liberals, the revolutionists and the peasantry alike. But it can plausibly be argued that although he underestimated the revolutionary potential of the Social Democrats his underlying diagnosis was subsequently vindicated in Russia just as it later was in Germany. In neither case, as he clearly saw, were there present at the beginning of the twentieth century the necessary prerequisites for a liberal parliamentary democracy; and without them, the collapse of the monarchy was bound to lead in the end to a bureaucratic, authoritarian, single-party state either of the Right or of the Left. He would never have claimed to be able to predict just when or how this would come about. But his assertion in 1906 that 'Only a disastrous *European* war would lead to a decisive overthrow of the autocracy'[2] did, of course, turn out to be prophetic.

[1] Below, pp. 224 and 268. [2] Below, p. 276n.

10 · *Politics as a Vocation*

What can politics as a vocation offer in the way of inner satisfaction, and which personal qualities does it presuppose in anyone who devotes himself to it?

Well, it offers first of all the sense of power. Even in positions which are, formally speaking, modest, the professional politician can feel himself elevated above the everyday level by the sense of exercising influence over men, of having a share in power over their lives, but above all by the sense of having his finger on the pulse of historically important events. But the question which he has to face is this: through which personal qualities can he hope to do justice to this power (however narrow its limits in his particular case) and so to the responsibility it lays on him? At this point we enter the domain of ethical questions; for it is in this domain that the question arises: what kind of man must one be to venture to lay hands on the spokes of the wheel of history?

Three qualities above all, it might be said, are of decisive importance for the politician: passion, a sense of responsibility and judgment. By 'passion' I mean *realistic* passion – a passionate commitment to a realistic cause, to the god or demon in whose domain it lies. I do not mean 'passion' in the sense of that state of mind which my late friend Georg Simmel used to call 'sterile excitement' – a state which is characteristic of a certain kind of intellectual, especially of Russian intellectuals (though not perhaps all of them!), and which now plays such a large part amongst our own intellectuals in this carnival which is dignified with the proud name of a 'revolution'. It is a kind of 'romanticism of the intellectually interesting' which lacks any realistic sense of responsibility and runs away to nothing. For it is not enough merely to have the passion, however genuinely felt. That alone does not make a politician, unless it is used to further some real cause and so makes a *sense of responsibility* towards this cause the ultimate guide of his behaviour. And that requires the decisive psychological quality of the politician – *judgment* – the ability to contemplate things as they are with inner calm and composure before allowing them to affect one's actions, or in other words, an attitude of *detachment* towards things and people. Lack of detachment, purely as such, is one of the mortal sins for every politician, and one of those qualities which would condemn our rising generation of intellectuals to political impotence if they were to cultivate it. The problem, therefore, is simply how hot passion and cool judgment can be made to combine within the same personality. Politics is made with the head, not with other parts of the body or mind. And dedication to politics can only be born from passion and nourished by it, if it is not to be a frivolous intellectual game but an authentic human activity. But that firm discipline of the personality which is the hallmark of the passionate politician and distinguishes him from the political dilettante who is merely possessed by 'sterile excitement' is achievable only through the habit of detachment, in every sense of that word. The 'strength' of a political 'personality' is to be found above all in the possession of these qualities.

The politician has daily, even hourly, to overcome in himself a wholly banal and all-too-human enemy: the *vanity* which is so common and which is the deadly enemy of all concrete commitment and of all detachment (in this case, detachment towards oneself). Vanity is a very widespread characteristic, and perhaps no one is altogether free of it. In academic and scholarly circles, indeed, it is a kind of occupational disease. But equally, in the case of a scholar, however distasteful its manifestations may be, it is relatively harmless in the sense that it does not, as a rule, interfere with his scholarly activity. In the politician's case, things are quite different. In his work, the urge for *power* plays an inescapable part. The 'power instinct', as it is often called, belongs therefore among his normal attributes.

The point at which someone in his profession begins to sin against the Holy Ghost, however, is the point at which this urge for power becomes *detached from reality*, and becomes a means of purely personal self-intoxication instead of being applied exclusively in the service of some realistic cause. For there are ultimately only two sorts of mortal sin in the political world: lack of realism and lack of responsibility (which is often, though not always, identical with it). At its most powerful, vanity – the need to occupy the limelight as much as possible – tempts the politician to commit one or both of these sins. The temptation is all the greater, in that the demagogue is forced to take into account the 'effect' which he produces: indeed just because of this he runs a constant risk of becoming a play-actor, making light of the responsibility for the consequences of his actions and asking only what 'impression' he is making. His lack of realism leads him to seek the glittering semblance of power rather than the reality of it, while his lack of responsibility leads him to enjoy power purely for its own sake, without any substantive purpose. For although, or rather precisely *because*, power is the inescapable instrument of all politics, and the urge to power is therefore one of the driving forces behind all politics, there is no more pernicious way to distort the political drive than for a politician to boast of his power like a parvenu and luxuriate conceitedly in the sensation of power – in short, to worship power for its own sake. The pure 'power-politician', extolled in the cult which has its zealous adherents even in our own society, may operate with impressive effect, but in the event his operations lead only into a meaningless void. In that respect, the critics of 'power-politics' are absolutely right. In the sudden inner collapse of some typical representatives of this way of thinking we have been able to see what inner weakness and impotence is concealed behind their ostentatious but totally empty posturing. It results from an utterly cheap, superficial and *blasé* attitude towards the *meaning* of human activity – an attitude lacking all awareness of the tragic element with which all action, but especially political action, is in fact intertwined.

It is undeniably true, indeed a fundamental truth of all history (though not one to be explored more closely here), that the final result of political activity often, nay, regularly, bears very little relation to the original intention: often, indeed, it is quite the opposite of what was first intended. But, for this very reason, if the activity is to have any kind of inner balance, the intention of serving some real cause must be present. It is a matter for the politician's own fundamental beliefs what *form* this cause, for the sake of which he seeks power and uses power, should take. He can seek to promote national or universal, social-cum-ethical or cultural, secular or religious causes. He can be carried away by enthusiasm for 'progress' (in whatever sense) or he can coolly reject this sort of belief. He can insist on standing firm in the service of an 'ideal', or he can reject such pretensions on principle and choose to serve the more external goals of everyday life. At all events, some belief or other must always be there. Otherwise, there will weigh on him in the event, it is perfectly correct to point out, the curse of futility to which all finite creatures are subject, even in what seem from the outside to be is greatest successes.

With what has just been said we have . .dy begun to consider the last problem which concerns us this evening: the *ethos* of politics as a 'cause'. What sense of vocation can we find in the profession of politics itself, quite independently of any goals it may serve within the general moral economy of life? In which area of ethics, so to speak, is it at home? Here, to be sure, we find a confrontation of ultimate conceptions of life, between which in the end a *choice* must be made. Let us resolutely approach this problem, which has recently been reopened, although in my view in an extremely distorted form.

But let us first rid the question of an utterly trivial attempt to cloud the issue. Ethics can, of course, first appear on the scene playing a part which, from the moral point of view, is absolutely fatal. Let us consider some examples. You will seldom find a man who has fallen out of love with one woman and in love with another who does not feel the need to justify his action to himself. He will say that the first was not worthy of his love, or that she deceived him, or whatever other 'reasons' of the same general kind there may be. There is a lack of gallantry here; which is still further compounded by the 'justification' which he invents for the unfortunate fact that he doesn't love her any more and that the woman must simply put up with it. In virtue of this justification, he claims to exonerate himself and tries to shift not only the suffering but also the blame on to her. The man who is successful in winning a woman's love behaves in exactly the same way: his rival must be less worthy than himself, otherwise he would not have lost. And of course the case is no different when after a victorious war the victor claims, in an unworthy desire for self-justification: 'I won, because I was in the right'. Or take the case of someone who suffers a mental breakdown because of the sheer horror of war and then, instead of straightforwardly admitting that it was indeed too much for him, feels the need to justify his war-weariness to himself by substituting the feeling that he could not bear the war because he had to fight for a morally evil cause. It is the same with the defeated in war. Instead of looking, like old women, for the 'guilty men' after a war (and, after all, it is the structure of the society which led to the war), it would be more manly and austere to say to the enemy: 'We lost the war, you have won it. All that is now over and done with: now let us talk about the conclusions to be drawn, as far as they concern the *real* interests involved, and, most importantly, in the light of the responsibility towards the *future*, which concerns the victor above all.' Everything else is undignified and one only has to pay for it in the end. Damage to its interests a nation will forgive, but not damage to its honour, least of all when caused by a canting self-righteousness. Every new document which comes to light decades later leads to the revival of the undignified howls, the hatred and the anger, instead of allowing the war and its outcome to be at least *morally* buried. This can be done only if we adopt a realistic and chivalrous, but above all a *dignified* attitude. It cannot be done by insisting on 'morality': that really means no more than a lack of dignity on both sides. Those who do so are occupying themselves not with the true concerns of the politician – the future and his responsibility towards it – but instead with politically sterile, because undecidable, questions of past guilt. It is *here*, if anywhere, that political guilt lies. In so doing, moreover, such people overlook the inevitable distortion of the whole issue by thoroughly material interests – the interest of the victors in extracting the greatest possible advantage, both material and moral, and the hope of the defeated that they may gain some advantage by acknowledging their guilt. If anything is 'vulgar', that is, and it is the result of using 'morality' in this way as a means of 'getting one's due'.

But what is the nature of the real relation between ethics and politics? Have they, as has sometimes been said, nothing whatever to do with each other? Or, on the contrary, is it correct to say that the *same* ethical standards apply in political life as in every other area of activity? The view has sometimes been taken that these two propositions present us with mutually exclusive alternatives: either the one or the other is correct. But is it true that any ethical system in the world could impose *identical* rules of conduct on sexual, commercial, familial and professional relationships; on one's relations with one's wife, greengrocer, son, competitor, friend and defendant? Should it really matter so little, in deciding on the ethical standards required in politics, that the specific instrument of politics is power, backed up by *violence*? Don't we see that the Bolshevist and Spartacist ideologues achieve exactly the *same* results as any military dictator you care to mention, precisely because they use this essential instrument of politics? What difference is there between domination by the Workers' and Soldiers' Soviets and that by any ruler of the old regime, apart from the persons of the power holders and their dilettantism? What difference is there between the polemics of most of the representatives of the so-called 'new morality' themselves against the opponents whom they criticise and those of any demagogue you care to mention? Someone will say: the nobility of their intentions. Fine! But what we are talking about here is the means which they use; and the opponents whom they attack claim likewise, with equal honesty from their point of view, that their ultimate intentions are noble. 'They that take the sword shall perish with the sword', and war is war wherever it is fought.

Well then, what about the ethics of the Sermon on the Mount? The Sermon on the Mount, or, in other words, the absolute ethics of the Gospel, is a more serious matter than it is believed to be by those who are nowadays so keen to cite its requirements. It is not something to trifle with. What has been said about the causal principle in science holds equally good of it too: it is not a cab which one can hail at will, to get in or out of as one thinks fit. What it really means, if it is not to be reduced to a set of trivialities, is: all or nothing. Take, for example, the rich young man who 'went away grieved: for he had great possessions'. The commandment of the Gospel is unconditional and clear: give what thou hast – *everything*, categorically. The politician will say that this is a socially meaningless demand, so long as it does not apply to *everyone*. So we must have taxes, tolls, confiscations – in short, compulsion and regulation applied to *everyone*. The ethical commandment simply pays *no* attention to that: that is its very essence. Or what about 'Turn the other cheek'? The commandment is unconditional: we are not to ask questions about the other's right to strike the blow. It is an ethic which denies all self-respect – except for a saint. That is the point: one must be a saint in everything, at least in intention: one must live like Jesus or the Apostles or St Francis or their like, and *then* this code of ethics will have meaning and express value. Otherwise, it will not. For if the consequence to be drawn from the other-worldly ethics of love is 'Resist not evil with force', the contrary proposition is true for the politician: 'Thou *shalt* resist evil with force' (otherwise you are *responsible* for the victory of evil). Anyone who wants to act according to the ethics of the Gospel should not go on strike, since strikes are a form of coercion: he should join one of the unaffiliated trades unions. But above all he should not talk about 'revolution'. For the ethic of the Gospel certainly does not teach that civil war is the one legitimate kind of war. The pacifist who lives by the Gospel will refuse to bear arms or will throw them away, as pacifists were recommended to do in Germany, as a moral duty, in order to put an end to the war and so to all wars. The politician will say that the only sure means of discrediting war for all *foreseeable* time would have been to make peace on the basis of the *status quo*. Then the combatant peoples would have asked what the war was all for. It would have been reduced *ad absurdum* – which is not now possible. For there will have been political gains for the victors, or at least for some of them. And the responsibility for that lies with the attitude which made all resistance impossible for us. Now – once the period of exhaustion is past – it will be *peace* which is discredited, *not* war: that is the result of absolute ethics.

Finally, the duty to tell the truth. For absolute ethics this is unconditional. The conclusion has therefore been drawn that all documents should be published, especially those which lay the blame on one's own country, and that on the basis of this one-sided publication guilt should be acknowledged unilaterally, unconditionally, and without regard for the consequences. The politician will find that the result of this is not that truth is advanced, but rather that it is obscured by the misuses to which it is put and the passions which are unleashed; that the only approach which could be fruitful is for impartial umpires methodically to set out the evidence in a way which takes all sides into account. Every other procedure can have consequences for the nation which adopts it which would be impossible to make good even after several decades. But absolute ethics is not even *concerned* with 'consequences'.

That is the decisive point. We must be clear that all activity which is governed by ethical standards can be subsumed under one of two maxims, which are fundamentally different from, and irreconcilably opposed to, each other. The ethical standards may either be based on *intentions* or on *responsibility*. Not that an ethic of intentions is the same as irresponsibility or an ethic of responsibility the same as indifference to intentions. Naturally, there is no question of either of these two things. But there is a profound antithesis between actions governed by the ethics of intention, where to put it in religious language 'The Christian acts rightly and leaves the outcome to God', and actions governed by the ethics of responsibility, where one is answerable for the (foreseeable) *consequences* of one's actions. You may put a very plausible case to a Syndicalist who is a convinced believer in the ethics of intention, to the effect that the consequences of his actions will be an increase in the chances for reaction, increased oppression of his class, retardation of its progress; and all this will make not the slightest impression on him. If an action which results from a pure intention has evil consequences, then the responsibility lies not with the man who performed the action but with the world in general, the stupidity of other men – or the will of God who created them as they are. The man who acts according to the ethics of responsibility, on the other hand, takes into account just those ordinary faults in men; he has, as Fichte has justly said, no right whatever to assume their goodness or perfection and doesn't feel himself in any position to shift on to others the consequences of his own action, insofar as he could foresee them. He will say: 'These are the consequences to be imputed to my action'. The man who bases his ethics on intentions feels that he is 'responsible' only for seeing that the flame of pure intention, the flame of protest against the injustice of the social order, is not extinguished. The aim of his action, which, considered from the point of view of its possible consequences, is totally irrational, is to keep fanning this flame; the action can and should have only the value of an example.

But even here we have not finished with the problem. No system of ethics in the world can avoid facing the fact that 'good' ends in many cases can be achieved only at the price of morally dubious or at least dangerous means and the possibility, or even the probability, of evil side-effects. No system of ethics in the world can make it possible to decide when and to what extent the morally good end 'sanctifies' the morally dangerous means and side-effects.

For politics, the essential means is violence. The significance of the tension between means and ends from the ethical point of view can be judged from the fact that, as is well known, the revolutionary Socialists of the Zimmerwald faction, even during the war, professed a principle which could be formulated in the following pregnant words: 'If the choice which faces us is between several more years of war followed by revolution and immediate peace with no revolution, then we choose several more years of war!' If one had gone on to ask what this revolution was supposed to achieve, every scientifically trained Socialist would have replied that there was no question of a transition to an economic order which could be called 'socialist' in *his* sense; rather a bourgeois economy would arise yet again, rid only of its feudal elements and the remains of dynasticism. For this modest result, then, they were willing to face 'several more years of war'! One could well be excused for thinking that even someone with very firm socialist convictions might well reject an end which can only be achieved by such means. Exactly the same applies to Bolshevism and Spartacism, and in general to every kind of revolutionary Socialism. It is, of course, simply ridiculous for those on this side to express *moral* revulsion for the 'power-politicians' of the old regime on account of their use of the same means – however completely justified the rejection of their *ends* may be.

It is on this very problem of the sanctification of the means by the end that the ethics of intention in general seems to have run aground. Indeed, the only logical course open to it is to *repudiate all* activity which involves the use of morally dangerous means. I repeat, this is the only *logical* course. In the real world we do indeed constantly have the experience of seeing the believer in the ethics of intention suddenly turn into a millenarian prophet. For example, those who have just been preaching 'Love against Force', suddenly urge their followers to use force – for the *last* time, so as to bring about a situation in which *all* violence will be abolished – just as our military commanders said to their men before every offensive, 'This is the last one: it will bring victory and so peace'. The believer in the ethics of intention cannot accept the ethical irrationality of the world. He is a cosmic 'rationalist' in his ethical views. All of you who know your Dostoievsky will remember the scene with the Grand Inquisitor, where this problem is admirably analysed. It is impossible to reconcile the requirements of the ethics of intention and the ethics of responsibility, and equally impossible to lay down a moral rule for deciding which end is to sanctify which means, if one makes any concessions at all to this principle.

My colleague F. W. Foerster, whom I respect very much as a man for the undoubted purity of his intentions, but whose political views, I confess, I totally reject, believes that in his book he has circumvented this difficulty by the simple thesis that from good only good can come and from bad only bad. If this were so, then this whole set of problems would not exist. But it is truly amazing that 2,500 years after the Upanishads such a thesis can still see the light of day. Not only the whole course of world history, but every incontrovertible test of everyday experience makes it plain that the opposite is true. The development of all the world religions is due to this fact. The age-old problem of theodicy comes down precisely to this question: how is it that a power which is depicted as being at the same time all-powerful and loving has been able to create an irrational world like this one of unmerited suffering, unpunished injustice and irredeemable folly? Either the omnipotence or the benevolence must be lacking: or else life is governed by wholly different principles of compensation and retribution, principles which we can explain metaphysically or which are even hidden for ever from our understanding. This problem posed by the experience of the irrationality of the world has been the driving force behind all religious development. The Indian doctrine of Karma, Persian Dualism, Original Sin, Predestination and the *deus absconditus* have all grown out of this experience. The ancient Christians, too, knew very well that this world is ruled by demons, and that he who meddles with politics, who in other words makes use of the instruments of power and violence, concludes a pact with the infernal powers. They knew too that for such a man's actions it is *not* the case that from good only good, from bad only bad can come, but that often the opposite holds true. Anyone who cannot see that is indeed politically a child.

Religious ethics have come to terms in various ways with the fact that we are involved in different ways of life, governed by different sets of rules. Hellenic polytheism sacrificed to Aphrodite as well as to Hera, to Dionysus as well as Apollo, knowing full well that they were not infrequently in conflict with each other. The Hindu way of life made each of the different callings subject to a separate ethical code, a Dharma, and divided them off permanently as castes from each other. These castes were, moreover, organised into a strict hierarchy of rank, from which there was no escape for anyone born into it, except by rebirth in the next life, and by which different castes were placed at varying distances from the highest religious blessings of salvation. This made it possible to cultivate the Dharma of each individual caste, from the ascetics and Brahmins to the thieves and prostitutes, in a manner appropriate to the specific inherent laws of each calling. These included the professions both of war and of politics. You can find a classification of war within the total system of ways of life in the Bhagavadgîtâ, in the dialogue between Krishna and Arjuna. 'Do thou what must be done' – that is, do what is required by the Dharma of the warrior caste and its rules, that which is specifically necessary to achieve the aim of war. In this system of beliefs, work does not obstruct religious salvation but promotes it. From time immemorial, Indra's heaven was as sure a fate for those Indian warriors who met a hero's death as was Valhalla for the Germans. The Indian warrior would, however, have felt as much contempt for Nirvâna as the Germans would have felt for the Christian Heaven with its choirs of angels. This specialisation of ethical codes made it possible for Indian ethics to treat this royal art in a wholly consistent way, by following only the inherent laws of politics and even radically strengthening them. Truly radical 'Macchiavellianism', in the popular sense of that word, is classically expressed in Indian literature in the Arthashâstra of Kautilya (written long before the birth of Christ, ostensibly in the time of Chandragupta): compared to it, Macchiavelli's 'Prince' is harmless.

In Catholic ethics, with which Professor Foerster has close connexions, the *consilia evangelica*, as is well known, are recognised as a special code for those blessed with the charisma of the saintly life. A contrast is drawn between the monk on the one hand, who may neither shed blood nor pursue profit, and the pious knight or citizen on the other, of whom the first may shed blood and the second pursue profit. The way in which this ethic is reconciled with, and finds a place in, the system of salvation is less consistent than in India: this is a consequence, indeed a necessary consequence, of the basic presuppositions of the Christian faith. The idea that the world has been corrupted by original sin made it relatively easy to incorporate the use of force into ethics as a corrective against sin and the heretics endangering men's souls. But the purely other-worldly requirements of the Sermon on the Mount, according to which a man's intentions were of supreme importance, and the religious conception of Natural Law as an absolute requirement which was based on it, retained their revolutionary power and emerged with elemental energy at almost all times of social upheaval. They gave rise in particular to the radical pacifist sects. One of these in Pennsylvania made the experiment of a state in which there was no external power; but the outcome was tragic, in that when the War of Independence broke out the Quakers could not take up arms in defence of their own ideals for which the war was being fought.

Ordinary Protestantism, on the other hand, legitimised the state, and therewith violence as a means, as a divine institution in general and specifically as the legitimate government. Luther took the burden of moral responsibility for war away from the individual and transferred it to the government, which it could never be a sin to obey on any matter other than a question of faith. Calvinism, again, recognised in principle that force might be used in order to defend the faith, and so sanctioned the religious war which was from the beginning a vital element in Islamic life. Evidently, then, the problem of political ethics is definitely *not* simply a modern phenomenon arising out of the rejection of religious belief which originated in the hero-cult of the Renaissance. All religions have grappled with it, with very different degrees of success, and after what has been said it could not have been otherwise. It is the specific use by groups of human beings of the means of legitimate violence as such which determines the particular character of all ethical problems of politics.

Anyone who accepts the use of this means, to whatever ends (and every politician does so) is thereby committed to accepting its specific consequences. This is particularly true of the warrior of faith – religious or revolutionary. Let us steel ourselves to consider the present situation as an example. Anyone who wants to establish absolute justice on earth by *force*, requires for this purpose a following – a human 'apparatus'. To these followers he must hold out the prospect of the necessary internal and external rewards – a reward in heaven or on earth – or else the apparatus will cease to function. Take the internal rewards first: in the conditions of modern class-warfare, these are gratification of hatred and the desire for vengeance, and especially of feelings of resentment and the need for pseudo-moral self-righteousness and therefore of the need to slander and abuse the enemy. The external rewards are adventure, victory, plunder, power and the spoils of office. The leader, once successful, is totally dependent on the functioning of this apparatus which he creates. Thus he is dependent on *its* motives, not his own. And he is dependent therefore on his ability to guarantee these rewards to his followers – the Red Guard, the secret police, the agitators, whom he needs – *over a long period of time*. What he in fact achieves under such conditions is never in his own hands: it is dictated to him by the motives which inspire the actions of his followers, and from the moral point of view these are predominantly vulgar. His followers are only held in check as long as at least some of them (perhaps never, in this world, the majority of them) are moved by an honest belief in his person and his cause. But in the first place, this belief, even where it is sincerely felt, is very often in reality only a means of giving moral 'legitimacy' to the passion for vengeance, power, plunder and office: let us not labour under any illusions about that, for the materialist interpretation of history is also not a cab to be hailed at will, and it does not come to a halt just for revolutionaries! In the second place, and most important of all, emotional revolution is followed by traditionalist routine. The hero of faith, and, even more, faith itself fades away or becomes (which is even more effective) part of the conventional jargon of political philistines and technicians. This development takes place with especial speed in ideological struggles, because it is usually conducted or inspired by true *leaders*, the prophets of the revolution. For, as with every apparatus of leadership, so here, one of the necessary conditions of success is to empty the ideas of all content, to concentrate on matters of fact, and to carry through a process of intellectual 'proletarisation' in the interests of 'discipline'. The followers of a warrior of faith, once they have achieved power, tend to degenerate with particular ease into a thoroughly commonplace class of office-holders.

Anyone who wants to take up politics in general, and especially politics as a vocation, must be conscious of these ethical paradoxes and of his own responsibility for the changes which may be brought about in *himself* under pressure from them. I repeat, he is meddling with the infernal powers which lie in wait for him in every use of violence. The great virtuosi of other-worldly love of mankind and saintliness, whether from Nazareth or Assisi or the castles of Indian kings, have not employed the instrument of politics, force. Their kingdom was 'not of this world', although they worked and still work in this world: the figures of Platon Karatayev and the saintly characters in Dostoievsky are still the closest approximations to them. The man who is concerned for the welfare of his soul and the salvation of the souls of others does not seek these aims along the path of politics. Politics has quite different goals, which can only be achieved by force. The genius, or demon, of politics lives in a state of inner tension with the God of love, even with the Christian God as the Church depicts Him, and this tension may at any time erupt into irresoluble conflict. This was known to men even in the time when the Church was dominant. The interdict in those days represented an enormously greater power over men and their souls' salvation than the (to use Fichte's words) 'cold sanction' of Kantian moral judgment: it lay time after time on Florence, but still the citizens of Florence fought against the Papal states. And it is with such situations in mind that Macchiavelli, in a beautiful passage in (if I am not mistaken) his *History of Florence,* makes one of his heroes extol those citizens to whom the greatness of their native city is more important than the salvation of their souls.

If, for native city or 'native land', which not everyone nowadays may consider to represent clear values, you substitute 'the future of Socialism' or even 'international peace', then you have the problem in its current form. For to seek to achieve all such ends by *political* activity, using force as a means and acting in accordance with the ethics of responsibility, is to endanger the 'welfare of the soul'. But when the goal is pursued in accordance with the pure ethics of intention in a war of faith, it can be damaged and discredited for generations to come, since no one takes responsibility for the consequences. For then the infernal powers which are involved remain unrecognised. These powers are inexorable: they create consequences for a man's activity, even for his own inner personality, to which he is helplessly surrendered if he does not see them. 'The Devil is an old man' (and it is not age in years of life that the proverb refers to), 'so become old in order to understand him'. I have never allowed myself to be trumped in debate by the date on a birth certificate: the sheer fact that someone is twenty, while I am over fifty, can certainly never lead me to think that that alone was an achievement before which I should swoon with awe. It is not age that counts. What matters is the disciplined dispassionateness with which one looks at the realities of life, and the capacity to endure them and inwardly to cope with them.

It is true: politics is made with the head, but certainly not *only* with the head. In that respect those who advocate the ethics of intention are absolutely right. No one can tell anyone else whether they *ought* to act

223

according to the ethics of intention or the ethics of responsibility, or when they should follow the one and when the other. One thing only can be said. In these days of an excitement which, in your opinion, is *not* 'sterile' (though excitement is certainly not always the same thing as genuine passion), when suddenly the politicians of intention come forward *en masse* with the watchword, 'It is the world which is stupid and vulgar, not me; the responsibility for the consequences doesn't concern me, it concerns the others whom I serve and whose stupidity and vulgarity I shall eradicate', then, I often think, we have to ask first how much *inner strength* lies behind this ethics of intention. I have the impression that, in nine cases out of ten, I have to do with windbags, who do not really feel what they profess to feel, but are simply intoxicating themselves with romantic sensations. This does not interest me very much from the human point of view and impresses me not at all. But it is enormously impressive if a *more mature* man (whether old or young in years) who feels his responsibility for the consequences genuinely and with all his heart and acts according to the ethics of responsibility, says at whatever point it may be: 'Here I stand: I can no other'. That is an expression of authentic humanity and stirs one's feelings. For the *possibility* of this sort of situation occurring at some time or other must indeed exist for *any one* of us who is not inwardly dead. To that extent, the ethics of intention and the ethics of responsibility are not diametrically opposed, but complementary: together they make the true man, the man who can have the 'vocation of politics'.

And now, ladies and gentlemen, let us agree to discuss this point again *ten years from now*. If by that time, as I am sorry to say I cannot help but fear will be the case, for a whole series of reasons, the period of reaction will have long set in and little – perhaps not nothing at all, but at least little that is visible – of what certainly many of you and, as I freely confess, I too have wished and hoped for will have been achieved – if, as is very probable, that is what happens, it will not demoralise me, but it is to be sure an inner burden to be aware of it. In that event, I should very much like to see what has 'become' (inwardly) of those of you who now feel that you are genuine followers of 'the politics of intention' and share in the frenzy which this revolution amounts to. It would be nice if the situation were such that Shakespeare's Sonnet 102 were true:

> Our love was new, and then but in the spring,
> When I was wont to greet it with my lays;
> As Philomel in summer's front doth sing
> And stops her pipe in growth of riper days.

But that is not how things are. It is not 'summer's front' which lies before us, but first of all a Polar night of icy darkness and severity, whichever group may be outwardly victorious at present. For where there is nothing, it is not only the Kaiser but the proletarian too who has lost his rights. When this night begins slowly to fade, who will be left still living of those whose spring has now, to all appearances, been clad in such luxuriant blossom? And what will by then have become of the inner lives of you all? Embitterment or philistinism, simple apathetic acceptance of the world and of one's profession or, third and far from least common, mystical escapism in those who are gifted in that direction or, as is frequently and regrettably the case, force themselves into it to follow the fashion? In every such case I shall conclude that such people were not suited to their field of activity, not able to cope with the world as it really is and with the routine of their daily lives. Objectively and factually, in their innermost hearts, they did not have the vocation for politics which they thought they had. They would have done better to promote brotherly love between man and man in a simple, straightforward way; and for the rest to have worked in a purely down-to-earth way at their everyday tasks.

Politics is a matter of boring down strongly and slowly through hard boards with passion and judgment together. It is perfectly true, and confirmed by all historical experience, that the possible cannot be achieved without continually reaching out towards that which is impossible in this world. But to do that a man must be a leader, and furthermore, in a very straightforward sense of the word, a hero. Even those who are not both must arm themselves with that stoutness of heart which is able to confront even the shipwreck of all their hopes, and they must do this now – otherwise they will not be in a position even to accomplish what is possible today. Only someone who is confident that he will not be shattered if the world, seen from his point of view, is too stupid or too vulgar for what he wants to offer it; someone who can say, in spite of that, 'but still!' – only he has the 'vocation' for politics.

(*Gesammelte Politische Schriften*, 2nd edn, Tübingen, 1958, pp. 533–48. First published in 1919.)

11 · *The Nature of Charismatic Domination*

I. THE ESSENCE OF CHARISMA AND ITS WORKINGS

Bureaucracy, like the patriarchal system which is opposed to it in so many ways, is a structure of 'the everyday', in the sense that stability is among its most important characteristics. Patriarchal power, above all, is rooted in the supply of the normal, constantly recurring, needs of everyday life and thus has its basis in the economy – indeed, in just those sections of the economy concerned with the supply of normal everyday requirements. The patriarch is the 'natural leader' in everyday life. In this respect, bureaucracy is the counterpart of patriarchalism, only expressed in more rational terms. Bureaucracy, moreover, is a permanent structure and is well adapted, with its system of rational rules, for the satisfaction of calculable long-term needs by normal methods. On the other hand, the supply of all needs which go beyond the economic requirements of everyday life is seen, the further back we go in history, to be based on a totally different principle, that of *charisma*. In other words, the 'natural' leaders in times of spiritual, physical, economic, ethical, religious or political emergency were neither appointed officials nor trained and salaried specialist 'professionals' (in the present-day sense of the word 'profession'), but those who possessed specific physical and spiritual gifts which were regarded as supernatural, in the sense of not being available to everyone.

In this context, the concept of 'charisma' is being used in a completely 'value-free' way. The ability of the Nordic 'Berserker' to work himself up into an heroic trance, in which he bites his shield and his person like a rabid dog, eventually dashing off in a raving blood-lust (like the Irish hero Cuculain or Homer's Achilles) is a form of manic attack, artificially induced, according to a theory long held about the Berserkers, by acute poisoning: in Byzantium, indeed, a number of 'blond beasts' with a talent for inducing such attacks were kept, in much the same way as war elephants had previously been. Shamanic trances, likewise, are connected with constitutional epilepsy, the possession of which, once confirmed, constitutes the charismatic qualification. Thus, both kinds of trance have nothing 'uplifting' about them to our way of thinking, any more than does the kind of 'revelation' to be found in the sacred book of the Mormons which must, at least in terms of its value, be considered a crude swindle. Such questions, however, do not concern sociology: the Mormon leader, like the heroes and magicians already referred to, is certified as charismatically gifted by the beliefs of his followers. It was in virtue of possessing this gift or 'charisma' and (if a clear concept of god had already been formed) in virtue of the divine mission embodied therein that they practised their art and exercised their domination. This was as true of healers and prophets as of judges or leaders in war or great hunting expeditions. We have to thank Rudolph Sohm for having worked out the sociological features of this type of power-structure in relation to one particular case of great historical importance (the historical de-velopment of the power of the Christian Church in its early stages) in a way which is intellectually coherent and so, from a purely historical point of view, necessarily one-sided. But the same situation in all its essentials is repeated everywhere, even though often expressed in its purest form in the religious domain.

In contrast with all forms of bureaucratic administrative system, the charismatic structure recognises no forms or orderly procedures for appointment or dismissal, no 'career', no 'advancement', no 'salary'; there is no organised training either for the bearer of charisma or his aides, no arrangements for supervision or appeal, no allocation of local areas of control or exclusive spheres of competence, and finally no standing institutions comparable to bureaucratic 'governing bodies' inde-pendent of persons and of their purely personal charisma. Rather, charisma recognises only those stipulations and limitations which come from within itself. The bearer of charisma assumes the tasks appropriate to him and requires obedience and a following in virtue of his mission. His success depends on whether he finds them. If those to whom he feels himself sent do not recognise his mission, then his claims collapse. If they do recognise him, then he remains their master for as long as he is able to retain their recognition by giving 'proofs'. His right to rule, however, is not dependent on their will, as is that of an elected leader; on the contrary, it is the duty of those to whom he is sent to recognise his charismatic qualification. When the Emperor's right to rule is said, in the Chinese theory, to depend on recognition by the people, that is no more a case of the acceptance of popular sovereignty than is the requirement of the early Christian Church that prophets should be 'recognised' by the faithful. Rather, it is a sign of the charismatic charac-ter of the monarch's office, based as it is on personal qualification and proof. Charisma may be, and obviously often is, qualitatively specialised, in which case qualitative limitations are imposed on the mission and power of its bearer by the internal character of his charisma, not by external regulation. The meaning and content of the mission may be (and normally are) directed to a human group which is defined geographically, ethnically, socially, politically, occupationally, or in some other way; its limits are then set by the boundaries of that group.

Charismatic domination is diametrically opposed to bureaucratic in all respects, and hence in its economic sub-structure. Bureaucracy depends on constancy of income, and so *a fortiori* on a money economy and money taxation, while charisma lives in the world, but is certainly not of it. The true meaning of this remark needs to be understood. Frequently there is a completely conscious sense of horror at the possession of money and at money incomes as such, as in the case of St Francis and many like him. But of course this is not the general rule. The domination exercised even by a gifted pirate may be 'charismatic' in the value-free sense of that term used here, and charismatic political heroes seek booty, above all in the form of money. But the important point is that charisma rejects as dishonourable all rational planning in the acquisition of money, and in general all rational forms of economy. In this it is sharply contrasted also with all 'patriarchal' structures, which are based on the orderly foundation of the 'household'. In its 'pure' form, charisma is not a private source of income for its bearer, either in the sense of being economically exploited in the fashion of an exchange of services or in the other sense of being salaried; equally, it is without any organised levying of tribute to provide for the material needs of the mission. Rather, if its mission is a peaceful one, its requirements are economically provided either by individual patrons or by the donations, contributions or other voluntary services given by those to whom it is directed. Alternatively, in the case of charismatic war heroes, booty furnishes both one of the goals of the mission and a means of supplying its material needs. 'Pure' charisma is opposed to all forms of regulated economy – in contrast with all kinds of 'patriarchal' domination in the sense of that term used here: it is a, indeed *the,* anti-economic force, even (indeed precisely) when it seeks to obtain possession of material goods, as in the case of the charismatic war hero. This is possible because charisma, by its very essence, is not a permanent 'institutional' structure, but rather, when it is functioning in its 'pure' form, the exact opposite. Those who possess charisma – not only the master himself but his disciples and followers – must, in order to fulfil their mission, keep themselves free of all worldly ties, free from everyday occupations as well as from everyday family responsibilities. The prohibition against accepting payment for ecclesiastical office laid down in the statutes of the Jesuit order, the prohibition against owning property imposed on members of an order, or even, as in the original rule of the Franciscans, on the order itself, the rule of celibacy for priests and members of knightly orders, the actual celibacy of many bearers of prophetic or artistic charisma – all express the necessary 'alienation from the world' of those who have a share ('κλῆρος') in charisma. The economic conditions of having such a share may, however, seem from the outside to be opposed to each other, depending on the kind of charisma and the way of life which expresses its meaning (religious or artistic, for example). When modern charismatic movements of artistic origin suggest 'those of independent means' (or, putting it in plainer language, *rentiers*) as the persons normally best qualified to be followers of someone with a charismatic mission, this is just as logical as was the vow of poverty taken by the medieval monastic orders, which had precisely the opposite economic implications.

The continued existence of charismatic authority is, by its very nature, characteristically unstable: the bearer may lose his charisma, feel himself, like Jesus on the cross, to be 'abandoned by his God', and show himself to his followers as 'bereft of his power', and then his mission is dead, and his followers must hopefully await and search out a new charismatic leader. He himself, however, is abandoned by his following, for pure charisma recognises no 'legitimacy' other than that conferred by personal power, which must be constantly re-confirmed. The charismatic hero does not derive his authority from ordinances and statutes, as if it were an official 'competence', nor from customary usage or feudal fealty, as with patrimonial power: rather, he acquires it and retains it only by proving his powers in real life. He must perform miracles if he wants to be a prophet, acts of heroism if he wants to be a leader in war. Above all, however, his divine mission must 'prove' itself in that those who entrust themselves to him must prosper. If they do not, then he is obviously not the master sent by the gods. This very serious conception of genuine charisma obviously stands in stark contrast with the comfortable pretensions of the modern theory of the 'divine right of kings', with its references to the 'inscrutable' decrees of God, 'to whom alone the monarch is answerable': the genuinely charismatic leader, by contrast, is answerable rather to his subjects. That is, it is for that reason and that reason alone that precisely he personally is the genuine master willed by God.

Someone who holds power in a way which still has important residual charismatic elements, as the Chinese monarchs did (at least in theory), will blame himself if his administration does not succeed in exorcising some calamity which has befallen his subjects, whether a flood or a defeat in war: openly, before the whole people, he will condemn his own sins and shortcomings, as we have seen even in the last few decades. If even this penitence does not appease the gods, then he resigns himself to dismissal and death, which is often the method of atonement. This is the very specific meaning of the proposition found, for instance, in Mencius that the voice of the people is 'the voice of God' (according to Mencius, this is the *only* way in which God speaks!): once he is no longer recognised by the people, the master becomes (as is expressly said) a simple private citizen, and, if he aspires to anything more, he is a usurper and deserves to be punished. The situation expressed in these phrases, with their extremely revolutionary resonance, can also be found, in forms which carry no hint of pathos, in primitive societies, where authority has the charismatic character to be found in almost all primitive authority, with the exception of domestic power in the strictest sense, and the chief is often simply deserted if success deserts him.

The purely *de facto* 'recognition', whether active or passive, of his personal mission by the subjects, on which the power of the charismatic lord rests, has its source in submission by faith to the extraordinary and unheard-of, to that which does not conform to any rule or tradition and is therefore regarded as divine – a submission born from distress and enthusiasm. In genuine charismatic domination, therefore, there are no abstract legal propositions and regulations and no 'formalised' legal judgments. 'Objective' law, in such a case, flows from concrete and intensely personal experience of heavenly grace and a semi-divine heroic stature: it means the rejection of the bonds of external organisation in favour of nothing but the ecstasy of the true prophet and hero. It thus leads to a revolutionary revaluation of everything and a sovereign break with all traditional or rational norms: 'it is written, but I say unto you'. The specifically charismatic method of settling disputes is a revelation through the prophet or oracle, or the 'Solomonic' judgments of a charismatically qualified sage based on evaluations which, while extremely concrete and individual, yet claim absolute validity. This is the true home of 'Kadi-justice', in the proverbial rather than the historical sense of that word. For, as an actual historical phenomenon, the judgments of the Islamic *Kadi* were bound up with sacred traditions and their often extremely formalistic interpretation: they amounted in some situations, to be sure, to specific, rule-free evaluations of the individual case, but only where these sources of knowledge had failed. Genuinely charismatic justice is always rule-free in this sense: in its pure form it is completely opposed to all the bonds of formalism and tradition and is as free in its attitude to the sanctity of tradition as to rationalistic deductions from abstract concepts. There will be no discussion here of the relation of the reference to '*aequum et bonum*' in Roman Law and the original sense of the term 'equity' in English law to charismatic justice in general and the theocratic Kadi-justice of Islam in particular. However, both are products in part of a system of justice which is already highly rationalised and in part of the abstract concepts of Natural Law: the phrase '*ex fide bona*' contains in any case an allusion to good commercial 'morality' and so has as little to do with genuinely irrational justice as does our own 'free judicial opinion'. To be sure, all forms of trial by ordeal are derived from charismatic justice. But to the extent that they substitute for the personal authority of a bearer of charisma a rule-bound mechanism for the formal determination of the divine will, they already belong to the domain of that 'bringing down to earth' of charisma which is shortly to be discussed.

As we saw, bureaucratic rationalisation can also be, and often has been, a revolutionary force of the first order in its relation to tradition. But its revolution is carried out by *technical* means, basically 'from the outside' (as is especially true of all economic reorganisation); first it revolutionises things and organisations, and then, in consequence, it changes people, in the sense that it alters the conditions to which they must adapt and in some cases increases their chances of adapting to the external world by rational determination of means and ends. The power of charisma, by contrast, depends on beliefs in revelation and heroism, on emotional convictions about the importance and value of a religious, ethical, artistic, scientific, political or other manifestation, on heroism, whether ascetic or military, or judicial wisdom or magical or other favours. Such belief revolutionises men 'from within' and seeks to shape things and organisations in accordance with its revolutionary will. This contrast must, to be sure, be rightly understood. For all the vast differences in the areas in which they operate, the psychological origins of ideas are essentially the same, whether they are religious, artistic, ethical, scientific or of any other kind: this is especially true of the organising ideas of social and political life. Only a purely subjective, 'time-serving' evaluation could attribute one sort of idea to 'under-standing' and another to 'intuition' (or whatever other pair of terms one might care to use): the mathematical 'imagination' of a Weierstrass is 'intuition' in exactly the same sense as that of any artist, prophet or, for that matter, of any demagogue: that is not where the difference lies.[1] If we are to understand the true meaning of 'rationalism', we must emphasise that the difference does not lie in general in the person or in the inner 'experiences' of the creator of the ideas or the 'work', but in the manner in which it is inwardly 'appropriated' or 'experienced' by those whom he rules or leads. We have already seen that, in the process of rationalisation, the great majority of those who are led merely appropriate the external technical consequences which are of practical importance to their interests, or else adapt themselves to them (in the same way that we 'learn' our multiplication tables or as all too many jurists learn the techniques of the law): the actual content of their

[1] And incidentally they correspond completely with each other also in the 'value'-sphere, which does not concern us here, in that they all – even artistic intuition – in order to make themselves objective and so in general to prove their reality, imply 'grasping', or, if it is preferred, being 'grasped' by the claims of the 'work', and not a subjective 'feeling' or 'experience' like any other.

creator's ideas remains irrelevant to them. This is the meaning of the assertion that rationalisation and rational organisation revolutionise 'from the outside', whereas charisma, wherever its characteristic influence is felt, on the contrary exerts its revolutionary power from within, by producing a fundamental change of heart ('*metanoia*') in the ruled. The bureaucratic form of organisation merely replaces the belief in the holiness of what has always been – the traditional standards – with sub- mission to deliberately created rules: everyone knows that anyone with sufficient power can always replace these rules with others, equally deliberately created, and so that they are not in any sense 'sacred'. By contrast, charisma, in its highest forms, bursts the bonds of rules and tradition in general and overturns all ideas of the sacred. Instead of the pious following of time-hallowed custom, it enforces inner subjection to something which has never before existed, is absolutely unique and is therefore considered divine. It is in this purely empirical and value-free sense the characteristically 'creative' revolutionary force in history.

Although both charismatic and patriarchal power rest on personal submission to 'natural leaders' and personal exercise of authority by them (in contrast with the 'appointed' leaders of bureaucratic systems), the submission and the authority take very different forms in the two cases. The patriarch, like the bureaucratic official, holds his authority in virtue of a certain established order: the difference between this order and the laws and regulations of the bureaucracy is that it is not deliberately created by men but has been accepted as inviolably valid from time immemorial. The bearer of charisma holds his authority in virtue of a mission held to be incarnate in his person: this mission need not always or necessarily be of a revolutionary nature, dedicated to the subversion of all hierarchies of value and the overthrow of existing morality, law and tradition, but it certainly has been in its highest forms. However unstable the existence of patriarchal power may be in the case of any particular individual, it is nevertheless the structure of social domination which is appropriate to the demands of everyday life and which, like everyday life itself, continues to function without regard to changes in the individual holder of power or in the environment. In these respects it may be contrasted with the charismatic structure which is born of extraordinary situations of emergency and enthusiasm. Both kinds of structure may, in themselves, be suited to any sphere of life: many of the old German armies, for instance, fought patriarchally, divided into families each under the leadership of its head. The ancient colonising armies of Eastern monarchs and the contingents of small farmers in the Frankish army, marching under the leadership of their '*seniores*', were patrimonially organised. The religious function of the head of the house- hold and religious worship within the household persist alongside the official community cult on the one hand and the great movements of charismatic prophecy, which in the nature of the case are almost always revolutionary, on the other. Along with the peacetime leader who deals with the everyday economic business of the community, and the popular levy in times of war involving the whole community, there is found nevertheless, among the Germans as well as the Indians, the charismatic war hero, who takes the field with his volunteer force of followers; even in official national wars the normal peacetime authorities are very often replaced by the war-prince, proclaimed as '*Herzog*' on an *ad hoc* basis because he has proved himself as a hero in such adventures.

In the political sphere, as in the religious, it is traditional, customary, everyday needs which are served by the patriarchal structure, resting as it does on habit, respect for tradition, piety towards elders and ancestors and bonds of personal loyalty, in contrast with the revolutionary role of charisma. This holds likewise in the economic sphere. The economy, as an organised permanent system of transactions for the purpose of planned provision for the satisfaction of material needs, is the specific home of the patriarchal structure of domination, and of the bureaucratic structure as it becomes increasingly rationalised to the level of the 'enterprise'. Nevertheless, even here there may be room for charisma. In primitive societies, charismatic features are often found in the organisation of hunting, which was at that time an important branch of the provision of material needs, even if it became less important as material culture increased: hunting was organised in a similar way to war, and even at a later stage was long treated in much the same way as war (even up to the time of the Assyrian royal inscriptions). But even in specifically capitalist economies the antagonism between charisma and the everyday can be found, except that here it is not charisma and 'household', but charisma and 'enterprise' which are opposed. When Henry Villard, with the aim of pulling off a coup on the stock exchange involving the shares of the Northern Pacific Railroad, arranged the famous 'blind pool', asked the public, without stating his purpose, for fifty million pounds for an undertaking which he refused to specify any further, and got the loan without security on the basis of his reputation, his action was an example of grandiose booty-capitalism and economic brigandage which, like other similar examples, was fundamentally different in its whole structure and spirit from the rational management of a normal large capitalist 'enterprise', while on the other hand resembling the large financial undertakings and projects for colonial exploitation, or the 'occasional trade' combined with piracy and slave-hunting expeditions, which have been known since earliest times. One can only understand the double nature of what one might call 'the spirit of capitalism', and equally the specific features of the modern, professionalised, bureaucratic form of everyday capitalism if one learns to make the conceptual distinction between these two structural elements, which are thoroughly entangled with one another, but are in the last analysis distinct.

Although a 'purely' charismatic authority in the sense of the word used here cannot, to the extent that it preserves its purity, be understood as an 'organisation' in the usual sense of an ordering of men and things according to the principle of ends and means, nevertheless its existence implies, not an amorphous, unstructured condition, but a well-defined form of social structure with personal organs and a suitable apparatus for providing services and material goods for the mission of the bearer of charisma. The leader's personal aides and, among them, a certain kind of charismatic aristocracy represent a narrower group of followers within the group, formed on principles of discipleship and personal loyalty and chosen according to personal charismatic qualification. The provision of material goods, though in theory voluntary, non-statutory and fluctuating, is regarded as a bounden duty of the charismatic ruler's subjects to an extent sufficient to cover what is required, and such services are offered according to need and capacity. The more the purity of the charismatic structure is maintained, the less the followers or disciples receive their material means of support or social position in the form of prebends, stipends, or any form of remuneration or salary, or in the form of titles or places in an ordered hierarchy. As far as material needs are concerned, to the extent that individuals have no other means of support, the master, in a community under authoritarian leadership, shares with his followers, without any form of deduction or contract, the wealth which flows in, according to circumstances, in the form of donations, booty or bequests; in some cases, therefore, they have rights of commensality and claims to equipment and donations which he bestows on them. As for non-material needs, they have a right to share in the social, political and religious esteem and honour which is paid to the master himself. Every deviation from this sullies the purity of the charismatic structure and marks a step towards other structural forms.

Together with the household community (though distinct from it), charisma is thus the second great historical example of communism, if that term is taken to mean a lack of 'calculation' in the *consumption* of goods, rather than the rational organisation of the *production* of goods for some kind of common benefit (which might be called 'socialism'). Every form of 'communism' in this sense which is known to history finds its true home either in traditional or patriarchal societies (household communism) – the only form in which it has been or is now a phenomenon of the everyday – or amongst charismatic modes of thought far removed from the everyday: in the latter case, when complete, it is either the camp-communism of the robber band or the love-communism of the monastery in all its varied forms and its tendency to degenerate into mere 'charity' or alms-giving. Camp-communism (in varying degrees of purity) can be found in charismatic warrior societies in all periods, from the pirate-state of the Ligurian islands to the organisation of Islam under the Caliph Omar and the warrior orders of Christendom and of Japanese Buddhism. Love-communism in one form or another is found at the origins of all religions, and lives on amongst the professional followers of the god, or monks; it is also to be found in the many pietistic sects (Labadie, for instance) and other extremist religious communities. Both the genuine heroic disposition and genuine sanctity, as it seems to their true advocates, can only be preserved by maintenance of the communistic basis and absence of the urge towards individual private property. In this they are right: charisma is a force which is essentially outside the everyday and so necessarily outside economics. It is immediately threatened in its innermost being when the economic interests of everyday life prevail, as always tends to happen: the first stage in its decline is the 'prebend', the 'allowance' granted in place of the earlier communistic mode of provision from the common store. Every possible means is used by the proponents of true charisma to set limits to this decline. All specifically warrior states – Sparta is a typical example – retained remnants of charismatic communism and sought (no less than religious orders) to protect the heroes from the 'temptations' presented by a concern for possessions, rational industry, and family cares. The adjustments achieved between these remnants of the older charismatic principles and individual economic interests, which enter with the introduction of prebends and are constantly hammering at the doors, take the most varied forms. In all cases, however, the limitless freedom to found families and acquire wealth which is finally given marks the end of the domination of true charisma. It is only the shared dangers of the military camp or the loving disposition of disciples who are withdrawn from the world which can hold communism together, and it is only communism in its turn which can ensure the purity of charisma against the interests of the everyday.

All charisma, however, in every hour of its existence finds itself on this road, from a passionate life in which there is no place for the economic to slow suffocation under the weight of material interests, and with every hour of its existence it moves further along it.

II. THE ORIGIN AND TRANSFORMATION OF CHARISMATIC AUTHORITY

Charismatic domination in the 'pure' sense which has just been described is always the offspring of unusual circumstances – either external, especially political or economic, or internal and spiritual, especially religious, or both together. It arises from the excitement felt by all members of a human group in an extraordinary situation and from devotion to heroic qualities of whatever kind. It follows directly from this, however, that it is only in the very early stages that the bearer's own faith in his charisma and that of his disciples (whether the charisma is prophetic or of some other kind) and the devout belief of those to whom he feels himself sent in his mission normally operates with unbroken force, unity and vigour. If the tide which once elevated a charismatically led group out of the routine of everyday life flows back into everyday channels, then charismatic domination, at least in its pure form, is undermined in most cases: it becomes 'institutionalised' and changes course, until it either becomes purely mechanical or is imperceptibly superseded by totally different structural principles or becomes mingled and blended with them in a variety of forms; and when this happens, it becomes in fact inseparably bound up with them, often deformed beyond recognition, an element in the empirical historical structure which can be separated out only in theoretical analysis.

'Pure' charismatic domination is thus unstable in a quite specific sense, and all its transformations derive in the last analysis from one and the same source. It is usually the wish of the master himself, and always that of his disciples and, even more, of his charismatically led followers to change charisma and the charismatic blessings of his subjects from a once-for-all, extremely transitory free gift of grace belonging to extraordinary times and persons into a permanent, everyday possession. The inexorable concomitant of this change, however, is a change in the inner character of the structure. The mode of existence of charisma is always overtaken by the conditions of everyday life and the forces which dominate them, especially economic interests; and this is so whether we consider the development of a war hero's charismatic following into a state, the development of the charismatic community of a prophet, an artist, a philosopher or an ethical or scientific innovator into a church, sect, academy or school, or the development of a charismatically led group of followers of a cultural idea into a party or even a mere apparatus of newspapers and periodicals. The turning-point always comes when the charismatic followers and disciples become first – as in the Frankish king's '*trustis*' – the lord's table companions, marked out by special rights, then vassals, priests, public functionaries, party officials, officers, secretaries, editors and publicists, or publishers, wanting to make a living out of the charismatic movement, or else employees, teachers or other professional interest groups, prebendaries, holders of patrimonial offices and the like. The charismatically ruled, on the other hand, usually become tax-paying 'subjects', contributing members of the church, sect, party or club, soldiers conscripted, drilled and disciplined according to the rules and regulations, or law-abiding 'citizens'. Charismatic preaching inevitably – even despite the Apostle's admonition not to 'damp down the spirit' – declines, according to circumstances, into dogma, doctrine, theory, regulations, legal judgments, or petrified tradition.

In particular, there is a consistent interrelationship between the two forces of charisma and tradition, which are at base so alien and hostile to each other. It is easy to understand that neither force depends on planned and purposeful rules or the knowledge of such rules, but rather on belief in the specific sanctity, whether absolute or relative, of the authority of concrete persons, which must be totally accepted by the ruled – the child, the client, the disciple, the follower or the vassal – and on submission to the relationships and obligations of piety due to these persons, which in both cases always has about it an air of religious solemnity. Even the external forms of the two structures of domination resemble each other, often to the point of identity. It is impossible to judge by external criteria whether the sharing of meals between a war-prince and his followers is 'patrimonial' or 'charismatic' in character: it depends on the 'spirit' which inspires the community, that is, on the foundation on which the master's position rests – whether it is the hallowed authority of tradition or personal belief in himself as a hero. And the path which leads from the former to the latter is a slippery one. As soon as charismatic domination loses the character of passionate belief, which distinguishes it from the traditionalism of everyday life, and its purely personal basis, then a link with tradition becomes, not perhaps the only possibility, but certainly by far the most appropriate and, especially in periods in which the techniques of living are insufficiently rationalised, usually the inevitable one. The essence of charisma would seem to be finally given up and abandoned in this process, and this is indeed what actually happens as far as its pre-eminently revolutionary character is concerned. For the main feature of this recurrent pattern of events is that charisma is overtaken by the interests of those in positions of economic or social power in giving legitimacy to their possession of power by deriving it from an authority and source which is hallowed because it is charismatic. Thus, instead of revolutionising, in accordance with its true meaning, all that is traditional or rests on 'legitimate' legal acquisition, as in its early stages, it now works in the opposite direction as the legal basis of 'acquired rights'. And it is in this function, so alien to its whole inner essence, that it becomes an element in the everyday. For the need which it meets in this way is universal, primarily because it is to be explained in terms of universal reasons.

The earlier analysis of the everyday powers of the bureaucratic, patriarchal and feudal structures of domination explained only how these powers *function*. But the question of the criteria on which the holder of the supreme power in the hierarchy, whether bureaucratic or patriarchal, is himself chosen has not yet been settled. It is conceivable that the head of a bureaucratic machine could also be simply the highest official, occupying his post in accordance with some general rules or other. But it is no accident that in most cases this is not so, or that at the least the rules which determine his position are not the same as those which determine the position of the officials who occupy subordinate positions in the hierarchy to his. It is simply a consequence of the pure type of bureaucracy, as a hierarchy of appointed officials, that there should be some level of authority which is not occupied by someone who is in turn 'appointed' in the same sense as the others. The person who is to hold power in the household is self-evident in the nuclear family of parents and children, and in extended families is normally defined by clear traditional rules. But this is not true without qualification of the head of a patriarchal state or a feudal hierarchy.

On the other hand, the first and fundamental problem which evidently confronts charismatic domination, if it is to be transformed into a permanent institution, is likewise precisely the question of the succession to the prophet, hero, teacher or party-leader. It is precisely at that point that charisma inevitably turns on to the path of statute and tradition.

In the first place, once it is a matter involving charisma there can be no question of a free 'election' of a successor, but on the contrary only of a 'recognition' that charisma is present in the claimant to the succession. One possibility is to wait for the epiphany of a successor or earthly representative or prophet who can personally prove his qualification – examples are the incarnations of the Buddha and the Mahdis. But such a reincarnation is often not to be found or is ruled out on dogmatic grounds – as in the case of Christ and, originally, in that of Buddha. Only true (Southern) Buddhism has in fact drawn the radical conclusion from this concept: here, the Buddha's disciples remained after his death, a community of mendicant monks with a minimum of any kind of organisation and formal association, preserving the character of their community, as far as possible, as an amorphous body which only occasionally came together. Where the ancient ordinance of the Pali texts was really observed – as was the case in many places in India and Ceylon – there was not only no patriarch but also no established association of individuals in a concrete monastic community. The 'dioceses' are only a geographical framework established to make it more convenient to define the area within which monks come together for the few common ceremonies, from which all elements of formal ritual are absent. The 'officials' of the monastery are limited to wardrobe-keepers and a few similar functionaries, and the principle that both individuals and the community as such should not own property and that needs should be supplied 'maecenatically' (by donations and begging) is observed as far as this is generally possible in the conditions of everyday life. 'Precedence' in seating and speaking at meetings is conferred only by seniority as a monk and the relation between a teacher and the novice who acts as his attendant. Anyone may freely leave the community at any time and it is only admission to membership which is subject to a number of very simple conditions, such as an apprenticeship, an attestation of reputation and freedom from the teacher, and a minimum of ceremonies. There is no true 'dogma' and no class of professional teachers or preachers. The two half-legendary 'councils' of the early centuries have had no successors.

This extremely amorphous character of the monastic community has certainly contributed to the disappearance of Buddhism in India. It was only possible in general in a pure monastic community and indeed one in which it was entirely up to the individual to achieve his own salvation by his own efforts. For in any other kind of community such behaviour, combined with the purely passive expectation of a new epiphany, naturally endangers the cohesion of the charismatic community, which requires the bodily presence of the master and leader. When this longing to have a bearer of charisma permanently in one's midst is satisfied, an important step in the direction of the everyday has been taken. The constant renewal of the incarnation results in a kind of 'bringing down to earth' of charisma. The person called to be its bearer must now be sought out systematically according to some criteria which manifest his charisma – that is, according to 'rules', as with the new Dalai Lama, who is chosen in basically the same way as the bull of Apis. Or else there must be available some other means for finding him which, being explicit, must follow equally definite rules. To this category belongs the belief which naturally suggests itself that the bearer of charisma himself is qualified to designate his successor, or if like Christ he can by his very nature only be a unique incarnation, his earthly representative.

The creation by the master of his own successor or representative is a very adequate method of preserving continuity of domination for all organisations with charismatic origins, whether prophetic or military. But of course it marks a step away from free domination based on personal charismatic power towards a 'legitimacy' based on the authority of the 'source'. In addition to the well-known religious examples, these charismatic features were also preserved in the form of the ceremony used in the creation of the Roman magistrates – nomination of one's own successor in authority from the ranks of those qualified and acclamation by the army which had been called together for this purpose. This continued to be so even when the office was subject to delay and to the previous consent, or 'election', of the citizen army in accordance with a laid-down procedure, as a means of limiting its power. The nomination of dictators in the field as a matter of necessity, which required men of more than everyday stamp, continued for a long time to be a typical relic of the old 'pure' type of creation. The Roman Emperorship, which originally developed out of the acclamation of the victorious hero as '*imperator*' by the army and which, by the '*lex de imperio*', became, not indeed a monarchy, but an office laying lawful claim to domination, permitted during its most specific period only the designation of colleagues and followers as a 'legitimate' succession to the throne. To be sure, this designation regularly took the form of adoption, as, conversely, in the Roman household the custom spread of the totally free nomination by its head of his own heir, who would then succeed to the place of the *paterfamilias*, once dead, as (in the eyes of the gods) holder of his position in the family and of his wealth. In the practice of succession by adoption there was some hint of the idea of the heritability of charisma, although in the time of the true Roman military Empire this idea was never really recognised as a principle. On the other hand, the position of Emperor always retained the character of an office: the Emperor always remained an official, with an ordered and regulated sphere of bureaucratic competence, as long as the military Empire retained its Roman character. It was the work of Augustus to have given the position this official character: it was seen by contemporaries as the preservation and restoration of Roman traditions and liberties, as opposed to the Hellenistic idea of monarchy which Caesar may have had in mind.

If, however, the bearer of charisma himself has not designated a successor, and if there are no clear outward signs, such as are usually present in incarnations, then the ruled may naturally come to think that it is those who participated in the domination, the *clerici*, or disciples and followers, who are most competent to recognise those qualified. It is then not difficult for these followers, especially since they alone have possession of the means of power, to appropriate this role to themselves as a 'right'. Admittedly, the source of the effectiveness of charisma lies in the faith of the ruled, and so the recognition of the designated successor cannot dispense with it. Rather, recognition by the ruled was originally all-important. Even in the time when the college of electors had defined itself as the panel for preparing the elections, it was still an important question, even from the practical point of view, which of the electors was to present the motion of election to the assembled army. For, in principle at least, he was in a position to obtain the acclamation for his own personal candidate, against the wishes of the other electors.

Designation by the closest and most powerful followers, followed by acclamation by the ruled, is thus the normal procedure in this kind of succession. In the patrimonial and feudal everyday state, this right of designation by the followers, which springs from charismatic roots, takes the form of a 'right of pre-selection' by the most important patrimonial officials or vassals. In this respect, the elections of the German kings are modelled on the elections of bishops in the Church. The 'election' of a new king, which, like that of a Pope, bishop, or priest, took the form, first, of designation by the disciples and followers (electors, cardinals, diocesan priests, chapter, elders) and then of acclamation by the people, was thus not an 'election' in the sense of a modern election of a president or parliamentary deputy, but at least in its true sense something of a totally different kind: the acknowledgment or recognition of the presence of a qualification which did not come into existence as a result of the election but already existed – in other words, a charisma, to the recognition of which the person who is to be elected as its bearer has a claim. Hence there can be, at least according to the original principle, no question of the will of a majority, since a minority, however small, can be just as likely to be right in recognising true charisma as the largest majority can be wrong. Only one decision can be correct: those who dissent in their choice are thus guilty of a misdeed. All the rules for electing a Pope seek to achieve unanimity. An indecisive election for a king, however, is equivalent to a schism in the Church: it obscures true knowledge of the one who is called, and this obscurity can only be removed by a trial by ordeal involving personal combat with physical or magical means, of the kind which has become institutionalised for settling disputes between claimants to the throne in African tribes (especially when they are brothers) and elsewhere.

ꟾWhen the majority principle has been accepted, the minority are under a moral 'obligation' to acquiesce in the right proved by the outcome of the election and subsequently to accept the majority decision꟦Naturally, however, despite the charismatic structure of domination, this kind of determination of the succession must, once the majority principle has been introduced, begin to move towards an authentic system of election. ꟾNot every modern method of choosing rulers, even in democratic societies, is free of all traces of charisma.꟦At all events, the democratic system of so-called plebiscitary domination, which is the official theory of French Caesarism, has in its conception charismatic features, and the arguments of its supporters consist of an emphasis on this aspect of it in particular. The plebiscite is not an 'election' but a recognition of a claimant as the personally qualified, charismatic ruler, either for the first time or (as in the plebiscite of 1870) as a renewal. But even Periclean democracy, which its creator saw as the domination of a demagogue by means of the charisma of spirit and rhetoric, contained a characteristically charismatic element precisely in the election of one of the generals (and also in the drawing of lots for the others, if Eduard Meyer's hypothesis is correct). In the long term, wherever an originally charismatic community has moved in the direction of electing its rulers, the electoral process has become associated with rules. This happens in the first place because, with the atrophy of the true roots of charisma, the everyday power of tradition and the belief in its sanctity again gains the upper hand, and it is only by observing it that the correct choice can be guaranteed. The acclamation by the ruled then begins increasingly to take second place to the rights of pre-selection of clerics, court officials or great vassals, which are based on charismatic principles, and this leads to the eventual emergence of an exclusive oligarchic body of electors. This is as true of the Catholic Church as of the Holy Roman Empire. The same phenomenon can, however, be found wherever a group with political experience has the right of proposal or pre-selection. It is especially the case in most urban societies, at all periods, that the ruling families have come to acquire a *de facto* right of co-optation, and so have been able both to remove the masters from their dominant position, transferring it to a mere 'first among equals' such as an archon, a consul or a doge, and to exclude the community at large from participating in the appointment. In the present day, the tendencies shown in the development of senatorial elections in Hamburg, for instance, represent parallel phenomena. From the formal point of view, this is by far the most frequent 'legal' route to oligarchy.

On the other hand, however, acclamation by the ruled can develop into a regular 'electoral procedure', with a 'right of suffrage' defined by rules, either direct or indirect, elections based on local constituencies or proportional representation, 'electoral classes' and 'electoral circles'. It is a long way before this point is reached. Only in the United States has this development gone so far that even the formally supreme rulers are themselves elected, and there, of course, one of the most essential aspects of the business of an election is seen inside the 'nomination' campaigns of each of the two parties. Elsewhere, it has never gone further than the election of the parliamentary representatives which in turn determines the nominations for the post of Prime Minister and his colleagues. The development from charismatic acclamation to true election of the ruler directly by the community of the ruled has taken place in the most varied cultural stages, and every advance in the rational treatment of the process, freed from emotional faith, is bound to help in bringing about this change. On the other hand, it is only in the West that the election of rulers has gradually evolved towards the representative system. In the ancient world, for example, the Boeotarchs were representatives of their own local community (just as the members of the English House of Commons originally were) rather than of the electors as such; and when, as in the Athenian democracy, officials were really only the mandated representatives of the common people and the electorate was divided up into wards, the principle which was applied was that of rotation rather than the true idea of 'representation'. If this principle is ruthlessly applied, the one who is elected is formally, just as in direct democracy, merely the delegate and so the servant of those who voted for him, not their elected 'master'. Once this has happened, the charismatic basis for the structure has been completely abandoned. However, it is always only in part that it is possible to introduce the principles of 'direct' democracy in this ruthless fashion under conditions where there are large administrative bodies in existence.

Even from a purely technical point of view, the principle of the 'imperative' mandating of the representative can be realised only incompletely, because of the constant changes in the situation and the continual emergence of unforeseen problems. The 'recall' of the representative by a vote of no confidence from his electors has up to now been only sporadically attempted; and the scrutiny of Parliamentary decisions by the 'referendum' chiefly results in nothing but the strengthening of all the irrational forces of inertia, since for technical reasons it normally rules out bargaining and compromise between interested parties. Frequent elections, finally, are ruled out because of their increasing costs. All attempts to subject the popular representatives to the will of the electorate in effect have only one long-term consequence in most cases: they strengthen the power, which is anyway growing, of the party bureaucrats over the popular representatives, since only the party organisation can set the 'people' in motion. Both the material interest in the flexibility of the parliamentary apparatus and the power interests alike of the popular representatives and of the party functionaries combine to promote the conception of the 'popular representatives' as, not servants, but elected 'masters' of their electorate. Almost all systems express this in the form that, like the monarch, the popular representative is not answerable for his decisions and that he 'represents the interests of the whole people'. His actual power may be extremely varied. In France, the individual deputy is in practice not only normally the controller of patronage for all offices, but in general in the truest sense 'master' of his constituency – hence the resistance to proportional representation and the lack of centralisation in the parties; in the United States, the overriding power of the Senate stands in the way, and the Senators have a similar position; in England, and even more in Germany, the individual member is, as such, more his constituents' clerk than their master as far as their economic interests are concerned, and it is the influential party chiefs as such who control patronage.

We cannot go any further at this point into the technical reasons for the way in which the electoral mechanism distributes power: these reasons lie in the historically determined nature of the structures of domination and to a large extent obey their own laws. Only general principles concern us here. Any 'election' may take on a purely formal character without real meaning. This happened with the Roman *comitia* during the early Empire and in many Greek and medieval cities, as soon as the means of political power fell into the hands either of an oligarchic club or of a tyrant, who would then compulsorily designate the candidates to be elected to each office. Even where this was not formally the case, however, it is as well, whenever there is talk in the historical sources of the 'election' of princes or other holders of power by the populace (as for instance among the Germans), to take the expression in a different sense from modern usage: it should be taken to mean rather a simple acclamation of a candidate who has in reality been designated by someone at a higher level and who, moreover, must be chosen from one of a few qualified families. Also, of course, there is in general no question of an 'election' when a vote for a supreme ruler takes a plebiscitary (that is, a charismatic) form, since in that case what is involved is not a choice between candidates but the recognition of a pretender's claims to power. Even a normal 'election', however, may always become merely a decision between several pretenders, who have been picked out and presented to the electorate as alone worthy of consideration – a decision which is worked out on the battlefield of electoral agitation by means of personal influence and appeals to material and non-material interests, and in which the electoral regulations are to some extent merely the rules of the game for this formally 'peaceful' contest. In that case, the business of designating those candidates who are alone worthy of consideration becomes primarily the concern of the parties. For it is not of course the amorphous communal action of the voters, but the party leaders and their personal followings who organise the electoral contests and so the patronage of offices. Even now in the United States, the direct and indirect costs of electioneering within a four-year period amount to almost the same as those of a colonial war, and they are rising in Germany too for all parties which cannot rely on the cheap labour of priests, feudal or bureaucratic notables, or paid trades union officials and other forms of secretarial staff.

Along with the power of money, the 'charisma of rhetoric' becomes more important too. Its power is not in itself confined to any particular cultural situation. The assemblies of Indian chiefs and African palavers are familiar with it, too. In Greek democracy it had its first tremendous qualitative flowering, with immeasurable consequences for the development of language and thought; but from the purely quantitative point of view, modern democratic election contests, with their 'stump speeches', have outdone all that has gone before. The more the aim becomes to influence the masses and the more rigidly bureaucratised the organisation of the parties becomes, the less important becomes the meaning of the content of the speech. For, except in those cases where simple class situations and other economic interests are in question and so must be rationally taken into account and dealt with, its effect is purely emotional, on a level with the party processions and festivals: the aim of all these is to bring to the attention of the masses the idea of the party's power and certainty of victory and above all of the leader's charismatic qualification. It is also a consequence of the fact that all attempts at emotionally influencing the masses necessarily have certain 'charismatic' features that the increasing bureaucratisation of the parties and elec- tioneering can experience a setback at the precise moment when it reaches its peak, as a result of a sudden outbreak of charismatic hero- worship. The charisma of the hero turns out in such a case, as the Roosevelt campaign of 1912 showed, to conflict with the everyday power of the party as a continuing 'enterprise'.

It is the universal fate of all parties, which almost without exception originated as charismatic followings, either of legitimate rulers or of Caesarist pretenders or of demagogues in the style of Pericles or Cleon or Lassalle, when once they slip into the everyday routine of a permanent organisation, to remodel themselves into a body led by '*notables*'. Indeed, one might say that up until the end of the eighteenth century they almost always became federations of nobles. In the Italian cities of the Middle Ages, since the fairly large feudal bourgeoisie was admittedly almost completely Ghibelline, there was often a 'reduction to the ranks' of the *nobili*, equivalent to disqualification from office and deprivation of political rights. Nevertheless, it is very exceptional, even under the '*popolani*', for a *non*-noble to hold a leading office, even though here, as everywhere, the financing of the parties was bound to be done by the bourgeoisie. The decisive factor at that time was that military support for the parties, which very often aspired to direct power, was provided by the nobility: in the case of the Guelphs, for instance, there was an estab- lished register. Any party of the period before the French Revolution – the Huguenots or Catholic League, or any of the English parties, includ- ing the 'Roundheads' – reveals the same typical pattern: a transition from a charismatic period of excitement, in which the barriers of class and status group are broken down in the common support of one or more heroes, to the development of associations of notables, led for the most part by nobles. Even the 'bourgeois' parties of the nineteenth century, the Radicals not excepted, always fell into the old pattern of domination by notables for the simple reason that it was only the notables who could direct either the state itself or the party without pay, but also, of course, because of their social or economic influence. Whenever a landowner on the plains changed his party, both in England and later (up until the seventies of the nineteenth century) in East Prussia, it was taken for granted that not only his patrimonial dependants but also – except in times of revolutionary upheaval – his peasants would follow him. In the towns, at least in the smaller ones, a more or less similar role was played by the mayors, along with judges, notaries, advocates, parsons and teachers and often also, before the workers became organised as a class, the factory owners. It will be explained in another connexion why the latter, even apart from the class situation, are relatively less qualified for this role. In Germany, the teachers are the stratum who, because of the 'status' attached to their profession, act as unpaid electoral agents for the specifically 'bourgeois' parties, just as the clergy normally do for the authoritarian parties. In France it has long been the advocates who have acted for the bourgeois parties, partly because of their technical qualifications, and partly, both during and after the Revolutionary period, because of their status.

Some groupings in the French Revolution, which did not, however, exist for long enough to develop a definite structure, show the first signs of bureaucratic organisation, which was beginning to prevail everywhere by the last decades of the nineteenth century. The swing of the pendulum between charismatic obedience and submission to notables has now been replaced by the struggles between the bureaucratic party organisation and the charismatic party leadership. The party organisation has fallen more and more securely into the hands of the professional party officials the further the process of bureaucratisation has gone and the larger have become the direct and indirect prebendal interests and chances that depend on it, and this is so whether these officials are direct agents of the party or originally free entrepreneurs like the American bosses. In their hands lie the system of personal connexions with ward chairmen, agitators, controllers and other indispensable personnel, the lists, papers and all the other materials which must be known about if the party machine is to be kept under control. It is thus only possible successfully to influence the conduct of the party and, in some cases, successfully to secede from it if one controls such an apparatus. The deputy Rickert's possession of the lists of ward chairmen made possible the 'Secession'; the fact that Eugen Richter and Rickert each controlled his own apparatus made it likely that the Progressive Party would split; and the fact that the 'Old National Liberals' were able to provide all the materials for controlling a party was a more serious symptom of their real intention to secede than all the rumours which circulated beforehand. On the other hand, attempts at mergers between parties always founder on the impossibility of personal mergers between rival apparatuses rather than on any concrete differences, as German experience at any rate shows.

This more or less consistently developed bureaucracy now determines the behaviour of a party in normal times, including the decisively important choice of candidates. But even in such highly bureaucratised structures as the North American parties, as the last Presidential campaign showed, the charismatic type of leadership occasionally comes to the fore again in times of great excitement. If there is a 'hero' available, he seeks to break the domination of the party machine by imposing plebiscitary forms of designation, and in some cases by transforming the whole machinery of nomination. Whenever charisma gains the ascendancy in this way, it naturally runs up against the resistance of the normally dominant apparatus of the professional politicians, especially the bosses who organise leadership and finance and keep the party functioning and whose creatures the candidates usually are. For it is not only the place-hunters whose material interests depend on the selection of party candidates. The material interests of the party's patrons – banks, contractors and trusts – are also, of course, very deeply involved in the choice of persons. The large contributor who finances a charismatic party leader in particular cases and expects from his electoral success, according to circumstances, state commissions, tax-farming concessions, monopolies or other privileges, but above all the repayment of his advances with appropriate interest, has been a typical figure since the days of Crassus. On the other hand, however, the normal party organisation depends on the support of such patrons. The party's regular income from members' subscriptions and possibly deductions from the salaries of officials who have obtained their posts with the help of the party (as in North America) is seldom sufficient. Direct economic exploitation of the party's power may enrich those directly involved without necessarily filling the party's own coffers at the same time. Frequently, membership subscriptions are for propaganda purposes either abolished altogether or made to depend on self-assessment: when this happens the large contributors become, even in formal terms, the rulers of the party's finances. The regular leader of the party organisation and genuine specialised expert, the boss or party secretary, can only rely on their money completely, however, when he has firm control of the machinery of the party. Every upsurge of charisma is thus a threat to the regular organisation even from the financial point of view. We thus have the frequent spectacle of competing bosses or other leaders of rival parties agreeing amongst themselves in the common interests of business to suppress the rise of charismatic leaders who would be independent of the regular party machines.

It is as a rule easy for the party organisation to achieve this castration of charisma: in America it has been done successfully time and again, even in the conduct of the 'presidential primaries', with their plebiscitary and charismatic character, since the professional organisation, because of its very continuity, remains tactically more than a match for emotional hero-worship in the long run. Only extraordinary conditions can enable charisma to triumph over the organisation. The peculiar relationship of charisma and bureaucracy which split the English Liberal Party over the introduction of the first Home Rule Bill is well known: Gladstone's completely personal charisma, so irresistible in its appeal to puritan rationalism, forced the majority of the caucus-bureaucracy, in spite of the most determined hostility on specific points and dire forebodings about the election, to swing unconditionally behind him, so leading to the split in the machine created by Chamberlain and as a result to the loss of the electoral contest. The same kind of thing happened last year (1912) in America.

We can accept that the chances of charisma in its struggle with bureaucracy in a party depend to some extent on the general character of the party. The chances of charisma are very different in a simple 'unprincipled' party – that is, a party of place-hunters which formulates its programme *ad hoc* in the light of the opportunities offered by the particular electoral contest – from what they are in a party which is primarily an association of notables based purely on status, or a class party, or a party which to a greater extent still preserves its idealistic 'programme' or 'ideology' (all such contrasts being, of course, relative). In certain respects, its chances are greatest in a party which is primarily of the first type, since in such a party it is much easier for impressive personalities to win the necessary following, other things being equal, than in such petty bourgeois organisations of notables as the German parties, especially the liberal parties with their inflexible 'programmes' and 'ideologies', whose adaptations to temporary demagogic opportunities may always signify catastrophe. But it is impossible to generalise about this topic. Each individual case is affected by too close an association between the intrinsic laws of the particular party machine and the economic and social conditions prevailing in the concrete situation.

As these examples show, charismatic domination is by no means only to be found at primitive stages of development: the three basic types of structure of domination cannot simply be arranged in a linear order of development, but are found in the most varied combinations with each other. It must be admitted, however, that charisma is fated to decline as permanent institutional structures increasingly develop. In the early stages of social relationships, as far back as we can reach, every social action which goes beyond the provision of traditional needs in the household economy is charismatic in structure. Primitive man sees in all those influences which determine his life from the outside the working of specific powers, which belong to things, animate or inanimate, and to men, dead as well as living, and give them power to act for good or ill.

The whole conceptual apparatus of primitive peoples, including their myths about nature and animals, proceeds on such assumptions. Such concepts as *mana* and *orenda*, as interpreted in ethnography, refer to such specific powers, which are 'supernatural' simply in the sense that they are not available to everyone, but are inseparable from their personal or material possessors. Every event which is out of the everyday run allows charismatic powers to blaze up, and every unusual capacity arouses charismatic beliefs, which then again lose some of their meaning in everyday routines. In normal times, the power of the village headman is extremely small: he is little more than an arbitrator and a representative. The members of the community generally speaking do not consider that they have an authentic right to depose him, because his power is based on charisma and not election. But on occasion they may desert him without hesitation and settle elsewhere. This sort of contempt for a king on account of his lack of charismatic qualification is found among the Germanic tribes. Anarchy, regulated only by continued observance of accepted custom, either through lack of thought or through fear of some ill-defined consequences of innovation, may be seen as almost the normal condition of primitive communities. Much the same is true in normal everyday conditions of the social power of the magicians. But when there is some special event – a great hunting expedition, a drought or other threat from the anger of the demons, but especially the danger of war – the charisma of the hero or magician is immediately able to begin to function. The charismatic leader in hunting or war is often a separate figure alongside the peacetime chief, who has primarily economic functions, and hence acts mainly as an arbitrator. If a permanent cult develops in order to influence the gods and demons, then the charismatic prophet and magician evolves into the priest. If the state of war becomes chronic, necessitating the technical development of military leadership to allow for the systematic training and recruitment of warriors, then the charismatic leader of the army becomes the king. The Frankish royal officials, the count and the *sakebaro*, were originally concerned only with military and financial matters: their other functions, especially the administration of justice, which had originally been left entirely to the old charismatic people's arbitrator, were not added until later.

The emergence of a class of war-princes as a permanent structure with a permanent apparatus marks a decisive step to the stage at which the concepts of 'king' and 'state' can appropriately be used, as opposed to that of the 'chief', who may, according to circumstances, exercise primarily economic functions in the interests of the communal economy and the economic regulation of the village or market community, or else may have primarily magical (cultic or medical) or judicial (originally arbitrational) functions. On the other hand, it is arbitrary to follow

Nietzsche in making kingship and the state begin with the subjection of another tribe by a victorious people and the creation of a permanent apparatus to hold the subjects in dependence as tributaries. For precisely the same differentiation between those who are fit to serve as warriors and are exempted from tax and those who are not fit and so are liable to tax can easily develop within any tribe which is chronically under military threat – not necessarily in the form of patrimonial dependence of the latter on the former, but very often without that. The following of a chief can then join together into a military guild and exercise political rights as lords, so that an aristocracy of the feudal type emerges; or else the chief may increasingly begin to pay his followers, first in order to make raids for plunder, and then in order to rule the other members of his own people. (There are many examples of the latter, too.) What is true is that kingship is normally what results from the development of the charismatic war-prince into a permanent institution, with an apparatus of domination to control the unarmed subjects by force. Admittedly, and quite naturally, this apparatus is most rigidly developed in foreign territory acquired by conquest, where it is required by the constant threat to the ruling stratum. The Norman states, especially England, were not by accident the only Western feudal states with a genuinely centralised and technically developed administration, and the same is true of the Arabian, Sassanid and Turkish warrior-states, which were most rigidly organised on conquered territory. Exactly the same is true, moreover, in the area of hierocratic power. The rigidly organised centralisation of the Catholic Church developed in the mission-field of the West and was completed after the historic local powers of the Church had been destroyed by the French Revolution: the technical apparatus of the Church was created during its period as the 'church militant'. But royal and high-priestly power in itself may be found even without conquest or mission, if one sees the decisive characteristic as the permanent institutionalisation of domination and therefore the existence of a continuous apparatus of domination, be it bureaucratic, patrimonial or feudal in character.

> (*Wirtschaft und Gesellschaft*, 4th edn,
> Tübingen, 1956, II, pp. 662–79.
> First published in 1922.)

12 · *Socialism*

What, in this context, do we mean by *socialism*? The word has, as argued earlier, many meanings. But the opposite of socialism which usually comes to mind is the private enterprise system: that is, the system in which the provision of economic needs is in the hands of private entrepreneurs and so is effected in such a way that these entrepreneurs provide themselves, by means of contracts of sale and wage contracts, with material plant, a clerical staff and a manual labour force, and then, at their own economic risk and in expectation of profit for themselves, cause goods to be produced which they then sell on the market. This private enterprise system has been labelled in socialist theory 'the anarchy of production', because it allows the provisioning of those who need the goods produced to depend on the outcome of the workings of the private interest in making a profit which the individual entrepreneurs have in selling their products.

The question of which of a society's requirements should be supplied entrepreneurially – that is, by private enterprise – and which should not be supplied in this way but, in the widest sense, socialistically, that is, by planned organisation, has had various answers in the course of history. In the Middle Ages, for instance, republics like Genoa allowed their great colonial wars against Cyprus to be waged for them by limited liability companies, the so-called *Maone*. They put up the money which was required, hired the appropriate number of mercenaries, conquered the territory, secured the defence of the republic, and, of course, exploited the land thus acquired for their own ends, either by establishing plantations or by exacting tribute. In much the same way, the East India Company conquered India for Britain and exploited it for its own ends. The *condottiere* of the late Italian Renaissance belonged to the same category. Like Wallenstein, the last representative of this type, he recruited his army in his own name and at his own expense, his coffers were enriched by a share of the booty plundered by the army and, naturally, he would stipulate that the prince, or king, or emperor paid him a fixed sum in recompense for his services and to cover his costs. Even as late as the eighteenth century, the colonel, though rather less independent, was still an entrepreneur who levied recruits on his own account and was responsible for their clothing. Some requirements, it is true, were met

251

from the prince's own stores, but the colonel always had to a large extent to manage at his own risk and for his own profit. The conduct of war by private enterprise, which to us today would seem monstrous, was in other words considered perfectly normal.

On the other hand, it would have been unthinkable for any medieval city or guild simply to abandon to the free market the provision of the city's corn or the supply of the imported raw materials which were indispensable for the work of the masters of the guild. Beginning in the ancient world, most notably in Rome, and right through the Middle Ages, it was the city's responsibility to provide these things: they were not left to the free market, which played only a supplementary role. In somewhat the same way as now happens during times of war economy, large sectors of the economy worked together under a policy of 'state interventionism', to use the currently preferred phrase.

The characteristic feature of our present situation is that private enterprise, which is associated with a private bureaucracy and therefore with the separation of the worker from the means of production, controls a domain which has never before in the history of the world possessed both these characteristics together to the same extent – namely the domain of industrial production. Furthermore, this process goes together with the mechanisation of production within the factory, which results in local concentration of workers in one and the same space, bondage to the machine and a common work discipline within the machine shop or mine. It is this discipline, above all, which gives its particular tone to the present-day form of 'separation' between the worker and the means of production.

It is from this situation, from the discipline of the factory, that modern socialism has emerged. There have been the most varied kinds of socialism at all times and in all the countries of the world, but it is only on this foundation that the distinctive features of modern socialism are possible.

This subjection to work discipline is so deeply felt by the industrial worker because, in contrast even to a slave-plantation or a socage-farm, the modern industrial enterprise is based on an extraordinarily rigorous process of selection. A present-day factory manager does not simply take on every worker who comes along, merely because he is willing to work, even for low pay. Rather, he puts the man on piece-work on the machine and says, 'Right, do some work and I will see how much you deserve'; if the man shows that he is not capable of earning a certain minimum wage, he is told, 'Sorry, you are not cut out for this kind of work, we can't use you'. He is dismissed, since the machine is not being used to full advantage if it is not manned by someone who knows how to use it to full advantage. This, or something like it, happens everywhere. In

252

contrast with the slave enterprises of the ancient world, where the master was bound to his slaves, since if one of them died, that meant a loss of capital for him, every modern industrial enterprise depends on this principle of selection. The selection, moreover, becomes extraordinarily rigorous because of the competition between entrepreneurs, which compels each individual entrepreneur to fix a definite maximum wage: to the necessity of discipline there corresponds the necessity of a minimum level of earnings for the workers.

If nowadays the worker comes to his boss and says 'we cannot live on this wage and you could afford to pay us more', then in nine out of ten cases (I mean in peacetime and in those sectors of the economy in which there is really severe competition) the boss is in a position to open his books and prove to the workers that this is out of the question, that his competitor pays such and such and that, if he were to pay them only so much more per head, then all the profits would disappear, he couldn't pay the shareholders, and he couldn't carry on with the business since he wouldn't get any credit from the bank. In saying that, he would very often be saying nothing but the naked truth. A final point is that under the pressure of competition, profitability depends on eliminating as much human labour as possible, especially that of the highest paid workers, and replacing it in the most expensive operations by new labour-saving machines: that is, on replacing 'skilled' workers by 'unskilled' or by 'semi-skilled' workers trained directly on the machine. This is an inevitable development, which is going on all the time.

All this is seen by socialism as the 'domination of people by things', in other words, the domination of the end (the supply of needs) by the means. Socialism sees that, whereas in the past there were individuals who could be made answerable for the fate of clients, bondsmen or slaves, that is no longer possible today. It therefore does not concern itself with individuals, but with the system of production as such. The scientifically trained socialist will absolutely refuse to make any individual entrepreneur responsible for the fate which befalls the worker, saying rather that it is a result of the system, of the situation of constraint in which all those involved, entrepreneur as much as worker, find themselves placed.

In positive terms, however, what would socialism, as opposed to the present system, amount to? In the widest sense of the word, what is usually referred to also as a 'collective economy'. That is, first of all, an economy without profit, in other words, without the direction of production by private entrepreneurs on their own account and at their own risk. Instead, the economy would be in the hands of the officials of a public corporation, who would take over control in respects to be discussed presently. Secondly, and in consequence, an end to the so-called anarchy of production, that is, to competition between entrepreneurs.

There is at present, especially in Germany, a good deal of discussion about whether the war has already in reality taken us halfway along the road towards such a 'collective economy'. In view of this, it should be briefly remarked that there are two fundamentally different principles which might underlie the form of organisation of a particular nation's organised economy. The first is the principle nowadays referred to as 'state interventionism', which is undoubtedly familiar to all those good men who work in enterprises which are involved in the war effort. It is based on collaboration between the combined entrepreneurs in a particular branch of the economy and state officials, either military or civilian. By this means, the supply of raw materials, the provision of credit, prices and commercial intelligence can be extensively regulated in accordance with a plan, and the state can participate both in the profits and in the decision-making of these combines. It is believed that the entrepreneur is then supervised by these officials and that production is controlled by the state. Thus, by this system, we should already have 'true', 'genuine' socialism, or at least be on the way towards it. In Germany, however, this theory has encountered widespread scepticism. I have no opinion to offer on the question of what may be true in wartime. Everyone who can count, however, knows that in peacetime, when we shall not be facing ruin, there cannot be such extensive control as there is at present, and that in peacetime this kind of state intervention, involving compulsory cartelisation of entrepreneurs in every sector and state participation in these cartels, so that the state takes a share of profits in return for extensive rights of control, would not in fact mean the control of industry by the state so much as the control of the state by industry. Indeed, this would take a very disagreeable form. Within the combines, the state representatives would sit at the same table as the managers of factories, who would be greatly superior to them in knowledge of the particular industry, in commercial training and in their personal stake in the industry. In Parliament, however, the workers' representatives would sit and demand that the state representatives concern themselves with high wages and low prices, as, they would say, they had the power to do. On the other hand, moreover, in order not to ruin its finances, the state, participating as it did in the profits and losses of the combine, would naturally have an interest in keeping prices high and wages low. And finally, the private members of the combine would expect the state to guarantee them the profitability of their enterprises. In the eyes of the working class such a state would thus appear as a class state in the truest sense of the word, and I doubt whether that is politically desirable; I doubt even more whether it would be wise to represent this state of affairs to the workers as 'true' socialism, tempting though this thought may certainly seem. For the workers would very soon discover by experience that the lot of the mine worker is not the slightest bit different whether the mine is privately or publicly owned. In the mines of the Saar, the worker's life is just the same as in a private mine: when the company is badly managed, so that it does not make much of a profit, then it also goes badly for the men. The difference, however, is that strikes against the state are impossible, so that in this form of state socialism the essential dependence of the worker is increased. That is one of the reasons why the Social Democrats reject this kind of 'state intervention' in the economy, or this form of socialism in general. The collective element in such a case is merely the cartel. Profit is still the decisive factor, as it was before; the important question which decides the direction to be taken by the economy is still that of the gains to be made by the individual entrepreneurs who have combined to form the cartel, of whom the state exchequer has now become one. The unfortunate thing would be that, whereas at present the political bureaucracy of the state and the economic bureaucracy of private enterprise, of the cartels, the banks and the large firms, exist alongside each other as separate bodies, so that, in spite of everything, economic power can be held in check by political, in the situation envisaged both sets of officials would form a single body with a solidarity of interests and would no longer be under control. At all events, profit as the goal of production would not have been abolished. The state as such, however, would have to share the burden of the workers' hatred, which at present is directed against the entrepreneurs.

The direct opposite of this system, in this last respect, could only be the kind of consumer organisation which sought to deal with the problem of which *needs* should be supplied by this state sector of the economy. As you know, many consumer cooperatives, especially in Belgium, have gone in for establishing their own factories. If one were to imagine this in a generalised form and under the control of a state organisation, then it would be a completely and fundamentally different species, a consumer socialism, of a kind which is today completely unknown, a system in which those in charge could be taken to task. But it remains a mystery where the interest groups are to be found which might one day give it life. For, judging by experience, consumers as a type have only a limited capacity for organisation. People who have a specific interest in making money can easily be brought together, once they are shown that combining in this way will help them to realise a profit or to guarantee profitability: it is on this that the possibility of creating the kind of producer socialism, of which state interventionism is one example, depends. On the other hand, it is extraordinarily difficult to persuade people to join together when they have nothing more in common with each other than a desire or intention to buy something or to provide for their needs, since the whole situation of the consumer stands in the way of socialisation. Even

starvation, in Germany at least, has not persuaded (or has hardly persuaded) the great mass of ordinary housewives to accept the meals prepared in the special wartime kitchens in place of their own amateurish
individual cooking, even though everyone has found the publicly-
prepared meals to be excellently made and tasty, and even though they
are incomparably cheaper.

So much by way of introduction. I now come to the kind of socialism
which is today associated with the programmes of the socialistic mass
parties which presently exist, and so with that of the Social Democratic
Party in Germany. The fundamental document of this kind of socialism
is the Communist Manifesto of 1847, published and circulated in January
1848 by Karl Marx and Friedrich Engels. This document is in its own
way, however much we reject its fundamental theses, as I at least do, a
scientific achievement of the first order. That cannot and should not be
denied, since no one believes it and since it cannot be denied with a good
conscience. Precisely in those theses which we today reject there is an
error of genius, which has had far-reaching, and perhaps not always very
pleasant, political consequences, but which has been very fruitful from
the scientific point of view – more fruitful than is often the case with what
is correct but uninspired. One thing must be said at the outset about the
Communist Manifesto: it refrains from moralising, in intention at least,
if not always in execution. It never occurs to the authors of the Communist Manifesto to denounce the world's wicked and ignoble ways – or
at least so they claim: in reality, they were human beings with strong
passions who did not by any means always stick to their intentions. It was
also, in their opinion, no part of their task to say that the world is
arranged in such and such a way, but it ought to be changed and
arranged thus and so. But the Communist Manifesto is a *prophetic* document: it prophesies the collapse of the private enterprise system – of
capitalism, as it is usually called – and prophesies that this society will be
replaced first, as a transitional stage, by a dictatorship of the proletariat.
Beyond this transitional stage, however, lies the authentic and final hope:
the proletariat cannot free itself from serfdom without making an end
of *all* domination of man over man. That is the real prophecy, the key
proposition of the Manifesto, without which it would never have been
written. The proletariat, the mass of the working class, will through its
leaders seize first political power, but that is only a transitional stage which
will lead to what is called an 'association of individuals', which is thus
the final goal.

What this association will look like is a question on which the Communist Manifesto and all the programmes of all the socialist parties are
silent. We are told that this is unknowable. All that can be said is that
this present society is condemned to collapse, that it will break down in

accordance with scientific law and will be replaced first of all by the dictatorship of the proletariat. But what comes next cannot be predicted, except to say that there will be no domination of man over man.

What reasons are given for the inevitable and scientifically predictable collapse of the present society? For it is supposed to occur in a way completely governed by scientific laws: that was the second key proposition in this pathetic prophecy, the one which won for it the ecstatic faith of the masses. In one place Engels uses the image that, just as in time the planet Earth will crash into the Sun, so present capitalist society is doomed to collapse. What grounds are given for this prediction?

The first is this: a social class like the bourgeoisie (by which is meant primarily always the entrepreneurs and those who directly or indirectly share a community of interest with them) – such a ruling class, then, can only maintain its domination if it can guarantee to the subject class, the wage earners, at least the bare minimum required for life. In the view of the authors, that was the case under slavery and also under the socage system and in other instances. In all these cases, people were guaranteed at least the bare minimum and so the system of domination could persist. That, however, is not possible for the modern bourgeoisie. It cannot achieve it because competition between entrepreneurs requires more and more price cutting and the throwing of more and more workers onto the streets to starve as a result of the introduction of new machines. The bourgeoisie must have available a large stratum of unemployed workers – the so-called 'industrial reserve army' – from which it can select, at any time and in any number required, the appropriate workers needed for its enterprises, and precisely such a stratum is created by the increasing use of automated machinery. The consequence is, however – so the Communist Manifesto claims – that a constantly growing class of the permanently workless, of 'pauper ', appears and undercuts the minimum required for existence, so that the proletariat is not guaranteed even the bare necessities of life by this social system. Where that is the case, however, a society becomes indefensible – that is, sooner or later it will collapse in revolution.

This theory of increasing misery, as it is called, has nowadays been explicitly and universally abandoned in this form as incorrect by all sections of the Social Democratic movement. It has been explicitly admitted in the Jubilee edition of the Communist Manifesto by its editor Karl Kautsky that society has developed in a different direction from this. The thesis is now presented in a different, modified form (which itself, incidentally, has not gone undisputed), but at all events it has been stripped of its earlier pathetic character. Be that as it may, however, what do the chances of success of the Revolution depend on? Could it not be condemned to a constant succession of failures?

At this point we come to the second argument. Competition between entrepreneurs means that those who are stronger, whether in capital or in commercial ability, but especially in capital, will come out on top. That means that the number of entrepreneurs will be constantly diminishing, since the weaker will be eliminated. The smaller the number of entrepreneurs becomes, the greater, both relatively and absolutely, becomes the number of the proletariat. At some point, however, the number of entrepreneurs will have shrunk so far that it will be impossible for them to maintain their domination. Then it will be possible to expropriate these 'expropriators', perhaps in a perfectly peaceful and polite manner – by pensioning them off, say – since they will see that the ground beneath their feet has become so hot, and their numbers have diminished so far, that they can no longer assert their domination.

This thesis is still put forward today, if already in modified form. It has, however, been shown that, at least nowadays, it does not hold good in general in any of its forms. First, it does not hold for agriculture, where on the contrary there has very often been a marked improvement in the condition of the peasantry. Furthermore, it has proved not so much mistaken as different in its consequences from what was expected in relation to broad sectors of industry, where it has turned out that a simple shrinkage in the number of entrepreneurs is not the whole story. The elimination of those who are weak in capital takes the form of their subjection to finance capital, cartels or trusts. These very complex processes are accompanied, first, by a rapid increase in the numbers of office workers, the bureaucrats of the private enterprise system: their numbers increase at a much faster rate than those of the manual workers, and their interests clearly do not by any means lie in the direction of proletarian dictatorship. A further consequence is the creation of a network of interest groups of the most varied kinds, a network so complex that it certainly cannot be maintained at the moment that the number and strength of the direct and indirect interests which people have in the preservation of the bourgeois system is declining. At all events, the situation in the meantime is not such that one could confidently assert that in future a mere half dozen, or a few hundred or thousand, capitalist magnates will stand alone in opposition to millions upon millions of proletarians.

Finally, the third argument was based on a calculation of the effects of crises. Because of the competition between entrepreneurs (at this point in the classical socialist writings there is an important, but intricate, piece of argument which I must here spare you), there would inevitably be more and more frequent periods of overproduction, which would be resolved by means of bankruptcies, crashes and so-called 'depressions'. As Marx merely hinted in the Communist Manifesto, but as was later to be developed into a comprehensive theory, these periods follow one another according to a regular cycle, governed by law. It is in fact true that over almost a century there has been such an approximate cycle in the succession of such crises. The causes of this are a subject of disagreement even among the foremost scholars in our discipline, so it would be out of the question to discuss them here.

It was on these crises that classical socialism based its hopes. Above all, it hoped that these crises would, in accordance with scientific law, increase in intensity and in their power to generate a destructive and terrifying revolutionary atmosphere, accumulate and multiply and eventually create such an atmosphere that there would no longer be any attempt, even in non-proletarian circles, to preserve the present economic system.

This hope has today been in essence abandoned. For the risk of crises, while it has certainly not disappeared, has diminished in relative importance, since the entrepreneurs have moved from ruthless competition to cartelisation, or in other words to the attempt to eliminate competition to a large extent by regulating prices and sales; and since furthermore the big banks, including, for example, the German State Bank, have moved to the point of seeing to it, by regulating the granting of credit, that periods of over-speculation also occur to a much lesser extent than before. Therefore, although it cannot be said that this third hope of the Communist Manifesto and its successors has actually been 'disproved', it is certainly true that many of its underlying assumptions have been radically shifted.

The lofty hopes placed, in the Communist Manifesto, in the collapse of bourgeois society have therefore been replaced by much more prosaic expectations. Amongst these is, first, the theory that socialism is by its very nature the next phase in evolution, since the productive activity of the economy is becoming increasingly 'socialised'. What this means is that the individual entrepreneur is being replaced by the joint stock company with its appointed managers, and that enterprises are being established by the state, by communities and by purposive associations which no longer depend, as before, on the risks and profits of an individual, or more generally a private, entrepreneur. That is quite true, with the qualification that the joint stock company often conceals one or more financial magnates, who control the shareholders' meeting: every shareholder knows that, shortly before the general meeting, he gets a letter from his bank, asking him to transfer the voting rights attached to his shares to the bank, if he does not wish to come and vote in person, as would indeed be pointless when faced with a capital of millions of crowns. Above all, however, what this form of socialisation means is a proliferation of officials, that is, of office staff with their specialist commercial or

259

technical training, on the one hand and, on the other, a proliferation of *rentiers*, that is, of the class which lives on dividends and rents alone, without, like the entrepreneur, performing any mental work, but has a stake in the capitalist system in virtue of its interest in all its sources of income. In public enterprises, however, and those established by purposive associations, the powerfully and exclusively dominant figure is the *official*: it is not the worker, who has a harder task to achieve anything by striking in this kind of organisation than when dealing with a private entrepreneur. It is the dictatorship of the official, not that of the worker, which, at present anyway, is on the advance.

Second is the hope that the machine, in replacing the older specialist workers, the trained craftsmen and the kind of highly skilled worker who used to fill the ranks of the old British craft unions, by unskilled workers, thus making anyone at all capable of working on any machine at all, will bring about such unity in the working class that the old division into different trades will cease, the consciousness of unity will become overwhelming and the struggle against the possessing class will be advanced. The answer to this is not entirely simple. It is true that the machine does tend to a large extent to replace precisely the highly paid and skilled workers, since obviously every industry seeks to introduce just those machines which will replace those workers who are hardest to obtain. The section of workers which is most often to be found on the increase in present-day industry is the so-called 'semi-skilled': in other words, not the skilled workers trained in the old way by a special course of instruction, but workers who are placed directly on the machines and trained on the spot. For all that, they too are often to a large extent specialists. For instance, it still takes some years before a 'semi-skilled' weaver reaches the peak of his skill, and so before he utilises his machine to the best advantage for his employer and earns the maximum wage. Admittedly, with other categories of worker the typical normal period of training is considerably shorter than in the case just cited. Nevertheless, this increase in the numbers of the semi-skilled, although it means a marked weakening in specialisation between different trades, does not mean the end of specialisation altogether. On the other side, moreover, there is an increase in specialisation and in the requirement of specialised training for all levels *above* that of manual worker in the productive process, down to foremen and overseers, and an increase at the same time in the relative numbers of persons employed at these levels. It is true that they too are 'wage-slaves'. But usually they are not on piece-rates or a weekly wage, but a regular salary. Above all, the worker naturally hates his foreman, who is in constant daily contact with him, much more than he hates the factory owner, and hates the factory owner more than the shareholder, even though it is the shareholder who really gets money without working for it, whereas the factory owner has very arduous mental work to do and the foreman comes even closer to the worker. The same thing happens in the army too, where it is usually the corporal who attracts the strongest antipathy, or at least has the chance to do so, as far as I have been able to observe. Anyway, the development of the general system of stratification is very far from going in an obviously proletarian direction.

Finally, there is an argument based on the increasing standardisation of production, in the sense of increasing uniformity. Everywhere there seems a general tendency, accelerated to an unusual degree by the War, towards greater and greater uniformity and interchangeability between products and an increasing schematisation of jobs. It is only among the top layer of entrepreneurs, it is said, and even there to a constantly decreasing extent, that the old free pioneering spirit of the bourgeois entrepreneurs of the past still reigns. In consequence, so the argument goes on, it becomes more and more possible to control production, even without the specific entrepreneurial qualities which bourgeois society claims to be indispensable for managing an enterprise. This is said to be so especially in the case of cartels and trusts, which have substituted an enormous staff of officials for the individual entrepreneurs. That is again quite correct. But again only with the same proviso, namely that this standardisation also increases the importance of a particular social stratum, the officials who have already been mentioned so often, who require a very definite kind of education and who therefore, as must now also be said, acquire the character of a definite status group. It is no accident that we see a general mushrooming of commercial high schools, trade schools and specialist technical schools. At least in Germany, there is the desire among the students at these schools to join a fraternity, to acquire a few duelling scars, to become accepted as a duelling partner and so fit to be a reserve officer, and subsequently in the office to become a preferential candidate for the hand of the boss's daughter: in short, to assimilate oneself to the rank of what is called 'society'. Nothing is further from the thoughts of this class than solidarity with the proletariat; they are much more concerned with increasing the gap between the proletariat and themselves. The same is true, to varying degrees but nevertheless quite plainly, of many of those employed at lower levels than these office workers. All aspire to at least a similar *status*, whether for themselves or for their children. There is no clearly discernible tendency towards proletarisation today.

However that may be, these arguments in themselves already show that the old hope for a revolutionary cataclysm, which gave the Communist Manifesto its power of enchantment, has mellowed into an evolutionary conception, that is, a conception of a gradual development of the old economy, with its entrepreneurs competing on a massive scale, into a regulated economy, whether the regulation is done by state officials or by cartels in which officials participate. It is this system, no longer the elimination of individual entrepreneurs by competition and crises, which is now seen as the first step towards the genuinely socialist society, the society free of domination. This evolutionary approach, which expects from this slow transformation the development of the socialist society of the future, had already before the War become part of the thinking of the trades unions and also of many socialist intellectuals in place of the old 'catastrophe' theory. The familiar conclusions have been drawn from it. 'Revisionism', as it is called, has emerged. The leaders of this movement have had at least some awareness of the grave step they were taking in depriving the masses of their faith in the sudden advent of the future paradise – that faith which their gospel had given them when it said to them, as was said to the ancient Christians: 'this very night salvation may come'. It is very easy to dethrone such a creed as that of the Communist Manifesto and the later catastrophe theories, very hard then to replace it by something else. Meanwhile, this debate with the older orthodoxy, arising from the scruples of conscience which were felt about the orthodox beliefs, has in the course of development long been left behind. It is mixed up with the question of whether and how far the Social Democrats as a party should engage in 'practical politics', in the sense of entering into coalitions with bourgeois parties, accepting ministerial posts and so taking part in the political responsibilities of government, and in this way striving to better the present conditions of the working class, or whether they would in so doing be 'class traitors' and political heretics, as the convinced believers in the catastrophe theory would be bound to regard the matter. Meantime, other questions of principle have emerged and on these the thinkers of the party are divided. Suppose that by a gradual process of evolution, in other words by general cartelisation, standardisation and bureaucratisation, the economy changed its character in such a way that at some point it became technically possible to replace the present private enterprise system, and so the system of private ownership of the means of production, by a system of regulation in which the entrepreneur had no part. Who would then take control of and direct this new economy? On this point the Communist Manifesto is silent, or rather has expressed itself extremely ambiguously.

(*Gesammelte Aufsätze zur Soziologie und Sozialpolitik*, Tübingen, 1924, pp. 500–11. First published in 1918.)

13 · *Economic Policy and the National Interest in Imperial Germany*

It has always been the case that, when a class has achieved *economic* power, it begins to think of its expectations of *political* leadership. It is dangerous and, in the long run, contrary to the national interest for an economically declining class to retain political dominance. But it is even more dangerous when economic strength and so the hope of political power come the way of classes which are not yet sufficiently mature in political terms for the leadership of the state. Both these menaces threaten Germany at the present time and are in reality the key to the present dangers of our situation. Furthermore, the shifts in the social structure of the East, with which the phenomena discussed in the first part of this lecture are connected, belong in this wider context.

Right up to the present day, the dynasty in Prussia has been politically dependent on the Prussian *Junker* Estate. It is only in cooperation with it (though admittedly also in opposition to it) that it has been able to build the Prussian state. I am well aware that, to South German ears, the word 'Junker' has a joyless ring. Perhaps it will be felt that I am speaking in too 'Prussian' a fashion if I say a word in their favour. I do not know. Even today in Prussia that Estate has many opportunities for achieving power and influence, or for reaching the ear of the monarch, which are not open to every citizen. It has not always used this power in a way which could be defended before History, and I do not see why a bourgeois scholar should feel any love for it. Nevertheless, and for all that, the strength of its political instincts used to be one of the most important sources of capital for promoting the interests of the state and its power. It has done its job and lies today in its economic death-agony, from which no state economic policy can restore it to its former place in society. Moreover, the tasks of the present are not those which it could perform. For a quarter of a century, the highest office in Germany was in the hands of the last and greatest of the Junkers. Future generations will find in his career as a statesman, not only incomparable grandeur, but also an inherent element of tragedy which at present increasingly escapes many people's notice. The tragic element in his career will be seen in the fact that under his rule his own creation, the nation, to which he gave its unity, slowly and inevitably changed in its economic structure, to the point where it became a different kind of people, requiring other institutions than those which he had given it and in which his imperious nature could find a place. In the end, it was precisely this which brought about the partial shipwreck of his life's work. For this life's work should have led, not only to the external unity of the nation, but also to an inner unification, and we all know that that was not what was achieved. It could not be achieved by this means. And when in the winter of that last year, trapped in the snare of his monarch's favour, he entered the Imperial capital, decked out as it was in all its finery, there were many (as I am well aware) who felt as if the Sachsenwald were opening up its innermost secrets like a latter-day Kyffhäuser. However, not everyone shared this feeling. For it seemed as if in the air of that January day could be sniffed the chill breeze of historical transience. We were overcome by a peculiarly oppressive feeling – as if a ghost had come down among us from a distant past and was wandering amidst a new generation and through a world which had become strange to him.

The estates of the East were the bases of the Prussian ruling class, scattered as it was over the region: they were the point of contact between officialdom and society. But inevitably, as that class declined and as the old landed nobility began to lose its special social character, the centre of gravity of the political intelligentsia shifted to the towns. This shift was the decisive *political* factor in the agrarian development of the East.

But whose are the hands into which the political function of the Junkers is passing, and what kind of political vocation do they have?

I am a member of the bourgeois class: I feel myself to be such and have been brought up on its opinions and ideals. But it is the solemn vocation of our science to say things which people will not like to hear – alike to those above one, below one and of one's own class. When I ask myself, therefore, whether the German bourgeoisie is at present ready to be the dominant political class in the nation, I cannot *at present* answer 'Yes'. It was not from the special resources of the bourgeoisie that the German state was created; and when it was created there stood at the head of the nation that Caesar-like figure who was not from bourgeois stock. Grandiose exercises in power-politics were not again imposed on the nation; it was only much later that bashfully and half unwillingly there began to be pursued overseas a 'power-politics' which was not worthy of the name.

After the unity of the nation had been achieved in this way and political 'satisfaction' was assured, the growing tribe of the German bourgeoisie, intoxicated with success and thirsty for peace, was overcome by a peculiarly 'unhistorical' and unpolitical mood. German history seemed at an end. The present represented the complete fulfilment of the preceding millennia: who cared to ask whether posterity might reach a different conclusion? World history – or so it seemed – could not, in all modesty, move on from these successes of the German nation to the minutiae of its everyday course. Nowadays we have become more sober: we ought to try to lift the veil of illusions which cloaks the true position of our generation in the historical development of our fatherland. I think we shall then judge differently. History has bestowed on us as a baptismal gift the most burdensome curse which it could give to any people: the harsh fate of *following* the period of political greatness.

Wherever we look in our country, are we not even now confronted by its wretched countenance? In the events of recent months, for which bourgeois politicians are mainly answerable, in all too many remarks made in the last few days both in and to the German Parliament, we could recognise with passionate anger and sorrow – those of us who retain the capacity to hate what is petty – the paltry manoeuvrings of political *epigoni*. The blazing sun which shone at Germany's zenith, and which caused the name of Germany to shine in the furthest corners of the earth – this sun was, so it almost seemed, *too* strong for us; it had burned away the bourgeoisie's slowly growing capacity for political judgment. For what do we see?

A section of the *haute bourgeoisie* longs, all too frankly, for the appearance of a new Caesar to protect it: to protect it from below, against the rising popular masses, and from above, against the social and political assaults which they suspect the German dynasties of making against them.

Yet another section has long sunk into that political philistinism from which the mass of the *petite bourgeoisie* has never stirred. Even early on, in the time after the wars of unification, when they were confronted with the first of the positive political tasks facing the nation, the idea of overseas expansion, they lacked even such an elementary grasp of *economics* as would have enabled them to see what it might mean for German trade in distant seas if the German flag were to be planted on their shores.

The blame for the political immaturity of large sections of the German bourgeoisie does not lie with economic factors, nor even with the much-criticised 'politics of interest', with which other nations are as familiar as we are. The source of its immaturity lies in its unpolitical past: a century's work in political education could not be made good in a decade, and the dominance of a great man is not always a means of political education. The serious question for the political future of the German bourgeoisie is now whether it may already be too *late* to make good the deficiency. No *economic* factor can compensate.

Will other classes be the bearers of a politically greater future? Proudly, the modern proletariat presents itself as the heir to bourgeois ideals. How do things stand with its aspirations towards the political leadership of the nation?

265

POLITICS

Anyone who would today say to the German working class that it was politically mature or on the way to political maturity would be indulging in flattery in an attempt to gain the dubious crown of popularity.

Economically, the upper strata of the German working class are much more mature than the egoism of the property-owning classes might admit. Justifiably, therefore, they demand freedom, even by means of organised and open struggles for economic power to defend their interests. *Politically*, the working class is infinitely less mature than the clique of journalists who aspire to monopolise its leadership would have it believe. Much play is made with memories of a century ago in the circle of these *déclassés* bourgeois: the result is that here and there the more timid souls see in them the spiritual descendants of the men of the Convention. However, they are infinitely more harmless than they appear to themselves: there is in them no glimmer of that Catilinarian energy of the *act*, nor certainly does there breathe in them any of that storm of *national* passion which blew through the halls of the Convention. They are pathetic experts in political triviality: they lack the deep instincts for *power* of a class which has been called to political leadership. It is not only the vested interests of capital, as the workers are led to believe, which are today behind the political opposition to granting them a share in power in the state. They would find few signs of any community of interests with capital if they were to investigate German academic circles. Nevertheless, we ask *them too* about their *political maturity*. If we are the political opponents of the working class, it is because there is no greater disaster that can befall a great nation than leadership by a *politically* uneducated *philistine class*, and because the German proletariat has not yet lost this character. Why is the proletariat of England and France to some extent differently constituted? The reason is to be found not only in a longer period of *economic* education, resulting from the organised struggle of the English working class for its interests. It is rather a matter of the reverberations of world-power status, which constantly confronts the state with great problems of power-politics and which provides the individual with continuous political schooling. This kind of schooling only becomes pressing for the individual in our case when our frontiers are threatened. It is also crucial for *our* development whether the pursuit of policies on the grand scale would again be able to bring before our eyes the meaning of the great questions of political power. We must grasp that the unification of Germany was a youthful spree, indulged in by the nation in its old age; it would have been better if it had never taken place, since it would have been a costly extravagance, if it was the conclusion rather than the starting-point for German power-politics on a global scale.

The *menacing* feature of our situation, however, is this: that the bourgeois classes, as bearers of the interests of the nation as a *power*, seem to be declining and that there is as yet no sign that the working class is ready to take their place.

The danger does *not* lie in the *masses*, as those who stare transfixed into the depths of society believe. The nub of the social and political problem is not the *economic* situation of the *ruled*, but rather the *political* qualifications of the *ruling* classes and those classes which are *rising* to power. The aim of our social and political work is not universal charity, but the *social unification* of that nation which modern economic development has created, in preparation for the difficult struggles of the future. Should it ever come about that a 'labour aristocracy' should be created to be the bearer of the political intelligence which is missing from the present-day labour movement, then it might be possible to lay on those broad shoulders the spear which the arms of the bourgeoisie have become too feeble to carry. But it seems we still have a long way to travel before we reach that point.

For the moment, however, one thing is clear, that we must carry out a colossal programme of *political* education. We have no more solemn obligation than this, that each of us, in his own sphere, should become aware of the need to work together on the political education of our nation. This must remain the ultimate goal, too, of our science in particular. The economic development of transitional periods threatens the natural political instincts with atrophy; it would be unfortunate if even economic science were to lead to the same result, by cultivating a feeble eudaemonism, in however ethereal a form, behind the illusion of independent 'socio-political' ideals.

To be sure, we should also for this reason remember that it is the opposite of political education to seek to embody in legal formulae a vote of no confidence in the peaceful social future of the nation; or for the secular arm to grasp the hand of the Church in order to support the temporal authorities. But there are also other obstacles to political education, such as the mechanical yapping of the steadily swelling chorus of (if you will excuse the expression) 'backwoods' social politicians; or that soft-headed attitude, so agreeable and even admirable from the human point of view, but nevertheless so unutterably philistine, which thinks it possible to replace political with 'ethical' ideals and innocently imagines that this is the same as optimistically hoping for the best.

Moreover, in view of the profound distress of the masses in our nation, which is so burdensome to the more acute social conscience of the new generation, we must frankly accept that today there weighs upon us still more heavily our answerability *before history*. It is not given to our generation to see whether the struggle in which we are engaged bears fruit, whether posterity will acknowledge us as its forerunners. We shall not succeed in exorcising the curse laid upon us, the curse of being born *after* a period of political greatness. It is essential therefore that we should know how to become something else, the forerunners of a greater period. Will that be our place in history? I do not know: I can only say that it is the right of youth to be true to itself and its ideals. And it is not years which make a man a greybeard: he remains young as long as he is capable of experiencing the *grand* passions which nature has implanted in us. So (and here I must draw to a close) it is not through carrying the burden of thousands of years of glorious history that a great nation grows old. It remains young, as long as it has the capacity and the heart to be true to itself and the great instincts with which it has been endowed; as long as its dominant classes are able to raise themselves up into the hard clear air in which the sober work of German politics prospers but which is pervaded by the stern magnificence of our national feelings.

> (*Gesammelte Politische Schriften*, 2nd edn, Tübingen, 1958, pp. 19–25. First published in 1895.)

14 · *The Prospects for Liberal Democracy in Tsarist Russia*

What lies at the root of the Liberal Democrats' reservations about agrarian reform is this: there is no doubt that the great mass of the *peasants themselves* could never be won over to an agrarian programme which was 'individualistic' in the West European sense. However true it may be that decisions about the allocation of land can be the product of an extremely bitter class struggle, it is certainly not only economic class interests which influence the administration of the commune but also deeply-rooted conceptions of 'natural justice'. For it is as obvious as it could be that the necessary decision to reapportion land is not reached only with the votes either of those who hope to better their positions by it or of those who have been intimidated by violence or boycott. On the other hand, it has to be admitted that it is equally certain that this very re-allocation of land, which seems from the outside to be the most important element of agricultural democracy in this form of social organisation, very often exists, insofar as it can be thought of as a piece of effective 'social policy', only on paper. The rich peasants lease, alienate or bequeath their lands (naturally, only within the commune), relying on there being no decisions about re-allocation; or, alternatively, they are in a position to control other members of the commune who are in their debt, and the re-allocation serves in practice to increase their power. And since it is *land* which is allocated rather than livestock or capital, apportionment is compatible with the most ruthless exploitation of the weaker members. But it is precisely this discrepancy between law and fact which leads to a growth in the most bitter radicalism among the poorer peasants as land values and social differentiation increase.

The decisive point seems to be that this communistic radicalism is, so far as one can judge, bound clearly to *increase* precisely *if* the lot of the peasants is improved – that is, if their burdens are lightened and the disposable land of the communes increased. In those districts (of which, as is well known, there were quite a few) in which the burdens imposed on the allocations of land exceed the profits from them, landownership is thought of even today as an obligation which every villager seeks to avoid; whereas in places where the profits exceed the burdens the poorer peasants are, on the contrary, in favour of land apportionment. The districts with the best land are, therefore, those in which the poorer peasants have the most compelling interest in re-allocation, and the well-to-do peasants have the very strongest interest against it. Every remission of taxes and imposts, such as the present remission of redemption fees, must therefore – if the commune remains firm on the matter – *multiply* these sources of communistic interests and social conflict. It is also well known that the German peasants of South Russia, for instance, were in many ways the first to introduce the rural commune in the strict sense, at the time when the government increased their landholdings. The reasons for this are perfectly intelligible. The outcome of a restoration of the *nadyel* ('apportionment') must generally speaking be nothing other than a powerful increase in the belief in communism. In this hope, so far as one can judge from the outside, the Social Revolutionaries will be proved right.

Accordingly, this programme of restoring the *nadyel* cannot at present be rejected by any honest agrarian reformer. The Constitutional Democratic party, in its agrarian programme (points 36 to 40), has therefore committed itself to the respective demands of the 'Liberation League' and of the Liberal Agrarian Congress, and has made concessions to the objections of the Social Revolutionaries which are in part still more far-reaching. These comprise: (i) the demand that expropriated landowners should be compensated *not according to the market-value of their land*, but according to its 'fair price' (point 36); (ii) the firm demand for a legal guarantee of renewal of tenure, if necessary, of the right of the tenant to compensation for improvements, and, above all, for the creation of *judicial* institutions (on the Irish model) for reducing 'disproportionately high' rents for tenancies (point 39); (iii) the creation of an agricultural inspectorate to supervise the administration of labour legislation as it applies to agriculture. The principles according to which the expropriated land is to be assigned to peasants (personal or collective allocation for ownership or use) are to be determined 'in conformity with the special character of land-tenure and land-use in the different regions of Russia'.

All in all, therefore, the implementation of the reform programme of the Liberal Democrats would be likely to lead to a powerful intensification of agrarian communist and Social Revolutionary feelings among the peasants. These feelings are already so strong that the great mass of peasants, at least, would certainly have nothing to do with an individualistic programme of the kind that Struve, for example, used to advocate in his day. It is a peculiar feature of the Russian situation that in this case intensified 'capitalist' development, accompanied by simultaneous increases in the price of land and of agricultural products, *can* lead, not only to a further growth of the industrial proletariat and so of 'modern' socialism, but also to an increase in something so 'unmodern' as agrarian communism. The prospects for future development in the realm of intellectual activity seem equally unclear as yet.

There is certainly a break in the mists of Russian Populism (*Narod-nichestvo*), which still permeate all factions of the intelligentsia of all classes and political programmes. But the question is, what is to take its place? A purely objective view of the situation, such as that of the reformist Liberals, will not be able without a struggle to fetter the 'expansiveness' of the Russian spirit. For the romantic radicalism of the Social Revolutionary intelligentsia has another side to it: because of its character, which, for all their protests, is close to that of 'state socialism', it is extremely easy to make the leap from it into the authoritarian and reactionary camp. We have often been told by observers who, although usually foreign, are at the same time conscientious about the relative frequency with which extreme radical students are 'metamorphosed' into highly authoritarian officials – a process which, even assuming these reports are correct, need not, as others have pointed out, imply any innate disposition or ignoble self-seeking on their part. For the opposite process has' also taken place several times in recent years – that is, an abrupt change from convinced support of the kind of pragmatic bureaucratic rationalism advocated by Plehve and Pobyedonostsev to support of the extreme Social Revolutionaries. It is, however, the pragmatic rationalism of those who think in this way which *in general* leads them to yearn for 'action' in the service of absolute social and ethical values and, starting from the ideals of that agrarian communism which still exists, to vacillate between 'creative' action 'from above' and 'from below'. The result is that their romanticism takes sometimes a reactionary, sometimes a revolutionary, form.

What then will the peasantry do in the elections? Their power to resist the influence of officials and conservative clergy is obviously extremely great. It seems to be greatest, as is understandable, not in the really distressed areas, but for instance in the South, in the Cossack villages, in the Chernigov and Kursk regions (*guberniyas*). In these districts and also in some parts of the industrial belt, the peasants have often made the most sharply worded proposals, in spite of the presence either of officials of the state police or of Marshals of the Nobility, and have submitted petitions covered with thousands of signatures for the removal of bureaucratic supervision and for permission to elect popular repre-sentatives. It is their determined view, moreover (*though one which has nothing at all to do with modern parliamentary ideas*) that these represen-tatives should deal directly with the Tsar, without the intervention, as under the present system, of paid officials. In other words, they want the abolition of the autocratic bureaucracy, but (as the Slavophils rightly point out) they have no desire for it to be replaced by a bureaucracy directed by Parliament.

The strength of this anti-bureaucratic movement is at present considerable. There have been several reports of cases in which the peasants have rejected the 'loyal' resolutions prepared beforehand by the officials for the Congress (*Skhod*); in other cases, they have accepted them while the officials were present but have subsequently recanted, or else they have sent back the publications of the reactionary leagues which have been sent to them. But it is hardly likely that this mood would be strong enough to prevail in the elections against the authority and the overt compulsion of the officials. The electoral law, even as formulated on 11 December, attempts to prevent all free electioneering: it permits meetings of electors and delegates who wish 'in a preliminary way' to discuss the character of the candidates – meetings from which, indeed, the police are excluded – but on principle allows only the enfranchised inhabitants of the ward or the delegates in question to attend the meetings, the police having control over the admission of participants! Incredible though it may sound, however, an exception is made to this principle in favour of the presiding official (the Marshal of the Nobility or his representative), *even when he himself is neither an elector nor a delegate*. Moreover, the principle of election 'from one's own group' or 'from the number of those entitled to take part' is maintained.

The *de facto* application of this principle in elections in the United States led, as is well known, to a sharp decline in the standard of the legislatures, and this is undoubtedly one of the aims of the present regulation. In the towns, it is all largely a formality; but everyone must decide for himself what will be the significance of this control of election meetings in rural areas, especially among the peasants. Above all, the peasants themselves must decide, since their *cardinal demand* is the abolition of supervision by officials. The government, for whom, clearly, *only* its *short-term* effects are important, has thereby *consistently* presented the radicals with the most convenient (and legitimate) argument for their purposes. The regulation will, in all probability, 'produce' conservative representatives for the peasants. But every peasant will know that they do not represent *him*; and so the number of reasons for hating the bureaucracy is increased by one.

No one can say, therefore, how the peasant elections for the Duma will turn out. Generally speaking, foreigners tend to expect that, so far as the peasants are concerned, the Duma will be composed mainly of extreme reactionaries; Russians, on the other hand, expect in spite of everything that it will be composed mainly of extreme revolutionaries. Both could be right in the end, and, what is more important, both outcomes could have identical consequences. In modern European revolutions, the peasants have generally swung from the most thorough-going radicalism imaginable either to apathy or all the way to political reaction, depending on the way in which their immediate economic demands have been satisfied. In fact, there can be no doubt that *if* a whole or half decree of the autocracy satisfied the peasant demand for land or if, during a period of anarchy, they seized the land themselves and were allowed one way or another to retain it, then all further issues would be settled as far as the majority of them were concerned and they would lose all interest in the form of government.

The view of the representatives of Liberal Democracy, and especially of Struve, is, on the contrary, that the desire of the peasants for land cannot be satisfied by a reactionary administration, since it would mean the economic dispossession not only of the lower nobility but also of the Grand Princes and ultimately of the Tsar himself. The interests of the peasants would be incompatible with the interest of these powerful men in their own survival. Yet despite the enormous extent, taken by itself, of the land belonging to the Imperial house, it is not very great in comparison with the land in private ownership, and it is precisely against the latter that the enmity of the peasants is directed. But then the question arises which, and how many, of the peasants' demands the Democracy for its part will be able to fulfil. Struve, naturally, has spoken out very forcibly against a simple confiscation of land. But naturally also, the manifesto setting out the programme of the Constitutional Democrats contains the point that those expropriated should *not* be compensated at the market value of the land on the 'liberal' interpretation of 'confiscation': the 'free-market principles' of the defenders of our political heritage have in this case taken a decidedly revolutionary turn. Prince Trubetskoy was already afraid that Chuprov's proposal would drive the liberal nobility into Shipov's camp. There does seem despite this to be a section of the nobility (which is internally an extremely heterogeneous stratum, stretching as it does, in the words of one of Nicholas I's Ministers of Education, 'from the steps of the throne to the ranks of the peasantry') which is not reluctant to surrender its land in the present situation: one would be better to 'live freely in a manor without land than, as at present, with land in a fortress', said Prince Dolgorukov at the Liberal Agrarian Congress in Moscow. But the Congress of agricultural employers in Moscow in December 1905, which was held behind locked doors, demanded unconditional repression.

In any event the land is costing a government which is not particularly strong untold sums of *money*. There is colonisable land available, especially in the South-East, but also in the North-East of the vast Russian Empire, as long as enormous capital sums are forthcoming for irrigation and (in Siberia) clearance of forests. The abolition of redemption fees, the remission of taxes to the peasants, the Civil List which was to take the place of the Imperial family's landholdings, losses in revenue from rents, the cost of capital improvements – all this amounts to a significant loss of income to the state and an equally significant increase in demand on its resources, in short to problems of cash of a hitherto unprecedented kind. Finally, since the increase in land is by itself no solution to the agrarian problem, this policy, as long as it is thought of as the *only* way out, might very well endanger 'technical progress':[1] we must reckon with serious disillusionment among the peasants once all their demands have been fulfilled. At their present level of development, the peasants could turn out to be important not as 'pillars' or 'supports' of agrarian policy but as its actual 'objects'. The party which has to carry out that reform by *legal* methods is not, therefore, to be envied in its task.

The road taken by the reformist Russian Liberal Democrats involves many sacrifices. They have no choice but to put forward an unconditional demand for universal equal suffrage, both because of their conception of their duty and because of considerations imposed on them by the demagogic behaviour of the old regime. And yet their own ideas could in all probability achieve political influence only in an electoral system similar to that of the District Council (*Zyemstvo*). They must, as a matter of duty, champion an agrarian reform which is more than likely to add enormous strength, not to an economically and technologically 'progressive' kind of voluntaristic socialism, but to the peasants' essentially archaic form of communism. This in turn will favour, not an economic selection of those who are 'commercially' fittest, but an 'ethical' levelling of opportunities, both as an economic practice and as a popular economic theory; and it will inevitably retard the development of that Western European individualistic culture which most of them regard as inevitable.

Such a movement is bound to strike the type of 'satisfied' German, who finds it unendurable that he should not be on whatever is for the moment the 'winning side' and who is all puffed up with the profound awareness of his talent for *Realpolitik*, as deserving only of pity. Moreover, its outward means of exerting power are naturally few, as the extreme Social Revolutionaries never fail to point out with scorn. The fact is that no one knows what the situation would be today if the autocracy had not been intimidated by the deaths of Plehve and Grand Prince Sergei. The only

[1] All specifically peasant policies leave quite untouched, above all in the cereal-exporting regions, the problem of *employment* created by the shortness of the growing period. The decline of the handicraftsman and of peasant domestic industry which is the consequence of capitalism, together with the ability of the money economy to supply all requirements, raise at this point, as the 'Populists' quite rightly say, direct questions about the existence of peasant economies.

similar means of exerting power available to the Liberals lies in the fact that the officers could not consent for long to act as executioners of families from which they themselves have for the most part come. In fact the tactics approved by the Liberals have often produced the right effect, not through provoking the troops to fight by the use of bombs and armed resistance, as one wing of the Social Revolutionaries has done time and again, but rather through placing themselves unarmed in the troops' path. It has, on the other hand, to be admitted that when confronted with a determined military leadership, this approach would have its limitations, and the brief uprising in Moscow will have a *very* beneficial effect on the discipline of the army.

To this there can now be added another, specifically 'bourgeois', instrument of power, though not one which is available to the Russian Liberals. If foreign financial powers had not spoken very forcibly (not perhaps in so many words, but in substance), it is possible that the charter of 17 October would either not have been followed through or else have been soon revoked. All the anxiety aroused by the anger of the masses and the mutiny of the army, all the weakening of the authoritarian regime resulting from the defeat in the East, only had any effect when combined with the pressure exerted on the autocracy by the cool, hard hand of the banks and stock exchanges. This explains the attitude of politicians like Vitte and Timiryashev. For when the Social Democratic '*Nachalo*' called Count Vitte 'an agent of the stock exchange', there of course lay behind this primitive idea a germ of truth. Vitte has hardly any firm convictions of any kind about the constitutional question and the conduct of domestic policy. At any rate, his various statements on the matter stand in the most flagrant contradiction with each other. His habit still is to deny remarks attributed to him by people of undisputed integrity on the ground that he has been 'misunderstood'; and he does this even when the remarks were made not in confidential conversations but in discussions with party delegates. His real interest is in matters of economic policy. Whatever one might normally think of him, he has, for example, had what from his point of view is the 'nerve' to incur the serious odium in the eyes of the reactionary bureaucracy and the reactionary democrats alike of defending peasant private ownership. In the same way, he is now the object not only of the increased hatred of the Slavophils but of the personal antipathy of the Tsar besides – an antipathy which is only increased by his 'indispensability'. Without any doubt he is 'capitalistically' minded, as are all the Liberals of Struve's stamp. Instead of attempting, like Plehve, to govern with the aid of the masses (under authoritarian leadership) against the 'bourgeoisie', he would undoubtedly much prefer to establish an understanding with the propertied classes against the masses. He, and perhaps he alone, is in a position to uphold the credit and the currency of Russia at the moment, and it is certain that he has the will to do so. He undoubtedly knows very well that it is an essential prerequisite for achieving this that Russia should be transformed into a constitutional state with assured constitutional guarantees; and he would probably so conduct his domestic policy, if he could, as to enable him not to have to sacrifice his life's work, the financial power of Russia.

The further thought naturally occurs to one that a Liberal regime which was to a certain extent 'respectable' would also strengthen politically the alliance with France. But these motives for adopting a liberal policy cannot of course carry unlimited weight for Vitte, and certainly not for the Tsar and his associates; and the question arises where their breaking-point would be found and the idea of a military dictatorship as a precursor of sham constitutionalism gain the upper hand. Such an idea is perfectly practicable in the immediate future. If even a tenth of the officer corps and the troops remained at the disposal of the government – and the fraction would, if the need arose, be nearer nine-tenths[1] – then any number of insurgents would stand no chance against them. The stock market greeted the first blood shed in the streets of Moscow with a boom, and everything which has happened since has shown how powerfully this has served to strengthen the self-confidence of the reactionaries and to convert Vitte to their point of view. The economic hardship which is bound to result from the fearful destruction of industry will in this case, as it generally does, first disabuse the proletariat of their political illusions and then paralyse their fighting spirit. And a government which in reality upholds the power of the centralist *bureaucracy* – which is the important thing – is bound meanwhile, in spite of everything, to seem to foreign observers to be perfectly viable. For even the social forces which have supported the regime up to now are undoubtedly already much better organised than it seems from the outside. Their recovery was all the more likely in view of the fact that the 'professional Socialists', with their sectarian and petty bourgeois attitudes, even when faced with the terror squads organised by police officials fighting for their lives, directed the frontal attack of their supporters mainly against their 'rivals', the Liberal Democratic parties. Moreover, in perfect consistency with this attitude, they gave free rein to their need to hurl abuse – an activity which, however understandable from the 'human' point of view, is, as we in Germany know only too well, politically sterile and, more important still, stunts all growth towards a capacity for effective political action. They may very well rejoice at the prospect that either the reactionaries will gain the upper hand entirely

---

[1] The course of the Moscow uprising which recently flared up is proof of this. Only a disastrous *European* war would lead to a decisive overthrow of the autocracy.

or the majority of the propertied classes will move over into the camp of the 'moderate' parties, with the result that they will feel entitled to wallow for a further generation in grandiose rhetoric – as in Germany – and to intoxicate themselves with the thought 'What terribly wicked people there are in the world'.

On 20 November 1905 the law and order party offered their help in strike-breaking to Count Vitte in the event of the impending walk-out of post and telegraph employees. Such groups are comprised partly of moderate members of the Duma and Councils, partly of the authentic bourgeoisie (bankers and big industrialists), and partly of people who, like Krassovsky, when the agitation at the congress of the Councils was beginning, represented the view that no constitution was possible but that a legal guarantee of freedom of the person and of the press should be demanded – without being able, of course, to specify what such a guarantee would amount to in practice without a constitution. What they all have in common, apart from a recognition of the manifesto of 17 October, which the old conservative officials answered, as is well known, with the butchery of the Black Hundred, and perhaps had hoped to thwart in any case, is an undisguised religious indifference. Otherwise, the only certain fact about them all is that they are unconditionally for 'peace' and in favour of anything which may bring this about by any means: the St Petersburg 'Law and Order League' is in favour of enfranchising the Jews – 'that', they say, 'will satisfy them'; the St Petersburg census-electors were, after long debate, in favour of the autonomy of Poland for the same reason; in other associations of census-electors the radical demand for separation of Church and State was rejected in favour of continued instruction in 'the law of God' (the catechism) as indispensable for the maintenance of order. All of them accordingly ended up by being satisfied with whatever concessions the Tsar thought fit to make to them. It is understandable that the number of these people has shown a marked increase under the pressure of the peasant and military revolts, the threat of the general strike, and the prevailing putschism of the Social Democrats. And it was only to be expected that the government, and especially Vitte, should hope that anarchy would have this effect and that, as Vitte put it, 'society itself' would demand that order be re-established and – it might be added – that there would be a place for the watchword '*Enrichissez-vous*'.

So indeed it turned out. But this development took place, of course, at the expense of constitutional Council democracy. The time of the congress of the Councils was over, remarked Prince Dolgorukov resignedly. It was indeed: the hour of the ideological gentry was past – the power of material interests had begun to operate as normal. This process led to the elimination, on the Left, of political idealism, and on the Right, of the moderate Slavophilism which sought to extend the old Council self-government. Neither was likely to cause Vitte much distress. All the same, it is probable in practice that Vitte's policy of wait and see has done other people's work for them, or rather, that he did not have the power to do anything else. In the eyes of the Court he is essentially nothing more than a man to fill the post, who cannot at present be dispensed with because of outside pressures, especially from the stock exchange, and also because of his intelligence. For in the minds of those elements in the government who are close to the *Court* there has not been a trace of doubt. In a few individual cases, the higher administrative officials of those regions in which, according to reports which neither can be nor have been denied, the police have taken the initiative in organising civil war, have been taken to task out of concern for international opinion. But the only result has been that they, like our Prussian 'Canal Rebels', have been 'kicked upstairs'. Count Vitte, on the other hand, has made no serious attempt at all (and indeed may well be unable to do so) to break down the ruthless obstruction of the provincial bureaucracy, who for the time being have no intention whatever of believing in the permanence of a constitutional regime.

If the Liberals saw this as a failure of 'honour' on Vitte's part, that is understandable. But it is not, perhaps, quite accurate: as the saying goes, 'a rogue gives more than he has' – the obstacle lies somewhere at a higher level. Many of the measures taken by the Ministry of the Interior, which one could read about in the newspapers, could have no other effect than that of alternately provoking the masses and then allowing the reins to appear to go slack until the Red terror had reached such a pitch that the time for the White had arrived. It must *not* be thought that this policy was *exclusively* the product of weakness and confusion: a 'revenge for the 17 October' was called for. The result, moreover – indeed the inevitable result – must undoubtedly be, in the long run, to discredit all libertarian movements, but especially the kind of bourgeois constitutional *anti-centralist* Liberalism whose importance in public opinion and whose position in the self-governing administrative bodies have for decades inspired the hatred of both the reactionary and the rationalist elements in the central state bureaucracy. Undoubtedly, it would have even less to hope for if there were a period of total anarchy than if the autocracy were to recover; and as things stand at present, anarchy would surely precede such a recovery.

It is quite certainly the case that the congenital flaw, not only, as has been said, in every radical policy, but in every ideologically orientated policy in general, is their capacity for 'letting opportunities slip past them'. When Vincke in his time refused to enter into private negotiations with the Ministers of the 'New Era' in Prussia about the Army Bill which was to be introduced, on the ground that this was morally impermissible for a deputy; and similarly, when in 1893 the Liberals were too late by a fraction of an hour in coming to the decision which they nevertheless took after the dissolution of the Reichstag – both occasions marked fateful turning-points for the cause of Liberalism. It is tempting to suppose, and some remarks of Vitte directly suggest this diagnosis, that the Russian Liberals are open to a similar criticism from the point of view of their party policy. I myself in the autumn formed this impression at first sight. However, the more closely one looks into the state of affairs, the more one is led to suspect that the Liberal politicians made a more accurate diagnosis of what they had to expect than that contained in these remarks of Count Vitte's. In both the examples cited above it was a matter of negotiations which were undoubtedly 'sincerely' intended. In the present case, however, *no* 'opportunity' was offered at all to the 'most moderate' constitutional Council Liberals. Plainly, therefore, it was simply not in their power to alter the course of destiny. Their case was like that of Bennigsen in 1877, when he, with what our historians generally concede to have been a much better reason, declined to join Bismarck's ministry. For, just as Louis XVI did not want under any circumstances to be 'rescued' by Lafayette, of all people, so nothing seems more certain than that the Court and the Bureaucracy would as soon make a pact with the Devil as with the Council Liberals. Political antagonisms within the same social stratum or between rival social strata are often the most intensely felt.

On the government side, the most far-reaching 'counter-move' was Count Vitte's invitation to the Moscow Town Council (*Uprava*) to send representatives of the Council party to him for consultations. This took place on 27 October (Old Style) between Vitte and the delegates Golovin, Prince L'vov and Kokoshkin. There was still a vital difference of opinion between the two sides on that occasion. Count Vitte wanted to abandon the idea of introducing universal equal suffrage with a secret ballot, extending to representation of the working class, for elections to the Imperial Duma; and he explicitly held out the prospect of his cooperation in return. The delegates, on the other hand, insisted that a constituent Duma, based on that franchise, should be summoned as the only means of securing peace. But behind this ostensible difference there lay, apart from the long-standing mistrust felt for the Council party, one set of circumstances which plainly stands in the way of *any* agreement. This was that at that time Trepov was still in full possession of his powers; that subsequently Durnovo, when accused by eminent people in public, circumstantially detailed letters to the press of having received money for services rendered 'even in small amounts' (1,200–1,500 roubles),[1] took his place and remained in it; and that the precise declaration of the terms of the Manifesto of 17 October which had been entirely constitutionally requested *failed to appear*. Vitte's assurance that he felt himself 'very close to' the Constitutional Democratic party in the Councils could hardly gain sufficient credence in these circumstances, especially after his 'confidential memorandum' of 1899, which stressed the incompatibility of the Councils with the autocracy and so frustrated the proposed generalisation of the Council system. The situation of Russia cries out above all for a 'statesman'; but the dynastic ambitions of the autocracy allow as little room there for a great reformer – if such a person were to be found – as anywhere in the world, perhaps even in Germany.

It seems for the time being absolutely certain that the Tsar has not for a single moment had the intention of reaching a truly lasting and sincere agreement with these men, to whom he referred as recently as six months ago in extremely unparliamentary language. If one treats this 'factor' as a 'datum' in the calculation, then it is without any question true that Russia is not 'ripe' for a genuine constitutional reform – although this is not the fault of the Liberals. For one is bound also to conclude that under these circumstances, as long as 'guarantees' of an altogether different kind were not given, the very idea of reaching an 'agreement' with the government could have no political meaning whatever for the Council Liberals. Their representatives could do no more than 'keep their escutcheons clean', once they had carried out their 'mission' to the extent and in the sense in which that was possible under present conditions. It is quite possible, although not certain, that in the immediate future they will have to come to terms with the fact that the Liberal Council movement, brilliant as it is of its kind, of which Russia has just as much reason to be proud as we Germans have to be proud of the Frankfurt Parliament, meanwhile perhaps 'belongs to history' in the form in which it has existed up to now.

This would, moreover, be likely to be better for it in the future than a 'March Ministry'. Only in this way can 'ideological' Liberalism remain a 'force' on the plane of ideas beyond the reach of any external power; and only in this way does it seem possible to restore the recently broken unity between the 'bourgeois' intelligentsia, which draws its strength

---

[1] There were also a number of stories told in private with full details, and on the evidence of completely reliable informants. Although Durnovo clearly *cannot* legally deny the criticisms which have been made of his conduct, even in public meetings, he has just been decorated and promoted. It is the strength – *and* the weakness – of Tsarism, as against the 'ideologues', that unlike them it has (and *must* have) a 'use' for this kind of 'gentleman' too. As things are now, it cannot dispense with the low peasant cunning of such loyal subjects for a single moment, and the Tsar is compelled to shake hands with people whom every independent 'bourgeois' would refuse to greet.

from its ownership of property, its wide-ranging culture and its political experience, and the 'proletarian' intelligentsia, whose importance rests on its numbers, its close connexions with the 'masses' and its recklessly combative spirit. This unity can only be restored after the 'proletarian' intelligentsia has ceased to undervalue the real importance to it of the 'bourgeois' element, which it finds 'sentimentally' antipathetic – an importance deriving from the disillusionments which are in store for it.

The further development of capitalism will ensure the disintegration of 'populist' romanticism. Its place will, no doubt, largely be taken by Marxism. But the intellectual resources of Marxism are simply not adequate for work on the massive and fundamental agrarian problem; and that work alone is capable of bringing both strata of the intelligentsia back together. Clearly, the problem can be solved only by the self-governing administrative bodies and for precisely that reason it seems vital that Liberalism should find its vocation, in the future as in the past, in opposing both bureaucratic and Jacobin *centralism* equally and in seeking to spread among the masses the old individualist principle of 'inalienable human rights' which to us in Western Europe seems as 'trivial' as black bread is to the man who has enough to eat.

These axioms of 'Natural Law' give as ambiguous a guideline for a social and economic programme as they give an answer to the question whether they are themselves the product of any set of economic conditions – or at least, 'modern' economic conditions – *alone*.

On the contrary; to the extent that the struggle for such 'individualistic' values has to reckon at every stage with the 'material' conditions of the environment, to that extent it is impossible to leave their 'realisation' to 'economic development'. It would be extremely harmful to the chances of 'democracy' and 'individualism' today, if we were to rely for their 'development' on the 'lawlike' operation of *material* interests. For the latter point as clearly as could be in the opposite direction, towards the American 'benevolent feudalism', the German so-called 'welfare institutions', the Russian factory system. Everywhere, the *casing of the new serfdom* is ready. Its final completion awaits only the stage at which the slowing-down of technological and economic 'progress' and the victory of loan interest over commercial profit, in conjunction with the exhaustion of the remaining 'free' land and 'free' markets, make the masses 'docile'. At the same time, the process is helped along by the mounting complexity of the economy, by partial nationalisation or 'municipalisation', by the territorial extent of nations, by constantly increasing paper work, and by increasing occupational specialisation and formalised administrative training – in other words, by caste. Those American workers who were against 'Civil Service Reform' knew what they were doing: they preferred to be governed by parvenus of doubtful morality rather than a formally qualified mandarinate. But their protest is in vain.

In view of this, those who live in constant anxiety lest there might in the future be *too much* 'democracy' and 'individualism' in the world, and too little 'authority', 'aristocracy' and 'respect for office' or the like, may take heart: all too much care has been taken to make sure that the trees of democratic individualism do not grow to the skies. All our experience suggests that 'history' continues inexorably to bring forth new 'aristocracies' and 'authorities' to which anyone who finds it necessary for himself – or for the 'people' – can cling. If we had *only* to take account of 'material' conditions and the collective interests 'created' directly or indirectly by them, then the opinion of every reasonable man would be that all the *economic* weather signs point in the direction of increasing 'unfreedom'. It is utterly ridiculous to suppose that it is an 'inevitable' feature of our economic development under present-day advanced capitalism, as it has now been imported into Russia and as it exists in America, that it should have an elective affinity with 'democracy' or indeed with 'freedom' (in *any* sense of that word), when the only question to be asked is: how are all these things, in general and in the long term, *possible* where it prevails?

They are so, in fact, only where, over a period of time, they are supported by the resolute *will* of a nation not to allow itself to be led like a flock of sheep. We 'individualists' and supporters of 'democratic' institutions are swimming 'against the stream' of material developments. Anyone who wishes to be the weather-vane of 'developmental trends' might as well abandon these outdated ideals as quickly as possible. The historical origins of modern freedom presupposed a certain conjunction of unique and unrepeatable conditions. Let us list the most important of them. The first is overseas expansion: this wind from across the sea blows through Cromwell's armies, through the French Constituent Assembly, through our common economic life even today. But a new continent is no longer available. It is the vast inland territories of the North American continent on the one hand and of Russia on the other on whose monotonous expanses, so favourable to schematic ideas, the brunt of the population of Western civilisation advances inexorably, just as it did in late antiquity. The second is the peculiar economic and social structure of the 'early capitalist'[1] epoch in Western Europe; and the third is the conquest of life by science, 'the return of Spirit to itself'. But the

[1] Sombart has, in my opinion, given an absolutely correct account of the meaning of this expression in all important respects. There are no 'finally valid' historical concepts. I avoid, however, the present-day literary conceit of treating someone else's terminology as one might his toothbrush.

task of achieving a rational organisation of outward life is today, at least 'in principle', complete (even though countless 'values' have undoubtedly been destroyed in the process). Its universal consequence, under the present conditions of 'commercial' life, has been to make our outward life-style uniform by means of the 'standardisation' of production; and 'science', purely as such, no longer creates today the 'universal personality'. Finally, certain ideal values which grew out of a particular concrete historical situation, dominated by distinct religious beliefs, working together with numerous equally specific combinations of political circumstances and the material preconditions mentioned above, impressed their particular stamp on the 'ethical' character and the 'cultural values' of modern man.

One needs only to pose the question whether any material developments, including those of the present advanced stage of capitalism, could preserve or even recreate these unique historical conditions, in order to know the answer. There is not a shadow of plausibility in the view that the economic development of society, as such, must nurture the growth either of inwardly 'free' personalities or of 'altruistic' ideals. Do we find the slightest hint of anything of that kind in those who, in their own opinion, are borne forward by 'material development' to inevitable triumph? Among the masses, the 'respectable' Social Democrats drill the spiritual parade, and instead of directing their thoughts to an otherworldly paradise (which according to Puritanism should *also* inspire respectable achievements in the service of this-worldly 'freedom'), they turn their minds to a paradise in this world, and thereby make of it a kind of vaccination for the vested interests of the existing order. They accustom their pupils to a submissive attitude towards dogmas and party authorities, or to indulgence in the fruitless play-acting of mass strikes or the idle enjoyment of the enervating howls of their hired journalists, which are as harmless as they are, in the end, laughable in the eyes of their enemies. In short, they accustom them to an 'hysterical wallowing in emotion', which replaces and inhibits economic and political thought and action. The only plant which can grow on this infertile soil, once the 'eschatological' age of the movement has passed and generation after generation has vainly clenched its fists in its pockets or bared its teeth towards heaven, is that of spiritual apathy.

Yet time is pressing: 'we must work, while it is still day'. If, in the course of succeeding generations, as long as the economic and intellectual 'revolution', the much-abused 'anarchy' of production and the no less abused 'subjectivism' continue unabated, the individual citizen who through them, *and only through them,* has been left to depend on himself fails to conquer certain spheres of freedom and personality as his 'inalienable' possessions, then he will *perhaps* never conquer them, once the world is for the time being economically 'satiated' and intellectually 'content'. This at least seems likely, as far as our weak eyes can penetrate into the dense mist of the future course of human history.

> (*Gesammelte Politische Schriften*, 2nd edn, Tübingen, 1958, pp. 45–62. First published in 1906.)

V · Economic and Social History

Introduction

Writing, as he said, as 'someone who is himself the offspring of modern European civilisation',[1] Weber approached his historical studies concerned above all to establish what accounts for the emergence of that civilisation in post-medieval Europe and nowhere else. This involves a twofold contrast: first, between post-medieval Europe and the other civilisations in which an industrial revolution might also have occurred but didn't; secondly, between post-medieval Europe and the civilisation of ancient Rome where many of the conditions for capitalist industrialisation were also present but failed to bring it about until after the complete dissolution of the Roman Empire and the long dominance of the system of social organisation now known to us as feudalism.

A part of Weber's answer lay, as we have seen, in the distinctive economic ethics of European Protestantism and, more generally, the 'rationalisation' of thought and behaviour which he held to be peculiar to the West. But this is far from the whole of the story. He also sought to identify the other conditions which could be held to have been necessary for the emergence of industrial capitalism, ranging from double-entry book-keeping (which was an invention of the Italian bankers of the Renaissance) to the development of the concept of citizenship to the supply of a formally free labour force emancipated from the land. Much of what he said on these matters had already been covered by other writers and would be agreed to have been significant by the great majority of economic historians writing today. But on two topics, his contribution is of particular interest: bureaucracy and the city.

Towards bureaucracy, as towards charisma, Weber's attitude was ambivalent. His discussion of it has been influential chiefly through his delineation of an 'ideal type' of bureaucracy as a form of administration distinctively characterised by continuity, hierarchy, clearly defined regulations, the separation of public office from private ownership or control over resources, the use of documentary records and the salaried employment of full-time professional experts with career-long tenure.[2] These characteristics Weber saw as making bureaucracy overwhelmingly more efficient in the performance of its assigned tasks than non-centralised, non-professional, 'patrimonial' or 'prebendal' forms of administration. Yet at the same time, he also saw it as involving a transfer of power to the expert from the leader and therefore as tending to reduce the capacity of organisations, institutions or societies to change. Likewise, in his sociology of law he sees the rise of the professional expert and the development of a tradition

---

[1] Below, p. 331.
[2] See *Economy and Society*, III, 956–63 (the passage which immediately precedes the concluding selection in this section).

of formalism as at the same time a part of the ongoing process of 'rationalisation' and also an entrenchment of a body of '*honoratiores*' whose purely logical jurisprudence often stood in the way of the interests of a rising commercial bourgeoisie or an 'enlightened despot'. The historical significance of bureaucracy, therefore, is a function of its whole social context. As Weber points out, England, which had the most advanced capitalist economy in Europe, also had the least bureaucratised and 'rational' judicial system. Conversely, ancient Rome, which was the cradle of 'rational' law, failed to develop as it might because, among other things, bureaucracy strangled its incipient potential for industrial capitalism.

Weber's analysis of the city similarly rests on a twofold contrast between ancient and modern Europe and between Europe and the rest of the world. His distinctive contribution, which despite some qualifications seems now generally acknowledged, was to stress the importance of the contrast between cities which are centres of consumption and cities which are themselves producers. In this respect, the medieval *Stadt* differs alike from the ancient *polis* (and Rome itself) and from the great cities of India, China or the Islamic world. Weber devoted what became a whole section of *Economy and Society* to the topic of the city. But the significance of the medieval European city was already brought out in his long essay of 1909 on 'Agrarian Relations in the Ancient World' from which the first selection in this section is taken. The essay is of broader interest than its title implies: much of it is explicitly directed to the question of the non-emergence of industrial capitalism and to the importance of military as opposed to economic considerations in the ancient world. Weber's approach was on the whole disregarded by ancient historians in favour of the work of Rostovtseff; but interest in it has more recently been revived.[1]

When he came to look at China, then, as I have already remarked, Weber grossly underestimated what are now known to have been its impressive and even spectacular achievements in science and technology. But this of course only further sharpens the question why Europe and not China achieved an industrial revolution; and the question becomes more difficult still when such other preconditions as the supply of credit, the cheapness of commercial transport, the disappearance of serfdom and the capacity for overseas trade and/or colonisation are examined also. Weber's views about Chinese social structure – ideology apart – have been disputed on several points. He is now held to have assumed more than the evidence warrants about the 'patrimonial' nature of Chinese bureaucracy, the monolithic character of central government and the divisive effects of the examination system. He is also held to be guilty of using materials from different periods to support his argument in a not strictly historical way.[2] But on two points he appears to have been right: the role of the *literati* and the significance of kinship groups. A conclusive answer to what Weber himself calls 'the old question'[3] has still not been reached, and perhaps never will be. It is, after all, even more difficult to explain why something didn't happen than why it did. Nor could it any longer be claimed, as it was by C. K. Yang in 1951, that

[1] See in particular M. I. Finley, *The Ancient Economy* (London, 1973).
[2] See Otto B. van der Sprenkel, 'Max Weber on China', *History and Theory*, III (1963).
[3] Below, p. 330.

Weber's essay on 'Confucianism and Taoism', from which the second selection in this section is taken, is 'more richly endowed with vital ideas and hypotheses on the structure and value system of traditional Chinese society than any other volume available today'.[1] But nevertheless it can certainly be agreed with Yang that Weber's essay retains its relevance both for the study of Chinese society and for the comparative sociology of religion.

[1] In his 'Introduction' to H. H. Gerth's translation *The Religion of China* (Glencoe, Illinois, 1951), p. xl.

15 · *Urbanisation and Social Structure in the Ancient World*

From the third century onwards, the progress of urbanisation encountered constant and manifestly increasing impediments. Before touching on the causes of them, let us examine yet again the special characteristics of the ancient city-state, and ask in particular how it is related to the medieval 'city'. A number of features are discernible in the beginnings of the medieval city which we have already observed in the early days of the ancient city-state. In both, the basic requirement for citizenship is the combination of landownership and participation in the market; there is a tendency towards the accumulation of landholdings through the investment of trading profits; the landless are treated as 'resident aliens' (or 'metics'); public service to the city is imposed as an obligation on the lords of the city; the citizen body is organised along military lines, especially the members of those trades which are of military importance; and there is a social division between those who fight on horseback and those who fight on foot. However, the differences are also enormous. Admittedly (and this cannot be stressed enough) it is important to bear in mind how widely the medieval cities differ from one another in their social structure. To anticipate one important point about the relationship to the knightly nobility, which was generally important in the ancient city and was always central to their development: there were obviously major differences between such cities as Genoa, where this held more or less good in its early period, Florence, where the burgesses forced the '*incasamento*' of the landed nobility and at times practised a kind of political 'reduction to the ranks of the patriciate' on it, the numerous cities which directly or indirectly compelled the nobles to join the guilds, Freiburg-im-Breisgau and other places where the nobility were, on the contrary, forbidden to settle in the town, and, finally, those numerous towns, including most of the large ones, in which a knightly patriciate emerged from the ranks of the middle class. The following generalisation may, however, be permissible: the Mediterranean coastal cities in which purely commercial interests and resources were dominant came closest in character to the large city of antiquity; the secondary, purely agricultural, townships were broadly similar to the small city of antiquity; while, by contrast, the *industrial* cities were of a type which was markedly different from the ancient city-state. Fluid as these distinctions between economic types, however great, always are, there is a great deal of truth (despite Goldschmidt's assertion to the contrary) in Lastig's thesis that it was industrial cities such as Florence which were chiefly responsible for the specific legal innovations relating to industrial capital. It is clear that the legal regulation of labour, the social power of the guilds and the organisation of labour relations by guilds, and therefore the first organisation of free labour were achievements, essentially, of these 'industrial cities', for although there had been the beginnings of free labour in the ancient world, they remained beginnings only, which never reached fruition.

The Carolingian empire recognised and regulated the market in slaves, and the slave trade persisted in the inland regions of eastern Europe, as it did in the Mediterranean coastal cities such as Genoa. But it declined in the inland industrial cities. It was not that bondage had been unknown among these from the beginning: on the contrary, craftsmen and even merchants who migrated to a newly licensed city were, to a legally significant degree, bondsmen whom the lord, like the ancient slave-owner with his 'people who lived apart', allowed into the city so as to profit from their taxes and bequests. Gradually at first, and sometimes only after centuries, these bondsmen achieved complete personal freedom. Like the slaves of the ancient world from whom their lord received money as '*peculium*' they too settled among their free colleagues, according to their trade. The difference, however, is that in the medieval case free and unfree labourers together formed a 'purposive association' within which differences of status were ignored and from which, furthermore, there emerged an autonomous community with specific legally defined freedoms. It was they therefore – that is, those who were taxed on their land or their persons – who represented the 'city', and not, as in the ancient world, the lords: this was undoubtedly true of this type of 'inland industrial city', and in general of all those cities in which the guilds achieved some influence.

The term 'inland city' does not, of course, refer to a city in a district totally without commercial links with the outside world: in such a district urbanisation does not occur at all. Rather, it means a city whose production and consumption are mainly dependent on the growth of a *local* market. Again, it goes without saying that the term 'industrial city', in the medieval context, does not refer to a city whose requirement for agricultural produce is paid for by the sale of its industrial products alone. Rather, it is a city in which the concentration of free industry both gives it an effective basis on which to provide for its food supplies and at the same time distinguishes it from a completely rural area. Those cities which depend for their existence on income from such 'inland' sources as land and slaves (as Moscow did up to the present century) and those cities at the opposite economic pole, which rely, like Genoa, on profits from maritime trade, overseas capital investment and colonial plantations, both come closer to the ancient city-state than the kind of city which lies between these two extremes – the medieval industrial city in the sense just explained.

It is certainly true that industrial and commercial cities tended to merge into one another (as is shown by the examples of Venice and, even more, Flanders and several South German and Rhineland cities), and likewise that in the ancient world industry could be of great importance in the development of the city-state. Nevertheless, the difference remains enormous. The most important and decisive factor is that the position of ancient industry, both social and economic, did not improve as wealth accumulated. It never reached the level of the great medieval industrial centres, whereas the whole development of a specifically modern form of capitalism, namely industrial capitalism, is connected with the legal forms created by these same 'industrial cities', and so with the very thing which was lacking in the ancient city-state. The craftsman of the early period of the ancient city-state declined as capital was increasingly invested in slaves. On the other hand, that mixture of free and unfree small tradesmen which constituted the 'artisan' class, and which, in the early Middle Ages, had been as much despised as in the ancient world, and as much excluded by comparison with the merchants from public office, made steady economic and political progress. Admittedly, as the work of Liebenam and Ziebarth has shown, artisan corporations were known in the ancient world. But whereas in the early period of ancient society, as in the Middle Ages, those artisans whose work was of military importance formed political bodies for voting and defence, in the 'classical' period of ancient civilisation the artisan guilds were of no real importance. It was only as commercial slavery began to decline that there emerged artisan associations of any social consequence – but without the typical legal rights of the medieval guilds. As L. M. Hartmann has rightly pointed out, the beginnings of the latter only became noticeable in the final period of all, after the total collapse of ancient capitalism.

Just as there is no trace in the ancient city-state of precisely the most characteristic feature of the development of the medieval city, namely the struggle between the guild and the patriciate and the establishment of specifically 'guild-cities', so there is virtually no analogue in the medieval city of what was most characteristic in the development of the ancient free city, namely the struggle of the peasants against the patriciate and the establishment of what was referred to above as the 'hoplite state' (a city dominated by those peasants wealthy enough to bear arms). The typical medieval city at first excluded peasants from participation in citizenship; and when, later on, it wanted to take them under its protection as 'external citizens', it was to be prevented from doing so by the nobles and princes. Moreover, the land acquired by the citizens as they accumulated wealth did not constitute an extension of territory. Of course, there are intermediate cases here, as there generally are in history. As the foregoing outline showed, the 'hoplite state' was nowhere found in a really pure and distinct form in the ancient world, neither in Athens after Cleisthenes and Ephialtes nor in Rome after the *Lex Hortensia*, nor anywhere else. Furthermore, we must not lose sight of the fact that the 'hoplite' class included, as a very important component, the urban lower middle class, and in particular the householders. (The craftsmen and their role have been considered in the earlier account.) The importance of the rural lower middle class in the Middle Ages should not, on the other hand, be forgotten: nor should the role played in the administration of the law by the 'separated communities' in the cities, nor, finally, the significance of the territories attached to the Italian city-states. But anyone who does not see it as the exclusive object of 'history' to make itself redundant by proving that 'there is nothing new under the sun' and – what is certainly true – that all, or almost all, differences are differences of degree, will emphasise the changes which occurred *despite* all the parallels. He will make use of analogies only to bring out what was distinctive of each of the two sequences of development by comparison with each other – which is, however, already a formidable enough task.

Whereas in the Middle Ages the guilds took over power in the city and, in pursuit of their political purposes, forced the patricians, as the class holding political rights, to enrol in a guild and to allow it to tax and supervise them, in the ancient world it was the '*demos*' (that is, the population of the villages) which made use of a similar power for political ends (for instance, over almost the whole of the area ruled by Athens). Whereas in the ancient world the duty of bearing arms was organised by classes defined by ground-rent, in the Middle Ages it was organised by guilds. The difference is extraordinarily striking and shows by itself that the medieval city, in the sense of the form of city which was specific to the Middle Ages, was in crucial respects economically and socially constituted in a totally different way from the ancient city. This holds precisely in the sense in which the Middle Ages came closer than did the ancient city-state to our kind of capitalist development, even long before the emergence of capitalist forms of organisation.

This becomes clear in various places in the way in which the battle-lines of social conflict were drawn. In the ancient world, the typical opposition was simply one of property: big landlord against smallholder. The conflict primarily concerned political equality and the distribution of the burdens of civic obligations. Where there was an element of economic antagonism between classes then, apart from the question of public land, it came down in the last resort almost entirely to an opposition of one of two kinds: either landowners versus the *déclassés*, or the preliminary to it – creditors versus debtors. The debtors, moreover, were mostly, though not entirely, drawn from the rural peasantry outside of the cities. Now it is certainly true that there are many points of comparison between the opposition of the guilds to the great families in our high Middle Ages (thirteenth to fourteenth centuries), at least in their early stages, and this kind of conflict in the city-states of the ancient 'middle ages': deprivation of political rights, financial oppression and discriminatory use of common land come especially to mind. But it is not so much the rural peasants outside the city as the urban artisans inside it who provide the crack troops of the opposition. And since capitalist development was by then in its early stages, the opposition in the conflicts of this period was no longer based, as it had been in the ancient world, purely on size of landholdings or simply on relations between creditors and debtors. The more clearly the tensions which developed were of a specifically economic character, the more definitely there emerged a sort of conflict which had simply not been feasible in the ancient world – that between merchants and artisans. The peasant in the ancient world was unwilling to be reduced to the status of a debt-slave working the land of a town-dwelling *rentier* who lived off income from land and money-lending. The artisan in the late medieval town was unwilling to be reduced to the status of a cottager working in the industrial undertaking of a capitalist entrepreneur. After the victory of the guilds, however, there emerged yet another social contrast unknown to the ancient world, that between 'master' and 'journeyman'. The forced labourer in the ancient East 'went on strike' with the cry: 'Give us our bread' (the bread due to him by tradition). The agricultural slave in the ancient world revolted in order to regain his freedom – we hear nothing of rebellions or conflicts involving *industrial* slaves in the ancient world. It was industry, indeed, which offered the most favourable position to slaves in the ancient world: in contrast with agricultural slaves, the industrial slave had some chance of manumission. Moreover, from the point of view of social demands, there was no point in 'brotherhoods of free artisans', since there were no 'brothers' anyway (or at least where they did exist,[1] they did not form a socially relevant class). Almost all ancient social conflicts, especially in the city-states, were in the last analysis struggles for possession of, or rights to, land – a problem which simply did not exist in the Middle Ages

[1] For, as was said earlier, we should not deny unconditionally that they did exist. Those assistants of Attic vase painters who later rose to be independent 'masters' might, for example, be described in this way. We simply do not know what legal form the relationship took – wage labour or partnership.

as a problem for the *city*. It was, on the contrary, essentially a matter of conflicts between the classes which lived on the land, between the peasants and their non-urban social superiors (landlords or political rulers as the case might be), as these worked themselves out in the struggles for freedom waged by the peasants of England, France and Germany, with varying fortunes but for the most part unsuccessfully. To be sure, the cities often took sides in these conflicts: in Italy they overthrew feudalism, in Germany they opposed it (though in the long run without success). But only in some of the larger Italian city-states was this a struggle *within* the city community or its territory.[1] The only medieval parallels to the struggles of the hoplite class against the urban patriciate in the West of the ancient world were perhaps the struggles of the popular forces in Switzerland against the feudal knights and the territorial lords.[2]

This difference underlies one of the most important contrasts between the development of the ancient and the medieval city: the difference in place of residence and character of the nobles and princes. The development of the ancient city-state began with the rule of a monarch residing in the city. This system was first overthrown by the urban patriciate, and this in turn was followed by the political emancipation of the rural areas, which came to dominate the city. By contrast, the development of the medieval city began with a nobility which owned and lived on the land and with a specifically *landed* royal and princely class: the history of the medieval city is one of the emancipation of the urban middle class from manorial dependence on these non-urban centres of power, a dependence which was given an explicit legal form. Admittedly, in this case too the contrast should not be treated as absolute. It was often precisely in the large commercial centres on the southern fringes of the development of the medieval city (such as Pisa, Venice, Genoa and a number of large French and Spanish cities) that the seats of nobles were found, or came to be so. In Italy, this process finally went so far that in eighteenth-century Tuscany a '*città*' was distinguished from a '*borgo*' and a '*castello*', partly by ecclesiastical criteria (whether it was the seat of a bishop or not), but partly also in terms of the rank of the noble who

---

[1] And then it was a struggle between the bourgeoisie and the nobility, rather than between the peasantry and the nobility.

[2] The struggles of the Swiss are most reminiscent of those of the Israelites against the Philistine nobility, and can also probably be compared to those of the Sabellian mountain peoples against Rome. But there is a difference in the latter case. It was the peasant hoplite class of Rome which was fighting for the possession of their land in the plains against the incursions of mountain peoples, and which drove back and eventually defeated the Samnites through their disciplined and on that account superior military techniques. By contrast, in the later Middle Ages it was the Swiss who were, like the Spartans, the *virtuosi* of infantry fighting: there was a direct connexion between their agrarian situation and their use as mercenaries. (Besides, it is well known what role was played in the Swiss struggles by the urban middle class.)

resided there. Furthermore, the sworn brotherhoods which usurped the autonomy of the town in such places, as the '*compagna communis*' did in Genoa, clearly call to mind, despite all the differences in their social composition, the formation of ancient towns from the union of village communities. At least, there are points of comparison: in these Latin cities of the early Middle Ages, too, the noble was involved, indeed took the lead. Connected with this, moreover, is the fact that the economic basis of the emerging urban patriciate in these cities was essentially similar to that of the leading families in the ancient city-state. Their wealth came partly from overseas trade, sometimes in the form of the *commenda* (as in the ancient East), and partly from large holdings in land, which grew as their trading profits increased. This last similarity in economic structure between the patriciates of the medieval city and of the early period of ancient society applies fairly generally to the cities of the Middle Ages. On the other hand, relationships with the authentically *feudal* powers in the great majority of medieval cities, especially the industrial cities of northern Europe and the continent, are quite different from those in the free city-state of the ancient world, both in the manner in which they first emerged and in their later development. This is the result of the fact that the medieval city grew up in the midst of large feudal states which, although very loosely unified, were nevertheless unified to some degree. It was thus subject to concessions and privileges granted by princes and lords of the manor, surrounded on all sides by their territory, and limited in the type and scale of its development, however much the bonds of dependence might slacken, by the need to compromise with them. It was precisely from this that there emerged a definite 'bourgeois' character, founded on profits derived from industrial monopoly and retail trade, such as those extracted by the Mediterranean patriciate from their involvement in maritime trade. It is this distinctively 'economic' character which distinguishes them very sharply from the outset from the ancient city-state of the classical period: in this respect, the Hellenistic cities and those of late antiquity are much more like them.

Most medieval cities grew up as a result of settlement on the lands of a prince or lord of the manor, who expected to receive from the town ground-rents, market dues and legal charges. In this way, the city was a direct successor to the straightforward concession of land for a market, through which the same aims had previously been pursued. In some cases, speculation in the foundation of cities misfired, as it had previously done in the case of markets. It succeeded in those cases in which the land granted by the lord was occupied by a mixture of free and unfree settlers, who obtained a plot of land to build a house, a garden, a share of produce from the common land and the right to trade at the city market; such commercial privileges as a staple, a precinct and so forth were soon added. Either immediately or after a short time, the settlement would be fortified and it would gradually acquire a degree of independence from its founder. In some cases, indeed, the degree of independence was very great, sometimes amounting to total separation and sometimes to complete autonomy in economic and police matters. In the large cities, this always followed the rule that the city had full internal and, according to circumstances, external autonomy subject to the maintenance of the lord's rights to ground-rent and jurisdiction. This ensured that the lord always remained interested in the city both politically and, above all, economically (as collector of tolls and dues).

The progressive extension of the autonomy of the urban middle classes within the overall unity of the state, up until the fifteenth century, as compared with the progressive diminution of the autonomy of the Hellenistic and Roman cities within the monarchical states, is a consequence of the differences in structure of the political institutions within which each functioned. The monarchical state of the ancient world was, or came to be, a bureaucratic state. In Egypt, as we saw, the universal domination of the bureaucracy had grown out of the royal *clientela* as early as the second millennium B.C. Its domination, together with the theocracy, stifled the development of the free city-state in the East; the areas ruled by the Romans went the same way under the Empire (see below). In the medieval West, the transformation in the role of ministers within the administrative system ran parallel with the development of territorial power. This development began, essentially, in the thirteenth century, was firmly established by the sixteenth, and finally, from the fifteenth century onwards, progressively undermined the autonomy of the city, incorporating it into the dynastic bureaucratic state. Throughout the whole of the early and high Middle Ages, however, the developing city was allowed to evolve its distinctive characteristics. In this period it was not only the mainstay of the money economy, but also (and consequently) of the administration, in virtue of its official obligations: it was surrounded on all sides by hierarchy, in the form of those power relations which were latent in feudal and service relationships – power relations in which (generally speaking) its own citizens as such had no part. This had important consequences: in the city-state, which was organised into tribes, phratries, and economically graded military classes, and in which, to all intents and purposes, militarism pervaded everything, military service and civic rights were simply identical. Furthermore, absolutely everything – trading monopolies, opportunities for profit from land, and finally and above all landownership itself – depended on military success in that chronic state of war in which each city was engaged, in the last resort, against all others. The city-state in the classical period was the most complete military organisation that the ancient world produced. It was founded essentially for military purposes, just as most medieval cities were founded essentially for economic purposes.

There are analogies to the militarism and the ruthless expansion by force of arms of the ancient city-state in the sea-port cities of Italy: the merciless destruction of Amalfi by Pisa, the crippling of Pisa by Genoa, the struggle of Genoa against Venice, are all, in both their ends and the means used, just like the politics of the ancient city-state. There are also analogies in the inland territories: the devastation of Fiesole, the subjugation of Arezzo, the crippling of Siena by Florence, and also the policies of the Hansa are all reminiscent of ancient politics. On the whole, however, especially in the inland territories of France and Germany, on the continent and in England, it was from a very early stage simply not feasible for a city to engage in a policy of war and plunder. The city was not, as in early antiquity, the most complete military organisation: inland cities, during the period of knightly wars in our Middle Ages, could do no more than win and retain their independence and the public peace in defence of their commercial interests, and even this was only possible if they made common cause with each other. It was not until the time of the *condottieri* and of mercenary armies that, even in Italy, their financial power gained the ascendancy in those places where capitalism was sufficiently developed to provide the means. (What is more, even the war of independence of the Netherlands cities was conducted on land entirely by means of mercenaries, except for the defence of their own city walls: this is just like the expansion of Florence.) The inland city, even when all due weight has been given to the military valour of its citizens, was from the beginning, and pre-eminently, of a 'bourgeois' character, designed for the peaceful acquisition of a market. The medieval 'burgher' was, from the very beginning, much more of an 'economic man' than the citizen of an ancient city-state either wished to be or could be. Above all, and in the sharpest contrast to the ancient city-state, the medieval burgher had no thought whatsoever of acquiring colonies, for the simple reason that there were no prospective takers for them: there were no peasants who had become *déclassés* because they had lost their land or fallen into debt, or who wanted land in order to provide for their heirs, and so could provide the driving force impelling the city into such a policy, however much the city patriciate, just as in the ancient world, might invest its money in the purchase of land.

Even when one considers the advance of the peasants themselves into the virgin forest and towards the East, expansion by force of arms in order to occupy land, after the ancient fashion, was ruled out in the Middle Ages by the position of the peasantry within the feudal system. Such expansion was now controlled by the landowners and territorial lords. As a goal of policy for a normal medieval city, the establishment of colonies, which was normal for the ancient city-state, would have been both a military and an economic impossibility. The interests of the medieval bourgeoisie, except in the few larger cities which exploited connexions in trade and colonies, became and remained directed towards the peaceful extension of trade within their own locality and with neighbouring localities. Of course, as Sombart rightly emphasised, in the latter part of the Middle Ages emergent capitalism found relatively large opportunities for profit also in those places where it acquired tax-farming concessions (as in Genoa or Florence) or, better still, was in a position to satisfy monarchical needs for finance. But this process, and all those groups who depended on it – the Acciajuoli, Bardi, Peruzzi, Medici, Fugger and their like – were nothing new in comparison with the ancient world, where they had been known and had been just as important from the time of Hammurabi's 'money-men' to that of Crassus. It is not here, and not in the nature of the process of primitive capital accumulation, that there lies the problem of the origin of the distinctive characteristics of the late medieval and modern economic system – that is, of modern capitalism. The decisive questions are rather, on the one hand, those concerning the development of the market – how did there develop in the course of the Middle Ages a body of consumers for the products of industry in its later capitalist form? – and on the other, those concerning the regulation of production – how did the tendency to realise capital lead to the creation of organisations of 'free' labour of a kind different from any known in the ancient world?

These problems will not be debated here: I shall simply add to what has already been said a few comments on contrasts between the development of the ancient and the medieval world so far as agricultural conditions are involved. The slow but steady improvement in the economic situation of the medieval peasantry, which came to an end with the stagnation of the process of internal colonisation in the forests and to the East, meant the emergence, in the course of the Middle Ages, of a slowly expanding market for the cities, just as the development of the cities in turn meant the growth of new openings for the sale of the peasants' produce. This economic improvement depended, as might be gathered from the preceding discussion, on the conditions of life secured for the continental peasantry at that time by the feudal social system as it was established outside the cities – just as did the 'bourgeois' development, so characteristic of the medieval as opposed to the ancient city, which was mentioned earlier. It seems appropriate at this point to take a brief look at the contrasts between this development and parallel phenomena in the ancient world.

We have seen the great importance of feudal elements throughout the whole of ancient society. We have seen, for instance, how all-powerful were

the relations of clientship in Egypt, infused as they were with religious ·
sentiment; and, so enormously powerful was the influence of religion in
the everyday life of the ancient world, where even the division of society
into artificial and purely rational 'tribal' and similar groupings immediately took on religious significance, that even in the later period the
tenacity of relationships of feudal allegiance should not be underestimated. Moreover, the point from which feudal development begins is in
both cases the same. In the Middle Ages, as in the ancient world, the
development begins with the following (*trustis*) of a local prince, which
reappears, on a higher level, as the following of the king, who, as in the
ancient world, was often seen as a stranger to the land or, at least, as
standing outside the local laws, protected by the royal power of expulsion.
In both cases there can be found the beginnings of royal control of store
houses, the provisioning of the army from the store houses (*cap. de villis*),
a famine-relief policy and so on. In both cases, finally, it was the knightly
nobility which developed out of that following (although also out of a
number of legal institutions different in character from it) whose power
and indispensability placed increasing constraints on the king, making
him dependent on it, at times reducing him to the position of a merely
elected monarch and coming to dominate the territory. But just as the
king was not an urban king, so the nobility was not an urban nobility;
nor did it become so in the Middle Ages, at least in the continental areas
– in partial contrast with those of the Mediterranean. The same is true
of the large estates. In the ancient world, up to the time of the Roman
Empire, these provided the basic source of income for *rentiers* living in
the cities. This is primarily to be explained by the simple fact that what
we call 'ancient civilisation' was the cultural zone surrounding the coasts:
in the large estates of Thessaly we already begin to see something more
of the medieval character, and the first mention of the true inland plains
is to be found in the Hellenistic period and especially under the Roman
Empire. In the Middle Ages, on the other hand, the centre of gravity
of the continuous historical development which leads from the Pharaohs
to our own civilisation shifts to the inland areas. Most estates were not
suburban but rural: they were meant for landowners actually living on
the land with their dependants (princes and free vassals with knights to
act as their ministers). The estates did not always, or in the case of the
large ones even predominantly, fulfil this function exclusively in the form
of a *natural* economy. On the contrary: the king, the princes and the great
vassals all wanted also to engage in profitable commerce. The origins of
markets and towns, as already mentioned, were indeed to be found in
speculation in taxes and rents by princes and lords. Nevertheless, nobles
and lords were not, as in the ancient world, citizens of the city as such.
Quite the reverse: they sought to isolate their manors in order to protect

them against inclusion in the 'free' brotherhood of the city, and to take away the cities' right to incorporate 'external citizens'.

Rural and urban spheres of interest thus sought to differentiate themselves from each other. It goes without saying that they were a long way from achieving complete success; but they came nearer to it than was ever even remotely possible in the ancient city-state, which was a military parade ground and permanent encampment. Furthermore, the internal social structure of the feudal classes was different from that existing in the ancient world. The feudal tenants of the Oriental princes, the helots, servants, clients, holders of *precaria* and tenant farmers of the Mediterranean landlords, were, during the feudal period of ancient civilisation, as we saw, small men who accompanied an individual warrior as camp followers or, at best, lightly armed foot-soldiers: the warrior himself, however, travelled to battle in a chariot. In the period of hoplite armies, the fully armoured heavy infantryman frequently employed one or two people (helots or slaves) as bearers and servants, whereas the cavalrymen of the ancient world (who were without stirrups right through into the classical period!) remained technically inferior until the time of the Parthians. By contrast, the feudal army of the Middle Ages was a cavalry army from the beginning and over the whole period of its existence: its armour, arms and discipline, moreover, were continually improving. Even the servants who stood at the lowest end of the feudal hierarchy, if they were armed and taken to war, could not be offered the kind of peasant allotments cultivated by the warrior caste and their like in the East or, it is plausible to suppose, by clients in Rome: in short, they could not take up the kind of social position occupied by feudal vassals who stood in the ancient kind of relation of clientship. Their way of life was always bound to give them some tinge of 'chivalric' values. Everything associated with the peasantry remained below this social level, which was necessarily, and of its essence, a stratum of '*rentiers*'.[1]

The nature of the development of the continental peasantry in the early Middle Ages is essentially a result of the fact that even the lowest stratum of the hierarchy, overlapping with the peasantry, was a social class of *rentiers*, whose interests were not purely economic, while the peasants themselves became, on the other hand, an increasingly unmilitary class. This peasantry had made territorial conquests of enormous extent, as large as those acquired by any hoplite army in the ancient world, but, in the same way as the city, they had done so by essentially peaceful means and, furthermore, essentially in the service of feudal *rentiers*. The clearing of the forests and the settlement of the colonisable land in the East were both brought about through the interests of the ruling class in increasing

[1] I am somewhat simplifying here a situation which was in reality much more complex.

its revenues. This enormous task of 'internal colonisation' could not have been achieved by the use of slave labour for three reasons: first, there would have been sheer lack of sufficient numbers of slaves; secondly, the feeding of the slaves would have resulted in higher, and mounting, costs; thirdly, and most important of all, slave labour would not have been qualitatively good enough to be used to advantage in establishing peasant settlements in the 'wilderness' or on the sandy soil of the East. Every settlement, therefore, meant an enormous increase in the numbers of 'free' peasants – that is, in this context, peasants who paid basically steady tributes. The individualistic squatter's rights of the Germanic 'Bifanc' in the virgin forest worked in precisely the opposite way to the rights of occupation on the conquered territories of Rome (which resulted in the creation of large estates) and in a completely contrary way to the creation of new land by canal building in the early Oriental states, which was necessarily under bureaucratic direction. The peasantry of the Middle Ages remained an expanding and ascending class as long as there stood over it the purely feudal ruling class of the purely feudal state, which sought revenue from its estates rather than trading profits from the market. The pressure of the natural economy on the inland regions, which were vast in terms of the means of transport of the past, held back the pace of development of distant markets for agricultural produce for sufficient time to enable the peasant economy to conquer central Europe. Towards the end of the Middle Ages, the typical farmer was the peasant who was subject to a landlord but was normally burdened only with traditional duties, and whose local town was his normal market; and since the city had monopolised trade for itself so far as it was able and had as far as possible squeezed out the 'intruder' and the rural manufacturer, he himself was the normal, but secure, consumer of most of the city's industrial products. The feudal army and the feudal state had helped to create the medieval peasant and the medieval city – both of which were expansionist purely in economic terms.

The intervention of modern capitalism, both in manufacturing and in agriculture, is bound up with this state of affairs. Admittedly, this intervention at the same time brought about its gradual downfall. Nevertheless, one should not underestimate the importance for the development of capitalism of the commercial underpinnings brought into existence through titles, privileges, cooperative associations, rights of control, of staple, of expulsion and of market, all enmeshed with one another in a thousand different ways, and above all through the traditional or enforced regulation of prices. All these things, although they imposed restraints on capitalism's drive for profit, nevertheless provided support for its need for rational calculation, which could not have been built on the shifting sands of oriental bargaining. At all events, the medieval organisation of trade, bound together as it was by a thousand threads, and made possible by the theocratic and feudal framework of the world as it then existed, was one of the components of a market in goods to which rational calculation could be applied. In the same way, the class of free peasantry and petty bourgeoisie which was clamped into that organisation provided the broad, relatively stable, body of consumers which modern capitalism needed for its wares.

The contrast which is so evident between the development of the bourgeoisie and the peasantry in the West in the Middle Ages and in the ancient world is the result, first, of the change in the geographical scene of operations, and secondly, of the different military development of the Middle Ages, which is connected with the first by a variety of causal chains. Whereas the army of knights in the Middle Ages enforced the feudal social order, and its dissolution at the hands of the mercenary army and later (from the time of Moritz von Oranien onwards) the disciplined modern army brought about the triumph of the modern state system, there were two major revolutions in military technique in the ancient world. First, the introduction of the horse from the East (either from Iran or Turan) led, as in the Middle Ages, to the creation of the castle, the oriental type of state based on conquest and Mediterranean knightly society. Secondly, iron,[1] the stabbing weapon, and the disciplined hand-to-hand fighting of armoured hoplites brought into being the army of rich peasants and urban small property-owners and thereby the ancient 'citizen *polis*'. Everything else was thus a consequence of the scene of operations in which the *polis* was engaged. For it was from the first dedicated to war and conquest, to the acquisition of commercial monopolies and tribute-paying subjects, but also of land to provide for the needs of the rising generation of hoplites or of opportunities to increase the revenues of its small property-owners. It pursued these aims wherever the chance was offered, and it continued to do so at all times and in all places, except where its expansion was checked by superior political strength.

The economy and economic techniques, on the other hand, obviously made relatively little progress in the ancient world after the time of the Ramesids and Assurbanipal, apart from the invention of money. How much, or how little, was achieved in the way of technological innovations in the period of ancient civilisation which is illuminated by history it will only be possible to decide when we have an industrial history of Egypt and Mesopotamia (mainly of Egypt, to the extent that technology is involved) appropriate to the state of the sources presently available. It is very possible that, when we have such a history, we shall see the East as

[1] Of course, iron has been used since prehistoric times. But iron *weapons* first became predominant in the 'post-Homeric' period.

having been responsible for the great majority of the technological innovations introduced into industry up to the end of the Middle Ages, just as it gave birth to all the forms of commerce which prevailed up to the end of our Middle Ages (Babylon), to the socage-farm (Egypt), to unfree domestic labour (Egypt), to the exaction of compulsory public services in lieu of tax (Egypt), to bureaucracy (Egypt) and to the monastery and other ecclesiastical organisations (Egypt and Palestine). As far as agricultural techniques are concerned, we may note a number of individual innovations during antiquity which had the effect of increasing the area of land which could be cultivated with a given amount of labour in a given time, and so of saving labour, such as better tools for threshing, ploughing and harvesting (of which the last two were typically introduced after the end of the classical period and in the inland areas of Northern Europe). In industry, if one disregards as one should machines used in warfare and the lifting mechanisms associated with them, together with similar instruments used essentially in public works, progress, as far as can be seen, was made chiefly in the specialisation of individual workers' tasks, which did not, at least to any significant extent, have the effect of concentrating labour. And the same can be seen in the economic organisation of industry. Neither should occasion any surprise, in view of the nature of the internal structure of ancient industry and the interest which slave-owners had in exploiting their property.

On the basis of the medieval system of commerce and industry, partly alongside it, partly within it, but always, despite all the many conflicts with the guilds, using the procedures and legal forms created by it, modern capitalism created for itself the conditions of its growth. Out of the *commenda* which dominated commerce from the time of Hammurabi to the thirteenth century it fashioned the limited liability company (which had its beginnings in the ancient world, characteristically, only in the form of *state* monopolies). The joint liability of partners, which in the ancient world was found only in crude forms, similar to the Russian *artel*, was elevated to the already highly refined forms of the late medieval law of commercial and industrial companies: the 'peculiar', the firm and so on. In other words, legal forms were now created for ongoing capitalist commercial and industrial enterprises, whereas the ancient world, at least where purely private commerce was concerned, retained legal forms suitable for discontinuous, opportunistic investment of capital.[1] In the Middle Ages, as soon as capital began to be invested in industrial production, it immediately led to the amalgamation of small artisan enterprises. After organising first the market and then the supply of raw materials, capitalism moved inexorably into the very heart of the process

[1] It would, of course, be wrong to suggest that there was *only* such discontinuous use of capital to be found in ancient commerce in general: but it was the characteristic use.

of production: through the dispersal and recombination of the labour force new artificial kinds of units of production were gradually formed which were adapted to the rationalisation of techniques, more and more detached from the family, of increasing size and, generally speaking, internally articulated to an increasing degree. In the ancient world nothing[1] of this sort is to be found in purely private enterprises. As we have seen, the concentration of dozens, even of thousands, of slaves in individual private fortunes, even in cases where all the slaves belonged to the same branch of industry, did not amount to the creating of a 'large enterprise' in the economic sense – any more than nowadays the investment of capital in the shares of different breweries amounts to the creation of a *new* brewery.[2] For it was a matter of investing capital in the ancient case, too, as we saw, in such a way that the economics and technology of production were not affected by it at all: the slaves remained what they were – small artisans used either by a wealthy man as a source of income, or (the nearest approximation to a capitalist 'large enterprise') by an importer, such as Demosthenes, to work up his raw material. We saw how unstable these concentrations were, in the sense that fixed capital was of little importance, and how completely the fate of the 'enterprise' depended on the fate of the monies involved in it.

There is one further point to be added now: when we come across concentrations of artisans of different types in the property of some ancient slave-owner, such as Timarchus, then it is as far from being merely accidental as when we come across shares in the balance-sheet of a modern private fortune which are of extremely varied kinds and likely to yield a return under totally different conditions. As everyone knows, it is only prudent to spread one's investment among the most varied kinds of stocks and shares; but it was equally prudent in the ancient world to spread one's investment in slaves, except in cases like the employment of workers in such absolutely stable industries as the mining of precious metals (Nicias) or the disposal of personal merchandise (Demosthenes). In other cases it was a matter of simple prudence to buy a variety of artisans in the same batch: it provided a guarantee against loss, similar to the guarantee against loss of rents which we have already come across, where the same man would have a share in the ownership of parts of as many different houses as possible. It follows from

[1] This point, however often it is stressed, ought *a potiori* to be understood; the achievements of ancient capitalism did not lie in this direction. Literally without *any* kind of 'internal division of labour', a very considerable part of even such industry as was known in the ancient world could not have been carried on at all.

[2] An Attic vase may carry its maker's guarantee: 'He has made it in a way which N.N.' (his 'competitor') 'would never have been able to do.' But I may leave it to the reader, however economically untutored, to discover by personal reflection the world of difference which divides such a situation in meaning, means and effect from modern 'competition' and 'advertising', to which, at an abstract conceptual level, it is similar.

305

this, however, that ancient 'capitalism', in the industrial sphere, since it took the form of *rentier* capitalism, worked in a sense *against* the creation of 'large enterprises' producing one specific item. Moreover, the sale of industrial products, or at least their sale to external markets, was of too opportunistic a character, affected as it was not only by innumerable political upheavals, but above all, to an extent only seldom found in this form since the later Middle Ages, by fluctuations in the price of corn: the mass of people, whose needs it is which modern capitalism supplies, had in the ancient world so narrow and fluctuating a scope for expenditure on anything over and above what was absolutely indispensable, or in other words such minimal purchasing power for industrial products, that it provided too small a foundation on which to build a socially powerful corporate industry, even a few large 'cottage industries' or indeed 'factories'.

These assertions are perhaps somewhat over-emphatic – as they need to be, if the differences which undoubtedly exist are to be brought out. Certainly, it would be wrong to dispute that here and there among ancient industrial enterprises some approximation to a rational 'large enterprise' may be found. That topic would be well worth special research. But the characteristic feature of the ancient economy is a precisely opposite kind of development, one which does not approximate to modern industrial capitalism but is, on the contrary, remote from it. It was, moreover, basically the fact that the utilisation of capital in the ancient world was connected with slave labour which gave this development its direction. The difference in the medieval case resulted both from strictly historical causes and also, above all, from the change in the geographical scene of capitalist development. The needs to be satisfied developed in a quite different way[1] because of the climatic differences; Northern Europeans were confined to their homes for a large part of the year because of the climate, whereas the ancients lived outside in their public squares (the café life of present-day Spaniards and Italians is very similar to this); there were differences of temperament, which can be explained without recourse to any 'racial' hypotheses[2] directly in terms of the climatic living conditions experienced by each generation anew; above all, there were the numerous inland centres of commerce whose constantly expanding consumption and production ruled out any fits and starts. All these were new conditions, into which the technological traditions of the ancient world were introduced and with which the reawakened urge to utilise capital had to reckon. Not only was the use of slave labour

[1] It is only necessary to think what a worker in our climate, as compared with the *fellahin*, needs as a bare minimum from a purely physiological standpoint in order to be able to work in a constantly sedentary position.

[2] Though such hypotheses should not by any means be generally excluded from scientific consideration.

unprofitable in itself in the North, because of the high maintenance costs, but the military organisation of the Middle Ages described above ruled out the possibility that the cities – that is, precisely those places in which industry was located – should engage in slave-raiding wars in the fashion of the ancient city-states. The knightly feuds of the inland areas, moreover, although they brought with them, as the spoils of war, an exchange of masters for the tribute-paying peasantry and an extension of the knight's own land and territorial sovereignty at the expense of another knight, did not, as did the sea-raiding expeditions of ancient coastal civilisation, bring the enslavement of the populace. Slavery declined, at least relatively, as the level of civilisation in the inland areas rose, while the development of 'free' labour advanced further for all the causes enumerated above (a more detailed analysis would take us too far from our main theme). Finally, in all the struggles between city-states in the ancient world, right up to the end of the Roman Republic, every war meant in principle the forcible overthrow of the entire system of landownership, vast confiscations and new settlements: in this respect the ancient city-state remained unchanged in the same position as the Germanic migrations.

The Middle Ages, on the other hand, for all its passion for feuding, and the early modern epoch too, were nevertheless periods in which the community of nations was 'at peace', when measured by ancient standards, even those of classical Greece.[1] It is true that modern capitalism both in the Middle Ages and in more recent times, drew, as has already been mentioned above, its largest profits from supplying the necessities of war. But what was novel – the capitalist organisation of industrial production – depended on just this maintenance of peace: because of it, despite all the political upheavals, the continuity of economic development was preserved. In the maintenance of the peace, not only the great feudal states, but above all the common Church played their part. In the ancient world, on the other hand, even the act of founding a city-state was governed by political and military motives, and in the same way, its further development depended on military activities. In this context, accordingly, capitalism lived off politics: it was, so to say, only indirectly economic. The political ups and downs of the city-state, in which opportunities varied for tax-farming contracts and the acquisition of slaves and (especially in Rome) land as booty, were its element. When, in the Hellenistic period and under the Roman Empire, the whole civilised world was at peace, there grew up on the territory of the ancient city, which from then on became a centre of exclusively economic interest,

---

[1] Not, of course, in the sense that there was a decline in the amount of military activity, but in the sense that, in relative terms, the practitioners of private commerce, especially the cities and the citizen bodies, were increasingly 'pacified'.

the kind of fully-fledged occupational associations of traders and artisans which had hitherto existed only in embryonic form. Their history may be traced, through their exploitation by the state for its own purposes in late antiquity, right up to the first beginnings of the medieval guilds. But for ancient capitalism the death-knell had sounded: it was smothered, such as it then was, by the peace, the monarchical state, and the move from a coastal to an inland type of civilisation, even though one might have surmised *a priori* that this was more likely to help it to flower.

This transition to peace and an inland civilisation, however, was finally accomplished by Imperial Rome. With the Empire there came, in a preliminary way under Tiberius, and definitively after Hadrian, peace and an end to wars for booty in the form of land and slaves; at the same time, great tracts of inland territory were brought into the Empire – Gaul, the Rhine and Danube territories, Illyria and the whole interior of the Balkan peninsula, in addition to the old province of Macedonia. Peace meant that slave imports gradually dried up: speculative slave breeding and peaceful slave trade were not sufficient to make up for the wearing out of the slaves caused by the working of the plantations in accordance with Varro's ideals and by the needs of the mines. The price of slaves at first rose rapidly, because of insufficient supplies to the market; in the later Empire it was, by contrast, extraordinarily low, because in the meantime the demand had sunk considerably as a result of revolutions in economic organisation. Earlier, I tended to overestimate this factor of the shifting market for slaves: but one should not on the other hand *under*estimate it. It is a fact that there was a decline in the practice of making slaves live in barracks and a reintroduction of family life for them, and that the result was a contraction of capitalism in the large agricultural enterprises: this fact is connected, moreover, to a large extent with those same fluctuations in the market (references can be found in the sources to a 'shortage of hands'). The great estates of the vast inland expanses of the North with their poor communications could not, in any case, be cultivated on the model of the Carthaginian and Roman plantations. Already Tacitus, or his informant, in his time had seen, probably amongst the princes of the Ubii on the Rhine frontier, the natural manorial economy which was to predominate in Frankish times, and had contrasted it with the Roman slave barracks, organised along the lines of a military machine. Slowly, the Roman villa, which nevertheless represented a high level of civilisation, began to advance northwards, finally reaching the Scottish borders. In this process, the villa, as the sources also reveal, came to be based on an increasingly broad foundation: indeed, this was essential, since the needs of a 'seigneurial' existence called for an increasingly large area of land. The process of increasing the size of the great estates, which was already under way in the time of the Republic, continued and resulted in the gradual separation of the estates from the market, which became more and more dispensable as a source of supply for the estates' requirements (more will be said about this process in the article on 'The Colonate'). The Emperors sought to amalgamate the estates by force into urban communities – meeting increasing resistance from the owners, as our sources reveal. But the prevailing tendency was to escape from the cities. The aristocracy to a large extent lived on the land: in other words, the Middle Ages were already on their way, and the importance of the cities, both in social and economic terms, was declining.

In absolute terms, trade certainly increased dramatically in the three and a half centuries from Gracchus to Caracalla over the whole of that part of the world encompassed within the territories of the Roman Empire in the Imperial period. In relative terms, however, this would not seem to be the case, if one compares the volume of turnover with the extent of the territories and the number of people included either as citizens or as subjects within the area specific to ancient civilisation. For this area had vastly expanded. Ancient civilisation was developing from a merely coastal into an inland culture and, in proportion to the means of trade which were available, that must mean a relative decline in the intensity of trade. In the coastal areas, the maintenance and clothing of slaves in the great households could be wholly or partly supplied by the market. In the inland regions, of course, the slaves or tenant-farmers of the landowners lived in a natural economy: only the thin upper layer of landlords had needs which gave occasion for the making of purchases and were met by the sale of surplus goods. This kind of trade is a tenuous network spread over the underlying natural economy. The common people of the great cities, on the other hand, were not provided for by private commerce but by the state corn-doles. This development did not, obviously, prevent an absolute increase in the settlement and cultivation of land in the newly annexed inland areas: on the contrary, nothing could be more certain than that both took place to a high degree. But it was precisely this which *increased* the effect of cultural dislocation.

The distinctive character of inland culture was most marked in two respects: first, in the disarmament of the city-states, the final elimination of their political autonomy, and therefore of all the capitalist interests and opportunities for profit which had depended on that autonomy; secondly, in the importance of the class of large inland landowners and its interests in Imperial policy. The latter had important consequences of a strictly political kind. The decline in the offensive capacity of the Roman army, so clearly apparent in the dispersal of the entire body of troops along the full length of the Northern frontier, was certainly also a result of the increase in the standing of the class of resident provincial landowners, which required of the army above all the defence and protection of its property, and therefore a defensive posture. An additional factor was the monarchical character of the state, which brought in its train all the typical consequences of ancient monarchy. In its day, the league of Italian cities, with its citizen levies, had defeated the Celts, whose strength was easily as great as that of the Goths and Vandals (about 15,000 to 20,000 men), and had in the Hannibalic wars raised a military force which would have found it child's play to defeat the so-called 'migration of peoples'. But, quite apart from the question whether it would have been possible, given the *social* stratification of the Imperial period, to base liability for military service on the capacity of a citizen levy (that is, in the context of the ancient city-state, a peasant levy) to equip itself, such temporary and *ad hoc* citizen levies would have been unable to undertake the permanent defence of a land frontier running right across Europe, as the interests of the landowners and the tenants who leased their domains required. That could only be done by a standing army, which meant, in the circumstances of the ancient world, a professional army. What is more, these interests of the inland regions now opened up to civilisation were, here as generally, in harmony with the dynastic interests of the Emperors. The professional army and bureaucracy of the dynasty now took the place, on the model of Hellenistic Egypt, of the city-state system, which was totally inadequate for a world empire; and it was no more than the logical conclusion of this development when the monarchical state, by removing its seat to the East, expressly acknowledged that it was the heir to the Hellenistic system.

Admittedly, Augustus and all the outstanding figures of the first two centuries were Roman Emperors, cautious about the extension of citizenship, especially in the East, and mindful to preserve the privileges attached to being Roman. But in order to increase their own dominance over the dominant nation, they gradually disarmed it, as is shown clearly enough by the declarations of nationality made by veterans in their military diplomas. It thus became possible under the Severi for the dominance of the Romans to be broken, without fuss or resistance, by one simple *coup d'état*, and for a race with no cultural traditions of its own, like the Illyrians, to alternate with Orientals in seizing control of the Empire. The exclusion of those of Roman descent from posts as officers and officials and the atrophy of the sound old governmental traditions of the Roman nobility (not 'racial' influences, for which, in this case too, no tangible evidence exists) were bound to shatter the state to its foundations. This is in fact what happened, thanks to the donatives to the all-powerful army, which (as von Domaszewski shows) were increasing at an insane rate. The state was bankrupted, resulting in the collapse for a generation of the ancient money economy (the later regulations about 'treasure trove' show where the cash had been kept, as always in such cases) and the disintegration of the Empire which was then re-formed on a totally new basis.

The Roman monarchy, moreover, now became a state which based itself on the extraction of compulsory public services from its subjects, on the model of Hellenistic Egypt. The origins of this development can be traced well back into the second century. The stratification of classes undertaken by the Emperors, from the most highly privileged senatorial class down to the bourgeoisie formed from freedmen in the smaller towns, who were organised into a cult of 'purveyors to the court' (the *Augustales*), together with the system of organisation of municipal councils and the organisation of extra-territorial estates and domains, formed the social basis for the extension of citizenship by Caracalla to all these privileged classes of the Empire. In contrast to them stood those who paid poll-tax: the dependent peasantry of the Greek East, the Roman plebeians, the tenant-farmers and those who leased the imperial estates ('*tributarii*'). Those classes of '*possessores*' or landowners who were exempted from the *corvées* of the common people, now came to form officially what one might call the 'immediate' subjects of the Emperor. Already this situation, which was simply a continuation of the situation of subjects under the Republic, was beginning to bear the Hellenistic stamp: it matters little how far it was a case of direct borrowing, since the conditions of ancient monarchy brought such structures with them. The system of supplying provisions to the army and the grants of land to the legions, who now became in effect an hereditary class of married frontiersmen, was undoubtedly borrowed from the East, especially from Egypt; this is all the more true, of course, of such things as monopolies, state workshops, compulsory guilds and the system of joint responsibility of the municipal councillors for taxes and all other public obligations, which, like a tight net, entangled the individual and bound him to his function.

In this net the ancient state also, slowly but surely, strangled capitalism. For how did it come about that at least the first two centuries of the Empire, and the fourth century, after order and peace had been restored – periods of relatively profound peace such as was unknown in the whole 'classical' period of ancient civilisation – were not golden ages for a capitalist economy? Sound progress continued to be made in the monetary system at least up to the time of Marcus Aurelius, but a monetary system is not the same thing as 'capitalism'. Large landed estates were established and grew, while on the other hand the small traders and small artisans of the East pressed onwards into the West throughout the period of the Empire, even in its last days (when they were, indeed, the carriers of Christianity). But we hear nothing of progress in capitalist economic organisation, either in trade or in agriculture or, finally, in industry. On the contrary: the 'royal merchants' of the early Empire, who traded with the North, disappeared; small shopkeepers made progress; tax revenues from commerce dried up so completely during the great collapse of the third century that (as von Domaszewski shows) even the tax collectors were suppressed. And the evidence of the papyri makes it probable that this stagnation or decline dated from as early as the time of Marcus Aurelius. The ancient world had certainly known more serious states of war than the periods of disorder in the third century: so why did it not recover from them? Because ancient capitalism was rooted in *politics*: that is, it depended on the private exploitation of relationships of political domination in an expanding city-state, and with the suppression of this source of capital formation the latter came to an end.

The first act of the Caesars was to regulate the taxes and limit the discretion of the state-appointed tax-farmers. Like the Ptolemaic government, the Caesars could not at first dispense with the tax-farmers' capital and business experience. But of course, the more their own bureaucracy achieved the necessary control, the less reason they saw for allowing the tax-farmer his private profits where there was no necessity to do so. They went steadily further along the road to the 'nationalisation' of the means of collection, and, as von Domaszewski and Rostovtzeff have shown, the tax-farmer ended up as a civil servant. Through the defence of their subjects on the one hand, and through the pacification of the world on the other, the Empire of the Caesars brought capitalism to the point of extinction. The contraction of the slave-market, the dwindling of all the opportunities offered by the conflicts between city-states, the decline in the forcible monopolisation of trade routes by individual city-states, and in general the obstacles placed in the way of the private exploitation of domains and subjects – all these things served to drain away the life-blood from ancient capitalism. It is obvious, finally, that capitalism could find no Archimedean point on which to anchor its drive for profit in the Diocletianic state, which rested on the performance of compulsory services by the subject population. The bureaucratic system undermined not only all attempts at political initiative by subjects but also all *economic* initiatives, for which there were no suitable opportunities in any case. Every form of capitalism transforms the 'wealth' of the propertied classes into 'capital': the Roman Imperial state eliminated 'capital' and held on to the 'wealth' of the propertied classes, like the Ptolemaic state. No longer did the propertied classes serve the state with spear and armour, as they had done in the days of the ancient *polis*: now it was with their property that they had to serve, as guarantors of the state's revenues and requirements. Before this direct use of wealthy subjects to perform compulsory public services could be replaced by their indirect use in the form of the alliance between monarchy and capital in the mercantilist state of the modern period, it was necessary that industrial capitalism should develop and that there should be the example of the private capitalist wealth of the Netherlands and England. The choking-off of private economic initiative by the bureaucracy is not in any way peculiar to the ancient world.

Every bureaucracy tends to arrive by expansion at the same result. This is no less true of our own. And whereas in the ancient world the politics of the city-state had to serve as the 'pacemaker' for capitalism, nowadays capitalism serves as the pacemaker for the bureaucratisation of the economy. If we want to imagine how the situation of the later Roman Empire might be achieved, under a military-dynastic regime, but on the basis of a more advanced technology, we have only to think of coal, iron and all mining products, all sections of the metallurgical industry, spirits, sugar, tobacco, matches – in short, as nearly as possible all those mass-production industries which are today highly cartelised – being taken over by the state or coming under *de facto* state control; of a multiplication of crown lands, entails, and estates rented out under state control and the carrying through of the full implications of the 'Kanitz motion'; of the establishment of state workshops and consumer cooperatives to provide for the needs of the army and the civil service; of the linking up of inland water-transport with state haulage; of state control of sea-transport; of the nationalisation of all railways, etc.; of the regulation of textile imports by state contracts and their management by the state; of all these enterprises being brought into a bureaucratic 'system'; of state 'controlled' cartels; of everything else incorporated and regulated by innumerable certificates of competence of academic and other kinds; and of the generalisation of the prototype of the '*rentier paisible*'. The present-day German 'bourgeois' has about as little of the quality of his forefathers in the time of the League of Cities as had the Athenian in the time of the Caesars of the quality of those who fought at Marathon. The 'system' is inscribed on his banner – especially if he is a 'Social Democrat'. In Germany, as in the ancient world, the bureaucratisation of society will most probably some day overpower capitalism. In Germany too, when that day comes, the 'anarchy of production' will be replaced by that 'system' which is in principle similar to that which characterised the Roman Empire and, even more, the 'New Empire' in Egypt and the rule of the Ptolemies. And no one should imagine that military service in an army which lives in barracks and is provided with the instruments of war, clothed, fed, drilled and commanded by a bureaucracy could offer a 'counterweight', or that the modern military machine in dynastic states has in general any spiritual affinity with the civic courage of the distant past.

But these visions of the future have no place here. In the continuous development of Mediterranean and European civilisation up to the present day there are to be found neither distinct 'cycles' nor a clear 'linear' development. From time to time, buried elements of the civilisation of the ancient world have surfaced again at a later date into a world which is alien to them. On the other hand, just as the cities of later antiquity, and especially of the Hellenistic world, paved the way for the Middle Ages in industry, so did the estates of late antiquity in agriculture. That, and in what sense, this proposition is valid will be argued in another place.

(*Gesammelte Aufsätze sur Sozial- und Wirtschaftsgeschichte*, Tübingen, 1924, pp. 254–78. First published in 1909.)

16 · *Government, Kinship and Capitalism in China*

In the period of the Warring States, the politically determined capitalism which is common in patrimonial states, based on money-lending and contracting for the princes, seems to have been of considerable significance and to have functioned at high rates of profit, as always under such conditions. Mines and trade are also cited as sources of capital accumulation. Under the Han dynasty, there are reputed to have been multi-millionaires, reckoned in terms of copper. But China's political unification into a world-empire, like the unification of the known world by Imperial Rome, had the obvious consequence that this form of capitalism, which was essentially rooted in the state and its competition with other states, went into decline. The development of a purely market capitalism, directed towards free exchange, on the other hand, remained at an embryonic stage. In all sections of industry, of course, even in the cooperative undertakings to be discussed presently, the merchant, here as elsewhere, was conspicuously superior to the technician. This clearly showed itself even in the usual proportions in which profits were distributed within associations. The interlocal industries also, it is plain, often brought in considerable speculative profits. The ancient classical disposition to set a high value on agriculture, as the truly hallowed calling, hence did not prevent a higher valuation being placed, even as early as the first century B.C., on the opportunities for profit from industry than on those from agriculture (just as in the Talmud), nor did it prevent the highest valuation of all being placed on those from trade.

But that did not mean that there were any beginnings of development towards a modern capitalism. Precisely those characteristic institutions which were developed by the bourgeoisie which flourished in the medieval cities of the West have, right up to the present day, either been entirely absent or taken characteristically different forms. There did not exist in China the legal forms, or the sociological basis, of the permanent capitalist enterprise, with its rational depersonalisation of the economy, such as existed already, in its first unmistakable beginnings, in the commercial law of the Italian city-states. The liability of members of a kinship group for their fellow members, which had existed in China in the more distant past and had represented a first step towards the development of personal credit, was preserved only in fiscal and political criminal law.

Development proceeded no further. To be sure, the association of heirs in a business partnership, based on the household communities, played a similar role, precisely among the propertied classes, to that played by the Western household associations, from which later (at least in Italy) our 'public trading company' emerged. But its economic meaning was characteristically different. As always in a patrimonial state, it was the official, both in that capacity and as tax-farmer (as officials actually were), who had the best opportunities for accumulating wealth.[1] Discharged officials invested their more or less legally acquired wealth in the purchase of land. Their sons, in order to maintain the power derived from their wealth, remained in partnership as joint heirs and raised the means to enable some members of the family again to study, so as to make it possible for them to obtain lucrative posts and so once again enrich the members of the hereditary partnership and create posts for their kinsmen (for the greatest possible number, it goes without saying). Thus, on the basis of political accumulation of wealth, there developed a patriciate, however unstable, and a class of great landowners leasing out plots of land, which was neither feudal nor bourgeois in type but speculated in opportunities for purely political exploitation of office. As is typical in patrimonial states, therefore, the accumulation of wealth, especially of land, was dominated, not primarily by rational economic acquisition, but by trade – which again led to the investment of the money acquired in land – and above all by a form of capitalism based on the exploitation of internal political opportunities. For the officials acquired their wealth, as we have seen, by, among other things, speculation in taxes – that is, by arbitrarily fixing the exchange rate at which the due payments were to be converted at current prices. Examinations also gave the right to expect to be fed at this trough. As a result, they were constantly being freshly shared out among the provinces, although only exceptionally was there a fixed quota. Suspension of examinations in a particular province was an extremely effective, because economically painful, punishment for the families of notables who were involved. It is plain that this kind of familial business partnership tended to develop in a diametrically opposite direction to that of the rational economic enterprise. Above all, however, it was also very closely bound up with the kinship group. At this point we must attempt a connected discussion of the significance of the kinship associations, which has already been touched on a number of times.

Kinship, which in Western medieval society had virtually lost all sig-

[1] The '*hoppo*' (inspector and farmer of customs) in Canton was famous for his tremendous opportunities for accumulation: the income of his first year (200,000 *taels*) went to pay for the purchase of his office, that of the second year was spent on 'gifts', that of his third and last year he kept for himself (calculations from the 'North China Herald').

nificance, remained important in China both for the local administration of the smallest units and for the character of economic association; it had indeed developed to an extent unknown elsewhere, even in India. The patrimonial government from above clashed with the kinship organisations from below, which were firmly structured as a counterweight to it. A very significant fraction of all politically dangerous 'secret societies' has, even up to the present day, consisted of kinsmen.[1] The villages were often called after the name of a kinship group[2] which was either exclusively or predominantly represented in them. Or else they were actual confederations of kinship groups. The old boundary stones show that the land was not allotted to individuals, but to kinship groups, and the sense of community in the kinship groups preserved this state of affairs to a considerable extent. From the numerically most powerful kinship group was chosen the – often salaried – village headman. 'Elders' of the kinship groups stood at his side and claimed the right of dismissal. The individual kinship group, however, of which we must first speak now, claimed, as such and independently, the power to punish its members and exercised this power, however little the modern state authorities may have officially recognised it.[3]

The cohesiveness of the kinship group and its continued existence, despite the relentless encroachments of the patrimonial administration, with its mechanically constructed liability associations, its resettlements, redistributions of land and groupings of the population according to *ting* (individuals capable of work) was without doubt entirely dependent on the significance of the ancestor-cult, as the only undoubtedly classical and ancient 'folk-cult', performed, not by the Caesaro-papist government and its officials, but by the head of the household, in his capacity as house priest, assisted by the family. Already in the 'men's house' of the early militarist period the spirits of the ancestors seem to have played a role. It may be remarked in passing that this seems hardly compatible with true totemism, and perhaps points to the following, and the hereditary charisma of the prince and his retinue developed from that following, under the form of the men's house as the oldest form of organisation which we can infer with any degree of probability.[4] However that may

[1] This was so with the core of the Taiping 'rebels' of 1858–64. Even at late as 1895, the Hung Yi Tang, the kinship group of the founder of the Taiping religion, was persecuted as a secret society (source: 'Peking Gazette').

[2] E.g. (Conrady in Pflugk-Harkkung, ed., *Weltgeschichte*, iii), *Chang chia tsung* was the village of the family Chang.

[3] Official recognition was given only to the jurisdiction of the Imperial kinship group over its members and to domestic authority.

[4] Perhaps both types of men's house, the 'comradely' and the 'seigneurial', existed regionally side by side, for it is right to say, on the other hand, that the notes collected by von Quistorp (*Mitteilungen des Seminars für Orientalische Sprachen*, xviii (1915)) *on the whole* tend rather to suggest the former. Nevertheless, the legendary Emperor Yao

317

be, in the historical period the absolutely fundamental belief of the Chinese people has always been the belief in the spirits of one's ancestors (not only, but principally, one's own[1]), in their role, as attested in ritual and literature, as intermediaries for the wishes of their descendants with the spirit of Heaven (or God),[2] and in the absolute necessity of appeasing them and gaining their favour by means of sacrifices. The ancestral spirits of the Emperors were the following, almost equal in rank, of the spirit of Heaven.[3] A Chinese who had no male descendants must necessarily have recourse to adoption, and if he neglected to do so, then his family would undertake a posthumous fictitious adoption on his behalf[4] – less in his interest than in their own, so as to be at peace with his spirit. The social effect of these all-pervasive ideas is clearly evident. First, there was the enormous strengthening of patriarchal power.[5] Then there was the cohesiveness of the kinship group as such. In Egypt, where the cult of the dead, but not that of the ancestors, dominated everything, the cohesiveness of the kinship group broke down (as in Mesopotamia, but considerably earlier) under the pressure of bureaucratisation and

handed over his authority to his successor Shun in the temple of his ancestors. An Emperor threatens his vassals with the wrath of the spirits of their ancestors. Such examples, collected by Hirth in his *Ancient History of China*, support the latter hypothesis, as does the fact that the spirit of one of the Emperor's ancestors appears when he is guilty of misgovernment and demands an account; so also does the speech of Emperor P'an Keng in the *Shu Ching* (Legge, *Prolegomena*, p. 238). Survivals of totemism are collected in Conrady, *Weltgeschichte*, III: they are not really entirely convincing, though they are impressive.

[1] The protection given, as already mentioned, to the last descendant of an overthrown dynasty results from the concern to avoid annoying the spirits of his ancestors, who would after all be powerful, as former Emperors. (Cf. even the 'Peking Gazette' of 13 April and 31 July 1883: the complaint of the Chang Tuan, the representative of the Ming dynasty, about building on the Ming ancestral land.) Similarly with the official state sacrifices, mentioned above, for the spirits of those who have died without issue and (also discussed above) the adoptions.

[2] See the speech of the Prince of Chou in the *Shu Ching* (Legge, *Prolegomena*, p. 175) and the prayer offered for the sick Emperor – to his ancestors, not to Heaven (*ibid.*, pp. 391ff).

[3] That the spirit of Heaven was treated merely as 'first among equals' seems very clearly to follow from the evidence cited by de Groot in his *Universismus*. It was the 'spirits of the ancestors', according to the report published in the 'Peking Gazette' of 29 September 1898, who condemned the attempts at reform made by the Emperor and K'ang Yu-Wei, which had at that time come to grief. Heaven is concerned, not only with what is due to it itself, but also with what is due to one's ancestors (de Groot, *The Religion of the Chinese*, New York, 1910, pp. 27, 28). Hence also the Confucian doctrine that Heaven regards impassively the sins of a dynasty for a little while and only intervenes when total degeneration has set in. This was of course a rather convenient 'theodicy'.

[4] There are cases in which an adoption has been annulled, because the death sacrifices of the natural father have been endangered ('Peking Gazette', 26 April 1878).

[5] 'Patricide' was considered such a dreadful act (to be punished by a 'lingering death') that the Governor of the affected province was deposed in the same way as after natural catastrophes ('Peking Gazette', 7 August 1894). According to the 'Peking Gazette' of 12 July, 1895, a drunkard's murder of his grandfather in that year led to the punishment also of the murderer's father, for not bringing up his son in such a way that 'he could tolerate the most severe punishments from an elder'.

fiscalism. In China, it survived and grew stronger until it became a force equal to the political power.

In principle, every kinship group had (and still has up to the present) the hall of its ancestors[1] in the village. Apart from the ritual objects of the cult, it often contained a table of the 'moral rules' recognised by the kinship group. For the right to lay down its own statutes was never in fact questioned for the kinship group, and it was exercised not only independently of the law, but also in certain circumstances, even in regard to ritual questions, contrary to the law.[2] The kinship group maintained its solidarity in relation to the outside world. Although, as previously explained, joint liability did not exist outside the criminal law, it was usual for the group, whenever possible, to settle the debts of a member. Under the chairmanship of the elder, it pronounced sentences, not only of flogging and excommunication (which meant civil death), but also, like the Russian commune, of exile. The often pronounced need for consumer loans was likewise met essentially within the kinship group, where it was considered a moral duty for the members with means to help in times of distress. Admittedly, a non-member was also supposed to be granted a loan if he made sufficiently many kow-tows, for it was impossible to take the risk of calling down the vengeance of the man's spirit if, in his desperation, he committed suicide;[3] and no one seems readily to have paid back a loan of his own free will, at least if he knew he had a strong kinship group behind him. Nevertheless, a clearly regulated obligation to help the needy and system of assistance with credit existed primarily only within the kinship group. When necessary, the kinship group conducted feuds with outsiders:[4] the reckless bravery shown here, where it was a matter of personal interests and personal ties, contrasted in the most glaring way with the frequently mentioned 'cowardice' of the government armies, manned as they were by conscripts or mercenaries. Wherever necessary, the kinship group provided for medicines, doctors

[1] In some cases, subdivisions of the kinship group had their own subordinate hall of ancestors.

[2] According to classical ritual, adoption might take place only within the kinship group. But the family statutes made a variety of arrangements for this, even within the same village. Several modifications of the old ritual had come almost universally into vogue. For instance, the daughter-in-law no longer mourned only, as officially prescribed, for her parents-in-law, but also for her own parents. Or again, 'deep' mourning was now the custom, not only for the father, as officially prescribed, but also for the mother.

[3] Hence, A. Merx's reading, 'μηδένα ἀπελπίζοντες', in place of 'μηδὲν ἀπελπίζοντες' is very plausible: in this case too there is anxiety about 'crying' to God and, in the case of suicide, about the 'spirit' of the desperate man.

[4] Occasions for such feuds were offered by re-allocations of taxes, vendettas and especially by conflicts provoked by the *fêng shui*, or 'geomancers', among neighbours. It will be explained later that every building and, above all, every new grave could injure the spirits of the ancestors already buried in existing graves or agitate the spirits of the rocks, streams, hills and so on. In such cases, it was often almost impossible to settle such feuds because of the geomantic interests involved on both sides.

and the burial of the dead; it looked after the old and the widows, and above all it provided the schools. The kinship group owned property, especially landed property (*shih t'ien* or 'ancestral land'[1]), and often, if it was particularly well-to-do, extensive endowed lands. It utilised this by leasing it (usually by auction for three years), but alienation of such land was only permitted with the consent of a three-quarters majority. The revenue was assigned to the heads of households. The typical method was to grant every man and every widow one unit each, those from the age of fifty-nine upward, two units, and from the age of sixty-nine upward, three units. Within the kinship group the principle of hereditary charisma was combined with that of democracy. All married men had equal voting rights; unmarried men could speak in discussion, but had no right to vote; women were excluded both from inheritance (they had only a right to claim a dowry) and from taking part in the deliberations of the group. The elders, chosen annually according to families but by an electorate consisting of all members of the kinship group, functioned as an executive committee which had to collect revenues, utilise property and distribute the income, and most important of all take care of the sacrifices to the ancestors and the maintenance in proper order of ancestral halls and schools. The outgoing elders proposed the motion of election, according to seniority; in case of refusal, the next in order of seniority was offered the post.

Communal acquisition of land by purchase or lease and allotment to the heads of households has been usual up to the present day. Mandarins, merchants or others finally moving from the land were indemnified, received an extract from the family book as proof of it, remained subject to the jurisdiction of the group, but were able to buy back their right of participation. Where the old situation still prevailed, inherited land seldom passed into the hands of strangers. The women's domestic spinning, weaving and tailoring allowed only a modest independent textile industry to emerge, especially since the women also worked for the market.[2] Headgear and footwear were also for the most part domestic products. Because the kinship group (i) was responsible for those festivals which were most important for the individual (mainly the twice-yearly festival of the ancestors) and the subject of the family history to be written by the heads of households, (ii) has been concerned right up to the present to lend capital at a very low rate of interest to apprentices and wage-workers without resources of their own, to enable them to set

[1] In the 'Peking Gazette' there is a case, for instance, of the purchase of 2,000 *mou* for 17,000 *taels* (1 *mou* = 5.62 ares). Express mention is made in this case, not only of sacrifices, but also of the relief of widows and orphans and the maintenance of the children's school out of the rents (14 December 1883).

[2] On the foregoing, see Eugène Simon, *La cité chinoise* (Paris, 1885) and Leong and Tao, *Village and Town Life in China* (London, 1915).

themselves up as 'independent' craftsmen, and (iii) as stated already, the elders of the group chose those young men whom they regarded as qualified for study and met the costs of preparation, examination and the purchase of office – for all these reasons, this association obviously gave strong economic support to the self-sufficiency of the households (thus constraining the development of the market) and was at the same time socially the be-all and end-all of existence for its members, even those living outside its confines, especially in the city.[1]

As pointed out in a general way earlier, the 'city' was consequently never 'home' for the majority of its inhabitants, but always thought of as somewhere typically 'foreign'. All the more so in that it was distinguished from the *village*, which we shall now go on to discuss, by the already mentioned lack of any organised self-government. It can be said without too much exaggeration that Chinese administrative history is full of the recurrent attempts made by the Imperial administration to extend its authority beyond the urban districts. However, leaving aside compromises over the payment of taxes, it achieved this only for short periods: it could not achieve it for long, given its own size. Its size – the small number of genuine officials – was determined by its finances (and in its turn determined the financial situation). The official Imperial administration remained, in fact, an administration of urban districts and subdistricts. Here, where it was not confronted in the same way as outside the cities by the massive blood-ties of the kinship groups, it could operate effectively – provided that it maintained a certain relationship with the guilds and corporations. Beyond the city walls, its power ceased very quickly to be genuinely effective. For, besides the power of the kinship groups, which was large enough in itself, it was also faced here with the organised self-government of the village as such. Since peasants also lived in large numbers in the cities, they were mostly cities of 'citizen farmers', and so the difference is a purely technical administrative one: a 'city' is the seat of a mandarin without self-government; a 'village' is a place with self-government but without mandarins!

Settlement in villages[2] as such was based in China on the need for security, which the extensive administration of the Empire, lacking as it does any concept of 'police', has never been able to supply. The villages were usually fortified: originally and, it seems, often even today they were palisaded, like the ancient cities, but frequently they also had an encircling wall. To relieve the villagers of the need to take a turn on guard duty, they appointed paid guards. The villages often had many

---

[1] As late as 1899 ('Peking Gazette' of 12 October), it was impressed on the police that they must not treat people going to new districts, who still retained a share in their ancestral land, as 'unknown aliens'.

[2] Ownership of individual properties was often split into between five and fifteen lots, as a result of the partition of inherited land.

thousands of inhabitants, but they were distinguished from the 'city' by the fact that they attended to these functions themselves and had the appropriate vehicle for doing so, in contrast to the city.[1] Since there is no concept of a 'corporation' either in Chinese law or, of course, in the habits of thought of the peasants, this was the village temple,[2] usually dedicated in modern times to one or other of the popular gods: to General Kuan Ti (the god of war), Po Ti (god of trade), Wen Ch'ang (god of schools), Lang Wang (god of rain), T'u Ti (a non-classical god, to whom every death must be notified to ensure an escort for the deceased in the other world) and so forth. Which of these gods is chosen seems to have been to some extent a matter of indifference. For, as in classical antiquity in the West, the 'religious' significance of the temple[3] was limited to a few ritual manipulations and occasional prayers by individuals, and for the rest its significance lay only in secular social and legal activities.

The temple, like the hall of ancestors, owned property, especially landed property.[4] But very often, too, it owned money, which it loaned at rates of interest which were not always low.[5] This money stemmed above all from the traditional market dues: the market stalls were from ancient times under the protection of the local god, as almost everywhere in the world. The temple land, like the ancestral land, was leased, chiefly to those villagers who had no property; the rents derived from this and in general all the revenues of the temple were likewise disposed of annually to revenue-farmers and the net profit remaining after deduction of expenses was shared out. The maintenance of the positions of the temple administrators was, it seems, usually a civic obligation of the village heads of households: they went in rotation from house to house, the village being divided for that purpose into districts of from one to five hundred inhabitants. Alongside these administrators, however, stood the 'notables' of the village, the elders of the kinship groups and the literati, who received purely nominal remuneration. Only they were recognised as representatives of the village by the political authorities, who were opposed to any legalisation of corporations or corporation

---

[1] In which only the corporations had, as we saw, usurped the functions of self-government, which were often far-reaching.

[2] Here again, cf. the work already cited by the two Chinese bachelors (considerably better in the section concerned with the village: about the 'city' as a social structure there is indeed little to be said!). There are analogies in Germanic law!

[3] The village temple was not a place of Taoist worship (see below, *Gesammelte Aufsätze zur Religionssoziologie*, Ch. VII).

[4] Especially also for the temple priest. If he were installed by donors, they were rewarded by honorific titles, such as *shan chu* ('master of youth'). The priests lived on occasional emoluments and donations of grain: hence, the more temples there were, the poorer was the village. Only one of the temples, however, was the 'village temple'.

[5] It was regarded as meritorious to borrow from the temple. On this point, see Doolittle, *Social Life of the Chinese* (London, 1866).

surrogates. For their part, however, they acted in the name of 'the temple'. Through them, the 'temple' concluded contracts on behalf of the village. The 'temple' had jurisdiction in trivial cases and very often usurped such jurisdiction in cases of all kinds, without interference from the government, except where state interests were involved. It was this court, not the court authorities of the state, which enjoyed the confidence of the population. The 'temple' looked after streets, canals, defence, policing (through a rota of guard duties, which was usually in fact evaded), protection against robbers or inhabitants of neighbouring villages, schools, doctors, medicines and burial, insofar as the kinship groups were unable or unwilling to do so. The village temple contained the village armoury. Through the village temple, which did not exist to perform this function in the 'city', the village was able, both in law and in fact, to engage in collective action. Above all, the village, but not the city, was an association which was in practice ready to fight in defence of its inhabitants' interests.

The government has not always adopted a *laissez-faire* attitude to this unofficial self-government in the way it has in the latter stages of the old regime. Under the Han dynasty it sought, for instance, to dismantle Shih Huang Ti's purely patrimonial absolutism by means of the ordered introduction of the communal elders into posts in the institutions of self-government (*san lao*) and in this way to regulate and legalise the ancient self-government.[1] The village chief (*shou shih jen*) was to be elected and ratified, with guarantees from the landowners for his good conduct: only occasionally, however, was this so in practice. And the government again and again ignored the village as a unit. For again and again purely fiscal interests prevailed. Wang An-shih in particular, as already explained in another context, rationalised the system in this regard. Formally (as is still the case today) every ten families, who together formed a '*pao*', had their headman, and every hundred families, or '*chia*', had their chief, or '*pao chia*', usually called '*ti pao*'. On every house, in village or city, there was to be (and in fact was, wherever

---

[1] Besides the elders of the kinship groups, about whose existence data seem to be available from all periods, there were also at that time sub-departments, with varying types of organisation and with their own officials, as a rule elected: under the Han, they were elected from those of fifty years of age or more. These officials had responsibility for the security police, communal bail (with the duty of censure), supervision of sacrifices, apportionment of forced labour, collection of taxes (and so liability for taxes), in certain circumstances for local jurisdiction and popular education, and occasionally also for the mobilisation and organisation of training of the militia. Under the Han, in accordance with the reforms instituted at that time, nine times eight families officially constituted a '*li*', ten *li* made a '*t'ing*' under an elected elder, and ten *t'ing* a '*san*' under an elected *san lao*, whose main task was to be popular education. There was also the *shih fu*, or tax inspector and justice of the peace, and the *ju tse*, or police commissioner. The main purpose was military. On this, see A. Y. Ivanov, *Wang-An-Shi i yego reformy* (St Petersburg, 1906).

tradition survived) a notice containing the following details: number of the house, *chia, pao*, owner, name of the head of the family, place of origin of the family (right of domicile), its members and lodgers and their occupation, absent members (and length of absence), rents for the tenancy, tax liability, and numbers of rooms inhabited by the family and its sub-tenants. The *pao chia* was officially responsible for policing and for supervision of criminals and secret societies. Not the least important of his tasks was to take responsibility for the activities of the Imperial religious police, to be discussed later. This official of the self-government, the *ti pao*, was to establish a liaison between the central government authorities and the local self-government. In particular, it was usual for him, where and for as long as the system was in operation, to spend some time at the office of the *hsien* magistrate in order to keep him informed. However, in recent times this had all already become essentially formal: the office of '*ti pao*' had often (regularly, it appears from Chinese authors) been simply transformed into an unclassical, and so a less highly valued, state position. The forces with which the apparatus of the state had in reality to reckon were the elders of the kinship groups, who were behind the village administration: these might possibly act as a kind of secret tribunal, like the Germanic '*Vehm*', and in case of conflict could be dangerous.

In all this, the life of the peasant in a Chinese village should certainly not be pictured, to judge by all indications, as a harmonious patriarchal idyll. Not only was the individual's life menaced often enough by external feuds. But also, and above all, the power of the kinship groups and the administration of the village temple often failed to provide any sort of effective protection for property, especially the property of the better off. What one might call the 'effective' peasants (the *lao shih*, as they were called) were then more typically simply handed over to the arbitrary will of the *kuang kun* – the *kulaki* or 'fists' as they would be called in the language of the Russian peasants. This was not, however, as in Russia, domination by a 'village bourgeoisie' of money-lenders and those with common interests with them (as the *kulaki* were in Russia): against such people, as we saw, divine and human help would easily have been obtained. Rather, they were subjected to the bands of landless villagers[1] organised by the *kuang kun* – in other words, to what are called in Bolshevik terminology the '*byednyata*' or village poor: in such groups the Bolsheviks might indeed find a base for exerting influence in China. Against this organisation, any individual large property-owner, or even groups of such property-owners, were often completely defenceless and powerless.[2] And if in recent centuries larger estates have been the

[1] There are various details of this in A. H. Smith, *Village Life in China* (Edinburgh, 1899).
[2] The *kuang kun* was normally a trained gymnast; he sought to establish, like the *Camorrist* or the *Mafioso*, unofficial relations with the *yamen* of the *hsien* official, who was powerless

exception in China, a contributing factor has certainly been the existence of this kind of naive 'peasant Bolshevism', considerably moderated by ethical influences and the power of the kinship groups, which was simply the consequence of the failure of the coercive powers of the state to guarantee property. Below the level of the *hsien* district, which was nevertheless about the size of an English county, there existed only the local native administrators, who were officially supposed to hold honorary office, but in reality often operated as '*kulaki*'. But also, alongside the official administration of the districts, right up to provincial level, there existed very often boards of delegates, who were theoretically 'appointed' for a period of up to three years and who could be recalled at any time, but were in fact in office because of their recognised or usurped charisma, and 'advised' the officials.[1] Their structure is of no interest to us here.

Any official attempting, for instance, to raise the traditional taxes or to introduce any other kind of change was confronted with this board, constituted by a tightly knit group of local notables within the village, and had to come to terms with it if he was to achieve anything at all. For otherwise he was as certain to encounter stiff-necked obstinacy as, in the same situation, were the landowner, the lessor, the employer – in short, anyone in authority from outside the kinship group. The kinship group supported as one man any of its members who felt themselves to be wronged,[2] and its united resistance was naturally incomparably more effective than, for instance, a strike by a freely organised trades union in our society. That fact alone prevented the development of any kind of work discipline or free market selection of the labour force of the type found in the modern large enterprise, as it did that of any rational administration of the Western type. The strongest counterweight to the officials, with their literary education, was sheer seniority in age, without literary pretensions. The official, no matter how many examinations he had passed, had to submit unconditionally to the absolutely uneducated elder of his kinship group in all matters concerning the group, as determined by tradition.

At all events, the patrimonial bureaucracy was confronted by what was in practice a considerable degree of usurped and conceded self-government: on the one hand, in the form of the kinship groups, on the

in regard to him. A village employee – the village headman or an arbitrator – or, quite the reverse, a beggar might develop into a *kuang kun*; and the situation of the other inhabitants of the village became hopeless, if he had a literary education and perhaps a relationship with an official into the bargain.

[1] It is they who are meant when the decrees in the 'Peking Gazette' speak of 'gentry and notables', whose advice should be sought.

[2] Cf. the report in the 'Peking Gazette' of 14 April 1895 of the release by two kinship associations of a man arrested by the tax collector.

other, in these organisations of the poor. Its rationalism here found itself face to face with a determined traditionalist power, which was, on the whole and in the long term, more than a match for it, because it operated continuously and with the support of the closest personal ties. Any innovation whatsoever could moreover arouse the anger of magical powers. The bureaucracy seems to have been suspected above all of fiscalism, and it met with sharp resistance. It would never have occurred to any peasant to think that the motives for such innovations were 'disinterested', any more than it would to the Russian peasants in Tolstoy's *Resurrection*. It was also – and this point is especially relevant to us here – the elders of the kinship groups whose influence was usually decisive for the acceptance or rejection of religious innovations, and was, of course, almost without exception on the side of tradition, especially when they scented any threat to ancestor-worship. The immense power of these kinship groups, with their strictly patriarchal leadership, was in reality responsible for the much-discussed Chinese 'democracy'. But it was only an expression, first, of the abolition of the system of feudal Estates, secondly, of the extent of patrimonial bureaucratic administration, and thirdly, of the all-pervasiveness and omnipotence of the patriarchal kinship groups, and it had absolutely nothing in common with 'modern' democracy.

Real or simulated relationships of personal kinship were the basis of almost all forms of economic organisation which went beyond the limits of the individual concern. First there was the *tsung-tsu* community. A kinship group organised in this form owned, not only the hall of ancestors and the school building, but also communal buildings for storing provisions and the tools used in processing rice, preparing conserves, weaving and other domestic industries, in some cases with a specially appointed administrator; in addition, it supported its members in need through mutual assistance and interest-free or cheap credit. It thus amounted to a cumulative household of the whole kinship group, extended into a producers' cooperative. On the other hand, there existed in the cities, along with the industrial enterprises of individual master craftsmen, specifically small-capitalist cooperative enterprises in communal workshops. In these enterprises, there was often extensive division of manual labour; often, too, there was thoroughgoing specialisation of technical and commercial management, with distribution of profits in proportion partly (and especially) to capital shares, partly to specific types of service performed (for example, commercial or technical). Similar types of organisation were known in Hellenistic and medieval Islamic civilisation. In China, such workshops seem to have been found mainly in seasonal industries, to sustain the community through periods when there was no market for its products, and also of course to facilitate the provision of credit and to make possible the division of labour in production. All these methods of creating larger economic units had, socially considered, a specifically 'democratic' character. They gave the individual some support against the danger of proletarisation and capitalist subjugation. From a purely economic point of view, the latter might certainly have infiltrated in the form of high investment by capitalists who were not themselves involved in production and the superior strength and greater share of profits of hired salesmen. On the other hand, the putting-out system, from which, in our society, capitalist subjugation began, seems to have remained fixed organisationally in the various forms of purely *de facto* dependence of artisan on merchant right up to the present day, when it has undergone significant quantitative development especially in industries working for distant markets. Only in individual trades had it advanced as far as domestic production with an admixture of workshops for finishing and a centralised sales office. The (as we have seen) extremely slender chances of compelling dependants to work at all, and above all to do work of a prescribed quality and quantity within a prescribed time, was decisive in this respect.

There seems to be scarcely any historical evidence for the existence of large factories owned by private capitalists; indeed, there would be unlikely to be any for articles of mass consumption, since there was no steady market for them. The textile industry could hardly compete against domestic production; only silk had its market, and that was a distant one. But the latter was monopolised by the caravans of the Imperial household. The metal industry could attain only modest dimensions because of the very poor productivity of the mines. This poor productivity in its turn was a consequence of those general causes which have partly been discussed already and must partly be discussed later. In regard to the processing of tea, there are pictorial representations of large workshops with division of labour, comparable to the ancient Egyptian pictures of a similar kind. The state factories normally produced luxury articles, as in Islamic Egypt; the expansion of the state metal industry for monetary reasons was short-lived. The guilds, which have already been mentioned, regulated apprenticeship. But we hear nothing of any separate journeyman associations. Only in isolated cases did the workers unite against their masters in a strike, but apart from that there seems to have been scarcely any hint of their developing into a separate class. The reasons were similar to those which operated in Russia up to thirty years ago. As far as is known, they belonged to the guilds on an equal footing. Or rather, it was appropriate, in view of the fact that industry was carried on by small craftsmen, but not usually by small capitalists, that in general there was no monopolistic exclusion of the rising generation from the guilds.

Similarly, the plan for liturgical closure of occupations, which was continually being put forward and seems at times actually to have been carried out, might have led to the formation of a caste system, but did not have this result in the event. The Annals speak especially of a fruitless attempt of this sort made at the end of the sixth century. A relic of this was certain magically 'impure' lineages and occupations. It is usual[1] to distinguish nine kinds of degraded 'castes': partly certain kinds of slave, partly certain descendants of slaves and colonists, partly castes of beggars, partly descendants of former insurgents, partly descendants of immigrant barbarians (guest tribes), partly musicians and certain actors involved in family ceremonies, and also dramatic actors and jugglers – just as in the Western Middle Ages. For the unclean occupations there existed, as in the Indian system, three types of custom – fixed, hereditary and saleable. Intermarriage, commensality and admission to the degrees remained forbidden to all degraded castes. Nevertheless, by authority of an Imperial edict, judicial rehabilitation for those who gave up an impure occupation was permitted (and was actually made use of, for instance as late as 1894, for some of these castes). Slavery arose after the ending of the wars of conquest through surrender or sale on the part of the parents or as a punishment inflicted by the government. The freedman owed his patron obedience, as in the West, and was ineligible to obtain degrees. The contract workers (*ku kung*) owed obedience during their service and were denied commensality with their masters.[2]

What remained of such caste-like phenomena up to the present day amounted to no more than a pathetic remnant of the structure of Estates which once existed, and whose practical effect consisted above all in releasing the privileged Estates (the *literati* and the 'great families' – the expression 'the hundred families' for 'the Empire' meant the latter stratum) from statutory labour and corporal punishment, which in their case was commuted to money fines and imprisonment. Degradation to 'plebeian' status was possible. The old structure of Estates, resting on hereditary charisma, was breached already at an early stage by the classification into pure property classes, which was constantly being undertaken afresh for fiscal purposes.

Along with the kinship groups, corporations and guilds, there flourished in modern China – for the past the outsider[3] has no reliable sources of information – association in the form of the club, or *hui*, in all areas

---

[1] S. Hoang, 'Mélanges sur l'administration' (*Variétés Sinologiques*, 21, Shanghai, 1902, pp. 120f).

[2] The colonists and farm labourers (formerly helots of the ruling stratum) did not belong to this category.

[3] I have not had access to some of the most recent good dissertations on this subject.

of life, even the economic (in the form of credit associations).[1] This is not a topic that need interest us here in any detail. At any rate in modern times, membership of a reputable club was both the aim of, and an incentive to, ambition and social legitimation for anyone who sought it, in egalitarian China as in democratic America. In just the same way, the certificate of membership in a Chinese guild which was pinned up on the stall was a guarantee to the customer of the quality of the wares.[2] The extent of the patrimonial bureaucratic administration, combined with the lack of any legally confirmed status structure, was also responsible for these phenomena.

Apart from a nobility of conferred titles, and leaving aside the strict separation of families registered in the Manchu levy (the expression of a foreign domination existing since the seventeenth century), there existed in modern times, as we saw, no further status differences of birth among the Chinese themselves. And after the 'bourgeois' strata, from the eighteenth century on, had secured considerable relaxation of the restrictions of the police state, there existed (and obviously had existed for a long time) in the nineteenth century freedom of movement, even though this had never been recognised in any official edicts. The right to settle and own land in a district other than that of one's origin was certainly, as in the West, a concession first extorted by force as a result of fiscalism. Since 1794, membership in a local community had been obtained by acquiring land and paying taxes for twenty years, and this meant loss of membership in one's native community.[3] There had also existed for a long time free choice of occupations, even though the 'Sacred Edict' of 1671 had recommended remaining in the same occupation. In modern times, neither passport, schooling nor military service has been compulsory. Neither have there been any laws restricting money-lending or any kind of trade in goods. In view of all this, it must be stressed again and again that this situation, which might seem so

[1] Especially also in the forms which are reminiscent of the Greek ἔρανοι. The arrangement might be that, through a credit association, or '*she*', money capital is accumulated and its yield is then put up for sale or lottery (Smith, *Village Life in China*, Edinburgh, 1899). Or else, the debtor of the loan given to him by the friends became club president, and would thus be spurred on by the honour of the club to pay back his debt by instalments to the other members, his creditors. Doolittle (*Social Life of the Chinese*, London, 1866) gives examples (pp. 147f) of such clubs. The recipients of the repayments were often decided by lot. This is an artificial substitute for the old neighbourhood credit, and also for the liquidator.

[2] Or a poster appropriate to the principle of fixed prices ('one price', 'truly one price', according to Doolittle, *Social Life of the Chinese*): but, in contrast with the Puritans, without any guarantee that the principle would really be put into practice.

[3] This question was of interest to the state on account of the notifications of examinations, since the number of prebends was shared out among the provinces. In the official lists, for example in the army list as early as the Han period, the names were always given together with an indication of membership of local and district communities (determined at that time without doubt by the place of origin of the kinship group).

conducive to the free development of bourgeois business enterprise, has nevertheless not led to the growth of a bourgeoisie of the Western type. As we saw, not even those forms of capitalist business enterprise which were already known in the West in the Middle Ages have grown to full maturity. From the small capitalist beginnings which have been discussed, there might well have grown (again, the old question), taking purely economic considerations into account, a purely bourgeois industrial capitalism. We have already learned several of the reasons why this did not happen. Almost all of them bring us back to the structure of the state.

(*Gesammelte Aufsätze zur Religionssoziologie*, 2nd edn, Tübingen, 1922, I, pp. 373–91. First published in 1916.)

17 · *The Origins of Industrial Capitalism in Europe*

It is both inevitable and right that someone who is himself the offspring of modern European civilisation should approach problems in world history with the following question in mind: through what concatenation of circumstances did it come about that precisely, and only, in the Western world certain cultural phenomena emerged which, as at least we like to think, represent a direction of development of universal significance and validity?

Only in the West is there a 'science' which has reached a stage of development which we today would accept as 'authentic'. In other cultures, especially in India, China, Babylon and Egypt, we can find empirical knowledge, reflection on the problems of the world and of life, philosophical and theological wisdom of great profundity (though the full development of a systematic theology is unique to Christianity, as influenced by Hellenistic thought, and is only hinted at in Islam and some Indian sects), and extremely sophisticated scholarship and observation. But Babylonian astronomy, like every other, lacked the mathematical foundations first laid by the Greeks: a fact which, indeed, makes the development of Babylonian astronomy in particular all the more astonishing. In Indian geometry there was no concept of rational 'proof' – another product of that Greek genius which also created mechanics and physics. Indian natural science, which was very highly developed in terms of empirical observation, did not have the concept of rational experiment which, although first found in the ancient world, is essentially a product of the Renaissance. Equally, the modern laboratory did not exist in India, with the result that medicine, which, especially in India, was highly developed at the empirical and technical level, lacked a biological, and especially a biochemical, foundation. There has been no rational chemistry in any civilisation except that of the West. Chinese historiography, for all its sophistication, lacks the pragmatic approach of a Thucydides. Macchiavelli had his precursors in India, but nowhere in Asian political thought do we find anything like Aristotle's taxonomy or rational concepts in general. The rigorous schemata and forms of thought necessary for rational jurisprudence, which are a feature of Roman law and the Western law derived from it, are not to be found elsewhere, despite suggestions of them in the Indian Mimamsa schools, comprehensive codifications of law, especially in the Near East, and numerous Indian and other legal texts. Such a structure as Canon Law, moreover, is known only in the West.

The same is true of the arts. Musical sensitivity seems to have been more highly developed in the past among other peoples than ourselves, or at any rate no less highly so. Polyphony of various kinds has existed in widely scattered parts of the world: ensemble playing by a number of instruments and descant, too, are found in other cultures. All our rational intervals of pitch have also been calculated and become well known elsewhere. But certain things are found only in Western music, such as rational harmonic music, including both counterpoint and chord-harmonics; or the organisation of tone material on the basis of the three triads with the harmonic third; or our chromatics and enharmonics, harmonically interpreted since the Renaissance in rational form rather than in terms of spatial intervals. Uniquely Western, too, is our orchestra, with the string quartet as its core and its ensemble organisation of the wind instruments; the continuo; our notation, which first makes possible the composition and performance of modern musical works, and so their whole continued existence; our sonatas, symphonies or operas (although programme music, tone-poems, modulation of tone and chromatics have existed as expressive devices in a wide variety of musical traditions); and finally, the necessary means for all this, our basic instruments – the organ, piano and violin.

The pointed arch as a means of decoration has also existed elsewhere, in the ancient world and in Asia; it has also been claimed that the combination of pointed arch and cruciform vault was not unknown in the East. But nowhere else do we find the rational use of the Gothic vault as a means of distributing stress and arching over spaces, however formed, and above all as the constructive principle of great monumental buildings and the basis of a style embracing sculpture and painting as these were conceived by the Middle Ages. Equally, although its technical basis came from the East, there is no trace elsewhere of that method of solving the problem of the dome and that kind of 'classical' rationalisation of all art – in the case of painting, by the rational use of linear and spatial perspective – which were produced, in our tradition, by the Renaissance. Products of the printer's art existed in China; but only in the West has there arisen a form of literature designed only for the printing press and only possible through it – above all, the 'press' and 'newspapers'. Institutions of higher education of every possible kind, including some with a superficial resemblance to our universities or academies, have also existed elsewhere, for instance in China and the Islamic world. But only in the West has there been a rational and systematic specialisation of knowledge and a body of trained specialists to any degree approaching the dominating importance which they have in present-day civilisation. Above all, it is only in the West that we find the specialist official, the cornerstone of both the modern Western state and the modern Western economy. No more than the beginnings of such a body can be found elsewhere: they never became in any sense so essential a part of the social order as they have done in the West. The 'official', even the official with a specialised task, is of course a very ancient figure, found in a wide variety of civilisations. But in no country and in no period in history has our whole existence, the very political, technical and economic foundations of our life, been confined in such an absolutely inescapable way inside the casing of a bureaucratic organisation of trained specialists as in the modern West: nowhere else have the most important everyday functions of social life been taken over in the same way by state officials with technical, commercial and, above all, legal training. Organisation of political and social associations according to status groups has occurred in many places. But only the West has known the peculiarly Western type of state based on status (the '*rex et regnum*'). In general, again, the Parliament of periodically elected 'popular representatives', the demagogue and the domination of party leaders as 'ministers' responsible to Parliament are uniquely Western institutions, even though there have naturally been 'parties', in the sense of organisations for winning or influencing political power, in all parts of the world. The 'state' in general, in the sense of a political institution with a rationally formulated 'constitution', rationally formulated laws and administration by means of specialist officials obeying rationally formulated rules or principles, is known only in the West in the form of this essential combination of defining characteristics, notwithstanding suggestions of it elsewhere.

The same is also true of that force in modern life which has most influence on our destinies, *capitalism*.

'Acquisitiveness', or the 'pursuit of profit', of monetary gain, of the highest possible monetary gain, has in itself nothing at all to do with capitalism. It is and has been found among waiters, doctors, coachmen, artists, tarts, venal officials, soldiers, brigands, crusaders, frequenters of gambling dens, beggars – one might say 'among all sorts and conditions of men', in all ages and in all countries of the world, wherever the objective possibility for it has existed or still exists in any form. Such a naive definition ought to have been given up once and for all at the nursery stage of cultural history. Unbridled avarice has no resemblance whatsoever to capitalism, still less to its 'spirit'. Capitalism may actually amount to the taming, or at least the rational moderation, of this irrational impulse. At all events, capitalism is the same as the pursuit of profit by means of continuing rational capitalistic enterprise: that is, for the constant *renewal* of profit, or '*profitability*'. It must be so. In the context of a capitalist ordering of the whole economy, an individual capitalist enterprise which did not direct its activities to opportunities for profitability would be doomed to go under.

Let us begin with some definitions which are rather more precise than those usually offered. By a 'capitalist' economic action we shall mean, first, one based on the expectation of profit from the utilisation of opportunities for exchange, that is, opportunities for acquisition which are formally peaceful. Acquisition which is formally and actually based on the use of force follows its own peculiar laws and it is inappropriate (though impossible to forbid) to put it in the same category as action which is ultimately directed to profit from exchange.[1] Where the pursuit of capitalist acquisition is rational, the corresponding action is organised around capital *calculations*. That is, it is ordered in such a way as to make planned use of material goods or personal services as a means of acquisition so that, when the balance-sheet is drawn, the final revenue of the particular enterprise in the form of goods with a monetary value (or, in the case of a continuing enterprise, the periodically estimated value of goods with a monetary value) should exceed the 'capital', that is, the estimated value in terms of the balance of the material means of acquisition utilised for acquisition by exchange (and that in turn means, in the case of the continuing enterprise, that the excess should continually increase). It is irrelevant whether it is a matter of a collection of merchandise given in natural form to a travelling merchant in the *commenda*, where the final proceeds may again consist of other merchandise traded in natural form, or of a manufacturing establishment, the constituent parts of which are buildings, machinery, reserves of cash, raw materials, half-finished and finished products, and claims offset against liabilities. The decisive thing is always that there is a capital calculation in monetary terms, either in the modern form of book-keeping or in some other form, however primitive and superficial. At the beginning of the operation, an initial balance is taken; before each individual transaction, there is a calculation; when checks are made to assess whether it is going well, there

[1] Here, as on a number of other points, I differ from our respected teacher Lujo Brentano (*Die Anfänge des modernen Kapitalismus*). The difference is in the first place terminological, but is also substantial. It does not seem to me to be useful to bring under the same category such heterogeneous things as acquisition by plunder and acquisition by direction of a factory. Still less is it useful to refer to any endeavour to acquire money as the 'spirit' of capitalism – in contrast with other forms of acquisition. In the latter case, in my opinion, all conceptual precision is lost, and in the former, all possibility above all of working out the specific nature of Western capitalism as compared with other forms. In Simmel's *Philosophie des Geldes*, too, 'money economy' and 'capitalism' are far too closely assimilated, to the detriment of his discussion of the facts. In Sombart's writings, especially the latest edition of his fine masterpiece on capitalism, the rational organisation of labour, which, at least from the point of view of my problem, is the specific feature of the West, very much recedes into the background in favour of developmental factors which have been active in all parts of the world.

is a repeat calculation; and when the operation is wound up, there is a final balancing of the books to confirm what 'profit' has been made. The drawing of the initial balance in the case of a *commenda*, for example, consists in the determination of a cash value of the goods in question which will be acceptable to the parties involved – insofar as they do not already take the form of cash; the final balance is the assessment on which the distribution of profit or loss at the end is based; as long as the operation is rational, calculation underlies every individual transaction between the partners to the *commenda*. In every form of capitalist undertaking, right up to the present day, in which the situation does not require exact reckoning, the calculations and estimates are never really exact but are conducted by guess-work or simply in a traditional or conventional form. But this affects only the degree of rationality of capitalist acquisition.

From the purely conceptual point of view, all that matters is that the actual concern with the comparison of income with expenditure, both calculated in no matter how primitive a way in monetary terms, should decisively determine the economic activity. In this sense, 'capitalism' and 'capitalist' undertakings, even with some rationalisation of capital calculation, have existed in all the civilised countries of the world for as far back as our economic documents can take us. They have existed in China, India, Babylon, Egypt, the ancient Mediterranean and the Middle Ages, as well as in modern times. There were not just individual undertakings completely cut off from each other, but whole economies engaged in a constant succession of individual undertakings and of continuous 'enterprises', even though trade in particular did not for a long time take the form of our kind of permanent enterprise, but rather of a series of individual undertakings: the first slow steps towards continuous operations in a particular sector were taken precisely by the large merchants. At all events, the capitalist undertaking and the capitalist entrepreneur, not only of the kind who engages in occasional ventures but also of the kind who undertakes long-term ventures, are both very ancient and well-nigh universal.

The West, however, has given capitalism a degree of significance such as it has never had elsewhere, for the reason that it has developed kinds, forms and tendencies of capitalism which there have never been elsewhere. Merchants have existed in all parts of the world, wholesale and retail, local and foreign; there have been money-lenders of all kinds, and banks with a variety of functions (although essentially similar to those of our banks, at least in the sixteenth century); sea-loans, the *commenda* and companies and associations of the limited liability type have been widespread, even in the form of continuing enterprises. Wherever public bodies have had monetary finances, the money-lender has appeared, whether in Babylon, Greece, India, China or Rome: he has financed, above all, wars and piracy, contracts and building of all kinds; he has figured in overseas policies as the colonial entrepreneur, acquiring plantations and working them with slaves or directly or indirectly impressed labour; he has farmed domains, offices and above all taxes; he has financed party chiefs in elections and *condottieri* in civil wars; and finally, he has operated as a 'speculator' in opportunities for monetary gain of all kinds. This kind of entrepreneurial figure, the capitalistic adventurer, has existed all over the world. With the exception of trade, and credit and banking activities, the basic opportunities sought by such men have been either in purely irrational speculation or in acquisition by violence, and above all in acquisition of booty, either in an actual war or by the fiscal plunder of subject-peoples over a long period.

Today in the West there are still some remnants of this to be seen in the capitalism of company promoters, large-scale speculators, colonisers and modern financiers, even in peacetime, but especially where capitalist activity is concerned with the waging of war. Some (though only some) aspects of large-scale international trade, now as in the past, also approximate to it. But alongside it, in the modern West, there exists a completely different form of capitalism, which has developed nowhere else in the world: the rational capitalist organisation of (formally) *free labour*. Only the first beginnings of this are to be found elsewhere. Even unfree labour has achieved some degree of rationality in its organisation only in the plantations and, in a very limited way, in the workshops of the ancient world, and to an even smaller extent in the early modern period in the socage-farms and the factories or domestic industries of the manorial estates, employing bondsmen or serfs. Only occasionally outside the West is there any well-confirmed evidence even of genuine 'domestic industries' employing free labour; and the use of day-labourers, which is of course universal, has, with very rare exceptions (and even those organised in a very different way from the modern type of continuing enterprise, as in the case of state monopolies), failed to lead to manufacturing industry or even to the type of rational organisation of apprenticeship found in the West in the Middle Ages.

The rational, organised enterprise, directed to the opportunities presented by the market rather than to those presented by political power or irrational speculation, is not, however, the only distinctive feature of Western capitalism. The modern rational organisation of the capitalist enterprise would not have been possible without two further important developments: the *separation of the household from the place of work*, which completely prevails in modern economic life, and, closely connected with that, the practice of rational *book-keeping*. Local separation of the place of work or commerce from the place of residence is also found elsewhere (in the Oriental bazaar and in the workshops of other civilisations). Then again, the formation of capitalist associations with separate accounting departments is found in the Far East, in the Near East and in classical antiquity. But compared with the modern independence of commercial enterprises, these examples represent only the first steps. The reason for this is, above all, that the internal basis for this independence, both our rational book-keeping and our legal separation of corporate from personal wealth, either did not exist at all or was only in the first stages of development.[1] Everywhere else, the tendency of development has been towards a situation in which the commercial enterprise forms part of the greater household (or '*oikos*') of the prince or landowner; and this, as Rodbertus had already recognised, is a very different pattern of development, even an opposite one, despite several apparent points of similarity.

The significance which all these peculiarities of Western capitalism have nowadays acquired, however, results in the last analysis from their connexion with the capitalist organisation of labour. Even what is usually called 'commercialisation', in the sense of the development of negotiable securities and the rationalisation of speculation by the stock exchange, is connected with this. For without the rational capitalist organisation of labour, all this, even the development towards commercialisation, would, so far as it was possible at all, have been far less important. This is especially true of its significance for the social structure and all the specifically modern, Western problems associated with it. Exact calculation, which is the foundation of everything else, is possible only where there is free labour. Furthermore, just as the world outside the modern West has not known any rational organisation of labour, so, and for that very reason, it has also known no form of rational socialism.

Granted, just as there have existed in the world municipal economic activities, municipal policies on food supply, princely mercantilism and

---

[1] Naturally, the contrast should not be thought of as absolute. Out of politically directed capitalism, especially tax-farming, there grew already in the ancient Mediterranean and Near East, but also in China and India, rational continuing enterprises, whose book-keeping (known to us only in scanty fragments) may well have had a 'rational' character. There were furthermore the closest of contacts between the politically directed 'adventurist' capitalism and the rational capitalism of the enterprise in the early history of the modern banks, even the Bank of England, the origins of which usually lay in transactions related to military policy. Significant in this respect is the contrast between the individuality of Paterson, for instance (a typical 'promoter'), and those directors of the Bank who were responsible for its long-term attitude and were very quickly dubbed 'The Puritan usurers of Grocers' Hall', as is also the blunder in policy of which this most 'solid' of banks was guilty at the time of the South Sea Bubble. In other words, the contrast is, as you might expect, extremely fluid. But it does exist. The rational organisation of labour has been as little the creation of the great promoters and financiers as it has been (again, in general and with individual exceptions) that of the typical representatives of finance and political capitalism, the Jews. It was the work of people who were quite different as a type.

welfare schemes, rationing, regulation of the economy, protectionism and *laissez-faire* theories (as in China), so there have also been communistic and socialistic economies of various kinds: communism organised on a familial, religious or military basis, state socialism (as in Egypt), monopoly cartels and consumer organisations of all kinds. But just as, despite the fact that there have everywhere existed municipal market privileges, guilds, corporations and a whole range of varied types of legal separation between town and country, there has been no concept of the 'burgher' outside the West and none of the 'bourgeoisie' outside the modern West, so there has been no 'proletariat' as a class – nor could be, precisely because there was no rational organisation of free labour in the form of the enterprise. 'Class struggles' have always existed in all parts of the world in the greatest possible variety of forms – creditors against debtors, landowners against the propertyless or the villeins or tenants, commercial interests against consumers or landowners. But even the Western medieval struggles between the putters-out and those whom they employed are found elsewhere only in their early stages. There is no trace at all of the modern conflict between the big industrial entrepreneur and the free wage-worker. Hence, there could be no trace either of the kinds of problem which confront modern socialism.

As we see it, then, even from the purely economic point of view, the central problem in a universal history of civilisation is ultimately not the development of capitalist activity as such, with its purely formal variations, whether it is of the adventurist type or is directed to opportunities for profit from war, politics or administration. Rather is it the emergence of the kind of capitalism which is characterised by the bourgeois enterprise with its rational organisation of free labour. Or to put it in terms of cultural history, it is the emergence of the Western bourgeoisie, with all its special features, which, although it is closely connected with the rise of the capitalist organisation of labour, is not, of course, simply to be identified with it. For a 'bourgeoisie', in the sense of a particular status group, already existed before the specifically Western form of capitalism developed, though admittedly only in the West.

Among the necessary conditions of capitalism in its specifically modern Western form is obviously, and very importantly, the development of certain technical possibilities. An essential condition of its present-day rationality is the calculability of those technically decisive factors which are the foundations of exact calculation. What that in fact means, however, is that it depends on the peculiar features of Western science, especially the mathematically and experimentally exact natural sciences with their precise rational foundations. In turn, the development of these sciences and the technology based on them has been, and still is, given a decisive impetus by the capitalist opportunities which reward their economic application. Of course, the origins of Western science are not to be found in such opportunities. Algebraic calculation, even with a positional notation, was in use among the Indians, the inventors of that system of notation, which in the West was first put to the service of the development of capitalism, but in India led to no modern system of calculation or book-keeping. Mathematics and mechanics, likewise, did not originate from capitalist interests. Admittedly, the technological application of scientific knowledge, which has so decisively affected the lives of the great mass of our people, has been influenced by the economic rewards offered in the West for precisely that kind of activity. These rewards, however, have themselves resulted from the special character of the Western social order. The question must therefore be raised, which elements of this character are responsible, for undoubtedly not all have been equally important.

One element which is certainly important is the rational structure of law and administration. For the modern form of capitalism, based on the rational enterprise, requires not only calculable technical means of production, but also a calculable legal system and administration in accordance with formal rules; without these, adventurist and speculative trading capitalism or any kind of politically determined capitalism may be possible, but not any kind of rational private enterprise economy with fixed capital and sure calculation. Only in the West has it been possible to base the conduct of economic life on such a system of law and administration, fully articulated both in the technical legal sense and formally. One must also ask: where did such a legal system come from? Other factors aside, capitalist interests have undoubtedly played a part in paving the way for the domination in law and the administration generally of the status group of jurists, with their specialised training in rational law. This is shown by all the research which has been done. But it was not by any means only or particularly such interests which led to this development. And they did not *create* such law by themselves. Quite different forces were at work in this development. And why was it that capitalist interests did not have the same effect in China or India? Why was it in general that in those countries neither scientific nor artistic nor political nor economic development followed the path of *rationalisation* which is unique to the West?

For, in all the cases mentioned, what is obviously at issue is the nature of a specific type of 'rationalism' peculiar to Western civilisation. This term may have a number of very different meanings, as will become clear again and again in the discussion which follows. For instance, it is possible to 'rationalise' mystical contemplation – in other words, a form of behaviour which, from the point of view of other areas of life, is specifically 'irrational' – just as much as the economy, technology, scientific work, education, war, the law and administration. Furthermore, any of these areas may be 'rationalised' from many different ultimate points of view and with many different purposes: what counts as 'rational' from one of these points of view may be 'irrational' from another. Thus, in all civilisations different areas of life have been rationalised in a great variety of ways. When it comes to distinguishing them for the purposes of cultural history, the essential question to ask is: which spheres of life were rationalised, and in what direction? Thus, the primary task is to recognise the special character of Western rationalism in general, and of modern Western rationalism in particular, and to explain its origins. In view of the fundamental importance of the economy, every such attempt at explanation must above all consider the economic determinants. But the causal relationship in the reverse direction should also not be disregarded. For the origins of economic rationalism depend, not only on rational technology and rational law, but also in general on the capacity and disposition which men have for certain kinds of practical rationality in the conduct of their lives. Where this was hindered by restraints of a spiritual kind, the development of an economically rational mode of life also encountered serious internal obstacles. Among the most important formative elements of the mode of life in the past, in all parts of the world, have been magical and religious forces and the concepts of ethical obligation which were anchored in the belief in such forces. This will be the topic of discussion in the following essays, which have been collected and supplemented by additional material.

(*Gesammelte Aufsätze zur Religionssoziologie*, 2nd edn, Tübingen, 1922, I, pp. 1–12. First published in 1920.)

18 · The Development of Bureaucracy and its Relation to Law

The social and economic preconditions for the modern form of bureaucratic administration are as follows.

(1) There must have developed a money economy to provide for the payment of officials, which nowadays is universally made in money. This is of great importance for the general mode of life of the bureaucracy, although it is not, on the other hand, in any way the decisive factor for its existence. In quantitative terms, the largest historical examples of a bureaucratic system which has achieved some obvious degree of development are: (a) Egypt in the time of the New Kingdom (though there were also marked patrimonial elements present in this case); (b) the later Roman Empire, but especially the Diocletianic monarchy and the Byzantine state which developed from it (though here again there were marked feudal and patrimonial elements present too); (c) the Roman Catholic Church, increasingly from the end of the thirteenth century onwards; (d) China, from the time of Shi Huang Ti to the present day, but with marked patrimonial and prebendal elements; (e) in an increasingly pure form, the modern European state and more and more public corporations, since the evolution of princely absolutism; (f) the modern large capitalist enterprise, which is more bureaucratic the larger and more complex it is.

Cases (a) to (d) are based to a very large extent, and in some cases mainly, on the payment of officials in kind. For all that, they reveal many of the characteristic features and effects of bureaucracy. The historical model for all later bureaucracies, the New Kingdom in Egypt, was also one of the greatest examples of an organisation based on a natural economy. The combination in this case, however, is explicable in terms of a unique set of conditions. For, on the whole, the very considerable reservations which one must make in counting that system as a 'bureaucracy' derive from the natural economy. A certain degree of development of the money economy is a normal precondition, if not for the creation of a purely bureaucratic administrative system, then for its unaltered continuance. For historical experience shows that, without such an economy, it is scarcely possible to avoid changes in the intrinsic character of the bureaucratic structure or even its replacement by something totally different.

The allocation of regular allowances in kind from the reserves in the lord's warehouse or from the revenue in kind resulting from them (the system which prevailed for millennia in Egypt and China, and played an important part in the later Roman monarchy and elsewhere) was already a first easy step on the road towards the appropriation of the sources of tax revenue and their yield by the officials as their own private property. Allowances in kind protect the official against the frequently abrupt variations in the purchasing power of money. If, however, the income which depends on taxes in kind comes in irregularly, as usually happens with such income whenever the lord weakens in the exercise of his power, then the official, with or without authorisation, will exert direct pressure on those liable to tax in the area under his control. The idea thus suggests itself of securing the official against such variations by the mortgage or transfer of taxes, and so of the power of levying them, or by the leasing of the lord's profitable lands for the private use of the officials. Every central power which is not organised in a completely rigid way is tempted to follow this path, either from choice or under pressure from the officials. When this happens, the official either draws on the income up to the level at which he has satisfied his claim for pay and then hands over what remains, or (since there are temptations inherent in this procedure which lead to results which are mostly unsatisfactory from the lord's point of view) it may mean that he is 'set at a fixed sum' – the system frequently found in the earlier stages of the German bureaucracy, though it was most fully developed in the satrapies of the East. In this system, the official hands over a fixed amount and keeps what remains.

He is then in a rather similar economic position to the tax-farmer; and indeed, there actually develops a regular system of office-farming, in which offices go to the highest bidder. In the private economy, the most important of the numerous examples is the transformation of the system of villeinage into a tenant relationship. In this way, the lord can also shift the burden of converting his income in kind into money on to the tenant or on to officials who are set at a fixed sum. This was evidently the case with several Oriental governors in the ancient world. This purpose is served most of all by the governor's farming out the gathering of public taxes instead of retaining it as his personal monopoly. The result is that it becomes possible to make the very important advance to the system of public budgeting in the organisation of finance: that is, instead of living from hand to mouth out of the incalculable income which may be received at any given time, as is typical in the early stages of all systems of public accounting, a firm preliminary estimate of receipts, and so of the corresponding expenditure, becomes possible. On the other hand, the lord thereby renounces control and full utilisation of the power of taxation for his own personal needs; indeed, depending on the amount of freedom given to officials or to office- or tax-farmers, he may even put their continued existence at risk through ruthless exploitation, since a capitalist does not have the same long-term interests in this matter as the lord.

In return for his renunciation, the lord seeks to secure his position by regulation. The organisation of the farming or transfer of taxes can thus vary greatly; indeed, depending on the relative strength of the lord and the office- or tax-farmer, either the farmer's interest in free exploitation of the power of taxing the subjects or the lord's interest in their continued existence may gain the upper hand. It was basically on the cooperation or opposition of the motives which have been mentioned – the elimination of fluctuations in revenue, the possibility of public budgeting, the desire to ensure the solvency of subjects by protecting them against uneconomic exploitation, control of the farmer's revenues to ensure the maximum possible appropriation by the state – that, for instance, the manner of organising the tax-farming system in the Ptolemaic kingdom depended. In that system, the tax-farmer was certainly still a private capitalist, as he was in Greece and Rome, but the collection of the taxes was carried out bureaucratically and controlled by the state, and the farmer's profits consisted only partly in any surplus which he might make over his fee (which was really a surety), while his risk was the possibility that the tax revenue might fall short of that fee.

The purely economic conception of office as a private source of income for the official may, if the lord comes to be in the position of needing capital rather than current income (for instance, in order to carry on a war or to pay off debts), lead directly to the purchase of office. This has been a regular institution in modern states themselves – in the Papal States as much as in France or England, and for sinecures as much as for such serious offices as military commissions: remnants of the system survived as late as the nineteenth century. In some cases the economic significance of such a relationship may change as a result of the fact that the purchase fee partly or wholly takes on the character of a security for the official's loyalty. But this was not the general rule.

This manner of allocating revenues, taxes and services which belong to the lord as such to the official for personal exploitation always means, however, that the pure type of bureaucratic organisation has been abandoned. The official in such a situation has personal rights of ownership over the office. This is even more the case when the relationship between official duties and payment is such that the official generally does not hand over the revenue from the objects allocated to him but disposes of such revenue for his own purely private purposes while, on the other hand, performing services for the lord: these services may be personal, military, otherwise political, or ecclesiastical. We shall use the terms 'prebends' and 'prebendal' organisation of office to refer to those cases in which payments of rent or essentially economic revenues from land or other sources, fixed in some tangible form, are allocated for life as payment for the fulfilment of real or fictitious official duties, those goods being assigned by the lord as economic security on a long-term basis.

The transition between such a system and a salaried bureaucracy is a fluid one. In the ancient world and the Middle Ages, though also up until modern times, the economic organisation of the priesthood has often been of this 'prebendal' form; but the same form has also been found in other areas and in almost every period. In Chinese religious law the specifically 'prebendal' character of all offices had the consequence that an official in mourning was forced, since abstinence from all enjoyment of property was prescribed during the period of ritual mourning for a father or other head of household (originally to avoid the ill-will of the deceased master of the house, to whom the property belonged), to renounce his office, which was looked on in a strictly prebendal way as a source of revenue. A further step away from a purely salaried bureaucracy has been taken when not only economic rights, but also rights of domination have been allocated for private use and personal services to the lord stipulated in return. The rights of domination allotted in this way may themselves be of various kinds: for example, in the case of political officials, they may be either of a more seigneurial or of a more official character. In both cases, but especially in the latter, the specific features of bureaucratic organisation are eliminated: we find ourselves in the sphere of a 'feudal' structure of domination.

All forms of such allocation to officials of services or revenues in kind as endowments have a tendency to slacken the bureaucratic mechanism, and in particular to weaken hierarchical subordination. In modern bureaucratic systems the most rigid forms of subordination have been developed. It is only in those cases where the subjection of officials to their lord is absolute at the purely personal level – that is, where the administration is carried on by slaves or by employees who are treated like slaves – that it is possible to achieve, given very energetic leadership, the same kind of precision as is found in the system of contractually employed officials as it exists in the West at the present time.

In the ancient world, among countries with a natural economy, the Egyptian officials were, if not in law, then in fact, the slaves of the Pharaoh. Roman landowners preferred to trust the direct management of their money, at least, to slaves, because of the possibility of putting them to torture. In China a similar result was sought by the frequent use of the bamboo rod as a means of discipline. The likelihood that such direct means of coercion will function consistently is, however, extremely poor.

Judging by experience, a secure money salary coupled with the opportunity of a career which does not depend solely on accident and whim, a form of discipline and control which, though strict, takes account of the sense of honour, and the development of a sense of social position and of the possibility of open criticism offer the best relative chance for the success and stability of a rigidly mechanised bureaucratic apparatus, which then functions more effectively in this respect than one based on legal enslavement. Indeed, a strong sense of status in the officials is not only perfectly compatible with a willingness to accept the most abject subordination to their superiors, but is a consequence of such willingness since it compensates them internally for their self-respect – as in the case of the army officer. The purely 'objective', professional character of the office, with its separation on principle of the official's private life from the sphere of his official activity, makes it easy for him to fit into the enduring, established and objective conditions of a disciplined machine.

Thus, even if the full development of a money economy is not an indispensable precondition for bureaucratisation, there is nevertheless one precondition for the development of a specifically permanent bureaucratic structure, and that is the availability of a permanent income to maintain it. Where this income cannot be supplied out of private profit – as with the bureaucratic organisation of large modern undertakings – or out of dependable ground-rents – as with landownership – a dependable system of taxes is therefore a precondition for the continuing existence of bureaucratic administration. The only secure foundation for such a system, however, is a thoroughgoing money economy (for general reasons which are well known). The degree of bureaucratisation has thus often been relatively greater in urban communities with a fully developed money economy than in the much larger states of the plains, even at the same period of history. Admittedly, once these latter states have been able to develop a regular system of taxation, they have developed a much more comprehensive bureaucracy than the city-states, which have generally tended, as long as their territory is only modest in extent, rather towards a plutocratic collegiate administration of notables. For the true basis for the bureaucratisation of administration has always been a specific type of development of administrative tasks, and principally:

(2) Their *quantitative* development. For instance, in the political sphere the classical basis for bureaucratisation has been the large state and the mass party. This does not mean, of course, that every genuine large state known to history has brought with it a bureaucratic administration. In the first place, the mere continued existence of a large state once it has come into being, or the homogeneity of its accompanying culture, have not always been bound up with a bureaucratic state structure, although both were, for example, found in large measure in the Chinese Empire.

345

The several large African kingdoms and similar formations have proved ephemeral mainly because of the lack of any apparatus of officials. Equally, the political unity of the Carolingian Empire collapsed with the collapse of its administrative organisation – though this organisation was admittedly mainly patrimonial rather than bureaucratic in character. Against this, if one takes only length of time into account, the Caliphate and its predecessors in Asia did last for a considerable period with an essentially patrimonial and prebendal administrative structure, as did the Holy Roman Empire despite its almost total lack of any bureaucracy: in both cases, too, these states displayed a cultural homogeneity almost as marked as that usually created by bureaucratic states. What is more, the ancient Roman Empire, despite increasing bureaucratisation – indeed precisely during the period when bureaucratisation was taking place – disintegrated from within as a result of the way in which the burdens of state were distributed in this process, which worked to the advantage of the natural economy. But the continued existence of the states first mentioned, from the point of view of their degree of purely political homogeneity, was essentially that of an unstable and nominal unit, whose cohesiveness was that of a conglomerate; and their capacity for political action on the whole steadily declined. Their relatively high degree of cultural unity was in part the result of an extremely homogeneous religious organisation, which in the medieval West became increasingly bureaucratic, and in part the result of a far-reaching community of social structure, which was in its turn an after-effect and a transformation of the former political unity.

Both these are manifestations of a cultural stereotyping which tends to lead to an unstable equilibrium and is closely bound up with tradition. Both were strong enough for even such grandiose expansionist adventures as the Crusades to be undertaken as a kind of 'private enterprise' in spite of the absence of any great degree of political unity; nevertheless, the failure of such attempts and their politically irrational conduct – an irrationality which was manifested in several ways – were a consequence of the lack of any underlying unitary or thoroughly developed state power. It is undoubtedly the case, moreover, not only that the seeds of the 'modern' type of thoroughly developed state in the Middle Ages are generally to be found associated with the growth of a bureaucratic structure, but also that it has been those political structures which have the most highly developed bureaucracies which have been finally responsible for the destruction of those conglomerates, resting as they essentially did on an unstable equilibrium.

One of the causes of the fall of the ancient Roman Empire was precisely the bureaucratisation of its military and administrative machine: this could only be achieved by the introduction at the same time of a method of distributing the burdens of state which was bound to lead to a growth in the relative importance of the natural economy. Individual factors, therefore, always have a part to play. Furthermore, a direct relationship between the 'intensity' of state action, both externally (in the drive to expansion) and internally (in state influence on culture), and the degree of bureaucratisation can only be stated as the norm, not as something holding true without exception. For two of the most expansionist political systems – the Roman Empire and the British worldwide Empire – were based, precisely during their period of expansion, only to a small extent on bureaucratic foundations. The Norman state in England introduced a rigorous organisation on the basis of the feudal hierarchy. Its unity and drive, however, came largely from its bureaucratisation of the Royal Exchequer, which was extraordinarily rigorous in comparison with other political systems of the feudal period. The subsequent failure of the English state to take any further part in the continental movement towards bureaucratisation and its retention of an administration of notables (a history similar to that of the Republican administration in Rome) was partly the result of its relative lack of a continental character but also of some purely individual conditions which can still be observed in England today, though they are on the point of disappearing. Among these special conditions was the lack of any need for a large standing army of the kind required in a continental state with land frontiers if it has similarly expansive tendencies. It was for this reason that in Rome bureaucratisation advanced along with the transition from a coastal to a continental Empire. Moreover, in the Roman structure of domination, the technical achievements of a bureaucratic apparatus (precision and consistency of functioning) were replaced in the administration, and in particular the administration of the areas outside the city of Rome itself, by the distinctively military character of the magistracy – a form unknown to any other people – and continuity was guaranteed by the similarly unique position of the Senate.

A further factor in the dispensability of the bureaucracy which should not be forgotten was, both in Rome and in England, the increasing tendency of the state to 'minimise' the range of its internal functions, that is, to limit them to those absolutely required by direct reasons of state. The powers of the continental states of the early modern period, however, had accumulated entirely in the hands of those princes who had most ruthlessly followed a policy of bureaucratisation of the administration. It is obvious that technically the large modern state is completely dependent on bureaucracy, that the longer this process goes on the further it goes, and that the bureaucratisation is all the more complete the bigger the state is, and above all the more it is or becomes a great power. The character of a state which is not bureaucratic, at least in the full technical sense, such as the United States, inevitably falls away and is gradually transformed into a bureaucratic structure, the greater the sources of external friction and the more pressing the need for internal unity of administration become. In the United States, furthermore, the partly non-bureaucratic form of the structure of the state is materially counterbalanced by the all the more rigorous bureaucratic structure of the organisations which are in fact politically dominant: that is, the parties, led by professional specialists in organisational and electoral tactics. The most conspicuous example of the importance of sheer size as a lever for the bureaucratisation of a social structure is precisely the increasingly bureaucratic organisation of all genuine mass parties: in Germany the chief example is the Social Democrats, while abroad the most important example is the two 'historic' American parties.

(3) The causes of bureaucratisation, however, lie much more in the intensive and qualitative expansion and internal development of the range of administrative tasks than in their extensive and quantitative growth. The direction and cause of this development may vary greatly. In the country which had the earliest bureaucratic state administration, Egypt, it was the technical and economic necessity for a common regulation of the water supply for the whole country from above which created the apparatus of scribes and officials, which then went on, from quite early times, to find its second great field of operations in the extraordinary building programme, organised along military lines. As mentioned earlier, bureaucratisation has been promoted most by those needs which come into existence as a result of the creation, for reasons of power-politics, of a standing army and the development of finance associated with it. In the modern state, however, the same process is also assisted by the general growth in those demands on the administration which result from the increasing complexity of civilisation. While significant external expansion, especially overseas, has also been achieved, precisely by states dominated by notables (such as Rome, England and Venice), 'intensity' of administration, by which I mean the tendency for the state to take under its own control as many tasks as possible for continuous operation and execution, is, as will be shown at the appropriate time, relatively weakly developed in large states administered by notables (especially Rome and England) as compared with bureaucratic states. To be precise, the structure of state power has had a very strong influence on the culture in both these cases; but it has not so much taken the form of state enterprise and state control. That is true all the way from the judiciary to education. These growing cultural demands are in turn, if also in varying degree, a result of the developing wealth of the most influential strata in the state. To that extent, then, increasing bureaucratisation is a function of an increase in wealth available for and

used for consumption and of a technology of the external organisation of life which is increasingly sophisticated and corresponds to the possibilities so created. The repercussions of this on the general needs of the community result in an increasing subjective sense of the indispensability of organised public interlocal (and therefore bureaucratic) provision for the most varied necessities of life, which were formerly either unknown or provided on a private or local basis.

Of the purely political factors promoting bureaucratisation, the most enduring is the increasing need felt by a society grown accustomed to stable and absolute peace for order and protection ('police') in all areas. There is a clear line of development from the simple use of religion or arbitration to influence the blood-feud, in which the only guarantee of justice and security for the individual lies in his kinsmen's vows of help and their obligation to avenge him, to the present position of the police as the 'representatives of God on earth'. Other factors working in the same direction include in the first instance the manifold tasks of 'social policy' which the modern state undertakes, partly under pressure from interested parties and partly by usurping them itself, whether from motives of power politics or of ideology. These are, of course, economically determined in the highest degree. Finally, the essentially technical factors include the specifically modern means of communication (public roads and waterways, railways, telegraphs, etc.) which have to be communally administered, partly by necessity and partly as a matter of technical expediency: they are among the pacemakers of bureaucratisation. In this respect they play a role today which is similar in many ways to that played in the ancient East by the canals of Mesopotamia and the regulation of the Nile. On the other hand, the degree of development of the means of communication is a condition for the possibility of a bureaucratic administration which, if not decisive in itself, is nevertheless extremely important. In Egypt, without the natural trade route provided by the Nile, bureaucratic centralisation on the basis of an almost totally natural economy would certainly never have been able to attain the extent which it in fact did. In modern Persia, the telegraph officials, as such, have been officially entrusted with the duty of reporting all events in their province direct to the Shah, over the head of the local governor; moreover, everyone has been offered the right of direct complaint by telegraph in order to advance the process of bureaucratic centralisation. The modern Western state can only be administered in the way it has come to be because it controls the telegraph network and has the posts and railways at its disposal.

This is in turn very closely associated with the development of mass trade in goods between different localities, which thus becomes one of the causal influences on the formation of the modern state. That has not always been absolutely true in the past, however, as we have seen earlier.

(4) The decisive reason for the advance of bureaucratic organisation has always been its purely technical superiority over every other form. A fully developed bureaucratic apparatus stands to these other forms in much the same relation as a machine does to non-mechanical means of production. Precision, despatch, clarity, familiarity with the documents, continuity, discretion, uniformity, rigid subordination, savings in friction and in material and personal costs – all these things are raised much more effectively to the optimal level by a strongly bureaucratic, especially a monocratic, administration with trained individual officials than by any form of collegiate, honorific or avocational administration. Where complex tasks are concerned, the work of a salaried bureaucracy is not only more precise but in consequence often cheaper than that of a formally unpaid honorific official. The work of an honorific official is work outside of his vocation: for that reason, it is usually performed more slowly, is less bound to routine and more formless, and so is less precise, less unified (because less dependent on acceptance by superiors), less continuous and also in practice very often expensive, since it is almost inevitable that the provision and employment of subordinate and clerical staff will be less economical. This is particularly the case when one takes into account not only the bare costs to the public treasury (which usually increase under a bureaucratic administration, especially as compared with an administration of honorary notables), but also the frequent economic loss caused to subjects through delay and lack of precision. The possibility of an honorific administration of notables normally only exists for any length of time when business can be adequately attended to 'as a sideline'. Once there is a qualitative increase in the range of tasks confronting the administration – as is happening now even in England – it reaches its limit. Work organised on a collegiate basis, on the other hand, gives rise to friction, delay and compromise between conflicting interests and opinions, and so proceeds in a way which is less precise and less dependent on superiors, and hence is less unified and slower. All the progress which has been and will be made by the Prussian administrative organisation is a result of the advance of the bureaucratic principle, especially in its monocratic form.

The demand for the greatest possible acceleration in the despatch of official business, combined with precision, clarity and continuity, is today imposed on the administration largely by the requirements of a modern capitalist economy. Large modern capitalist enterprises are themselves in most cases unrivalled models of strict bureaucratic organisation. Their commercial relationships are completely dependent on increasing precision, reliability and, above all, speed of operation. This in turn is made possible by the nature of modern means of communication, including the news service provided by the press. The extraordinary increase in the speed with which public announcements are transmitted, whether about economic or even purely political matters, has in itself created nowadays a continuous and intense pressure in the direction of the maximum possible acceleration in the time taken by the administration to react to situations as and when they arise: the best results in this respect are normally only achieved by strict bureaucratic organisation. (It is irrelevant in this context that the bureaucratic machine may, and in fact does, also in its turn create definite obstacles to the possibility of carrying out its task in a manner adapted to the individual case.)

Above all, however, bureaucratisation does offer the best chance of putting into practice the principle of division of labour in administration according to purely objective criteria; individual parts of the work may be allotted to functionaries who have had specialist training and will continually improve their skills by practical experience. 'Objective' execution of business in this context means execution which has 'no regard for persons' and which follows calculable rules. 'No regard for persons', however, is also the slogan of the 'market' and of all forms of the naked pursuit of economic interests in general. The consistent introduction of a bureaucratic structure of domination implies a levelling of 'status', and so, if there is no simultaneous restriction on the workings of the free-market principle, it implies the universal prevalence of the 'class situation'. If this consequence of bureaucratic domination is not universally found to an extent proportionate to the scale of bureaucratisation, the reason lies in the variety of possible principles on which the needs of political communities may be met. But the second element – the calculable rules – is the most important for a modern bureaucracy. The nature of modern culture, especially its technical and economic substructure, requires precisely such 'calculability' of consequences. In its fullest development, also, bureaucracy specifically conforms to the principle of 'neither fear nor favour'. Its distinctive characteristics, which make it so acceptable to capitalism, are developed all the more completely the more it 'dehumanises' itself: that is to say, the more perfectly it succeeds in realising the distinctive characteristic which is regarded as its chief virtue, the exclusion from the conduct of official business of all love, all hatred, all elements of purely personal sentiment – in general, everything which is irrational and resists calculation. In place of the lord of older societies, who was capable of being moved by personal sympathy, kindness, favour or gratitude, modern culture requires the external apparatus which supports it to be manned by the expert, who is all the more indifferent in human terms, and so all the more completely 'objective', the more complex and specialised the culture becomes. All these features, however,

351

are to be found in bureaucratic structures in a convenient combination. In particular, in the sphere of the administration of justice, it is normally the bureaucracy which first creates the basis for the introduction of a conceptually coherent and rational legal system, founded on 'statute', of the kind first created in a technically perfect form by the later Roman Empire. In the Middle Ages, the acceptance of Roman Law went together with the bureaucratisation of the administration of justice: the gradual introduction of rationally trained specialists to replace the earlier procedures tied to tradition or irrational preconceptions.

A 'rational' legal procedure, based on formalised legal concepts, may be contrasted with the type of procedure which is primarily bound up with hallowed traditions but settles those concrete cases which are not unambiguously decidable on this basis in one of the following ways: first, by means of concrete 'revelations' (oracles, prophecy, trial by ordeal) – this may be called 'charismatic' justice; secondly – and these cases alone are of interest in the present context – either by means of informal decisions based on concrete ethical or otherwise practical value-judgments (what R. Schmidt has aptly called 'Kadi-justice') or by means of decisions which are formal, but are not based on any subsumption under rational concepts: instead they refer to 'analogies' and copy or interpret concrete 'precedents' (this may be called 'empirical' justice). Kadi-justice involves no rational 'bases of judgment', and empirical justice, in its pure type, involves none which are rational in our sense. The character of Kadi-justice, based as it is on concrete value-judgments, can be pushed to the point of a prophetic break with all traditions; empirical justice, on the other hand, can be sublimated and rationalised into an art. For, as will be explained elsewhere, the non-bureaucratic forms of domination reveal a peculiar conjunction of a sphere of thoroughgoing traditionalism on the one hand with the arbitrary will and favour of the lord on the other: intermediate and transitional forms, combining elements of both principles, are thus very frequent. In England, for instance, as Mendelssohn has shown, there is even now a broad substratum of the administration of justice which is in fact 'Kadi-justice' to an extent which it is hard to conceive on the Continent. The German jury system, in which no statement of the reasons for the verdict reached is allowed, often functions in practice in precisely this way, as everyone knows: one must take care not to confuse 'democratic' principles of justice with 'rational', that is, formal, legal judgment. The two are quite different, as will be shown in another place. On the other hand, the administration of justice in the great central courts of England (and America) is always largely empirical, based particularly on precedents.

The reason for the failure of all attempts at the rational codification of law or the introduction of Roman Law in England lay in the successful resistance of the great centrally organised lawyers' guilds, a monopolistic stratum of notables, from whose number the judges of the great courts were drawn. They retained tight control of legal education in the form of training in an empirical art (highly developed though it was from a technical point of view), and successfully resisted all the attempts made especially by the ecclesiastical judges, and sometimes also by the universities, to create a rational legal system, which would have threatened their social and material position. The struggle of the Common Law advocates against Roman and church law and against the powerful position of the Church in general was thus largely motivated by economic considerations, by their interest in fees, as is clearly shown by the manner in which the King intervened in this struggle. But their position of power, which survived the struggle in which they were victorious, was the result of political centralisation. In Germany, for largely political reasons, there was no socially powerful estate of notables to constitute, in the fashion of the English lawyers, a national school of legal training, to develop the national law to the rank of an art with a controlled apprenticeship and to resist the infiltration of the technically superior training of those jurists who had studied Roman Law. It was not, indeed, the greater appropriateness of the *content* of Roman Law to the needs of emerging capitalism which was responsible for their victory on the Continent: all the specific legal institutions of modern capitalism are in fact alien to Roman Law and are of medieval origin. What was decisive was its rational *form* and above all the technical necessity of placing the conduct of trials in the hands of rationally trained experts (that is, university-trained experts in Roman Law), in view of the increasing complexity of actual cases and of the rational procedures of evidence which had replaced the original universal determination of truth by concrete revelation or religious guarantees and which were required by an increasingly rationalised economy. The situation was, of course, conditioned to a large extent by the changed economic structure. But this factor was operative everywhere, even in England, where rational procedures of evidence were introduced by the power of the King in order particularly to favour the merchants.

The main reason for the difference which nevertheless exists in the development of substantive law in England and Germany lay, as should already be obvious, elsewhere: it originates from the autonomous development of the two different structures of domination. In England there was centralised administration of justice combined with domination by notables; in Germany there was no political centralisation but a high degree of bureaucratisation. Thus the first country in modern times to have a highly developed capitalist economy, England, retained a less rational and less bureaucratic system of justice. The main reason why capitalism in England was able to come to terms so well with this situation, however, was that in that country the manner in which the courts were organised and the trial procedure, right up until modern times, were in fact tantamount to a virtual denial of justice to the economically weak. This fact, together with the time-consuming and costly procedure for conveyancing land, which is also the result of the economic interests of the lawyers, has in turn also deeply affected the agrarian system of England in the direction of the accumulation and immobilisation of land.

For their part, Roman legal judgments in the time of the Republic were a peculiar mixture of elements drawn from rational, empirical and even Kadi-justice. The appointment of juries and the *actiones in factum* given by the praetors, at first undoubtedly on a purely *ad hoc* basis, contained elements of the last kind. 'Cautelar' jurisprudence, and everything which developed from it, including some of the responses of the classical jurists, was 'empirical' in character. The ground was first prepared for the decisive advance to rationality in juristic thought by the technical mode of trial instruction based on the formulae of the praetorian edict, reformed in accordance with legal concepts. (Today, when the principle of substantiation prevails, so that what decides is the statement of the facts of the case regardless of the legal point of view from which they substantiate the indictment, there is not the same pressure to elaborate the scope of the concepts in clear formal terms as there was in the technically sophisticated culture of Roman Law.) To that extent, therefore, development was influenced by technicalities of trial procedure which were only indirectly connected with the structure of the state. But the rationalisation of Roman Law, which so sharply distinguishes it from anything created in the East or indeed by Greek civilisation, was achieved for the first time in the form of a closed system of concepts working on scientific principles during the period of the bureaucratisation of the state.

(*Wirtschaft und Gesellschaft*, 4th edn, Tübingen, 1956, II, pp. 564–72. First published in 1922.)

VI · Miscellaneous Topics

Introduction

The short selections which are included in this final section have been chosen partly to illustrate the wide range of Weber's interests but partly also for their intrinsic interest. They all deal with topics which, although peripheral to the major studies on which Weber's reputation rests, nonetheless reflect the same underlying presuppositions with which he approached all aspects of social organisation and culture.

The first selection is from the chapter in *Economy and Society* which Weber devoted to what he called 'communal relationships' of an 'ethnic' kind. Under this heading, he deals with what tend nowadays to be called 'race relations', including the question how far, if at all, these need to be understood in biological rather than sociological terms. But he extends the discussion to broader considerations of folk, tribal and national relationships and loyalties with which he considered ethnic relationships and loyalties to be closely connected. His view, like that of the overwhelming majority of later anthropologists and sociologists, was that inherited physical characteristics as such play no significant role in 'ethnic' relations. It is, however, consistent with Weber's general view of social stratification that he analyses them in terms not merely of cultural self-differentiation but also of attempted monopolisation by rival groups of social status and political power.

The second selection is from the first of two papers which Weber published on the methodological and substantive problems of an enquiry into the determinants of industrial workers' output which had been proposed by the Association for Social Policy and which Weber became involved in during 1908. The enquiry proved abortive. But Weber's two papers remain interesting on two counts: first, in setting out Weber's view of the relation between sociology and psychology with reference to a specific topic; secondly, in demonstrating Weber's capacity for quantitative empirical research of the kind which came to be extensively practised by industrial psychologists and sociologists, particularly in the United States.[1]

The third selection is the concluding passage of a two-part essay on the stock exchange which Weber published in 1894 and 1896. It is written from the same point of view as his Freiburg inaugural lecture of 1895 and his several studies of the agrarian economy of East Prussia, and reflects his same concern that a policy should be adopted which will best serve Germany's national interest. The article displays a characteristically thorough knowledge of the technicalities of the subject not only in Germany but abroad. It is also characteristic of Weber

[1] Cf. P. F. Lazarsfeld and A. Oberschall, 'Max Weber and Empirical Social Research', *American Sociological Review*, XXX (1965).

in the way in which it is equally contemptuous of greedy and witless speculators on the one hand and anti-capitalist conspiracy-theorists on the other.

The selection on the piano is from an essay which Weber wrote in about 1911 although it was not published until 1921. In it, he traces once again the all-pervasive influence of 'rationalisation' which he saw as distinctive of Western art no less than Western science.[1] But he also relates the development of Western music to such specifically sociological influences as the domestic life of the bourgeoisie of Northern, in contrast to Southern, Europe.

The selection on Freudianism is the text of a letter written by Weber to Edgar Jaffé, his co-editor, rejecting an article by a then well-known Freudian for the *Archiv für Sozialwissenschaft und Sozialpolitik*. It is interesting not only because it gives something of Weber's view of Freud's own writings, but also for the light it throws on Weber's own personal relationships and those of his milieu at Heidelberg. 'Dr X' was in fact Otto Gross (1877–1920), whose wife Frieda was a friend of Jaffé's wife Else. Gross became the lover both of Else Jaffé (who was later to become, it is now thought, Weber's mistress) and of her sister Frieda (who was later to marry D. H. Lawrence).[2] Weber, as his remarks in this letter show, was responsive both to the claims of a conventional ethic of responsibility and also to the arguments for sexual liberation: but it was characteristic of him to insist that it is impossible to have the best of both worlds.

The final selection is from an exchange between Weber and the biologist Ploetz which took place at the first meeting of the German Sociological Society held in Frankfurt in 1910.

[1] Cf. above, p. 332.
[2] For Gross's career, see Martin Green, *The von Richthofen Sisters* (London, 1974), pp. 32ff, and for Weber's relationship with Else Jaffé, *ibid.*, p. 366.

19 · Race Relations

I. MEMBERSHIP OF A 'RACE'

A much more problematic source of communal action than what has been mentioned so far is 'membership of a race', or in other words the possession, resulting from actual common descent, of similar inherited or heritable characteristics. Naturally, such common descent only expresses itself in the form of a 'community' when the individuals concerned have a subjective feeling of their common identity; and this in turn only develops when people of different races, living in close proximity to each other or associated together in some other way, are involved in some common activity (usually of a political nature), or alternatively when racially similar people share a common fate in virtue of their shared opposition to other groups who are markedly different from them. When communal action results in such a situation, it generally takes a purely negative form: those who feel themselves to have a common identity mark themselves off from the noticeably different group and despise them, or sometimes, on the contrary, regard them with superstitious awe. Some-one who is foreign in his external appearance, however he may 'act' or whatever he may 'be', is despised simply as such; or, on the contrary, if he remains in a superior position over a period of time, is regarded with superstitious veneration. Rejection is thus the primary and normal response. Two points, however, should be made about such rejection. First, it is not only found as a response of the anthropologically similar to those who are different from themselves, and the degree of rejection in no way depends on the degree of anthropological affinity. Secondly, it is by no means only a response to inherited differences, but may equally be a response to other conspicuous differences in external appearance.

If the degree of objective racial difference can be determined by purely physiological criteria – for instance, by ascertaining whether the reproduction rate of hybrids is roughly normal – then the intensity of subjective feelings of attraction and repulsion between races might be measured accordingly. It could be established, for instance, whether the members of the groups concerned formed sexual relationships willingly or only rarely and whether such relationships were normally permanent or in essence merely temporary and irregular liaisons. The presence or absence of intermarriage would then be a normal consequence of racial attraction or repulsion between communities with a developed sense of 'ethnic' separateness. The study of relationships of sexual attraction or repulsion between different ethnic communities on the basis of exact observation is at present only in its infancy. There is not the slightest doubt that factors connected with race, and so resulting from the fact of common descent, *do* play a part, and sometimes the decisive part, in determining the frequency of sexual relationships and the rate of intermarriage between members of different groups. But that sexual repulsion based on race is not 'primitive', even amongst races who are very sharply differentiated from each other, is shown plainly enough by the example of the several million Mulattoes to be found in the United States. Not only the direct prohibition of intermarriage in the Southern States, but also the sense of horror at any kind of sexual relationships between the two races (now felt on both sides, since the Negroes too have recently come to share it), are *socially* determined. They result from the claims made by the Negroes, since the emancipation of the slaves, to be treated as citizens with equal rights. In other words, they result from the tendency, with which we are already familiar in outline, to monopolise social power and status – a tendency which happens in this case to be associated with racial differences.

There is a variety of conditions for the presence of intermarriage in general, and so for the admission of the offspring of an enduring sexual union to an equal share in the collective activities of the father's community and in the benefits resulting therefrom for the members (whether the community is politically, socially or economically based). Under the system of unqualified patriarchy (discussed in another section), it was entirely within the father's discretion whether any children born to him by a slave were to be treated as possessing equal rights. Furthermore, the tendency to glorify the abduction of women by heroes meant that racial mixing became the norm in the ruling élite. The domination of the patriarch in this respect was first progressively limited by the tendency, with which we are familiar in outline, towards monopolistic exclusiveness on the part of communities based on political interests, considerations of social rank, or other common characteristics, together with the tendency towards monopolisation of the chances of marriage. This resulted in a strict limitation of the right of intermarriage to the children of enduring sexual unions between members of the same community (whether the community was based on rank, political interests, religious beliefs, or economic considerations). It also led, however, to a very high degree of inbreeding. In general, the 'endogamy' of a community is very much a secondary result of such tendencies. (By the term 'endogamy' is meant here not only the fact that enduring sexual relationships are primarily formed between members of an association, which is, as always, an organised one, but that the community acts in such a way that only the children born to a father who is a member of the community are allowed to share in communal activity on an equal footing with other members.) Incidentally, it is misleading to speak of 'endogamy' in the context of kinship groups. It does not exist, except as a way of referring to such phenomena as levirate marriage and the rights of heiresses, which are of secondary origin, either religious or political. The 'pure breeding' of anthropological types is very often a secondary consequence of such exclusiveness, which, as always, is limited. This is true as much of sects (in India) as of 'pariah peoples', by which I mean groups which are socially despised but are nevertheless at the same time sought after as neighbours because they have the monopoly of a special and indispensable skill.

Other factors than the extent of objective racial affinity help to create not only the fact, but also the degree, of awareness of real blood-ties. In the United States, the tiniest drop of Negro blood is sufficient to disqualify a person absolutely, while very large amounts of Indian blood are no disqualification at all. This distinction results in part, undoubtedly, from the fact that a full-blooded Negro is aesthetically even more alien in his appearance than an Indian. But without any question it arises also from the memory that the Negroes, as opposed to the Indians, were a people of slaves, or in other words a group disqualified in terms of social class. Differences in social status (that is, environmentally determined differences) and especially differences in 'upbringing' (in the widest sense of that word) are a much more formidable obstacle to conventional intermarriage than differences in anthropological type. By and large, purely anthropological differences (leaving aside extreme cases of aesthetic revulsion) play only a limited role.

II. ORIGINS OF THE BELIEF IN COMMON ETHNIC IDENTITY. COMMUNITIES BASED ON LANGUAGE AND CULT

Normally, however, the question whether differences which are felt to be particularly noticeable and therefore are a source of division result from 'heredity' or 'tradition' has absolutely no bearing on mutual attraction or repulsion. This applies to the development of endogamous intermarriage between different groups, and naturally still more to attraction and repulsion in 'intercourse' of other kinds. In other words, it applies to the question whether the members of such groups form friendships, or enter into relationships of a social or economic nature, or create associations of any kind easily and on the basis of reciprocal trust, and in so doing treat each other as mutually alike and equal in

mutual esteem; or whether they form such relationships only with difficulty and with the kind of precautions which give evidence of mistrust.
The degree of ease with which members of a community enter into
relationships of social intercourse (in the widest possible sense of that
word) is determined at least as much by the most superficial, though
long-established, differences in outward style of life, often the accidental
product of history, as by racial inheritance. In many cases, the decisive
factor, apart from the sheer strangeness of the alien custom in itself, is
an inability to grasp the' subjective 'meaning' of the alien 'custom',
resulting from the lack of the relevant key to the understanding of it.
But not all repulsion is a result of this kind of lack of common understanding, as we shall soon see. Someone in the grip of immediate
feelings of attraction or repulsion may make as few distinctions in degree
of 'importance' and 'triviality' between such things as differences in the
trim of beards and hair, style of dress, type of food, usual division of
labour between the sexes and other such immediately obvious differences
as the naive travel writer or Herodotus or the older kind of pre-scientific
ethnographer. Such differences can not only, in particular cases, arouse
feelings of repulsion and contempt for foreigners, but also, and more
positively, they can stimulate awareness of a common identity among
those who resemble each other: this consciousness can then as readily
become the basis of a community as, conversely, every kind of community,
from household and neighbourhood to political and religious communities, tends to be marked out by a shared set of customs.

All differences in 'custom' can nurture a special feeling of 'status' and
'worth' in the members of the relevant communities. The original causes
of the divergence in way of life are forgotten: the contrasting patterns
of life become established as 'conventions'. Just as every single community develops customs in this way, so each community also has a specific
effect on the selection of anthropological types, since it differentially
favours particular inherited characteristics in respect of the chances of
life, survival and reproduction. In other words, it controls breeding, and
in some cases extremely effectively so. The situation is the same with
regard to the way in which a community differentiates itself from outsiders as with regard to the way in which it maintains its internal balance.
The tendency, with which we are already familiar in outline, towards
monopolistic exclusiveness towards outsiders may be linked with any
factor, no matter now superficial. The universal strength of the desire
to 'imitate' usually has the consequence that purely traditional customs
change from one place to another only by gradual transitions, just as
anthropological types merge into one another through the mixing of
races. Thus, where there are sharp boundaries between the areas in which
markedly different ways of life are found, this is either a result of

conscious monopolistic exclusiveness, which seizes on minor differences and then carefully cultivates and deepens them, or else of peaceful or warlike migrations, in which communities which previously lived far away have moved into an area and adapted their traditions to the new and different conditions of life. The situation is the same, in other words, as in the case of strikingly different racial types, which have arisen through breeding in isolation, but which then, either through monopolistic exclusiveness or through migration, are found living in close proximity to each other but with a sharply defined boundary between their respective territories. Nevertheless, it has to be accepted that similarities and differences in customs and ways of life, whether they are biologically inherited or traditional, are in principle subordinated to the same conditions of communal life, both in their origins and in their development, and also that they are similar in their effect on the formation of a community. There are two main differences between them. First, there are enormous differences in the degree of instability of inherited, as compared with traditional, patterns of behaviour. Secondly, there are definite limits (though in any given case the limits may often not be known) to the possibility of breeding new inherited characteristics: by contrast, though there may be also marked differences in the extent to which traditions can be handed on, there is very much more scope for 'customs' to 'take hold'.

Virtually every kind of similarity or opposition in habit and way of life is likely to generate the subjective belief among the groups concerned that their mutual attraction or repulsion is based on some racial affinity or difference. Admittedly, not all beliefs in racial affinity are based on similarities of custom and habit. Even when there are marked differences in this respect, such a belief may develop and help to create a sense of common identity, as long as it is reinforced by the memory of some actual migration, whether in the form of colonisation or of individual voyages. For the change of habits and the memories of their youth continue to influence the emigrants and to induce feelings of nostalgia in them even when they have become so thoroughly adapted to their new environment that they themselves would find it intolerable to return to their old homes. (This is true, for instance, of most German-Americans.) In the case of colonies, the colonists' spiritual ties with their homeland survive, even if they have mingled almost totally with the original inhabitants of the colonial territory and even if both their traditions and their inherited biological type may have radically changed. A decisive factor in this, in the case of political colonisation, is the need for political support, as also, in general, is the persistence of the matrimonial connexions created by intermarriage. Finally, insofar as the pattern of 'custom' remains unchanged, the market relationships between homeland and colony (assuming that the needs of both sides remain constant) may become especially close – especially, indeed, in the case of colonies which are located in unfamiliar surroundings and in the midst of a politically alien territory. The belief in racial affinity may have important consequences for the formation especially of a political community, and these consequences will, of course, be quite independent of whether there is any objective foundation for the belief. We shall use the expression 'ethnic' groups to describe human groups (other than kinship groups) which cherish a belief in their common origins of such a kind that it provides a basis for the creation of a community. This belief may be based on similarities of external custom or practice or both, or on memories of colonisation or migration. The question whether they are to be called an 'ethnic' group is independent of the question whether they are objectively of common stock. The 'ethnic' group differs from the 'kinship group' in that it is constituted simply by the belief in a common identity, whereas a kinship group is a genuine 'community', characterised by genuinely communal activity. By contrast, the sense of a common ethnic identity (as that expression is being used here) is not itself a community, but only something which makes it easier to form one. It facilitates the formation of widely varying kinds of community, but chiefly, judging by the empirical evidence, of political communities. Conversely, it is often the political community, even when formed in a highly artificial way, which gives rise to beliefs in ethnic identity which survive even its downfall, unless there are such obstacles as extreme differences in custom and practice or, most important of all, in language.

The 'artificial' character of the origins of the belief in ethnic identity fits in perfectly with the pattern which we have already outlined, according to which rational social formations take on a new meaning as personal relationships within a community. Where there is little in the way of rationally grounded social action, virtually all forms of association, even those created in a purely rational way, tend to attract the sense of community in the form of sentiments of personal brotherhood founded on a belief in 'ethnic' identity. Even amongst the Greeks, every subdivision of the *polis*, no matter how arbitrarily it was created, developed into a personal association, which had at least a common cult, and often a mythical ancestor. The Twelve Tribes of Israel were subdivisions of the political community which took it in turns every month to undertake certain tasks, as were the Greek *Phylai* and their subdivisions. But even in the latter case, they were also considered as completely ethnic groupings, based on common descent. Certainly, the original division may very well have been connected with political or pre-existing ethnic differences. But even where the system was constructed completely according to a rational plan, as a result of the breakdown of old associations and the abandonment of locality as the basis for social cohesion, as in the reforms of Cleisthenes, the effect was the same – the development of a sense of ethnic identity. It is wrong, therefore, to infer from this that the Greek *polis* was either really or in its origins normally a state based on clans or families: rather, it is a symptom of the generally low degree of rationalisation of Greek community life in most cases. Conversely, it is a symptom of the greater degree of rationalisation of the structures of the Roman political community that its ancient systematic subdivisions, the *curiae*, took on to a much smaller extent this kind of religious meaning, based on myths about ethnic origins.

The belief in 'ethnic' identity very often, though not always, sets limits to a 'community', in the sense of a group within which social intercourse is permitted. A community in this sense, however, is not always identical with the endogamous community, within which intermarriage is practised, and the orbit of both can vary very considerably. The close connexion between them results simply from their similar basis: both are founded on a belief in a 'status' which is peculiar to their members and is not shared by outsiders. This is the 'ethnic status' of the members, whose affinity with the status conferred by social rank we shall discuss later. For the moment, it will be sufficient to make the following few points. A properly conducted sociological enquiry must always make much finer distinctions between its concepts than we make here for our limited purposes. A community may, for its part, engender a sense of common identity which then continues to exist for a long period, even after the community itself has disappeared, and is felt as 'ethnic'. This is true, above all, of political communities; but it is most directly true of the linguistic community, since such a community possesses its own special 'heritage of popular culture' and makes it possible, even easy, to achieve mutual 'understanding'.

A very special kind of sense of 'ethnic' community, capable of withstanding severe stress, undoubtedly exists in cases where, for one reason or another, the members of a community retain the memory for a long time of the establishment abroad of the community either by peaceful separation from the mother-community or by migration to some distant country (whether as colonists, or through being exiled as a form of religious sacrifice, or by some process of that sort). In such a case, however, the feeling is caused by shared political memories, or (a more powerful influence in earlier times) by a persistent attachment to the old cult-communities or the continuing strength of kinship ties and other groupings shared by both the old and the new communities, or finally, other enduring relationships with a continuing emotional basis. Where such relationships do not exist, or cease to exist, there can be no feeling of 'ethnic' community, no matter how close the ties of blood may be.

If one leaves out of account the possession of a shared language, which is by no means always confined to or characteristic of groups which either objectively are, or subjectively believe themselves to be, of the same blood, and shared religious beliefs, which are similarly independent of blood-relationships; and if one further disregards for the moment the effects of, and the memories of, a common destiny in the purely political sphere (something which, at least objectively, has likewise nothing to do with ties of blood), then one can ask in a general way which 'ethnic' differences are left. The answer is that what remains is, on the one hand, the aesthetically conspicuous differences in external appearance noted already and, on the other (and deserving of equal consideration), immediately detectable differences in the *manner in which everyday life is carried on.* Indeed, since, in dealing with the question of the foundations of 'ethnic' differences, it is always the most striking and immediately detectable external differences which count, what matters is precisely those things which may otherwise appear to be of only minor social importance. Clearly, a shared language and, after that, a common pattern of ritual regulation of life, based on shared religious conceptions, everywhere play an exceptionally important part in creating feelings of 'ethnic' affinity. This is so particularly in view of the fact that it is an elementary condition for the formation of a community that its members should be able to 'understand' the meaning of each other's actions.

But let us for the moment leave these two factors aside and ask what is then left. (After all, it must be granted that marked differences in dialect and in religious practices at least do not absolutely rule out all feelings of common ethnic identity.) Really striking differences in the conduct of economic life have played a part in creating a feeling of ethnic affinity, as also have at all times such forms of external self-expression as differences in type of dress, types of housing and food, the customary form of division of labour between the sexes and the division between the free and the unfree. All these things belong to areas of life in which questions arise about standards of 'propriety' and, above all, about matters to do with the individual's feeling of his own status and worth. In other words, these are all matters which we shall come across again later, when we shall see them to be connected with differences of social 'rank' in particular. In fact, the feeling of 'ethnic status', exactly like the conception of status based on social 'rank', feeds on convictions about the excellence of one's own customs and the inferiority of other people's. 'Ethnic' status is the form of status which is specifically open to the mass of the population, since it can be claimed by anyone who shares in the common ancestry which is subjectively believed to exist. In the period of slavery, it was the 'poor white trash', the propertyless whites of the American South, who often had to eke out a poverty-stricken existence because of the lack of opportunities for free work, who really felt a racial hatred which was quite alien to the planters themselves. This was precisely because their social 'status' could only be preserved if the blacks were relegated to the bottom of the class system. At the root of all 'ethnic' conflicts, of course, there is somewhere to be found the idea of a 'chosen people'. This idea is simply a parallel to ideas about differences of 'rank', but shifted into the horizontal plane. It owes its popularity to the very fact that, in contrast with distinctions of rank, which are always based on subordination, membership of the chosen people can be subjectively claimed on exactly the same footing by all members of each of the mutually contemptuous groups. Hence, in their feelings of ethnic repulsion, the members cling to every imaginable difference in standards of 'propriety' and make them into 'ethnic conventions'. Besides the factors mentioned already, which all have a close connexion with the economic system, even such things as the style of trimming beards and hair are seized on in the passion for 'conventionalisation' (a concept to be discussed later). These things serve to foster 'ethnic' conflicts, since they act as symbols of ethnic co-membership. Admittedly, repulsion is not always or only a result of the purely symbolic function of these distinguishing characteristics. According to ancient tradition, when the aristocratic ladies of Greece and Scythia attempted to make social advances to each other, their attempts came inevitably to nothing on both sides because the Scythian women greased their hair with rancid-smelling butter while the Greeks, on the other hand, used perfumed oil. The smell of the butter certainly had a greater divisive effect than even the most striking racial differences could have achieved – even the 'Negro smell' (which, as far as I can discover, seems to be entirely mythical, anyway). Generally speaking, 'racial characteristics' are only important in the formation of a belief in 'ethnic' identity, as limiting factors, in cases where the external type is so different as to be aesthetically unacceptable: they do not play a positive part in forming a community.

Marked differences in 'custom', on this view, play a part in the development of a sense of ethnic identity and beliefs about blood-relationships which is equivalent in every way to that played by biologically inherited appearance. Such differences, along with differences in language and religion, are an entirely normal result of differences in the economic or political conditions to which a human group has adapted itself. If we think of a situation in which there are no sharp linguistic boundaries or well-defined political or religious communities to give support to differences in 'custom' (a situation which actually exists in many cases over wide areas of the African and South American continents), then there will be only gradual transitions from one set of customs to another and no definite 'ethnic boundaries', except those which result from extreme spatial separation. Where there are sharp boundaries between the areas in which different customs, of an 'ethnically' relevant kind, hold good, and where these boundaries are not caused by political, economic or religious divisions, this is normally because migration or expansion has brought a number of groups into direct geographical proximity who previously lived at some distance from each other, either for a long time or even for a short one, and who accordingly became adapted to widely varying conditions. When the members of both communities become aware in this way of the distinct contrast between their modes of life, they usually come to think of each other as of 'alien blood', quite independently of the objective facts of the situation.

It is naturally very difficult to determine how much of an influence is exerted on the formation of a community by 'ethnic' factors, defined in this specific sense of a belief in the existence or non-existence of a blood-relationship, based on common or different elements in the outward appearance of persons and their mode of life, and their significance in each individual case is problematic. 'Ethnically' relevant customs operate usually in much the same way as custom in general (a topic to be discussed elsewhere). The belief in common ancestry, along with similarity of custom, facilitates the spread of any communal activity practised by some members of the 'ethnic' group to the other members, for consciousness of common identity encourages 'imitation'. This is especially true of the propaganda of religious communities. But apart from such vague remarks, little more can be said. The character of the sort of communal action which is possible on an 'ethnic' basis remains unclear. Correspondingly unclear are all those concepts which appear to imply some purely 'ethnic' basis for communal action in the sense of action dependent on a belief in blood-relationships. I have in mind such concepts as those of the 'nation', the 'race', or the 'people', each of which is normally used in the sense of an ethnic subdivision of the concept following it (except that the order may be reversed in the case of the first two). Normally when these expressions are used, there is also some implication of an existing political community, however informal, or of memories, preserved in the form of a common epic tradition, of a political community which used to exist at an earlier period; or else there may be some implication of a community of language or at least dialect, or finally of a common cult. In the past, it was especially the possession of a common cult which was the normal concomitant of consciousness of belonging to a 'race' or a 'people' believed to be bound together by their common blood. But when such consciousness was not expressed in the form of any kind of political community, whether past or present, the outer limits of the community and its exact extent were usually fairly vague. The cult communities to be found among the Germanic races, even as late as the Burgundian period, were indeed rudimentary political communities and so seem to have been reasonably well defined. On the other hand, the Delphic oracle was undoubtedly the religious focus for the Greeks' sense of themselves as a 'people', but the god gave advice to barbarians as well and even accepted their worship. At the same time, only some of the Greeks took any part in the administration of his associated cult, and it was precisely the most powerful of the Greek communities, considered from the political point of view, who took none at all. In general, then, the cult community, as an exponent of 'racial feeling', is either a relic of a narrower community which once existed but was scattered by schism and colonisation (usually of a political character), or else, as in the case of the Delphic Apollo, it is rather the product of a 'cultural community', brought into being by conditions which are not purely 'ethnic', but which then make it possible for the belief in common blood to arise. The whole course of history makes it plain with what extraordinary ease common political activity in particular leads to the idea of 'common blood' – as long as there are no differences of anthropological type, of *too* extreme a character, to stand in the way.

(*Wirtschaft und Gesellschaft*, 4th edn, Tübingen, 1956, I, pp. 234–40. First published in 1922.)

20 · *Industrial Psychology*

For all their intrinsic importance, the individual results of the work so far done in experimental psychology on the course of the processes of fatigue and training are not perhaps of much direct assistance to the compilers of this survey for their special purposes for the reasons already mentioned. Nevertheless, it might possibly be of some use to them to acquaint themselves with some of the simpler concepts commonly employed in the more recent studies in this field, even though, unfortunately, the precise meaning of many of them is at present a matter of dispute.[1] However, some of these concepts are sufficiently clear in meaning, represent measurable quantities, are of proven usefulness and can provide the compilers with a convenient summary of certain simple elements in personal qualifications for work, together, if necessary, with a handy terminology: for instance, such concepts as that of 'fatiguability' (measured in terms of the rate and degree of onset of fatigue); 'recuperability' (measured in terms of the rate of recovery of efficiency after fatigue); 'capacity for training' (in terms of the rate of improvement in performance in the course of the work); 'durability of training' (in terms of the extent of the residue of training left after breaks and interruptions in the work); 'stimulability' (in terms of the extent to which the 'psychomotor' influence of working itself improves performance); 'powers of concentration' and 'distractability' (in terms of the reduction or lack of it in performance caused by an unaccustomed environment or extraneous disturbances, and, in the case of a reduction, in terms of its extent); and, finally, 'habituation' (to an unaccustomed environment, extraneous disturbances, and – most important of all in principle – to the combination of different activities).

These concepts can perfectly well be used even in cases in which the extent to which work performance is affected by the particular factors to which they refer cannot be mathematically determined. Moreover, there is something to be gained from certain discussions within technical psychology: for instance, on the relationship between fatigue and change of job; on the subjective and objective consequences of 'application' to

---

[1] I have attempted to summarise the problems and to provide an abstract of the literature in *Archiv für Sozialwissenschaft und Sozialpolitik* (November–January issue), and can supply copies of this article for as long as the supply of offprints lasts.

a particular job; on the mutual adaptation of the different psycho-physical elements in training for complex tasks and combinations of activities, and on the differences between the sensory and motor bases of reaction, both in respect of their consequences for the quantity and quality of performance and in respect of their determination by differences in the psycho-physical foundations of 'personality'. All these and similar discussions within the specialism of psychology, little though they may have yielded as yet in the way of definitive proof on many issues, would serve in themselves to sharpen our awareness of a number of general problems, which extend into such extremely complex questions as the conditions of industrial efficiency and the effects of technical development, especially the 'division of labour' and similar phenomena. In particular, it would be of the greatest importance if some precise psycho-physical basis could be found for dealing with the question of change of job, both in regard to its effects and its preconditions. In this regard, it must of course be remembered that in the present survey even this problem is approached entirely from the point of view of profitability. Such a point of view is usually totally unsympathetic to the change of job, since by and large it is obviously a process which tends to have an adverse effect (often extremely adverse) on the continuous utilisation of assets employed. But it is favourable, on the other hand, in cases where, for instance, it becomes necessary, in a situation of extensive specialisation, to give the individual workers engaged in one stage of the work process the chance to get to know for themselves the consequences of their shortcomings through engaging in subsequent stages. At all events, it is always necessary to ask, in any case in which the change of job is found, what experiments have been made by the managers of an enterprise in a particular industry and with particular types of work to discover what effects a possible change of job within the enterprise has on productivity. What differences, moreover, are to be found in a particular worker's aptitude for his job according to the type of work which he has done immediately before taking up his present occupation, or earlier, or, finally, in his youth? These differences are often extremely important and are, furthermore, mathematically calculable, as we shall see below.

It would also obviously be necessary to consider the feelings and subjective attitudes of the workers themselves. This is plainly determined to the greatest extent by such rational factors as pay differentials, the convenience of the work and so forth. Where such factors are clearly the decisive ones, there can of course be no question of taking up any position on the issue of whether uniformity or change of job is preferable in itself, and of whether and how this might be determined by physiological or psychological influences. Further, the attitude of a worker to

371

a change of job, purely as such – that is, in cases where the different kinds of work do not involve any considerable differences in either amenities or pay – is naturally determined to a large extent by rational economic satisfactions. In every case in which change of job within an enterprise has a lastingly depressive effect on the level of performance (because of the 'loss of training' and the need to break oneself in all over again), it also depresses the level of earnings (to the extent that pay is based on a piece-work system). In industries with diversified production and little standardisation, during times of depression, when the individual tasks in themselves become smaller and the diversity of production per unit of time increases, a critical situation is created for the workers' chances of earnings in the form of more frequent changes in kind of occupation. In such cases, too, there can of course be no question of any physiological or psycho-physical determinants of their opinion of these developments. There is equally no question of such determinants, when it is observed that older married workers prefer uniformity of earnings in work which is continuous, even if it is also monotonous, whereas younger, single men prefer change, in the interests of broadening their training and so increasing the economic value of their particular skills.

However, besides these and similar cases (whose importance requires exhaustive study), in which the workers' behaviour is determined by considerations of economic purpose, there are many others in which their behaviour does not seem to be clearly determined by them, and sometimes even to be incompatible with any motive of this kind. It seems plausible, and has occasionally been observed, that they may regard a change of job as desirable, purely in itself – that is, in cases where economic opportunities and the pleasantness or unpleasantness of the job are *not* the decisive factors. It is equally certain, however, that there are other, well-attested, cases in which they do not find a change of job desirable, even when they have been given a firm guarantee that it would cause them no economic disadvantage; that the reason in such cases was not entirely accidental circumstances or a general conservatism of mind seems probable in view of the fact that such reluctance was sometimes found even in workers who found it easy, or even preferred, to change firms and place of work, as long as in their new location they could step into a similar kind of job. It cannot be decided *a priori* whether the explanation of such behaviour might be found in the concepts of 'habituation' and 'adaptation' to a particular type of work, whose significance for the work curve seems to be measurable by the methods of experimental psychology.

In such cases, and many like them, it seems that it is always possible that purely psycho-physical considerations would in general not enable a clear answer to be given, since the interplay of different motives is much too complex. This situation will be found over and over again. On the whole, the compiler will, in the present state of psychological enquiry, have fairly frequently to fall back on his own resources in almost all cases in which he has occasion to describe differences in the general 'mental' characteristics of workers in different kinds of occupation and coming from different origins – that is, differences in their 'characters' and in their 'intellectual' and 'moral' attitudes, things which are often of undoubted importance and are sometimes decisive in their influence on men's aptitudes for different kinds of industrial work. The old conception of the 'four humours' is nowadays usually replaced by that of the four possible combinations of intensity and duration of the momentary 'state of feeling'. The qualitative sense which was implicit in the old concepts, however, is thereby lost. It has so far not proved possible to replace the old concepts by a new classification of the 'humours', or in general to construct an interpretative classification of the manifold and psychologically extremely complex qualitative differences of attitude which we refer to as 'character', in any of the works of 'differential psychology', 'characterology', 'ethology', 'individual psychology' (or any of the other labels which we apply to such studies). The reasons for this failure lie in certain readily intelligible general difficulties of a methodological nature which are inherent in the task itself. A generally accepted classification of such differences does not exist at present, especially one which could be adopted without further ado as a basis for the purposes of the present survey. The psychological distinctions with which present-day psychiatry operates, moreover, are, for reasons inherent in the peculiar nature of that science, in part too simple and in part, on the contrary, too specific. The only advice which can be given to the compiler, therefore, is to observe in as much detail and as accurately as possible and to describe as simply and in as generally comprehensible a way as possible in everyday language the outward forms in which 'character differences' manifest themselves, insofar as such differences can genuinely and unambiguously be discerned: that is, those externally observable differences in an individual's mode of reaction which the compiler believes to be the behavioural signs of differences in character.

(*Gesammelte Aufsätze zur Soziologie und Sozialpolitik*, Tübingen, 1924, pp. 21–6. First published in 1908.)

21 · *The Stock Exchange*

From the point of view of the community at large, there is a more important question than that of whether and how the public can be protected against the consequences of its own gambling mania. This is the question of the influence exerted by the forms of commercial transaction, especially trading in futures, on the way in which the stock exchange discharges its most important function, that of controlling prices. In this respect, too, the advantages and drawbacks of futures trading are almost inseparably mixed. There is no doubt that it performs in a technically perfect manner the function of equalising prices, which is extremely useful and is indeed essential in speculative dealings. In buying cheap in Paris and at the same time selling dear in London, the arbitrageur increases demand in the one place and supply in the other, and so brings about a geographical redistribution of stocks. The speculator, following the harvest, expects a rise in prices in the winter, so buys grain per June; expecting a rise in prices in spring, he sells per June; thus he brings it about that there is in winter a section of those possessing grain who will not now sell it off locally at the low price, but will sell it at the June settlement date at the price which the speculator promises, and so will keep their grain in store until that date arrives. In this way, he diminishes the net supply at the moment and increases the stocks held in reserve for the future, so redistributing them temporally over the year.[1] The abrupt fluctuations in the general level of prices which would occur without speculation are thereby moderated. Admittedly, the large steep fluctuations in prices are replaced by smaller day-to-day variations. For speculation, since its success depends entirely on developments affecting the readiness to buy or sell of those concerned, is very sensitive to every occurrence in which there is any possibility, however vague, that it will influence the present or future readiness to buy. Every torrential rainstorm at harvest time makes itself felt in the grain futures prices, and every political news report (even false ones) affects the prices of numerous stocks. This volatility in prices, whose causes are often not entirely clear, is naturally inconvenient in some cases, especially in the case of products

---

[1] In real life, this effect does not usually come about as straightforwardly as this, but in a rather more complicated form, especially when *contango* arrangements are involved. But the principle and the outcome of the way in which it is achieved are totally identical.

used by manufacturers. This is the reason for the criticism, which is in a sense valid, that futures trading also makes it particularly easy to influence prices artificially in the selfish interests of the large banks or individual speculators. This is up to a point a result, first of all, of the fact that futures trading makes it easier even for a man without any of his own capital to engage in speculation. The great host of small speculators, equipped with little more than a good pair of lungs, a notebook and a pencil, and the less judicious members of the public generally have no choice but to follow the watchword given 'from on high' – in other words, by the big banks; if, therefore, dear bidding from that source for some reason pushes prices up, they are obliged for their part to engage in blind speculative buying. Everyone involved knows full well that this increase in prices will sooner or later be replaced by its opposite, but hopes that this will only happen when *he* has already realised a profit, so that the losses which are certainly to be expected will hit someone else (as in the case of 'Black Peter'). Besides this general reason for the ease with which futures prices can be influenced, there is also the special skill which speculators have, often based on the technical form of futures. The largest-scale forms of this kind of manipulation are the so-called 'corners' or 'tails'. These consist in attempts by an individual large speculator, engaged in dealings in a certain direction (especially bullish), or a group of speculators who combine for that purpose, to make it impossible for opposing interests to fulfil their obligations by the settlement date, so that they can then dictate to them a penal premium. Thus, the Russian Finance Minister, in order to ruin the bearish speculators in rouble notes on the Berlin stock exchange, had almost all the rouble notes which were available on the Berlin market bought up surreptitiously by a Berlin bank, so that the bears, who had not noticed this move, were not able, when the settlement date approached, to buy or borrow any notes to fulfil their obligations; finally, they had to turn to the Russian Finance Minister themselves and ask him to allow them to sell the notes through the aforementioned bank. For all that, such occurrences, which in Germany, even if one takes several decades into account, are to be numbered at most in their dozens, are phenomena of a transitory and feverish kind, ending with the collapse of some of the speculators and usually of the 'corner' itself; above all, they are in no way connected with the form of futures, but in Germany are usually brought about by means of cash transactions, in a way which I shall not discusss in detail at this point.

In general, the criticisms which might really be levelled at futures trading as such all relate to the ease with which it is possible to introduce speculators who lack both judgment and capital. This ease of admission, however, is only the reverse side of that 'widening of the market' which it produces, and whose positive importance for the national economy we earlier came to appreciate in its main features. National interests, both political and economic, make it impossible, on the grounds of these drawbacks, unilaterally to prohibit futures trading as such in a particular commodity, and thereby, instead of achieving the goal of suppressing speculation, merely to drive it, and therewith the decisive market for the commodity in question, to other countries whose financial power will thus be strengthened. The increased temptation to gamble which is thus placed in the way of the domestic public and the losses which they thereby incur must be accepted as part of the costs of the war between the nations for economic domination. If it is really desired to abolish dealings in futures in particular cases, then only an international agreement could have any point.[1]

In my view, a rational policy for controlling trade on the stock exchange, based on the international political interests of Germany, would have to pursue roughly the following aims (leaving aside such technical details as the form of quotation of exchange rates, the settlement of commission business and the regulation of conditions for dealings in grain futures): since it is useless, even harmful, for speculators without capital to work directly together in dealings on the stock exchange, it is desirable, though certainly far from easy to achieve, that evidence of wealth should be required before admission. Speculation in 'small' securities is harmful and should be prevented, though not only when it takes the form of trading in futures. Even when speculation takes the form of cash transactions, it is not easy to keep concealed for long the growth of a speculative market, so it could effectively be prevented by refusing to quote exchange rates and by banning all newspaper reports. There should be a rigid ban on the reporting by the German press of the quotations of any securities which are not acceptable on German stock markets, and also on any reports of them when there is, in the opinion of the relevant authorities, some grounds for suspicion that these stocks are coming into the hands of German capitalists by a route which circumvents the German stock markets. Furthermore, the state authorities should be given rights of supervision and veto against stock exchange dealings in any object in general, and against futures trading in particular. With reference to the latter, however, this authority should

[1] That there are such cases is beyond doubt. For reasons of space, however, I cannot go into them in detail here. In that category might perhaps be placed, for example, woollen slubbing, a semi-manufactured article: in such a case, as distinct from raw materials, whose production requires long harvest periods, every rise in price can easily lead to overproduction. At the moment, from the point of view of German interests, grain does not, in my view, fall into that category. The unilateral prohibition which the Reichstag imposed on domestic trade, without securing international agreement, was considered to be simply an electoral manoeuvre, and even from this point of view to be a foolishness.

generally be used only when international agreement on the particular objects whose prohibition seems desirable can be achieved. For the rest, it would merely be necessary to punish attempts to inveigle inexperienced or silly people into engaging in speculation, as has happened under the rules of the stock exchange.

The claims of pure moral theory can be met, for as long as nations, though militarily at peace, are engaged in a relentless and ineluctable economic struggle for national existence and economic power, only subject to the narrow limits set by the consideration that, even in economics, unilateral disarmament is impossible. A strong stock exchange cannot be a mere club for 'ethical culture', and the funds of the great banks are no more a 'charitable device' than are rifles and cannons. From the point of view of a national economic policy aimed at *this-worldly* goals, they could only be one thing – a weapon for achieving power in that economic struggle. If it can also achieve what is right and proper from the 'ethical' point of view in regard to these institutions, well and good; but it has a duty in the last resort to guard against the disarmament of its own nation by fanatical interest groups or the unworldly apostles of economic peace.

(*Gesammelte Aufsätze zur Soziologie und Sozialpolitik*, Tübingen, 1924, pp. 318–22. First published in 1896.)

22 · The History of the Piano

The second specifically modern keyboard instrument, the piano, developed from two historical sources which were technically very different from each other. On the one hand, there was the clavichord, which developed by an increase in the number of strings from the early medieval 'monochord', a single-stringed instrument with a movable bridge which was the basis of the rational tone-measurement which prevails across the whole of the Western world. In all probability, the clavichord was a monastic invention. Originally it had grouped strings for several tones, which could thus not be struck at the same time, and free strings only for the most important tones: the number of free strings, however, gradually increased from bottom to top, at the expense of the grouped strings. On the oldest clavichords it was impossible to strike c and e simultaneously – in other words, the third. However, the instrument had by Agricola's time (the sixteenth century) been brought from a range which in the fourteenth century encompassed twenty-two diatonic tones (from G to e' including b flat next to b) to a chromatic scale from A to b". Its rapidly fading tones encouraged figuration, and so it was pre-eminently an instrument suitable for genuinely artistic use. It was struck by jacks which simultaneously separated the sounding part of the strings and silenced them, and the peculiar sonorities which this gave the instrument at the peak of its perfection, especially the characteristic expressive 'tremolo' of its tones, allowed it to fall victim to the competition of the hammer piano only when the fate of musical instruments began to be decided, not by the requirements of a small stratum of musicians and musically sensitive amateurs, but by the market conditions of a capitalistic instrument-producing industry.

The second source of the piano is the 'clavicembalo', 'clavecin' or 'cembalo', derived from the psaltery, and the somewhat different English 'virginal', whose strings (one for each tone) were plucked by quills, and which thus did not permit modulation in volume or colour, though it did allow great freedom and clarity of touch. The clavecin shared with the organ the drawbacks mentioned earlier, and similar technical devices were used in an attempt to remedy them. Until the eighteenth century, organists were the normal makers of keyboard instruments, and they were thus the first to create a keyboard literature. Because the instrument's free touch favoured its use in rendering popular airs and dances, however, its specific public consisted essentially of amateurs, in the first instance, naturally enough, those belonging to sections of society which were confined to their homes – monks in the Middle Ages and then, in modern times, women, led by Queen Elizabeth. As late as 1722, a new and more complicated type of keyboard instrument was recommended on the grounds that 'even the ladies, if they have some practice in playing on the (customary) keyboard' are 'capable of managing it'. The clavecin undoubtedly played a considerable part in the fifteenth and sixteenth centuries in the development of music which was melodically and rhythmically clear, and it was at that time one of the means by which the simple harmonic sensibilities of folk music infiltrated at the expense of polyphonic art music. The sixteenth century, the age of general experimentation in the production of purely pitched instruments for compositions for many voices (theorists had instruments, especially of the keyboard type, specially built for their experiments), was essentially limited to the lute for accompanying singing, but then the cembalo gained ground and became the typical instrument first for accompanying vocal music and then for opera.

In the seventeenth and eighteenth centuries the conductor sat in the middle of the orchestra at the cembalo. In musical technique, the instrument remained very close to the organ right up to the end of the seventeenth century, at least as far as art music is concerned. Organists and pianists, who in the seventeenth century felt that, despite their distinctness, they yet had a solidarity of interests as artists and participants in the development of harmonic music (especially in opposition to the string instruments, which 'could not produce full harmony') withdrew on these grounds in France from the dominance of the first violin. Piano music was musically emancipated from organ styles, first by the influence of the dance on French instrumental music, a result of the French social structure, and then by the example of the beginnings of virtuoso violin playing. If the *Chambonnières*, in the seventeenth century, should be regarded as the first to compose works specifically for the piano, Domenico Scarlatti, at the beginning of the eighteenth, should be seen as the first to exploit in a virtuoso fashion the characteristic sonorities of the instrument. These beginnings of virtuoso playing, together with the emergence of a large-scale cembalo industry based on the demand from orchestras and – as it slowly built up – from amateurs, were responsible for the last great technical modifications to the instrument and its standardisation. The first great makers of cembalos (such as the Rucker family in Belgium around 1600) produced 'by manufacture' individual instruments to order for particular consumers (orchestras or patricians), so that the instruments were built in a great variety of ways to meet all the possible concrete needs of the clients, in exactly the same way as the organ.

The hammer piano developed by various stages, partly in Italy (the *Cristofori*), partly in Germany. But the inventions made in Italy remained at first virtually unexploited in practice there. Italian culture remained fundamentally different, almost up to the present day, from the 'indoor' character of Northern musical culture. *A capella* singing and opera – the latter so structured that its arias could meet the domestic need for easily understandable and singable melodies – remained the Italian ideal, because of the absence of the culture of the bourgeois 'home'. The centre for the production and further technical development of the piano consequently became Saxony, the region which at that time had the best (which means in this case the most widespread) musical organisation. The 'bourgeois' musical culture stemming from the choir schools, together with the virtuosi and instrument builders and the lively interest of the local court musicians, all helped to encourage the further development and popularisation of the instrument. Of the instrument's advantages, those which aroused greatest interest were the possibility of reducing and increasing the volume, the ability to sustain notes and the beauty of chords which could be struck in the form of arpeggios at any tone distance required; the disadvantage which loomed largest (particularly in Bach's eyes) was the lack of freedom in playing passages which characterised the piano early on by comparison with the cembalo and clavichord, and the likelihood that this defect could be overcome aroused considerable interest. In place of the gentle touch of sixteenth century keyboard instruments, a rational technique of fingering was developed, first for the organ and soon after for the cembalo also: admittedly, with its interlocking of the hands and overlapping of the fingers, this was to our way of thinking rather intricate and contorted, until the two Bachs put it on what one might call a physiologically 'tonal' basis by introducing the rational use of the thumb. Whereas in the ancient world the hand had had to display its greatest virtuosity on the aulos, the violin and, above all, the piano now presented the greatest challenge.

The greatest masters of modern piano music, Johann Sebastian and Carl Philipp Emanuel Bach, were still neutral in their attitude to the hammer piano, and the former especially wrote a considerable number of his best works for the older types of instrument, the clavichord and the cembalo, which, though tonally weaker, were more intimate and attuned to more refined ears. It was the international virtuosity of Mozart and the increasing needs of music publishers and concert impresarios for mass consumption of music under the conditions of a large-scale market which first brought about the eventual triumph of the hammer piano. Even as late as the eighteenth century, piano-makers, especially in Germany, were in the first instance great artist craftsmen (like Silbermann), who themselves physically collaborated and tested their instruments. Mechanised mass production of the instrument became dominant first in England (with Broadwood), and then in America (with Steinway), where the superior quality of the iron made possible the construction of iron frames and must have helped to overcome the considerable purely climatic difficulties which stood in the way of the piano's naturalisation (as they have also done in the tropics). Already by the beginning of the nineteenth century it had become a regular object of commerce and was produced for stock. The fierce competition between factories and virtuosi, using the specifically modern methods of the press, exhibitions, and even (following the analogy of the brewers' marketing techniques) the building by instrument factories of their own concert halls – a particular case in Germany was the Berlin concert hall – brought about that degree of technical perfection in the instrument which alone was capable of satisfying the ever-increasing technical requirements of composers. The older instruments were no longer adequate even for Beethoven's later compositions. Orchestral compositions were in general only made available for domestic performance in piano transcriptions. Chopin was an example of a composer of the first rank who confined himself entirely to the piano, and finally in the case of Liszt the intimate knowledge of the greatest of virtuosi elicited from this instrument every last possibility of expression which it concealed within itself.

The piano's present unshakeable position rests on its universal usefulness as a means of becoming acquainted at home with almost all the treasures of musical literature, on the immeasurable riches of its own literature and finally on its character as the universal instrument for the accompanist and the learner. As a learner's instrument, it has superseded the ancient cithara, the monochord, the primitive organ and the hurdygurdy of the monastic schools; as an accompanying instrument, the aulos of the ancient world, the organ and the primitive stringed instruments of the Middle Ages and Renaissance lute; as an instrument for the amateur musicians of the upper social classes, the ancient cithara, the harp of Northern Europe and the lute of the sixteenth century. The fact that our education is exclusively in terms of modern harmonic music is essentially due to it. This is true even in the negative sense, insofar as the way in which our ears – the ears of the listening public – have become accustomed to the tempering of pitch has certainly taken away from them some of that refinement in regard to melody which was the distinguishing characteristic of the melodic sophistication of ancient musical culture. In the West, singers were still trained in the sixteenth century on the monochord, and the aim of this, according to Zarlino, was to reintroduce perfect pitch. Today they are trained almost entirely on the piano, at least in our latitudes, and even the tonal training in schools for string instruments is carried out from the beginning on the piano. It is clear that it is not possible to achieve such a sensitive ear by this method as by teaching which uses instruments in perfect pitch. The notoriously greater impurity of intonation of Northern singers as compared with Italian must be largely a result of this. The idea of building pianos with twenty-four keys in the octave, as proposed by, for instance, Helmholtz, is not very promising, mainly for economic reasons. As compared with the comfortable twelve-keyed keyboard, it would have no market amongst amateurs and would remain a mere virtuoso instrument. Piano building, however, depends on mass sales. For the piano is by its very musical nature a bourgeois domestic instrument. In the way that the organ needs a vast enclosed space to display its charms to best advantage, the piano requires a modestly sized room. All the virtuoso successes of modern pianists cannot fundamentally alter the fact that the instrument, when it appears on its own in a large concert hall, is involuntarily compared with the orchestra and found, of course, to be too light. It is thus no accident that the representatives of piano culture are the Northern peoples, whose life, for purely climatic reasons, is house-bound and centred on the 'home', in contrast with the South. Because bourgeois home-comforts were, for climatic and historical reasons, not cultivated there to nearly such a great extent, the piano, a Southern invention, did not, as we saw, spread so quickly there as in the North. Even today, it has not to the same extent achieved the status of a piece of bourgeois 'furniture' which it has obviously had amongst us for a long time now.

(*Wirtschaft und Gesellschaft*, 4th edn, Tübingen, 1956, II, pp. 925–8. First published in 1921.)

23 · *Freudianism*

Heidelberg, 13 September 1907
... I am returning herewith the copy of Dr *X*'s article, with the suggestion that we do *not* accept it for the '*Archiv*'. I should also say, however, that I am prepared to be overruled on this. Personally, I could not on *any* account vote for acceptance. The obvious thing would be for me to inform Dr *X* of this myself, giving my reasons. But *cui bono*? I know that, *however* I might explain my position, I should be bound, in this as in *all* cases of difference of opinion, to seem to him, if only because of the nature of the terminology which I (indeed 'deliberately') adhere to, to be bound by convention and to hold ethical views which were identical with 'conventional' ethics, or with certain propositions of conventional ethics. I am unable to alter anything in that regard, *even* for someone whom I value so highly as a *human being* as I do Dr *X*, for that would call for extensive oral or written discussion, which I am afraid I am simply not capable of. And besides, I should have to be prepared to give offence by my remarks: we all have it in common today that we are much more ready to allow it to be said of us that 'we are in our theories ethical monsters' than that 'we are, quite simply, counsellors of confusion'. The latter, however, fits Dr *X* well – and, as far as I can see, it fits him *wherever* he steps outside the bounds of his specialism and puts over a 'world view': that is, wherever he becomes a 'moralist' instead of a 'scientific *investigator*'. And, at the risk of appearing, not merely a moral, but also an intellectual, Pharisee, I have to say this in all honesty. Of course, I must also give my reasons for saying it, at least briefly.

Freud's theories, which I now know of also from his major works, have admittedly changed considerably over the years, and I have the impression, speaking as a layman, that they have not yet by any means reached their final form: important concepts, such as that of 'abreaction', have unfortunately very recently been garbled and watered down until they have lost all precise meaning. (This happened first of all in the '*Zeitschrift für Religionsphilosophie*': I might remark in passing that this was a really sickening piece of work, made up of the 'good Lord' and of a variety of sexual nastinesses.) For all that, there is no doubt that Freud's line of thought *could* become very important in suggesting interpretations for whole series of cultural phenomena, especially in the area of the history of *religion* and morality: admittedly, when seen from the lofty vantage-point of the cultural historian, this importance is very far from being as universal as is assumed, in their very understandable enthusiasm and joy in discovery, by Freud and his followers. An essential precondition would be the creation of an *exact casuistics* of a scope and a certainty which, despite all assertions to the contrary, does not exist today, but will perhaps exist in two or three decades: one has only to follow through all the changes which Freud has made in one decade, and to see how alarmingly thin, in spite of everything, his material still is (all of which is very understandable and is certainly *no reproach*). But instead of this kind of work, which is of necessity specifically *specialist* in character, we see Freud's followers, especially Dr *X*, spending their time partly in metaphysical speculation, and partly (what is worse) on a question which, from the point of view of exact science, is a childish one, namely, 'Can one eat it?' – that is, cannot one construct a practical 'world view' from it? That is certainly no crime: *every* new scientific or technological discovery has had the consequence that the discoverer, whether of meat extract or the loftiest abstractions of natural science, has believed himself to have a mission to discover new values or to reform ethics – just as, for instance, the inventors of colour photography thought they were called to be reformers of painting. But I can see no need for the nappies of this seemingly inescapable baby stage of science to be washed in our '*Archiv*'.

'Baby's nappies', however, is what they are. For what else is one to say about an 'ethic' which, in Dr *X*'s terminology, is too 'cowardly' to confess that its 'ideal' must be the utterly banal healthy '*nerve-snob*'? Which believes it possible to discredit any ethical standards whatsoever by simply proving that their observance is not 'wholesome' for our precious nerves? And despite all the passionate protests which this interpretation would naturally provoke, the *ethical* content of the 'new' doctrine is no more than this: there is *nothing* more concrete behind it than this kind of philistinism. If *any* repression of affectually toned wishes and instincts leads to 'inhibition' (and this silly assertion is implicit at least in the form of *words* used), and if 'inhibition' as such is absolutely evil (allegedly because it leads to inner falsity, to 'error and cowardice', but really because, considered from the *specialist viewpoint of nervous hygiene*, it brings with it the risk of hysteria, obsessional neurosis, phobia, etc.), *then* this 'nerve-ethics' must, for instance, cry to the Boers fighting for their freedom, 'Take to your heels, or else you will "repress" your affect of anxiety and possibly earn Andreyev's "Red Laugh"'. Putting it in 'technical' language, 'become cowards' in the *conventional* sense, allow your affect of cowardice to 'abreact' by showing a clean pair of heels, so that you don't become 'cowardly' in Dr *X*'s ultra-modern psychiatric sense: that is, so that you don't 'repress' those affects and keep them 'below the threshold of consciousness', which will certainly be harmful to you and therefore immoral. It must cry to the husband or lover of a wife or mistress who is overtaken in all too rapid succession by fits of jealousy, 'Let them *abreact, à la* Othello, or by means of a duel – better to be "mean" (from the point of view of the "new" sexuality) than to resist them and so risk "illusion"'. It must in general have spirit enough to recommend that I 'abreact' *any* stirring of my appetites and my instinctual life, however craven its intention: and that means opening the way to any form of *gratification* which is in *any* way adequate, since otherwise my precious nerves might suffer. That is the true attitude, which we know so well, of the medical philistine!

Am I doing Dr *X*'s 'theory' some injustice? But on p. 9 of the article I find, explicitly expressed, the sentence about the *sacrifices* which are the *costs* of 'adjustment' (that is, the repression of 'wishes' for the sake of observing 'standards'), and these 'sacrifices' are precisely sacrifices of *health*. In other words, meanness is demanded of me, before I act in such a way as to believe it to be owing to my human dignity to calculate 'what it costs'. And am I to accept the psychiatrist as the authority in deciding whether the ethical value of my action compensates for the 'costs'? In this context, admittedly, there is the laughable assertion that these 'costs' (possible 'inhibitions' with their hygienic consequences) arise only as a consequence of the belief in *absolute* values. Now I have the gravest doubts whether Dr *X* has the slightest conception of what it means to 'believe in *absolute* values': but, as you are well aware, that is not a topic which can be explained precisely enough in one or two letters or in one or two conversations – but that is by the by. The decisive point is still that any ethic which is meant to be relativistic and at the same time 'idealistic' leads to exactly the *same* 'hygienic' consequences the moment it requires a particular concrete individual to will a value which has force for him (which, as far as I am concerned, means in fact *only* for him, only now in *this* situation, in other words, purely 'relatively' and 'subjectively'). Unless 'relativism' is to consist in the fact that the individual is always to leave his 'relative ideal' in the lurch in any case in which the pursuit of it costs something, that is, perhaps 'gets on his nerves'. *That* would be, to be sure, a kind of cheap shopkeeper's idealism, which I at least would be as unable to accept as undoubtedly in practice would Dr *X*.

All systems of ethics, no matter what their substantive content, can be divided into two main groups. There is the 'heroic' ethic, which imposes on men demands of principle to which they are generally *not* able to do justice, except at the high points of their lives, but which serve as signposts pointing the way for man's endless *striving*. Or there is the 'ethic of the mean', which is content to accept man's everyday 'nature' as setting a maximum for the demands which can be made. It seems to me that only the former category, the 'heroic ethic', can call itself 'idealism', and that to this category belong both the ethics of the *older* form of Christianity, before it lost its integrity, and Kantian ethics, both of which start, measured by their ideals, from a pessimistic assessment of the 'nature' of the average man to which, God knows, Freud's revelations from the realm of the Unconscious have *nothing* particularly 'terrible' to add. But to the extent that the 'psychiatric ethic' makes only the demand that one should confess what one is and what wishes one has had, it does not impose any really new demands of an ethical kind. The father confessor and the pastor of the old type had no other task in this direction than this, and Freudian therapy is simply a revival of *confession*, with somewhat different techniques. Only, the purpose here is *still* less 'ethical' than was the case in Tetzel's old method of letting off steam. Someone who is deceiving himself and wants to deceive himself, and who has learned to shut out from his memory those things in his life which he has to be ashamed of, and which he *can* remember in large part if he wants to, is not going to be helped *ethically* by lying for months on end on Freud's couch and allowing 'infantile' or other shameful experiences which he has 'repressed' to be recalled to consciousness. Freud's treatment may have *hygienic* value for him, but what for instance do I stand to gain ethically, if some sexual misdemeanour to which I have been provoked by a housemaid (Freudian examples!) or some smutty impulse which I have 'repressed' and 'forgotten' were to be revived? I don't know: for I fully admit (and without any feeling that there is anything 'terrible' about the admission) that absolutely nothing 'human' is or was foreign to me, so that I haven't learned anything which is in principle new.

Still, this is not really relevant, and I say it only to make the point that the Categorical Imperative, 'Go to Freud, or to us his pupils, to learn this historical *truth* about yourself and your actions, or else you are a coward' not only reveals a kind of childish 'departmental patriotism' of the psychiatrist and the modern type of professional '*directeur de l'âme*', but also totally debases itself from the ethical point of view because of the fatal admixture of purely 'hygienic' motives. I can, however, as I said, discover no other practical postulate in my reading of this article, which moralises from start to finish, except this 'duty of self-knowledge' with the aid of the psychiatrist. For *where* is there even the slightest trace of a hint of the *content* of the new, relativistic and yet *ideal* (N.B.) values, which are to provide the basis for the critique of the 'old', 'dubious' values? To look for them is like trying to grasp the air. And for good reasons: any attempt to delineate these values would expose them to criticism and show that the problem has simply been shelved, rather than solved. An idealistic ethic, which demands *sacrifices* and does not exclude *responsibility*, can never produce different results. But it will not do to criticise an ethic from any *other* basis than its *own* ideals: otherwise one simply gets into the domain of the cheapest kind of 'cost-accounting', and the 'ideal' then inevitably becomes, as I said before, the normal health-snob and the medically supervised philistine of macrobiotics.

If Dr *X* were to catch sight of the foregoing lines (I hope he doesn't, but I leave it entirely up to you: the question is, does he have a sense of humour? I doubt it – no moralist does), then he would certainly consider that I had shockingly trivialised his views. I certainly have! I have deliberately translated them into our beloved 'vulgar' German. The triviality which is thus revealed in them is his own fault, for it is the result of the combination of his medical researches with a totally confused reforming zeal. The whole article is absolutely bursting with noisy value-judgments, and I have no respect at all for supposedly scientific works which do not satisfy the requirement of sobriety and respect for facts – which are not 'value-free'. . . .

For a particular *branch* of science is a technique: it teaches certain technical methods. But where disputes about values come in, the problem is projected on to quite a different spiritual plane, one far removed from 'science'. To put it more precisely, the *question* is *posed* in a totally different way. *No* branch of science and no scientific knowledge, however important (and Freud's discoveries, if they are ultimately confirmed, I consider to be certainly of scientific importance) results in any 'world view'. And conversely, a specialist scientific journal is no place for any article which aspires to be a sermon, and which is a *poor* sermon at that.

This criticism[1] applies to this particular work – I am well aware of the high esteem in which competent judges hold other works by the same author. It applies *also* – be it said in so many words – to the *person* and his character. The fact that we two will *always* talk at cross purposes to each other cannot mean that, after the brief impression in *your* accounts, I should fail to recognise the noble trait in his character, which is certainly one of the most charming that one could meet today. But how much more *purely* would the nobility of his personal charisma and that 'other-worldly' love, before which I deeply doff my hat, have its effect if it were *not* concealed behind a dust of *specialist* jargon and the departmental patriotism of the nerve-hygienist, etc. etc. If only he could venture to be *what he is* – and that is to be sure something different and better than a follower of Nietzsche. And it is not even that part of Nietzsche's work which is of lasting value which he chooses to follow: not

[1] If you should find it not only superficial (as it necessarily is) but a little arrogant, then please re-read the article I am criticising. I don't see why I should be the *first* to get off my high horse, *if* a further tournament on it was *intended*.

the 'morality of superiority', but precisely the *weakest* part of Nietzsche, the biological trimming which he piles onto the core of his totally moralistic doctrine.

That is the basis of my vote.[1]

Warmest greetings,

Yours,

Max Weber.

> (Eduard Baumgarten, ed., *Max Weber: Werk und Person*, Tübingen, 1964, pp. 644–8.)

[1] I must retract my remarks at the beginning. I should be lacking in character if I were to allow myself to be overruled and I make use of my contractual veto.

24 · *Sociology and Biology*

Dr Ploetz has described 'society' as a living organism, on the basis of the familiar analogy, which he has himself impressively expounded, between societies and such things as cellular organisations. It may well be that, for Dr Ploetz's purposes, there is something of value in such an analogy: he himself, of course, is the best judge of that. But sociological enquiry never gains by the attempt to combine a number of relatively precise concepts into a single vague one. Such is the situation here. It is possible for us to understand the rational actions of individual human beings by re-living them in our own minds. If we sought to understand a human association of any kind only in the way in which one would investigate an animal community, we should be abandoning the means of knowledge which, as things are, are available to us in the case of human beings, but not in the case of animal societies. For this reason and no other, we can see no general advantage for our purposes in drawing the analogy which can undoubtedly be drawn between a bee-hive and any human political association of any kind, and in making it the basis for any sort of enquiry.

Finally, gentlemen, Dr Ploetz has said that social theory is a branch of racial biology.

[*Dr Ploetz*: Social biology, not social theory in general!]

Yes, well, admittedly, the fault may perhaps be mine, but it is not entirely clear to me what the distinction is supposed to be between social biology and racial biology, unless it is that the subject-matter of social biology is to be just the kind of study which I myself have carried out in the past of the relations between social institutions and the selection of certain qualities.

I should like to add only a general comment on that point. It does not seem to me to be profitable to demarcate domains and provinces of knowledge *a priori*, before the relevant knowledge exists, and to say that one thing belongs to our science and another does not. To do this is simply to multiply fruitless disputes. It would, of course, be possible to say that since, in the last resort, all social processes take place on Earth, and since the planet Earth is a part of the solar system, everything which takes place must, properly speaking, be the concern of astronomy, and that it is only an accident that it is studied by other means, since there is no point in

389

observing events on Earth with a telescope. But would there be anything to be gained by saying that? By the same token, I should like to question the idea that, just because some processes which concern biology – the processes of selection – are undoubtedly affected by social institutions, and in many cases, furthermore, by social institutions as influenced by hereditary racial characteristics, it therefore makes sense to appropriate any object or problem in that area for a science which has yet to be constructed for the first time *ad hoc* for this very purpose. What we hope for from the racial biologists – and what we shall certainly get from them some time, as I do not doubt, precisely because of the impression I have gained from the work of Dr Ploetz and his colleagues – is exact evidence of well-defined connexions in individual cases, and so of the decisive importance of completely specific hereditary qualities for particular concrete social phenomena. That, gentlemen, does not exist as yet. That is no reproach to a very young science, but the fact must be stated, and it may perhaps help to prevent the degeneration of the Utopian enthusiasm characteristic of the early days of such a new field of study to the point where its practitioners misjudge the actual boundaries of their enquiries. We can see this today in all fields. We have seen how it has been believed that the whole world, including, for instance, art and everything else, could be explained in purely economic terms. We see how modern geographers treat all cultural phenomena 'from the geographical point of view' – meaning by that, not that they show us what we might like to learn from them, namely which specific concrete elements in the particular cultural phenomena are determined by climate or similar purely geographical factors, but that they include among their 'geographical' statements such assertions as that 'The Russian church is intolerant'. When we then ask them how far this is a geographical assertion, they say, 'Russia is a geographical region; the Russian church is geographically spread; so, it belongs to the subject-matter of geography'. My view is that the individual sciences lose their point when each fails to perform that specific task which it, and it alone, can perform; and I should like to express the hope that this fate may not befall the biological approach to social phenomena.

(*Gesammelte Aufsätze zur Soziologie und Sozialpolitik*, Tübingen, 1924, pp. 461–2. First published in 1911.)

Suggestions for Further Reading

Of Weber's works themselves, *Economy and Society* is available in full in a three-volume translation by various hands edited by Guenther Roth and Claus Wittich (New York, 1968): this incorporates the separate portions previously published in English as *The Theory of Social and Economic Organization* (tr. T. Parsons, London, 1947), *Max Weber on Law and Economy in Society* (tr. E. Shils and M. Rheinstein, Cambridge, Massachusetts, 1954), *The City* (tr. D. Martindale and G. Neuwirth, Glencoe, Illinois, 1958), *Basic Concepts in Sociology* (tr. H. Secher, London, 1962) and *The Sociology of Religion* (tr. T. Parsons, Boston, 1963). Of the methodological essays, that of 1904 on '"Objectivity" in Social Science and Social Policy', that of 1906 on 'Critical Studies in the Logic of the Cultural Sciences' and that written for the Association for Social Policy's debate on values in 1914 but only published in 1917 as 'The Meaning of "Value-freedom" in Sociology and Economics' are available in E. Shils, ed., *The Methodology of the Social Sciences* (Glencoe, Illinois, 1949); 'Marginal Utility Theory and the So-called Fundamental Law of Psychophysics' has been translated by Louis Schneider in the *Social Science Quarterly*, LVI (1975); 'Roscher and Knies: the Logical Problems of Historical Economics' has been translated under that title by Guy Oakes (New York, 1975); and Weber's review of Stammler has been translated by Martin Albrow in the *British Journal of Law and Society*, II (1975). Of the essays on religion, both parts of 'The Protestant Ethic and the "Spirit" of Capitalism' together with the later 'Foreword' are in Talcott Parsons' translation (London, 1930); 'The Protestant Sects and the Spirit of Capitalism', together with the 'Introduction' to 'The Economic Ethics of the World Religions' and the linking essay 'Religious Rejections of the World and their Directions', may be found in H. H. Gerth and C. Wright Mills, eds., *From Max Weber* (London, 1947); the essays on 'Confucianism and Taoism', 'Hinduism and Buddhism' and 'Ancient Judaism' are available as *The Religion of China* (tr. H. H. Gerth, Glencoe, Illinois, 1951), *The Religion of India* (tr. H. H. Gerth and D. Martindale, Glencoe, Illinois, 1958) and *Ancient Judaism* (tr. H. H. Gerth and D. Martindale, Glencoe, Illinois, 1952).

Weber's various writings on politics are far from completely available in English. However, the lecture on 'Politics as a Vocation' and part of a pamphlet of 1917 on 'Democracy and the Franchise in Germany' are in Gerth and Mills' selection, the lecture on 'Socialism' is in J. E. T. Eldridge, ed., *Max Weber: the Interpretation of Social Reality* (London, 1971), and the set of articles 'Parliament and Government in a Reconstructed Germany' first published in the *Frankfurter Zeitung* in 1917 is translated as an appendix to Roth and Wittich's edition of *Economy and Society*. Of his remaining writings, the whole of the essay on

Suggestions for Further Reading

'Agrarian Relations in the Ancient World' is translated by R. I. Frank as *The Agrarian Sociology of Ancient Civilizations* (London, 1976); the 'Methodological Introduction' for the Association for Social Policy's proposed study of industrial workers is translated by D. Hytch in the volume edited by Eldridge; *The Rational and Social Foundations of Music* is translated under that title by D. Martindale, J. Riedel and G. Neuwirth (Carbondale, Illinois, 1958); the lecture of 1919 on 'Science as a Vocation' is in the volume edited by Gerth and Mills, as is the address to the St Louis Congress of 1904 on 'Capitalism and Rural Society in Germany'; the lecture delivered at Freiburg in 1896 on the decline of the ancient world is translated by Christian Mackauer as 'The Social Causes of the Decay of Ancient Civilisation' in *The Journal of General Education*, v (1950), reprinted also in the Eldridge volume, and as an appendix to Frank's translation of the *Agrarian Sociology*; and Weber's lectures of 1919–20 at Munich, based on the notebooks of students who attended them, are available in a translation by F. H. Knight as *General Economic History* (London, 1927). Finally, a number of Weber's incidental writings on the problems of the German universities have been translated and brought together by E. Shils in *Minerva*, xi (1973); Weber's exchange with Ploetz on race in 1910 has been translated by J. Gittleman in *Social Research*, xxxviii (1971); an unpublished fragment on Simmel has been translated by Benjamin Nelson, *ibid.* xxxix (1972); and a letter which Weber wrote in 1920 at the time of resigning from the National Committee of the German Democratic Party has been published by B. B. Frye, 'A Letter from Max Weber', *Journal of Modern History*, xxxix (1967).

There is unfortunately no single study of Weber's work as a whole which can be recommended without reservation. Raymond Aron's chapter on Weber in his *Main Currents in Sociological Thought*, ii (London, 1967) is a good short introduction. Also worth reading still is Talcott Parsons' discussion of Weber in his *The Structure of Social Action* (New York, 1937). Reinhard Bendix's *Max Weber: an Intellectual Portrait* (London, 1960) ignores the methodology entirely, but has useful synopses of Weber's substantive works. Methodology is ignored also in Donald G. MacRae's brief *Weber* (London, 1974). Perhaps the best general treatment, although not originally written for an English-speaking audience, is Julien Freund, *The Sociology of Max Weber* (tr. M. Ilford, London, 1968). Roth's 'Introduction' to *Economy and Society* is also very useful. Georg Lukacs, 'Max Weber and German Sociology' is translated by A. Cutler in *Economy and Society*, i (1972).

On Weber's life, the biography published by his widow in 1926 is available in a translation by H. Zohn: Marianne Weber, *Max Weber: a Biography* (New York, 1975). Arthur Mitzman, *The Iron Cage: an Historical Interpretation of Max Weber* (New York, 1970) is based on some speculative psychoanalysis but contains interesting material. Weber's relationship with Else Jaffé is discussed by Martin Green, *The von Richthofen Sisters* (London, 1974). Accounts of Weber by people who knew and admired him are to be found in Karl Jaspers, *Three Essays: Leonardo, Descartes, Max Weber* (tr. R. Manheim, New York, 1953), Karl Loewenstein, *Max Weber's Political Ideas in the Perspective of Our Time* (Boston, 1966) and Paul Honigsheim, *On Max Weber* (tr. D. K. Rytina, East Lansing, Michigan, 1968).

On Weber's methodology, see John Torrance, 'Max Weber: Methods and the

Man', *Archives Européennes de Sociologie*, xv (1974), H. H. Bruun, *Science, Values and Politics in Max Weber's Methodology* (Copenhagen, 1972) and W. G. Runciman, *A Critique of Max Weber's Philosophy of Social Science* (Cambridge, 1972). Attacks on Weber from an anti-Positivist standpoint are made by Leo Strauss in his *Natural Right and History* (Chicago, 1953) and Carlo Antoni in his *From History to Sociology* (London, 1962). Particular aspects of Weber's method are interestingly treated by P. F. Lazarsfeld and A. Oberschall, 'Max Weber and Empirical Social Research', *American Sociological Review*, xxx (1965) and Frederic Jameson, 'The Vanishing Mediator: Narrative Structure in Max Weber', *New German Critique*, I (1973). See also Guy Oakes, 'The Verstehen Thesis and the Foundations of Max Weber's Methodology', *History and Theory*, xvi (1977).

On Weber's relation to Marxism, Karl Löwith's now classic article 'Max Weber und Karl Marx' first published in 1932 has been partly translated by S. Attanasio as 'Weber's Interpretation of the Bourgeois Capitalistic World in Terms of the Guiding Principle of "Rationalization"' in D. Wrong, ed., *Max Weber* (Englewood Cliffs, New Jersey, 1970). Other useful articles are Norman Birnbaum, 'Conflicting Interpretations of the Rise of Capitalism: Marx and Weber', *British Journal of Sociology*, IV (1953), Guenther Roth, 'The Historical Relationship to Marxism', in Reinhard Bendix and Guenther Roth, eds, *Scholarship and Partisanship: Essays on Max Weber* (Berkeley, California, 1971), A. Giddens, 'Marx, Weber and the Development of Capitalism', *Sociology*, IV (1970), Richard Ashcroft, 'Marx and Weber on Liberalism as Bourgeois Ideology', *Comparative Studies in Society and History*, xIV (1972) and Carl Mayer, 'Max Weber's Interpretation of Karl Marx', *Social Research*, xLII (1975).

Weber's politics are treated by Wolfgang Mommsen, *The Age of Bureaucracy: Perspectives on the Political Sociology of Max Weber* (Oxford, 1974) and David Beetham, *Max Weber and the Theory of Modern Politics* (London, 1974), and more briefly by Anthony Giddens, *Politics and Sociology in the Thought of Max Weber* (London, 1972). Otto Stammer, ed., *Max Weber and Sociology Today* (Oxford, 1971) contains papers delivered at Weber's centenary congress by Raymond Aron on 'Max Weber and Power-politics' and Herbert Marcuse on 'Industrialisation and Capitalism' together with discussion of them; see also Vernon K. Dibble, 'Social Science and Political Commitment in the Young Max Weber', *Archives Européennes de Sociologie*, xv (1974).

On the concept of charisma, three general articles from different standpoints are Edward Shils, 'Charisma, Order and Status', *American Sociological Review*, xxx (1965), Claude Ake, 'Charismatic Legitimation and Political Integration', *Comparative Studies in Society and History*, Ix (1966), and Arthur Schweitzer, 'Theory and Political Charisma', *ibid.*, xVI (1974). Discussions relating it to political leaders of the mid-twentieth century include W. G. Runciman, 'Charismatic Legitimacy and One-Party Rule in Ghana', *Archives Européennes de Sociologie*, IV (1963), Richard Fagan, 'Charismatic Authority and the Leadership of Fidel Castro', *Western Political Quarterly*, xVIII (1965), Stuart Schram, 'Mao Tse-Tung as a Charismatic Leader', *Asian Survey*, II (1967), and David Apter, 'Nkrumah, Charisma and the Coup', *Daedalus*, xCVII (1968). On the religious rather than the political aspect of charisma, see P. L. Berger, 'Charisma and Religious Innovation: the Social Location of Israelite Prophecy', *American*

Suggestions for Further Reading

Sociological Review, XXVIII (1963), and on Mahdism, Richard H. Dekmejian and Margaret J. Wirszomski, 'Charismatic Leadership in Islam: the Mahdi of the Sudan', *Comparative Studies in Society and History*, XIV (1972). A study of the attitudes of the American electorate to the 'charisma' of Presidential candidates is reported by James C. Davis, 'Charisma in the 1952 Campaign', *American Political Science Review*, XLVIII (1954).

There is a large literature in English on the 'Protestant Ethic' but much less on Weber's treatment of the religions of India and China and Islam. For criticism of the 'Protestant Ethic' see H. M. Robertson, *Aspects of the Rise of Economic Individualism: A Criticism of Max Weber and his School* (London, 1933) and Kurt Samuelsson, *Religion and Economic Action* (Stockholm, 1957). For counter-argument against Samuelsson, see Niles M. Hansen, 'On the Sources of Economic Rationality', *Zeitschrift für Nationalökonomie*, XXIV (1964). S. N. Eisenstadt, ed., *The Protestant Ethic and Modernization: a Comparative View* (New York, 1968) is a useful collection of articles covering a wide range of topics. Other relevant articles are Gabriel Kolko, 'Max Weber in America: Theory and Evidence', *History and Theory*, 1 (1961), Niles M. Hansen, 'Early Flemish Capitalism: the Medieval City, the Protestant Ethic and the Emergence of Economic Rationality', *Social Research*, XXXIV (1967), Reinhard Bendix, 'Japan and the Protestant Ethic' in Bendix and Roth, eds., *Scholarship and Partisanship: Essays on Max Weber*, Rex A. Lucas, 'A Specification of the Weber Thesis and its Critics', *History and Theory*, X (1971), and Robert Moore, 'History, Economics and Religion: a Review of "The Max Weber Thesis" Thesis', in Arun Sahay, ed., *Max Weber and Modern Sociology* (London, 1971). A useful corrective to Weber on China is Otto B. van der Sprenkel, 'Max Weber on China', *History and Theory*, III (1963), and on Islam Maxime Rodinson, *Islam and Capitalism* (London, 1974; originally published in French in 1966), particularly Chapter 4; see also Bryan S. Turner, *Weber and Islam* (London, 1974). On Judaism, see I. Schiper, 'Max Weber on the Sociological Basis of the Jewish Religion', *Jewish Journal of Sociology*, 1 (1959). For a more general discussion, see R. Stephen Warner, 'The Role of Religious Ideas and the Use of Models in Max Weber's Comparative Studies of Non-capitalist Societies', *Journal of Economic History*, XXX (1970).

For discussion of Weber's treatment of the ancient world, see M. I. Finley, 'The Ancient City: from Fustel de Coulanges to Max Weber and Beyond', *Comparative Studies in Society and History*, XIX (1977) and the review of Frank's translation of the *Agrarian Sociology* by Arnaldo Momigliano, *Times Literary Supplement*, April 8, 1977. On stratification, see O. C. Cox, 'Max Weber on Social Stratification: a Critique', *American Sociological Review*, XV (1950) and Bryan Jones, 'Max Weber and the Concept of Social Class', *Sociological Review*, XXIII (1975); on law, M. Albrow, 'Legal Positivism and Bourgeois Materialism: Max Weber's View of the Sociology of Law', *British Journal of Law and Society*, II (1975); on bureaucracy, Helen Constas, 'Max Weber's Two Conceptions of Bureaucracy', *American Journal of Sociology*, LIII (1958); on authority, Peter M. Blau, 'Critical Remarks on Weber's Theory of Authority', in Wrong, ed. *Max Weber*; and on industrial psychology, J. E. T. Eldridge, 'Weber's Approach to the Sociological Study of Industrial Workers', in Sahay, ed., *Max Weber and Modern Sociology*.

Index

Index

Index